GUIDE TO
USED CARS

EDITORIAL CONSULTANT
M A I JACOBSON
C ENG, F I MECH E, M I PROD E
Chief Engineer, The Automobile Association

The contents of this publication are believed correct at the time of printing, but the current position may be checked through the AA.
The technical information and the price information are correct as at 1 February 1975. Price variations after this date may be checked with the AA by means of the Voucher on page 255.

Produced by the Publications Division of the Automobile Association, Fanum House, Basingstoke, Hants RG21 2EA

Editor: *Alice Clamp*
Designer: *Sheila-Elizabeth Still*
Contributors: V I Coles   P Denayer   B Francis   E Garrard
            P C Kippax   D Le Cornu   A W Sims and Staff
            J Stubbs   C Surridge
Phototypeset by Vantage Photosetting Co, Ltd
Printed and bound in Great Britain by Sir Joseph Causton & Sons Ltd
Illustrations by AA Design Staff and 'What Car?'
© The Automobile Association 1975   50377   ISBN 0 09 211580 2

In your Guide . . .

How durable are cars? When do they begin to deteriorate? What are the most common faults in individual models? How big a problem is corrosion? Will an expensive car last longer than a cheap one? Are foreign-made cars better than British-made? These and hundreds of other questions are posed almost daily by secondhand car buyers in Britain. The answers are all too often based only on hearsay or the off-hand remark picked up out of context when cars are being discussed with acquaintances or colleagues. This Guide aims to provide factual answers to these and other questions asked by the would-be car purchaser. It is the next best thing to a physical inspection by a qualified engineer of those cars likely to appear on your 'value for money' shortlist.

What VISAR means to you

The word 'VISAR' has been bandied about quite a bit recently. In the acronym-orientated world of today, we tend to accept these 'shorthand' forms without knowing what they really stand for. VISAR in fact means Vehicle Inspection: Systematic Analysis of Reports, which may leave you only slightly less puzzled. The best course is to begin at the beginning.

More than 65,000 cars inspected
The AA has been conducting inspections of its members' cars since 1946. For a period covering the last 4 years, however, the AA has kept a detailed record of every one of more than 65,000 vehicle inspections carried out for members who intended buying secondhand cars and those who were unhappy with their automobiles. Data from the inspections of 31,358 cars during 1973–4 have been computer analysed and compiled into a dossier covering 168 different makes and models. AA engineers have checked some 354 items on each car; these checks cover most major car parts and components, and the findings can give a general idea of what trouble, disappointment or repairs may lie around the corner

for the owners of both fairly new cars and those several years old.

Once the engineer has carried out his checks – a job that takes several hours – what happens to the inspection results? First they are listed under separate headings which identify defects in the major body structure, paintwork, and mechanical, electrical and hydraulic systems. 'Corroded front doors', 'noisy valve gear' and 'defective obligatory lights' are just three examples. Then a percentage is worked out which reflects the proportion of cars, by registration suffix (F/G, H, J, K, L, and M), suffering from the given defect. For example, if 254 of the 4,235 H registration cars inspected are prone to clutch judder, the figure 6 (per cent) will appear in the data table in the horizontal column marked 'clutch judder' and the vertical column marked 'H registration'. Once a percentage has been assigned to each of the categories of defects, and for each of the six registration groups covered by the survey, a basis exists for comparing individual makes and models of cars against the all-makes average. The more popular a car, the greater its

What VISAR reveals ALL MAKES

Sample: 31,358

All chart figures are percentages

	Age in years:	6–8	5–6	4–5	3–4	2–3	1–2
	Registration Suffix:	FG	H	J	K	L	M
Corroded front doors		19	13	10	6	4	3
Corroded rear doors		15	10	8	5	3	2
Corroded front wings		29	17	12	6	3	2
Corroded rear wings		21	13	10	6	3	2
Corroded front underwings		15	7	5	2	1	1
Corroded rear underwings		9	5	4	1	1	0
Corroded body sills		36	24	18	10	5	4
Corroded jacking points		17	10	7	4	2	1
Corroded floor		15	9	6	2	2	2
Corroded underbody frame members		23	13	9	5	3	2
Defective undersealing		31	18	14	11	10	9
Loose/misaligned driver's seat		6	5	5	3	3	2
Attend to engine mountings		6	3	2	2	1	0
Evidence of head gasket leaks		4	2	2	2	1	1
Noisy valve gear		23	22	21	21	19	19
Evidence of engine oil leaks		43	35	31	26	24	22
Attend to carburettor tuning		35	31	30	28	25	29
Evidence of fuel leaks		5	3	3	2	2	3
Final drive noise		8	6	6	5	5	5
Unsatisfactory gear change		7	8	7	4	3	2
Unsatisfactory auto gear change		13	9	7	6	5	3
Clutch judder		6	6	5	4	4	4
Attend to front wheel bearings		17	15	15	15	13	10
Attend to steering box/rack		12	11	10	8	8	10
Attend to footbrake		18	14	12	11	10	10
Attend to handbrake		22	18	17	14	11	10
Corroded brake pipelines		23	14	13	8	4	2
Defective obligatory lights		29	27	21	18	14	11
Attend to charging system		4	3	2	2	2	2
Attend to horn		9	6	4	3	2	2
Sample size by registration suffix.		5687	4235	5850	7573	6210	1803

influence on the level of all-makes average performance. The table for all makes appears on page 6.

We have selected 50 cars for discussion, but not at random. In fact, the 50 covered in this book represent 82½ per cent of the cars inspected – some 168 different makes and models – and in terms of sample size are the most popular. It would not be statistically meaningful to include all the makes and models inspected, as in a number of cases fewer than ten cars of a particular make were examined. In those instances where the sample size is less than ten for one of the 50 cars covered in the book, we have said no data are available. The data table for each of the 50 cars – headed 'What VISAR reveals' – reflects both the probability of some defect being found in a particular car and a particular age group *and* the performance of that particular model against *all* the cars inspected. For example, 20 per cent of J registration Ford Escorts suffer from corroded front wings. This percentage is greater than that for all 168 makes and models, and it is thus qualified as 'worse than average'.

Interpretation of statistics

These figures cannot stand alone, however. Like most statistics, they are open to interpretation. And in fact, they *must* be interpreted. For instance, it costs little to replace a blown bulb, but the expense of rectifying a noisy final drive can be great. Yet this is not always the case. In some final drive installations it may only be necessary to re-tighten the universal joint clamping bolts. In others, such noise may presage a costly repair bill. Knowing which to expect makes a world of difference. We thus attempt to distinguish between those percentages which should be taken as a warning, and those which represent problems fairly easily – and inexpensively – dealt with.

The following comments further bear out the need to explain the VISAR figures. Only about one in every nine cars is fitted with an automatic transmission. Some models are only offered with automatic transmission,

while on others there is no option for it. Therefore the total number of cars (all makes) on which comments on auto gear change quality are made is only 3,508. By the same token, there are a number of lights which are required by law to be operational at all times. The failure of any one of them is registered as a defect. VISAR views the defect rating as cumulative, *ie* four lights inoperative due to a blown fuse equal four defects as far as the law and AA statistics are concerned. Thus a car having four defective lights will be rated as equivalent to four cars having one inoperative light each.

These are only some of the factors which make up the interpretation of the VISAR figures. But they at least serve to indicate that there is more to the data than meets the eye. The engineers' comments accompanying each of the 50 data tables are an attempt, albeit in a limited space, to expand upon the VISAR findings.

Emphasis on cars' body

Great emphasis has been placed on the cars' body structure, their method of construction and rust protection, their paint system, and the rate of deterioration with age of major structural and mechanical components. Such items as battery contact breaker, exhaust system, fan belt and tyre life have not been discussed. And with good reason. These latter items all require regular, periodic replacement and are generally accepted as consumable items. The body of a car, on the other hand, is not replaceable in practical terms. The relationship of body to power unit and drive line can be expressed by the following example. Home improvements – new decoration, double glazing, central heating – are worthwhile only so long as the house itself is sound. The best central heating is useless if the house suffers from wet rot; once serious structural defects are found in a house, interior improvements are a waste of time and money. The same is true of a motor car. In general, it does not pay to renew the structure of either.

It is worth pointing out that the interpretation of these factual data is based on a good deal of accumulated field experience and engineering expertise. The AA is in a unique position to undertake the explanation of its findings. The Association is not commercially involved and thus does not have to defend a manufacturer's decision, it does not have to justify to its customers why certain repairs and component replacements are listed on the bill, and it does not have to make the crucial decision as to whether a car should be banned from the roads. The engineers' comments should thus be viewed in the light of these facts.

More than a guide to defects

This book does more than point out defects, however. It also gives a brief description of the 'road manners' of a popular model from each range of the 50 cars. The road test is based on some 1,000 to 2,000 miles of motoring carried out by the AA's road test engineers when the car is still relatively new. It will tell you whether the vehicle is a roomy or very compact one, how it handles under a variety of conditions, how comfortable it is, whether it is designed with acceleration or leisurely motoring in mind, the size and ease of loading of the boot, how easy it is to service and what kind of fuel consumption you can expect from it. In addition, there are specifications of each of the 50 cars tested: the principal technical data and a brief summary of significant model changes and variations.

The engineers' comments, VISAR revelations, road test reports and specifications form the heart of the book, but there is more. Features on corrosion, tyres, car electrics, the importance of maintenance and the Dealer Stock Inspection Scheme (the sale of AA-inspected used cars by motor traders) elaborate on significant aspects of the motor car – how it works, how you look after it, how you buy it secondhand. Having set the reader along the path of his choice, the AA *Guide to Used Cars* then discloses the results of its survey of prices, conducted by numerous technical experts countrywide. Variations in prices are shown region by region and

year by year, and a unique free valuation service is offered to keep these prices up to date regardless of when you purchased your copy of the Guide. In addition, there is a further listing of new and comparable used car prices for the person who has a specific sum to spend and wants to see what alternatives are available for it. In this section you are given at least three options.

Survey outside car's warranty period

Take i as a whole then, what is the purpose of this book? Quite simply, it is to give the would-be purchaser of a used car as much prior factual information as possible on a number of points about which dealers may be reticent or unable to comment. By and large, manufacturers monitor (via their dealer network) reasonably well the performance of their cars in the hands of the first buyer. They have a good idea of the car's reliability during the warranty period – but what happens after that? The significance of the VISAR survey lies in the fact that it covers cars *outside their warranty period?* What does this mean to the potential used car purchaser?

Shopping for a used car

Up to now, there have been two courses of action open to the individual who wants to buy a secondhand car. He may simply 'fall' for a particular car – its colour, shape or reputed performance – and settle for it then and there, ignoring all else. Or he may have a number of 'possibles' inspected by a qualified engineer. This can be costly and time-consuming. At last there is a third course of action. The AA recommends that you, the prospective car buyer, select the range of cars which is likely to appeal to your tastes and needs.

Make a short list of your personal requirements. If you have a large family and a dog, a sports car would be a poor bet. If you intend to tow, you need a larger car and a bigger engine than you would for short runs to and from the shops and school. If your family includes an elderly or infirm person, four doors are a must. If you intend to do the major part of the routine servicing yourself, stay clear of highly tuned, multi-carburettor cars unless you enjoy such endeavours, are fully capable of carrying out the tasks to complete satisfaction, and possess the equipment to do so. In general, the more complex a system, the more troubles it will have developed in someone else's hands. The previous owner may not have managed or bothered to have the 'kinks' ironed out before selling the car. In fact, irritation over the need to have small jobs carried out rather too frequently is often the prime cause for a 'very attractive car' being offered at a surprisingly low price.

Once you have listed those cars which would suit your way of life, compare their performance over the 8-year period of the VISAR survey – before you actually sit in them or take a test drive, let alone part with your money. If you intend to buy a 3-year-old car and expect to run it for another 3 years before re-selling it, look at the H and L columns of the data table and the engineers' comments as well. They may give you an idea of what the future might hold.

What about deterioration?

Finally, it is well to remember that you are buying a *secondhand* car – it will have been subjected to fair, or even unfair, wear and tear by one or more previous owners. Although all cars travel a one-way road to the scrapyard it may be useful to understand a bit more about how cars do deteriorate. First, both the percentage level of the defects found and the ratio at which this percentage increases as the car ages are important. The two are not the same; that is, the car does not necessarily deteriorate at the same rate as its components, nor is the rate uniform. For convenience, the rate of deterioration for all makes has been divided into five groupings; slow, moderate, high, very high, and ultra high.

Over the period of the VISAR survey, the following fall into the 'slow to deteriorate'

category; valve gear, including tappet clearance; front suspension, steering box or rack; clutch and fuel systems. Those in the moderate category include engine oil seals and gaskets, back axle and automatic gear boxes, footbrake and handbrake systems and light units.

A high rate of deterioration applies to cylinder head gaskets, underbody protection compounds, electric horn, fixing of driver's seat and – after a period of trouble-free operation, usually 4 years or so – the electric charging system. Also included in this group are corrosion of front and rear doors and underframe members, softening of engine flexible mountings and wear of synchromesh for the first 4-5 years of the car's life. Following component renewal, synchromesh wear slows down considerably, falling into the 'moderate' category.

The rate of rusting of front and rear wings, body sills, brake pipelines and valances is very high, and an ultra high rate of deterioration is suffered by door and boot sealing rubbers and jacking points.

These categories of deterioration are proof that ample room exists for manufacturers to improve materials and processes in order to slow down the rate of decay of today's motor cars. Routine maintenance and parts replacement help, but they cannot halt the progressive deterioration of the automobile.

Attraction of the secondhand market

Such inevitable decay, coupled with the current alarming increase of new car prices, is prompting more and more motorists to turn to the secondhand market. Used cars pose less of a drain on the wallet and they have already undergone the most serious period of depreciation.

This Guide should help you to get the right car for your needs and the best car for your money in the less-than-perfect world of motor cars.

Maintenance

Hindsight useless in a casualty ward

Maintenance can be neglected. If you are lucky, you can buy a secondhand car, put it on the road and run it for a year with only the occasional kick of the tyres and sniff of the dipstick. Sooner or later, though, the day of reckoning will arrive; one cold morning, on a wet motorway or possibly in a casualty ward you will have more time to consider the 'pros and cons'.

The maintenance of a car includes day-to-day running checks, routine servicing, and care of the bodywork. Each of these aspects requires active attention if a car is to give its best performance in terms of safety, economy and reliability. The responsibility for making sure they are carried out rests with the driver, whether or not he or she is the owner; even if you borrow a car for a short trip, there is a lot to be said for at least a quick check of the essentials.

Day-to-day checks

The following is a brief summary of the items that should be checked every week, or more often if high mileages are covered.

1 Tyre pressure: Set to the recommended pressure (when cold) for type of tyre, car and loading conditions. Check for cuts, bulges or other damage.
2 Engine oil level: Check the dipstick with the car standing on level ground; top up with correct grade of oil if required.
3 Brake fluid level: Check the level of fluid in the brake master cylinder as indicated in the car handbook. Investigate immediately if there is a marked drop in the level. Top up if necessary with clean hydraulic brake fluid of the correct type kept in a closed container.
4 Radiator level: Keep the radiator filled to the correct level as indicated in the car handbook. Do not remove the cap when the engine is hot, and top up with the appropriate water/anti-freeze mixture. Look out for split or bulging water hoses, and check the cause of any significant loss of coolant.
5 Battery: The level of the electrolyte in the battery should be kept about a quarter of an inch over the tops of the plates, usually visible when you remove the caps or cover. Use only purified water for batteries, such as distilled or de-ionised water.
6 Lights: Make sure that all lamps, flashers and stop lamps are working properly.
7 Windscreen: Check that the windscreen washers and wipers are in good order.

The above checks can be carried out quite quickly. If you keep a piece of rag and a tyre pressure gauge handy, they need only take 5 minutes – unless you find something wrong!

Routine servicing

The servicing required will need more detailed attention. The precise operations and the mileages at which they should be carried out will be given in the car handbook or service voucher book. They are usually listed in three groups: 3,000 miles or 3 months, 6,000 miles or 6 months, and 12,000 miles or 12 months, whichever is the shorter period in each case.

The routine servicing operations, if carried out properly in accordance with the manufacturer's recommendations, should ensure the safe and reliable running of the car as far as possible. If you buy a secondhand car, it is as well to assume that the servicing may not have been kept up to date. Have the major 12,000-mile service carried out by a dealer for the make concerned. Even if you do most of the normal servicing yourself, it is advisable to have at least an annual safety check made by a dealer, as he will have the current service information and specialist tools necessary to do this thoroughly. It is quite easy for an owner driver to become used to a fault in the car, such as excessive play in the steering; it can develop so gradually that the defect is not noticeable until an emergency situation occurs, and it may then be too late. The dealer should know what to look for, and will be advised by the manufacturer if any serious fault is found in a particular model that may require modification of vehicles in service.

DIY advice

If you decide to carry out some of the servicing yourself, first check the list of operations given in the handbook and make sure that you have the tools required and the parts that are likely to be necessary, and that you are confident of your ability to do the work properly. It is really not much good haphazardly doing those jobs that are easy, and leaving the others. It is positively dangerous to start adjusting the steering mechanism, for example, without detailed knowledge of what should be done.

3,000-mile service

The 3,000-mile/3-month service will include items such as brake adjustment, lamp alignment, a steering check and a check of the fan belt and battery connections, as well as the seven operations already listed. It therefore includes a number of important safety checks which must not be neglected.

Obviously the most important safety checks are the brakes, lights, steering and tyres. The brake hydraulic system should be checked for leaks at the master cylinder, the wheel cylinders or any of the unions. The flexible hoses leading to the wheels should be closely examined for abrasion, fraying, splitting or any other surface deterioration. Brake pedal travel should be checked to make sure it is not excessive and that pedal operation has not become spongy, as this might indicate the ingress of air into the system. The brakes should be adjusted if necessary.

The alignment of the headlamps should be checked, preferably with a beam tester. The steering should be examined for security of all the components and freedom from excessive wear. The amount of allowable free-play in the various parts depends on their design and should therefore either be checked in the workshop manual or referred to a dealer. If any of the protective gaiters are found to be split these should be replaced.

All the tyres should be inspected, over the whole tread pattern and both the inner and outer walls. Remove embedded objects and look for cuts, bulges or other damage. Make sure the tread depth is adequate; though the legal limit is 1mm, road grip in wet weather is markedly reduced when depth is below 2mm.

6,000-mile service

At 6,000 miles or 6 months, all the above work is repeated. In addition, the distributor, sparking plugs and tappets, carburettor settings and oil levels are adjusted, grease nipples are lubricated and brake lining thickness is checked. These mainly affect the economy and reliability of the car. For maximum economy, some vehicles may require more frequent attention to the engine settings, particularly when fitted with more than one carburettor.

The ignition system needs thorough maintenance to ensure reliability. If neglected, it is possibly more prone than other systems to cause breakdowns and it is therefore worthwhile to make sure it is in good condition. The spark plugs should be renewed if they have done more than 10,000 miles; otherwise, they should be cleaned and the points carefully reset. The contact breaker points in the distributor should be examined and renewed if there is any obvious pitting. If the surfaces are just slightly dirty, they can be cleaned with a petrol-moistened rag and the gap reset. This gap is important to the correct performance of the coil, as it determines the period of 'dwell angle' during which the points remain closed. After any such adjustment the ignition timing should be checked as indicated in the car handbook.

The valve tappets should be checked, as lack of adequate clearance can lead to valve failure and excessive clearance will cause a loss of power. When the tappets and other settings have been corrected, the carburettor can be adjusted. In most cases, this involves setting the idle speed and idle mixture, as these can have a considerable affect on the general running of the car.

12,000-mile service

The parts of the car requiring only occasional attention are included in the 12,000-mile or 12-month service. The checks listed in the 3,000 and 6,000 mile services are made, and in addition the water pump, steering box, front wheel hubs, gear box and rear axle are lubricated and the locks, hinges, drain holes, seat-belts and so on are checked.

Bodywork maintenance

The running checks and routine servicing so far mentioned will keep the car mechanically sound, but maintenance in the broader sense must include attention to the bodywork to prevent unnecessary deterioration. Cleaning is obviously a requirement; regular washing with plain water or a very dilute detergent will remove most harmful deposits from the surface of the paintwork. If left, they can cause deterioration of the finish and ultimately lead to corrosion. In normal road use, the paintwork will inevitably suffer some damage from stone chipping, and minor dents or abrasions can damage the paint film, leaving areas which sooner or later will show rust spots. Probably the best course of action, therefore, is to look out for such damage while washing the car, particularly around the wheel arches and on the front panel.

As soon as possible after any defects are noticed they should be repaired. If the paint film is broken, the immediate area should be rubbed down to the bare metal with 320 grit 'wet or dry' abrasive paper – use it well wetted – until every trace of rust has been removed. The metal should then be treated with a rust remover, primed and given three or four coats of finish paint; for small areas an aerosol can is convenient. Regular attention in this way will at least keep the car looking smarter, though unfortunately the more serious type of corrosion starts inside panels or underneath the car. Once established, it is not so easy to cure: simply treating the surface where it breaks through will not give any long-term benefit.

Maintenance of the car underbody should include an occasional thorough hosing. If it is done only once a year, the best time will be in late spring – when salt is no longer used on the roads – before warmer weather accelerates the corrosion. Heavy deposits of mud should be scraped out, and any loose underbody protection compound removed. Rust patches can then be wire brushed and treated with a good rust remover before priming and re-coating as necessary.

Equipment

The equipment required for home car maintenance need not be elaborate. As previously mentioned, the service data will be essential, and a well-lit garage will help – working outside is not ideal. The most useful tools will include a set of open-ended spanners, metric or AF according to the car. Sizes between 7mm and 17mm or $\frac{3}{8}''$ and $\frac{3}{4}''$ will cover most work; the correct plug spanner for the car is also necessary. A range of three or four conventional screwdrivers and a large and small cross-slot screwdriver, a set of feeler gauges and a strong pair of pliers will be required. If your car has grease nipples that require attention, you will find a high-pressure grease gun the most efficient, and a jack and axle stands are needed for work under the body .

It is quite justifiable to save money by carrying out your own maintenance. If you take on the responsibility of doing this work yourself, however, it must be done thoroughly. If you are not inclined to do any servicing, at least the day-to-day checks should be made. In either case, knowing something about the subject can make life easier in dealing with minor breakdowns or garage estimates. Making sure that the correct maintenance is carried out can avoid an unnecessary repair, a breakdown or possibly an accident.

Corrosion

Rust is your car's greatest enemy

Cars do not last forever. This fact is as true today as it was 20, 30 or 40 years ago, and even those on which great care has been lavished eventually end up in the scrapyard. Since the time when sheet steel replaced timber and fabric as construction materials for the passenger compartment, cars have gone rusty with monotonous regularity.

It is in the nature of things that iron and steel corrode in our everyday environment. In doing so, the metal completes the cycle from natural ores found in the earth to a strong, relatively durable structure and back again to an amalgam of iron oxides and carbonates, etc. In the weakened form of rusty components, the metal is of little practical use to man, except as the starting point of the process of making iron and steel parts once more.

Precisely when a car is relegated to the scrap-heap is a decision based on many considerations, mainly economic ones. Vehicle manufacturers are basically interested in satisfying first and second owners, when corrosion is not too obvious. They have therefore by and large adopted markedly similar techniques and products to achieve this end. They have not deliberately designed their cars either as a throw-away short-life commodity, such as children's mechanical toys, or as a vehicle with the potential long life expectancy of a merchant ship. The average lifespan – in economic terms – of most mass-produced cars is between 10 and 12 years in most of the highly motorised countries of the world, and this has remained constant for the last 20 years or more.

The motor manufacturers have made great strides over the years to improve the durability of engines, gear boxes, steering and suspension. Hence the major mechanical components of a car will still be fit for further use when the body of the car shows serious signs of rotting away. The rate of decay is initially quite slow. If no preventive maintenance is carried out by first owners, however, a small neglected defect may subsequently require a costly repair. At worst it could result in the car becoming both unroadworthy and unsaleable.

It is rarely appreciated that the technology of sheet-steel fabrication, metal pre-treatment, paint systems, underbody protection coatings and anti-corrosion compounds applied to closed sections of the bodyshell has barely been able to keep pace with the ever increasing severity of corrosion attack in our highly industrialised country. Other countries have a climate which is less injurious to the car body. This includes some of the Mediterranean as well as some of the land-locked Continental countries where daily and seasonal fluctuations of temperature, humidity, rain and slush are less pronounced. Cars produced in some of these countries have until quite recently had an anti-corrosion treatment applied at the factory which, while somewhat inferior, may nonetheless be completely adequate for the major portion of their market.

The environmental conditions which have a substantial effect on the rate of corrosion are many, and usually inter-related. In a dry atmosphere free of industrial pollution the rate of corrosion is slower than in a damp one. Similarly, months of motoring on packed snow do less harm than a few days' motoring in slush, which penetrates every nook and cranny of the car. Condensation on the inside of panels such as doors and pillars, under carpets, and in box sections is caused by an overnight temperature drop following a warm muggy day and this cycle can be as harmful as exposure to the rock salt used to prevent freezing of road surfaces.

In the UK, corrosion is a year-round, endemic disease. While it principally attacks iron and steel in mechanical components and the bodyshell, and magnesium and zinc alloy castings, it can also affect stainless steel and aluminium brightwork where these are joined to the basically mild-steel structure. It mars the appearance of chromium-plated steel bumpers, diecast door handles and wing mirror stems.

How corrosion occurs

For corrosion to take place several conditions must exist: oxygen and moisture must have access to the metal, there must be a small difference in electrical potential – $\frac{1}{4}$ volt is enough – between metallic surfaces in close proximity to one another, and there must be an electrolyte bridging them and a temperature sufficiently high to maintain the flow of ions.

In such a corrosion cell, which is analogous to a wet-cell car battery or a dry-cell torch battery, the negatively-charged ions on the free surface flow to the anode or positive pole. (See figure 1).

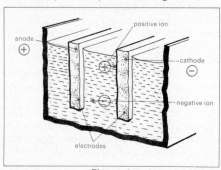

Figure 1

The result is that the positive ions concentrate round the cathode (negative pole) and the anode dissolves. The higher the temperature and the stronger the electrolyte solution, the greater the rate of electrochemical action. In the case of iron or steel poles we call this process rusting. Rusting stops if the electrolyte freezes or is very depleted but any increase in acidic content or temperature will reactivate it. Hence, the mud poultices or dirt and dust which so easily accumulate on vehicles are re-charged with road salt, industrial pollution and soil rich in agricultural chemicals and farmhouse manure, all of which constitute a major hazard.

Fighting back

The best way to combat corrosion is to liberally wash all surfaces on which mud and dirt can lodge, particularly the underside, and provide good ventilation; do not employ force drying or rely on polishes. The most destructive corrosion, which in fact weakens the body structure, is rusting from the inside of closed or box sections where it is particularly difficult to deposit paint or a rust inhibitor. (See figure 2).

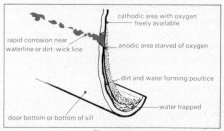

Figure 2

Since it is not feasible to change the operating environment, the engineers and technicians must try to retard the onset and rate of corrosion. In our everyday environment – on roads both in town and country – untreated steel corrodes rapidly. The purpose of all paint systems, as applied by manufacturers, is to retard this process rather than enhance the car's appearance.

The bodyshell is given a uniform acid etch in order to deposit on it a thin unbroken phosphate film, particularly inside difficult-to-paint closed or box sections. A primer paint coat is keyed onto this film and on visible surfaces this is further reinforced by one or more layers of colour coat. A further layer of clear lacquer may also be applied. Only if this protection system of steel+phosphate+primer coat were totally effective – over the entire structure of the car – in preventing the electrolyte from coming into contact with sheet steel would the car body be immune to corrosion. The ideal is rarely fully realised, however, and where this barrier system breaks down, local corrosion will be found. Generally the more localised the breakdown, the more serious the problem, because all the corrosion activity will be concentrated, usually in an inaccessible area. (See figure 3).

mud is thrown up by wheels and trapped, thus causing corrosion

Figure 3

Two approaches to the problem

Two methods of minimising the corrosion rate have found ready acceptance of late. The most common procedure used by manufacturers is to dip the complete bodyshell in a giant vat in which paint comprised of various resins and pigments forms a suspension in water. The phosphated steel body is immersed for $1\frac{1}{2}$ to 2 minutes, during which time all accessible surfaces receive a thin, uniformly deposited film of paint approximately $\frac{3}{4}$–$1\frac{1}{2}$ thousandths of an inch thick. This thin film is achieved by making the whole body the anode or positive pole. Unfortunately, the first generation of electro-coated bodies – sometimes referred to as electrophoretically painted – was deficient in film adhesion properties in the very sections where it mattered most from the point of view of structural safety, eg in the long box sections of small cross-sectional areas, which are principally underbody stiffeners, body sills and door pillars. This defect applies to some cars in the 5-10-year-old age bracket. Only within the last 2 to 4 years have most of the production problems been fully overcome by re-design of certain body pressings, better paint technology, and improved production control.

Some plants in the US and Sweden have adopted an entirely different approach; they galvanise these difficult-to-protect areas.

Galvanisation, which has been successfully applied to buckets and water tanks as well as to Landrover–type dual-purpose vehicles, relies on the sacrificial nature of the zinc deposited on the sheet steel. In a corrosive environment the zinc, being anodic in relation to the steel, is dissolved, *ie* it is sacrificed to save the sheet steel. This relatively more expensive process, and to a lesser extent the use of zinc–rich primer paints, give excellent service, healing over the abrasion when the zinc coating is damaged. Once the zinc coating is exhausted, however, the corrosion rate increases at a gallop! When local failure has set in, especially near weld joints, neither system succeeds in delaying serious trouble for long.

Local corrosion antidote

The best way to prevent local corrosion is to inject under high pressure one of the various types of petroleum- or wax-based corrosion inhibitors; these can add 3 to 5 years to the life of critical body-structure zones. By offering a thin unbroken film which attaches itself to the metal and covering paint film, the moisture-repellant inhibitor prevents moisture and oxygen gaining access and rust getting a foothold. It is essential that they never set completely hard, have good adhesion to metal and primer paint, and be capable of creeping into close fitting joints and crevices. However, it should be remembered that this process requires regular inspection and supplementary application after 1 or 2 years. Above all, it is important to note that it cannot be successfully applied to retard further corrosion once the flake type of corrosion, rather than a slight red-brown general surface rusting, has set in; at this stage, it will give preferential protection to the loose or partly lifted off flakes rather than the residual more or less sound steel pressing.

Looks aren't everything

Appearance is not everything, and waxes and polishes do not help to stave off the onset of corrosion.

Remember that the least effective part of

15

the complex protective paint system is the glossy top coat, which readily allows moisture and oxygen, as well as weak acids and alkalis, to permeate it.

If you are inspecting a used car and see signs of poor bodywork repair or an obvious area of respray, beware! If the metal preparation and etch priming have been skimped in the course of a repair job, while the outward appearance may be good at the time, general rusting and paint blistering will emerge in another 6 to 9 months. Always insist on a look beneath the carpet and underlay in the passenger compartment and the boot and compare its general state with the outward appearance of the car. No amount of paint can restore a vital section which has been structurally weakened by rust. It *is* possible to weld in complete sub-assemblies and large sections, however, provided the metal to which they are to be joined is still in sound condition and not badly rusted. Before contemplating such drastic surgery it is important to assess the cost against the life expectancy of the rest of the car. In most cases it is pointless to carry out a patchwork pattern of rebuilding.

Corrosion and . . .

. . . *exhaust systems*

Exhaust systems, particularly the tailpipe and rear silencer, are attacked internally by hot gases and externally by road slush and de-icing salts. In general, the more stop-go and short-distance motoring, the shorter the life of the system. The average life of a mild-steel silencer is rarely more than two winters; it must be considered a routine replacement item. Many manufacturers have been fitting longer life aluminised steel silencers on their most recent models and these give an extra 12 to 18 months' service life. A stainless steel tailpipe is not to be confused with the much more expensive long-life all-stainless steel exhaust systems which have yet to find acceptance on the mass market.

. . . *chrome-plated parts*

Modern plating technology uses a metallurgical process called 'micro-cracking' which, by offering many possible corrosion paths, spreads the electrical potential. If concentrated, this potential might be sufficient to cause a single deep pit, but in a diffused state it is insufficient to cause general rusting.

. . . *underbody protective compounds*

The application of relatively thick and non-hardening compounds before rust has set in can be effective in retarding corrosion. If applied too late, over rust, or if allowed to harden and crack, however, they can accelerate rather than retard rusting.

. . . *stone damage*

No stone chips should be ignored. The longer they remain without touch-in paint repair, the greater the risk of unsightly paint blistering. Such blistering indicates that rust beneath the paint layer is forcing an ever increasing amount of paint away from the metal it is supposed to be protecting. This occurs because rust takes up more volume than unaffected mild steel.

In areas where stone chipping cannot be avoided, some manufacturers apply a PVC, polyurethane or another type of plastic coating over the most exposed curved surfaces.

. . . *braking systems*

Corrosion affects not only the body structure, mechanical components and cooling system, but also the hydraulic braking system. Brake systems also suffer from both internal and external corrosion. Grit, corrosive salt and slush bombard the outside of brake pipes and unions; only a careful inspection of the underside of the car will establish whether this attack has been of sufficient severity to warrant replacement. It is false economy to delay replacement – your own and other people's lives may depend on a sound, reliable braking system. It is very important to check on the proper functioning of the hydraulic brakes and also the free working of the non-hydraulic handbrake mechanism. Internal corrosion is minimised by flushing out the hydraulic system once every 2 years, replenishing it with fresh fluid from an unopened tin and removing all air from the system by bleeding it.

AA Report Scheme

Buying a used car the easy way

The greatest danger to the purchaser of a secondhand car is the purchase of a secondhand car! Armed with his money and an absolute determination to go home with a 'new' car he is easy meat for the trade wolf.

With sales averaging two million cars a year there are bound to be rogues in the business; they exist in every trade and profession, and the motor trader is no exception. No established dealer, however, will risk his livelihood or his local reputation for a few pounds profit.

Independent examinations

For many years the AA, the RAC and firms of consultant engineers have inspected cars for prospective purchasers, and no self-respecting dealer with nothing to hide would refuse to agree a purchase subject to an examination by an independent body. In fact, like the doctor who seeks a second opinion, reputable dealers not only accept such examinations but often state in advertising that independent inspections are welcome.

Inspection prior to sale

Unfortunately, demand varies enormously and it helps neither the dealer nor the customer if a transaction is delayed for more than a few days while arrangements are completed. With this problem in mind the AA and, to a lesser extent, other organisations have made arrangements to inspect dealers' stocks prior to sales and to indicate to prospective customers that selected cars have been subjected to thorough examinations. The cost of inspection is met by the dealer who agrees beforehand to remedy all defects found by the AA inspecting engineer and listed by him as being in need of rectification. On completion of essential repairs the dealer is given a windscreen 'sticker' signed by the inspecting engineer, and is authorised to advertise the fact that an independent examination has been carried out.

On average, the cost to the dealer completing all the necessary repairs is around £50 but, as the Yorkshireman is reputed to say, no one does 'owt for nowt'. In return the dealer gets the goodwill of his customers and a considerable decrease in expenditure resulting from warranty claims.

Warranty responsibilities

As far as the AA is concerned, dealer stock inspections do not in any way relieve the dealer of his warranty responsibilities. In fact, the opposite applies as it is a requirement of the scheme that an adequate warranty is given and honoured. A detailed ten-page report is given to the dealer for each car inspected and this is made available to all existing members of the AA and other prospective buyers who agree to join the Association. In some cases dealers offer a year's membership as an incentive to the customer. The advantage to the AA member is that the report details other minor faults, commensurate with the age of the vehicle, which will require attention in due course.

Adequate repairs

Although non-members are not entitled to a report, the fact remains that the windscreen 'sticker' is not signed until the engineer is satisfied that adequate repairs have been carried out. Even so, like the surgeon who is never quite sure until he opens you up, no engineer can be absolutely sure that some of the internal mechanism has not suffered through previous misuse or, in the case of older cars, from fair wear and tear. That is why we recommend, in another section of this book, that you keep some cash in hand to deal with repairs and servicing.

A selection of some of the dealers operating the AA's stock inspection scheme is given on the following pages. A full list is available from local AA service centres.

Watch for the Stickers!

THE AUTOMOBILE ASSOCIATION
TECHNICAL SERVICES
INSPECTED
AA

A selection of dealers operating the AA Stock Inspection Scheme

AA
INSPECTED CARS SOLD HERE
please ask for details

Morris House Tel: Belfast
90–106 Victoria Street 32361
Belfast BT1 3GY

WH ALEXANDER LTD

Morris, Wolseley & MG Distributors

Britton Park Road Tel: Teignmouth
Teignmouth, S Devon 2501

COUNTY GARAGE
(TEIGNMOUTH) LTD

AUSTIN, MG, ROVER, TRIUMPH

VW–AUDI–NSU–MERCEDES

KINGSTHORPE GARAGE
Quality used cars

42–50 Harborough Road
Northampton NNS 7BA

JA GORDON & SON LTD
Stonehouse, Stroud
Gloucestershire
'Leaders in new and used cars'
STROUD
Tel: 2130 2139 Chrysler main dealer
2769

CHRYSLER MAIN DEALERS
Hillman–Humber–Sunbeam–Simca

BELLS OF RICHMOND
North Road, Tel: 01–876 2631
Richmond, Surrey 01–878 0271

GE HARPER LTD
Main dealer for Chrysler & Simca

1 London Road, Tel: Stevenage
Stevenage, Herts 54691
SG1 3LN

Clough Street, MAIN FORD DEALER
Hanley,
Stoke-on-Trent
Tel: 29591

A E CHATFIELD LTD

19

The electrical system

Neglect it – and invite breakdown

Although the highest percentage of car breakdowns is attributed to the car's electrical system, covering such things as a flat battery or damp ignition, normally the electrical system gives trouble only if it is not properly maintained. When mishandled it does not always fail at once – perhaps a week or so later a different part will go wrong because the system concerned has been disturbed. If something does go wrong with the electrics, it can be expensive to repair – and the damage can be increased by inexpert attention.

Current problems with the battery
The battery fitted to a car is of a type known as lead-acid. It is normally a 12-volt battery, although a few types of car have 6-volt batteries. As the name implies, a battery is a collection of cells; as each cell is able to produce 2 volts, a 12-volt battery has six cells and a 6-volt battery three. The cells are joined together and housed in the same package, but each functions as a separate unit.

If you allow a battery to remain discharged, the chemical action whereby the acid in the electrolyte is combined with the lead plates and sulphate is produced, runs wild. It forms crystals that grow and multiply on the lead plates, interfering with the action of the electrolyte by reducing the exposed area of the lead plate. As this sulphation continues, the plates expand, forcing lead sulphate into the pores of the separators. This fouling reduces the circulation of the electrolyte and the flow of current. In time, the crystals grow very large and the lead sulphate becomes extremely solid, making it very difficult to dissolve or return to its original state – which would normally happen during re-charging. If you fast-charge or boost-charge a battery in this condition, you often merely lift off the sulphated areas, thereby damaging the plates. A battery that has been left for 2 or 3 days in a discharged state is hard to reclaim. One that has been

left flat for a week or so is unlikely ever to be useful again.

Effect of low temperature
As the battery is a chemical device, it is greatly affected by lower temperatures experienced during winter. An additional strain is placed upon the battery for two reasons: its efficiency is reduced as the temperature drops, yet at the same time more power is needed to start the engine at lower temperatures. In addition, a higher lighting and heating load is normally demanded.

The ability of a fully charged battery to supply current at the necessary high starting rate is reduced by approximately 40% at freezing point. Very much more energy is needed to crank the engine at reduced temperatures, even when it contains SAE 20W oil; at freezing point, 75% more energy is needed than on a hot summer's day. When a battery is asked to start a car at freezing point, not only is its efficiency reduced by 40%, but one and three-quarters times the normal power is demanded from it.

Hydrometer reading (specific gravity)	Charge state of battery
1.270–1.290	Fully charged
1.230–1.250	70% charged
1.110–1.130	Discharged

The power-hungry starter motor
The starter motor is a powerful electric motor whose function is to start the engine crankshaft turning and keep it turning until the engine starts. More energy is needed to get something moving initially than to keep it moving once it is in motion. The amount of electrical energy required to enable the starter motor initially to turn the crankshaft is about equivalent to that needed to light 100 headlamp bulbs.

Because the starter motor needs such a lot of current, it makes the biggest demands on the battery. Although the lights and other parts may work well, a fairly flat battery is unlikely to be able to supply sufficient current to operate the starter motor properly. The battery connections are also important; if the battery terminals are dirty, a narrow passageway can exist and give all the symptoms of a flat battery. When this happens the dirty terminal will usually feel warm immediately after you try to start the car.

In addition to the earth strap from one side of the battery to the car body, all cars have another thick, braided earth strap somewhere between the engine and chassis (often underneath the car by the gear box); this is necessary to provide a good earth return back to the battery because the engine is supported on rubber mountings. If this earth strap is loose or missing, another current-limiting passage will exist and give symptoms similar to those of a flat battery. In this case the choke cables and throttle cables often get warm as the current tries to complete the circuit – via them – back to the battery.

Ignition – the spark of activity
The function of the ignition system is to produce and deliver current surges at high voltage to each of the sparking plugs in turn, at exactly the right moment, in order to fire the compressed fuel/air mixture in the engine cylinders. To do this there has to be a means of increasing the 12-volt output of the battery to the 10,000–20,000 volt pressure that is necessary to jump the current in the form of a spark across the gap between the plug electrodes. This is done by using a transformer – the ignition coil. The coil itself very rarely fails. There is very little that can go wrong. But it can overheat and be damaged if the ignition is left switched on for too long when the engine is not running.

The contact-breaker points are the biggest single cause of ignition problems. Over a period of time they become very dirty, burnt, and out of adjustment. The contact-breaker points in the average four-cylinder car travelling at 70mph are opening and closing about 10,000 times a minute, and in a 6,000-mile period they will open and close about 60 million times. If they fail to make a proper electrical connection just once or twice every minute, a misfire will be heard and – felt.

Dirt and dampness are the biggest enemies of the HT system (comprising the distributor cap, rotor arm, sparking plugs, and all the thick, heavily insulated HT – high tension – leads), as they can offer alternative routes for the spark current. Cracks in the rotor arm and distributor cap will also reduce their insulation and provide alternative paths for the current. Modern HT leads do not have metal wire cores for the HT current to travel along; carbon-impregnated string is used instead. Although the carbon is a resistor, the high voltage is able to move the current through it; at the same time the carbon leads act as radio and television interference suppressors, and this is why they are used. If these leads are pulled or stretched or in any way misused, the carbon string can be broken and misfires are likely to occur, particularly at high speeds.

The sparking plugs have an average life of 10,000 miles, after which it is sensible to change them.

Blowing your own horn
The electric horn is a very simple device. It comprises a thin sheet of metal (the diaphragm) – with a piece of metal (the armature) bolted to it – stretched across the front of the horn body behind a protective front cover.

In some systems the horn button is placed in the supply side of the circuit, and in some on the earth side. In either case, pressing the button completes the circuit and the horn will operate until the button is released. As horns demand a great deal of current to work efficiently, rapid and firm connections and disconnections are necessary to prevent 'arcing' at the switch or press-button contacts.

The main problem is keeping the terminal connections in good condition; they are often exposed to water and salt thrown up off the road. Otherwise the horn rarely gives trouble.

Tyres

Your life may depend on them

The tyre has to perform many different roles: it acts as a spring to soften road shocks, transmits all the power of engine and brakes and translates the steering wheel input into a change of direction. All this has to be transmitted through just four small but vital areas of contact between the moving car and the road – each about the size of the sole of an average man's shoe. In a moment of crisis the driver may have to rely on these four small areas for his very survival.

Just as there are many widely differing types of footwear, each best suited to a particular requirement, so there are different types of tyre. It is therefore unreasonable to expect a universal tyre to suit all purposes without some drawbacks.

All tyres are a compromise solution to a complex series of problems. None of them will fully satisfy the requirements under all possible conditions of operation. A tremendous, costly, and continuing effort has gone, and still goes, into design, research, development, testing, production, and yet more development in rubber grades and mixes, carcass construction, and tread patterns. There have been large strides forward during the past 15 years or so towards that elusive goal – the ideal motor car tyre.

Treading a narrow path

In order to steer a car round a corner, the tyre must produce a cornering force to push it away from the straight-ahead path. This cornering force is produced by that part of the tyre tread in contact with the road (known as the contact patch) becoming distorted and running at a small angle to the direction of travel of the wheel. This angle is known as the slip angle. When the car is not turning but travelling straight ahead, the tyre must produce a similar force against the effect of road camber or cross-winds.

The amount of slip angle on both the front and rear tyres will affect the handling of the car. If the front slip angles are greater than those at the rear, then the car is said to understeer; if the rear slip angles are greater than those at the front, the car is said to oversteer.

Although modern cars are designed to give, as near as is practicable, a neutral steering (ie, with no tendencies to either understeer or oversteer), this cannot always be achieved under all conditions of motoring. It is safer to have a vehicle with a tendency to understeer rather than oversteer. It is easier to control a vehicle with a tendency to understeer, as it will not be so liable to get into an uncontrollable spin, particularly on a slippery surface.

Tyre types and their make-up

Modern cross-ply tyres have casings made from plies of rayon, polyester, or nylon, laid at opposing angles to each other and at approximately 40 degrees to the circumference of the tyre. They are wrapped around two steel wire hoops or beads which prevent the tyre stretching and parting from the wheel. The tyre tread, which is moulded to the casing, is nowadays manufactured mainly from a blend of synthetic rubbers in order to provide a good road grip, especially in wet weather.

The need for a new tyre with an even longer life led in 1948 to the introduction of the Michelin X, the first of the present-day radial tyres. The construction of the radial-ply tyre reduces cornering wear and considerably increases the overall life of the tyre; but this is usually at the expense of a slightly harder ride at lower speeds. It gives greater high-speed cornering grip than cross-ply or bias-belted tyres of equivalent size.

The cords in the plies run from bead to bead across the crown at right angles, not diagonally as in the cross-ply tyre. This gives great pliability and comfort, but little or no directional stability. Stability comes from the tread-bracing layers, a belt of cords running round the circumference of the tyre beneath the tread. These cords are usually spun from rayon textile or fine steel wire, and are flexible but do not lose their tautness. This firmly restricts any lateral stretching of the tread.

Cross-plies versus Radials

The two conflicting requirements – that of providing fairly soft springing for comfort by means of flexible sidewalls, but a relatively stiff structure in the tread area for steering and stability – are difficult to achieve in a cross-ply tyre, due to its type of construction. The layers of cross-ply reinforcement extend throughout the tyre's sidewalls as well as the tread, resulting in a fairly homogenous structure in which the two requirements are inter-related. In the radial-ply tyre, these two requirements are dealt with separately by the very flexible radial-ply sidewalls and the inextensible bracing layer under the tread. This stiffening of the tread enables the radial-ply to provide the necessary force or cornering power at a much lower slip angle than the cross-ply tyre, because there is less scrubbing of the tread when cornering, thus resulting in a much-increased tyre life.

Slip angle varies according to the type of tyre; it is smallest in the radial-ply steel-braced tyre, and increases progressively from this to the radial-ply textile tyre, the radial-ply winter tyre, the cross-ply tyre, and finally the cross-ply winter tyre.

Because of the inextensible bracing layer under the tread, radial-ply tyres cannot be made and shaped as easily as cross-ply tyres and call for higher standards of accuracy in manufacture. These factors make them cost more. Nevertheless, because of the substantially increased tread life, tyre cost per mile is lower. They do, however, have some undesirable features; at low speeds they offer some resistance to steering movements, thus requiring more effort when making parking manoeuvres. They are also apt to transmit small vibrations caused by the relatively stiff tyre rolling over road joints or cat's eyes, but at higher speeds it is advisable to consult the vehicle manufacturer's agents before changing from cross-ply to radial-ply tyres.

Another feature which affects the performance of a tyre, either cross-ply or radial, is its aspect ratio; that is, the ratio of its cross-sectional height to its cross-sectional width when fitted to the appropriate wheel rim. In the early days the width of a tyre section was about the same as its height, thus giving an aspect ratio of 100%. The modern trend is to make tyres wider and shallower, reducing the height from tread to rim while increasing the width across the tyre's section. Gradually over the years the aspect ratio has been reduced – first to 95% in the cushion-type tyre, then to 88% in the medium-profile tyre, and down through 77% to 70% in the 70 series as used today on high-performance cars. On racing cars, with their extra wide wheels, the ratio can be much lower, going down as far as 30%.

Working under pressure

Correct tyre inflation pressures are vitally important for the safe handling of the car and also for attaining the maximum life from the tyres.

Always check inflation pressures with a reliable gauge at the start of a journey when the tyre is cold. The correct pressures will be found in the vehicle handbook. Do not rely on the appearance of the tyre – this can be deceptive, especially with radial-ply tyres which, because of their more flexible sidewalls, tend to look under-inflated. Even more important than ensuring correct inflation pressure is ensuring that tyres on the same axle have the same pressure reading – they should be within 2lb per square inch ($2lb/in^2$) of each other.

Tyre pressures increase fairly rapidly with the running of the vehicle; the faster the speed, the more rapid the increase. The amount of pressure increase depends on the surrounding air and road surface temperatures and the method of construction of the tyre carcass. Cross-ply tyres run hotter than radial-ply and so have a more rapid temperature rise. In this country, the increase on basic pressure of $24lb/in^2$ will, on average, be roughly as follows:

On a 1–2 mile trip to your local garage 2–4lb/in^2 cross-ply; 1–2lb/in^2 radial-ply

Over 10 miles in average traffic in town and country 3–5lb/in^2 cross-ply; 1–3lb/in^2 radial-ply

For high-speed motoring 6–10lb/in^2 cross-ply; 3–6lb/in^2 radial-ply

On the Continent, high-speed motoring in summer temperatures would produce an average increase of 8–14lb/in^2 cross-ply, and 4–8lb/in^2 radial-ply.

Never reduce pressures during a long journey, when hot tyres will have increased pressure from the cold setting.

Contrary to popular opinion, lowering the tyre pressure does not give you a better grip on wet roads, snow, or ice, since it tends to close the actual tread pattern and thus reduces the grip. Worst of all, because of excessive flexing and the heat built up in the carcass, it considerably reduces the life expectancy of your tyres.

A delicate balance

The engine is not the only part of a car that needs running-in. Tyres, particularly high-speed tyres, need a period of settling down. It is generally advisable to run tyres at no more than 50mph for the first 50 to 100 miles. Speed should be increased gradually over the first 250 miles, and severe cornering should be avoided.

A front wheel that is not properly balanced can set up disturbing vibrations that can be felt through the steering wheel and by the passengers – particularly at high speeds. If not corrected it also leads to excessive wear of wheel bearings and swivel joints. New tyres should always be balanced before being fitted, and – particularly in the case of radial-ply tyres – should be checked for balance after the first 500 miles. The balance of a wheel can be upset by damage to the wheel rim, and high-speed cornering causes rapid tread wear which in turn can affect the balance of the tyre.

What's the damage?

Under-inflation: Excessive wear on the edges of the tread with much less wear in the centre of the tread is a clear indication of a tyre constantly used with insufficient inflation pressure.

Over-inflation: The pattern of wear is the reverse, the excessive wear being in the centre of the tread, with less wear on the edges.

Camber wear: This shows as excessive wear of from a third to half of the tread, caused by wear in the steering linkages.

Misalignment: The feathered edge of the tread pattern indicates that the tread of the tyre has been scrubbed off because it has been dragged sideways as it rolled forward on a wheel out of correct alignment.

And now a word on neglect . . .

The VISAR survey of 31,358 cars tells an interesting but frightening story about tyres. Of the 158,790 inspected (five tyres per car), 3.35% were dangerous, unroadworthy or in need of immediate attention, 7.85% needed attention soon, 2.8% had tread depth less than the 1mm required by law, 7% were between 1mm and the AA's recommended minimum of 2mm, 1.6% were damaged, and 0.8% were unsuitable or an illegal mixture.

Signs of uneven wear were noted on 20.5% of front tyres, 11% of rear tyres, and 23% of spares. Six per cent of all tyres were remoulds, 37% were cross-plies and 63% were radials, showing clearly that more and more people opt for radial tyres both as original and replacement fitment.

The spare was generally in a poorer condition than the rolling tyres, particularly with regard to its state of inflation. The survey found that 18.5% of the spares were dangerous or in need of immediate attention, and 10% were in need of attention soon. Yet 43% of all spares inspected had hardly ever been in use, for they had well over 6mm of tread depth left compared with 39.5% of the front tyres and 35.5% of the rear tyres with over 6mm tread depth.

Austin Allegro 1300 Super

AUSTIN ALLEGRO
ENGINEERS' COMMENTS
Fair – after a slow start

This car, which has been rather slow in taking over from British Leyland's best-selling 1100/1300, has had its share of teething troubles and yet is not basically an unreliable car. Most owner complaints concern relatively minor faults and irritation with dealers. Difficulty in keeping water out of the boot has been a sore point for production engineers; the problem has persisted through L and M registration, with water penetrating where rear wheel arch, boot and rear seat scuttle join.

A great deal has been done to ensure that the car is given more anti-corrosion protection than many, although the metal preparation and painting techniques employed are no different from most of those currently practised by European and Japanese manufacturers. The body's primer coat is applied by electropherisis and the underbody is given a thorough sound-deadening and anti-corrosion protective coating. The extra treatment the Allegro receives, however, is as yet fairly uncommon in volume-produced medium priced cars. A wax-based anti-corrosion compound is injected into many of the hollow sections by special lances. The aim is to seal those sections where paint protection may be inadequate or impossible to apply, thus preventing moisture and oxygen coming into contact with the sheet metal. The body should therefore be well protected against corrosion.

Some early cars had a stone-chipping problem on front and rear valance and sills; the hard top coat was rather too brittle and it splintered off, resulting in small-scale surface rusting. The structural strength of the car is not affected, but in some respects this splintering has caused concern when the car has been towed away after a bump. A suspended tow without the use of special wedge blocks can produce some creasing of body panels. There are special instructions available at Austin dealers regarding where and how to apply jacks and lifting tackle. If this recommended practice is followed, unnecessary straining or damaging of the bodyshell is avoided. The car was designed as a lightweight to give good fuel economy. It has no subframe for the power unit; there is a controlled 'crushability' to absorb energy in frontal impacts and little extra sheet metal anywhere.

Some early five-speed gear boxes on the larger-engined cars are noisy, and clutch action tends to be rather fierce. These problems have been largely resolved on more recent models. Approximately one in ten cars suffers from gaiter leaks of the rack-and-pinion steering as a result of tears in the convolutions. In addition, some of the steering rack attachments tend to work loose. These faults can be remedied cheaply if attended to promptly.

Reference to front wheel bearing attention in the VISAR table should alert owners to the advisability of having the front suspension inspected. Don't automatically suspect faulty bearings, as it is usually only a matter of 'check and adjust'. Some front suspension arm bushes may show excessive movement, so if there is an audible 'knocking' noise from the front, it is best to see a local dealer promptly to have the front suspension checked and, if need be, have the lower arm bush replaced. This is not a major repair job.

Some of the early Hydragas suspension elements give trouble, but a visit to a franchised dealer will establish whether they need replacing. Some of them leak the inert gas which provides the 'springiness' of the interconnected suspension system. Basically, they differ from the elements of the Hydrolastic system in that they cannot be re-pressurised. If the car tends to lean when loaded, suspect such a systems failure and do not ignore it.

Noisy valve gears are usually confined to the OHV engines, with pushrods, tappets and rockers accentuating valve clatter. This can be readily minimised by tappet clearance adjustment. OHC engines, on the other hand, are basically quieter.

The virtue of the Allegro is its modest thirst for fuel. It is one of the highest 'mile per gallon' cars of its size and class.

Specification of AA tested car

See p. 28

Make & model	AUSTIN ALLEGRO
Production years	1973–present
Body alternatives	2-door Saloon, 4-door Saloon
Engine variants	1098cc OHV, 1275cc OHV, 1485cc OHC, 1748cc OHC
Data: AA test version	Allegro 1300 Super 2-door Saloon. 1974 model
Engine	In-line 4-cyl, watercooled, transverse front-mounted Bore 70.6mm, stroke 81.3mm, 1275cc. Comp ratio 8.8:1
Fuel system	1 SU variable-jet carburettor. Mechanical pump. 10.5-gallon tank
Transmission	4-speed & reverse, synchromesh on all forward gears. Front-wheel drive. Diaphragm-spring clutch, $7\frac{1}{4}''$ diameter dry plate, Hydraulically operated
Suspension front	Independent. Wishbone, Hydragas interconnected
Suspension rear	Independent. Trailing arms, Hydragas interconnected
Steering	Rack & pinion. $3\frac{1}{2}$ turns between full locks Turning circle $34\frac{1}{4}$ feet
Wheels	13" diameter, $4\frac{1}{2}$C rims
Tyres	145SR13 radial-ply (Dunlop SP68 fitted)
Brakes	Hydraulic, disc front/drum rear. Optional servo
Dimensions (overall)	Length 12'7$\frac{3}{4}$" Width 5'3$\frac{1}{2}$" Height 4'6" Wheelbase 8'0$\frac{1}{4}$" Ground clearance $5\frac{1}{2}$" Kerb weight (full tank) 17 cwts
Max speed (in gears)	First 29mph, second 45mph, third 71mph, top 86mph
Overdrive	Not applicable
Acceleration	0–60mph: 16.0 seconds; standing-$\frac{1}{4}$ mile: 20.6 seconds
Fuel consumption	overall: 34.7mpg steady 50mph: 41.6mpg (top gear) steady 70mph: 30.6mpg (top gear)
Fuel	Mixture 3-star

What VISAR reveals

Worse than average | Average
Better than average | No data

All chart figures are percentages

	Age in years: 6–8	5–6	4–5	3–4	2–3	1–2
	Registration Suffix: FG	H	J	K	L	M
Corroded front doors					3	3
Corroded rear doors					0	2
Corroded front wings					3	2
Corroded rear wings					2	2
Corroded front underwings					0	0
Corroded rear underwings					0	0
Corroded body sills					13	4
Corroded jacking points	N	N	N	N	3	1
Corroded floor	O	O	O	O	0	2
Corroded underbody frame members	–	–	–	–	0	0
Defective undersealing	T	T	T	T	14	10
Loose/misaligned driver's seat	C	C	C	C	6	1
Attend to engine mountings	U	U	U	U	0	1
Evidence of head gasket leaks	D	D	D	D	0	1
Noisy valve gear	O	O	O	O	15	26
Evidence of engine oil leaks	R	R	R	R	28	18
Attend to carburettor tuning	P	P	P	P	26	25
Evidence of fuel leaks					0	0
Final drive noise	N	N	N	N	13	5
Unsatisfactory gear change	–	–	–	–	0	0
Unsatisfactory auto gear change						
Clutch judder	T	T	T	T	6	8
Attend to front wheel bearings	O	O	O	O	22	9
Attend to steering box/rack	N	N	N	N	12	9
Attend to footbrake					9	4
Attend to handbrake					6	1
Corroded brake pipelines					0	0
Defective obligatory lights					12	11
Attend to charging system					3	3
Attend to horn					0	0

AUSTIN ALLEGRO 1300

From AA Road Test Report 329, 1974

Improved, but no panache

With its revolutionary suspension and superb space utilisation, the Austin 1100/1300 became the epitome of respectable family motoring. As acquaintance grew, however, so did complaints about its indifferent gear shift, underdamped ride and odd driving position, as well as the difficult mechanical access that put off the fleet operators. The Allegro is an attempt to re-think these problems and refine the entire concept.

In 1300 form it offers average performance with above-average economy. Slightly quicker than domestic rivals using conventional engineering, it is also tractable but a nasty grating afflicts it when accelerating in top; the testers detect installation problems which the 1500/1750 seems free from. Gear shift quality is a distinct improvement over its predecessor although the clutch still judders at times. Fuel consumption is slightly better than most in this class.

Hydragas suspension on the Allegro feels altogether softer, with pitch and roll showing in a way that the old 1300 studiously avoided. However, the vertical bounce has gone and although it clacks noisily and complains about the single pothole, it rides quite well compared with the Marina and most of that ilk. Comparison with the Maxi and some European competitors leaves the testers mildly disappointed nevertheless. By the same token, it feels less of a go-er round corners. Perhaps the peculiar steering wheel is partly responsible – it looks like a TV screen and feels like an accordion if one tries to twirl it quickly! Still, the car proves very sure-footed, with nicely progressive nose-drift under power turning to equally tame tuck-in if the accelerator is cut, with no drama or treachery. The brakes are fit for any situation but they have no dual-circuit protection.

The driving position and nice set of controls represent a considerable improvement over the old 1300, although a lot of people always swore they were comfortable. Triumph-style column stalks and pedals are well related to seat and wheel; instruments are legible and attractive. All-round vision is good and the dipping mirror is much nicer than the old one that used to sit on a plastic sucker. The continued omission of quick headlamp beam trimmers on these load-sensitive Austins, however, is an omission to be deplored. Apart from the nasty rasping that occurs at lower speeds, the Allegro 1300 is commendably quiet.

The back seat suffers from softness and shapelessness and legroom and headroom are restricted. It no longer elicits the appreciation of rear passengers as its predecessor did and is probably the Allegro's most serious retrograde feature. However, the boot is much more family-sized and the wheel is stowed erect, out of the way of luggage. The heater is simple to command and instantly responsive, giving good, fast warmth and cooler air from screen outlets at the same time. The fascia mounted ventilators are less convincing, especially in summer. More could be done to protect occupants from injury – the screen is non-laminated and visor mounts and roof padding are deficient.

Owing to the Allegro's 'Humpty Dumpty' profile, the paint along sills and lower door panels receives a peppering from the wheels. The undersealing was unconvincing and the wheel hub caps are too easy to savage against a high kerb.

Under-bonnet access is superb. Thoughtful details like the front-mounted radiator with electric cooling fan and 'Fabrostrip' wiring are also commendable. The cost of spares is less than most of its European rivals, yet the car somehow lacks their panache in the way it performs. However, the Allegro is a real improvement over its predecessor.

Austin Maxi 1750

AUSTIN MAXI
ENGINEERS' COMMENTS
Marked improvement with II

When the Maxi was introduced some 4 years after the very successful Renault 16, many hoped it would be Britain's answer to the French 16. But the very practical multi-purpose five-door family saloon was launched rather precipitously, leaving some fairly basic design and production problems unresolved. The Maxi had to be virtually presented afresh 18 months later, when it was given two engine options – a 1485cc and a 1748cc power unit – and different gear ratios because major irritations had arisen over the five-speed gear box and its gear shift mechanism.

Re-designed gear box
The original gear box attracted a good deal of legitimate customer complaint owing to its excessive noise and the difficulty of obtaining clean, positive gear selection. Despite a number of attempts to improve the action, leak resistance and durability of the lubricated armoured push-pull cable, only the eventual introduction of a re-designed gear box and a rod linkage resolved these problems. The marked effect this has had on gear shift quality can be seen by contrasting pre-J (Mark I) and post-J (Mark II) registration cars.

Unfortunately, Mark I and Mark II transmissions are not interchangeable.

Clutch judder
The below-average rating of early Maxis' footbrake system is in part due to brake squeal, which was cured on later models by altering machining sequences of the front disc unit and using a different brake pad material. On long hot summer days, early Maxi engines tended to boil when the car was driven long distances at maximum speed. Clutch action at times is still inclined to be juddery. In part this is due to the rocking movement of the engine transmission unit on its mounts as the throttle is closed and then opened wide again.

Engine mountings
The transverse mounting of any power unit of this size and output in a confined space presents technical problems. It has taken rather a long time for durable and utterly reliable solutions to these problems to be phased into production. Engine steadies have been employed since 1971 to reduce rock, but occasionally the bolts of the bracket to which they are connected work loose. An engine mount failure is a more serious matter. If not detected in time, the ▶

29

power unit can drop right out. Whereas the timely replacement of a suspect rubber-bonded unit or even of a cracked metal bracket is relatively easy and cheap, the consequences of neglecting to take prompt action can be very costly indeed.

Stone chipping

Stone chipping is responsible for slight damage to the paintwork of lower door panels and front and rear wings, boots, valances and above all, body sills. If these blemishes, usually quite small, are dealt by prompt touching-in with a small paintbrush, visual appeal suffers little and rust will not spread.

Low deterioration with age

The steering rack assembly tends to work loose and the steering gaiters need checking for oil tightness, but these are relatively easy and cheap service tasks. Carburettor tuning is usually only a case of re-setting idling speed and topping up the dashpot, except in the case of the twin SU 1748cc version, which requires additional balancing. Lack of owner attention to regular servicing may account for some of the fault percentages on F/G registration cars, but there are other factors. For instance, the relatively thick factory-applied bitumastic underbody protection compound, though still quite effective except possibly on subframes, begins to crack and lift at the edges. Engine seals and covers begin to leak oil. But the rate of deterioration of the car with age, in terms of body structure, appearance and mechanical parts, is generally low. The metal preparation, anti-corrosion treatment and paint are basically of sound quality. Improvements in sill protection inside and out – introduced some 3 years ago – should help to establish the Maxi as a good sturdy practical family car.

Specification of AA tested car

See p. 32

Make & model	AUSTIN MAXI
Production years	1969–present
Body alternatives	4-door Saloon
Engine variants	1485cc OHC (1969–present) – "1500"
	1748cc OHC (1971–present) – "1750"
Data: AA test version	Maxi 1750 4-door Saloon. 1972 model
Engine	In-line 4-cyl, watercooled, transverse front-mounted
	Bore 76.3mm, stroke 95.7mm, 1748cc. Comp ratio 8.75:1
Fuel system	1 SU variable-jet carburettor. Mechanical pump.
	9-gallon tank
Transmission	5-speed & reverse, synchromesh on all forward
	gears. Front-wheel drive.
	Diaphragm-spring clutch, $7\frac{3}{4}$" diameter dry plate,
	hydraulically operated.
Suspension front	Independent. Transverse link, Hydrolastic, interconnected
Suspension rear	Independent. Trailing arm, Hydrolastic interconnected
Steering	Rack & pinion. 4 turns between full locks
	Turning circle $30\frac{1}{2}$ feet
Wheels	13" diameter, $4\frac{1}{2}$C rims
Tyres	155SR13 radial-ply (Dunlop SP68 fitted)
Brakes	Hydraulic, disc front/drum rear. Servo
Dimensions	Length 13'$2\frac{1}{4}$" Width 5'$4\frac{1}{4}$" Height 4'$7\frac{1}{4}$" Wheelbase 8'8"
(overall)	Ground clearance $5\frac{1}{2}$" Kerb weight (full tank) $19\frac{3}{4}$cwts
Max speed (in gears)	First 32mph, second 50, third 74, fourth 90, top 90.
Overdrive	Not applicable
Acceleration	0–60mph: 14.6 seconds; standing-$\frac{1}{4}$ mile: 19.6 seconds
Fuel consumption	overall: 28.75mpg
	steady 50mph: 39.6mpg (top gear) 37.0mpg (4th)
	steady 70mph: 28.2mpg (top gear) 26.3mpg (4th)
Fuel	Premium 4-star

What VISAR reveals

All chart figures are percentages	6–8	5–6	4–5	3–4	2–3	1–2
Age in years: / Registration Suffix:	FG	H	J	K	L	M
Corroded front doors	16	13	12	8	2	0
Corroded rear doors	13	11	10	8	1	1
Corroded front wings	28	19	15	6	2	0
Corroded rear wings	21	19	15	8	2	0
Corroded front underwings	11	8	5	0	1	0
Corroded rear underwings	4	7	4	0	0	0
Corroded body sills	41	25	19	8	2	2
Corroded jacking points	18	8	8	5	1	0
Corroded floor	4	2	2	1	0	0
Corroded underbody frame members	21	2	4	4	0	0
Defective undersealing	36	16	9	5	6	4
Loose/misaligned driver's seat	7	6	5	5	3	2
Attend to engine mountings	4	6	14	9	8	1
Evidence of head gasket leaks	4	5	4	3	2	0
Noisy valve gear	36	21	18	19	13	10
Evidence of engine oil leaks	38	22	30	19	15	20
Attend to carburettor tuning	32	31	25	20	11	18
Evidence of fuel leaks	4	4	3	2	1	2
Final drive noise	4	2	4	3	1	2
Unsatisfactory gear change	21	23	8	10	6	2
Unsatisfactory auto gear change						
Clutch judder	4	7	5	7	5	9
Attend to front wheel bearings	0	4	8	2	1	2
Attend to steering box/rack	7	7	11	15	15	12
Attend to footbrake	21	14	11	6	8	0
Attend to handbrake	30	20	20	16	9	6
Corroded brake pipelines	15	8	16	12	3	2
Defective obligatory lights	34	24	23	10	8	0
Attend to charging system	0	3	2	1	2	0
Attend to horn	0	5	2	0	1	0

AUSTIN MAXI 1750

From AA Road Test Report 263, 1972

Five-door front ranker

The original 1500 Maxi received a lot of scathing comment about underdevelopment even though the basic design was sound. Fortunately, important changes were made, and the 1750 – apart from its bigger engine and altered gear ratios – was announced with those modifications of the smaller-engined model.

The 1750's engine, though even longer stroked, provides only a modest increase in power, but a lot more torque makes it much more responsive. Maximum speed is up by only 3mph, but acceleration is more competitive, putting the Maxi ahead of its Gallic rival the Renault 16TL. Revised gearing makes overdrive/fifth of more value, and a smooth though leisurely 23mph pullaway is possible; a timely top-to-third gear change makes quick overtaking safest, however – forget fourth gear. The latest rod-operated mechanism does take at least some of the springiness out of the former cable-operated shift, yet there is still the same old jerking in the lower gears if the accelerator is worked suddenly, on or off. The test car's fuel consumption averaged 28¾mpg, but 30mpg is easy to achieve out of town. Test figures ranged from 24–33mpg.

Suspension changes

Subtle changes to the Hydrolastic suspension reduce the ride's bounce and harshness, but occasionally surface faults will catch the suspension out, causing it to stiffen with an uncomfortable jolt. On most surfaces the car rides masterfully with a characteristic levelness and an arrow-straight course. A smaller wheel makes the already pleasant steering even better, and its feel and accuracy are hard to beat. The brakes are excellent.

The high-backed reclining front seats have a good range of adjustment, but need more lumbar thrust. A set of squarely-placed pedals and the neat steering wheel create a comfortable driving position, while wide, deep window space (plus a door mirror) make for easy vision front and rear. The attractive fascia contains two legible dials, but more could be done to improve the switches, which are difficult to find at night. The Maxi's versatile accommodation provides lots of rear lounging room for two, and the back seat is admirably comfortable considering its 'foldability'.

Vast cargo area

Removing the rear canopy and dropping the backrest provides a 6½-foot double bed, or the car can be made a two-seater with a vast cargo area. Ringing the changes isn't easy though, for one needs three hands to work the catches and the squab, the latter fouling the rear armrests unless the doors are open. Entry and exit are easy, while loading the rear is simplified by the assisted full-width tailgate and the absence of a rear sill. The latest upholstery and pile carpet add plushness to the interior, but the fibreboard side-trims in the boot scuff too easily. Equipment and appointments are none too generous. The heater is spoilt by its inability to mix hot with cold properly, so separate draughts emerge round the centre tunnel. It can certainly push out the heat though. The finely controllable fascia fresh-air vents cannot be boosted by the quiet two-speed fan, but are powerful anyway.

Apart from several fascia rattles and column creaks, the five-door body seems very sturdy. Paintwork is thoroughly applied and the underside well under-sealed. The Maxi is one of the best front-wheel-drive cars in respect of servicing access – only valve adjustment is tricky.

Seven years after Renault set the five-door style, the idea has really caught on, with the Maxi 1750 now in the front rank with the best of them. Compared with the 16, the Maxi is brisker, with better handling and more space. It lacks the Renault's soft refinement and plush pampering surroundings, however.

32

Mini 1000

AUSTIN/MORRIS MINI

ENGINEERS' COMMENTS
Newer is better

Minis have been around for such a long time that some of their good and bad points have become part of motorists' folklore. Few such myths still apply. The Mini has gained a reputation for early corrosion particularly around and behind door hinges, in the wing area, around and behind the headlamp unit, and in the rear subframe, jacking points, body sills and floor panels. While once true, minor design changes, better sealing materials and changes in the anti-corrosion treatment and paint technology have improved the model beyond all recognition. Thus H registration cars – and J and subsequent registration cars even more so – are rusting much more slowly. Rust weeping from behind the ungainly looking cover or capping strips and around light units has virtually ceased, underwings are better protected, and jacking points and floor pressings no longer suffer from early and extensive rusting. Stone-chip-induced surface rust spots on bumper valances and body sills are also less numerous.

Subframes are now relatively rust-free. But in many cases the water-based bitumastic underbody protection compound has been neither generously nor effectively applied.

Minis 7 to 8 years old or older can be seriously weakened by untreated corrosion in such structurally vital areas as the front bulkhead, floor and body sill junctions. However, it is possible to weld in new body pressings, provided the adjacent sheet steel is sound and free of rust. The radius arm bearings tend to deteriorate with age and seize up.

Engine overheating, cylinder head leaks and mixing valve seizure in the car heater box are not problems after H registration. The reliable engines fitted to Minis still suffer from oil weeps past seals and cover plates. Such oil seepage often adversely affects the rubber elements of the driveshaft inner universal joints, which then need periodic replacement due to oil swelling. Also, the U clamps need periodic re-tightening.

Clutch action has always been relatively fierce. First gear synchromesh was only introduced on H registration cars and the gear change linkage on many pre–1972 production cars after a time needs franchised dealer attention. These factors account for poor gear shift quality.

The Mini has an above-average tendency

to pull to one side during hard braking, which can be quite vicious on F/G registration cars. Owing to their exposed location, rear brake pipes suffer stone bombardment and are thus prone to surface corrosion. Brake pipes on older cars need replacing, since this surface attack eventually results in significant weakening of the hydraulic tubing. Brake maintenance means frequent adjustment; the handbrake in particular suffers from corrosion and seizure of the handbrake cable quadrant, which prevents the free return of the brake shoes. If the car looks lopsided when stationary or moving, the Hydrolastic units should be inspected for leaks or malfunction by a franchised dealer. He may be able to re-pressurise the system or fit new units.

Final drive noise can be due to bush wear on the idler gear. Any major repair to the engine, clutch, gear box and final drive units and the constant velocity joints at the road wheel end of the short driveshafts can be costly.

Rapid wear of the Mini's steering rack is often due to damaged gaiters, which allow lubricant to escape and dirt to enter. Wear in suspension and steering joints increases with age and mileage. Unless owners attend to routine maintenance and deal with accidental damage or age deterioration early on, the bills can be needlessly depressing.

On older Minis an up-and-down lift of the steering wheel is occasionally detected due to loosening of the lower pinch bolt on the steering column; this requires garage attention.

A good used Mini can give many years of faithful service at relatively little cost but a previous owner's harsh treatment and neglect often mean that the next owner will pay dearly for it.

Specification of AA tested car

Make & model	AUSTIN/MORRIS MINI	See p. 36
Production years	1959–present	
Body alternatives	2-door Saloon, 2-door Clubman Saloon, Estate	
Engine variants	848cc (1959–present), 970cc (1963–5), 997cc (1961–3), 998cc (1964–present), 1071cc (1963–4), 1275cc (1963–present) OHV	
Data: AA test version		
Engine	Mini 1000 Mk II, 2-door Saloon. 1969 model	
	In-line 4-cyl, OHV watercooled, transverse, front-mounted Bore 64.6mm, stroke 76.2mm, 998cc. Comp ratio 8.3:1	
Fuel system	1 SU variable-jet carburettor. Electric pump. 5.5-gallon tank	
Transmission	4-speed & reverse, synchromesh on all forward gears. Front-wheel drive. Diaphragm-spring clutch, $7\frac{1}{8}''$ diameter dry plate, hydraulically operated	
Suspension front	Independent. Wishbone, Hydrolastic interconnected	
Suspension rear	Independent. Trailing arm, Hydrolastic interconnected	
Steering	Rack & pinion. $2\frac{3}{4}$ turns between full locks Turning circle $28\frac{3}{4}$ feet	
Wheels	10" diameter, $3\frac{1}{2}$B rims	
Tyres	5.20×10 cross-ply (Dunlop C41 fitted)	
Brakes	Hydraulic, drum front/drum rear.	
Dimensions (overall)	Length 10'0$\frac{1}{4}$" Width 4'7$\frac{1}{2}$" Height 4'5" Wheelbase 6'8$\frac{3}{4}$" Ground clearance $5\frac{1}{4}$" Kerb weight (full tank) 13 cwts	
Max speed (in gears)	First 27mph, second 43mph, third 66mph, top 77mph	
Overdrive	Not applicable	
Acceleration	0–60mph: 25.2 seconds; standing-$\frac{1}{4}$ mile: 21.9 seconds	
Fuel consumption	overall: 35.3mpg steady 50mph: 42.1mpg (top gear) steady 70mph: 25.0 mpg (top gear)	
Fuel	Premium 4-star	

What VISAR reveals

Legend: Worse than average / Average / Better than average / No data

All chart figures are percentages

	6–8	5–6	4–5	3–4	2–3	1–2
Age in years: Registration Suffix:	FG	H	J	K	L	M
Corroded front doors	19	10	6	4	1	4
Corroded rear doors						
Corroded front wings	28	19	9	6	2	0
Corroded rear wings	15	11	9	6	4	1
Corroded front underwings	12	4	3	2	4	0
Corroded rear underwings	8	3	2	1	2	0
Corroded body sills	39	20	12	8	5	1
Corroded jacking points	20	11	3	4	2	0
Corroded floor	20	11	7	5	2	3
Corroded underbody frame members	27	13	7	5	4	1
Defective undersealing	39	24	19	12	14	15
Loose/misaligned driver's seat	5	2	4	3	1	0
Attend to engine mountings	5	3	2	1	1	1
Evidence of head gasket leaks	7	2	2	1	2	1
Noisy valve gear	23	17	12	21	19	13
Evidence of engine oil leaks	44	32	18	20	24	30
Attend to carburettor tuning	29	29	26	27	22	25
Evidence of fuel leaks	5	0	4	2	2	1
Final drive noise	8	8	5	3	1	5
Unsatisfactory gear change	11	21	18	9	0	2
Unsatisfactory auto gear change						
Clutch judder	13	10	9	10	9	11
Attend to front wheel bearings	13	15	6	9	7	9
Attend to steering box/rack	16	19	18	12	13	23
Attend to footbrake	24	15	18	15	16	11
Attend to handbrake	33	27	21	12	14	10
Corroded brake pipelines	29	18	15	12	6	3
Defective obligatory lights	24	19	14	13	5	7
Attend to charging system	6	4	3	1	2	4
Attend to horn	9	7	4	5	1	3

Quicker, quieter and still frugal

 The year 1967 saw the introduction of the Mark II Mini with its face-lifted body and numerous detail changes to the specification – including the availability of the Hornet/Elf 998cc engine.

Useful gains in performance result from this bigger engine. Five seconds are cut from 0–60mph, top speed is up by 5mph, and thanks to higher gearing, fast cruising is less frantic. Nevertheless, even the 1000 displays a harsh busyness when revved hard. It is flexible though, pulling smoothly from 20mph in top. The testers coaxed 51mpg out of the test car by driving gently, but most owners can expect 35–40mpg. In contrast to the short quick clutch, the remote-control gear lever has a stiff, sticky action and all the well-spaced ratios (except top) whine.

While the Hydrolastic suspension eliminates pitching, it induces a lot of vertical bounce on poor surfaces where potholes cause loud and firm thuds. On main roads the ride is flat and level, but tyre noise is as loud as ever. There is very little body roll and because of its tenacious grip and quicksilver steering response, the Mini can still outcorner practically anything on the road. It is a very stable car, but on cross-ply tyres it squirms badly on raised white lines. The brakes, though a little heavy, work very well, although more weight over the back wheels would prevent early locking. The handbrake works well, however.

The seats are still too erect and lacking in support (three sets of mounting holes cater for different sized drivers though) and the pedal pads are still too small. Apart from a corner blind spot on the windscreen when rain-covered, all-round vision is splendid. The central instrument panel is easily masked by the driver's left hand, but the fascia switches are less of a stretch now; only the heater controls are remote.

Climbing into the back past the tipped-up front seats calls for some agility, yet there is a surprising amount of space in so small a car. Kneeroom is adequate and two passengers can spread themselves in reasonable comfort, but the upholstery is pretty thin. Sliding windows are retained, there is a lot of painted metal in view and flimsy leathercloth trim panels abound, but nylon carpeting lends luxury to the floor. Safety features are minimal, however. All the minor controls protrude, the upper fascia rail is unpadded and the front seats have no anti-tip catches.

Heating is improved but rear passengers still receive little warmth and there is no face-level ventilation. Compared with the generous interior storage space the boot is really diminutive. Not so clever is that the spare wheel, tools and battery are hidden below the leathercloth mat.

The fit and finish of the Mini are basically very sound. It feels solid and has a comprehensive coating of paint (but unfortunately no undersealant) and most of the brightwork is rust-resistant. Neither the distributor nor the carburettor is particularly easy to get to, but most items requiring routine servicing are a piece of cake.

Those who are fans of the 850 Mini will like the 1000 even better. It is quicker, quieter, and better equipped and it maintains its reputation as a frugal four-seater.

Second thoughts – 5 years later
Hydrolastic didn't last long and the Mini reverted to 'dry' line suspension after 'floating on fluid' from 1965 to 1969. Current Minis benefit from Allegro-type gear change and driveshafts, which make for quieter and smoother cruising as well as smoother town driving, but the seats are no better. The latest 850 Basic is nippier too, and its consumption is 40–45mpg – similar to a Renault 5TL or a Datsun Cherry. The Mini still makes good economical sense, particularly in this 850 Basic, but the 1000 and Clubman look less competitive on the current scene.

Austin 1300

AUSTIN/MORRIS 1100/1300

ENGINEERS' COMMENTS

Maintenance history important

This range of transverse-engined car has been in production for a remarkably long time and has enjoyed a great deal of popularity. It has also attracted a fair share of criticism from owners, who fall into two basic groups: those who love it and will forgive most of its quirks and shortcomings, and those who are exasperated by it. The 1100/1300, of course, shares many of the features of the Mini – both good and bad.

Design and manufacturing changes have markedly improved the corrosion resistance of those cars produced in the last 4 to 5 years. Some earlier cars justifiably had a bad reputation, however. Contributing to it were the collapse of the rear subframes which house the Hydrolastic unit, bad underwing corrosion, rusting out around headlamp units, inside-out corrosion near wing, front scuttle and door pillar junctions, and underfloor and body sill junctions. On many of these pre-H registration cars the body sill is often holed where it joins the rear wing. Underfloor pressings, which received no factory protection other than phosphate and primer coat until very recently (M registration), suffer particularly

badly from corrosion, as do rear subframes and jacking points. The rear brake pipelines, exposed to grit bombardment, suffer erosion attack and the resultant early onset of corrosion even more than those on the Mini. Water ingress past various sealants into the passenger compartment has surprisingly not been eliminated to date.

The problem of engine rock owing to the comparatively short life of the engine mounts has not been resolved with complete satisfaction. This engine movement does not help when it comes to operating the clutch, and judder results. It has taken a rather long time for those factors associated with poor gear change quality to be satisfactorily dealt with. In fact, synchromesh durability and gear change linkage left a lot to be desired right up to late 1972. When it comes to the suspension, swivel joints tend to wear out with age and mileage. Bearings on the swinging rear subframe tend either to wear out prematurely, or seize up. Corrosion of the subframe is no longer the major problem it once was, when many motor traders' suspicions were aroused if they took an old 1100 in part exchange. Few can be pleased that the handbrake mechanism tends to corrode and seize up, particularly on the quadrant pivot. Uneven braking, which had been overcome, reappears as a problem on some M registration cars.

One can hardly blame the factory for the poor quality of dealer-applied underbody compounds and their lack of adhesion to the flat underfloor. Unfortunately, these materials crack and fill with moisture and salts, promoting, rather than retarding corrosion. The seats tend to work loose on their flimsy runners, but early tightening of the bolts can stop them from rattling.

Engine overheating, cylinder head gasket leaks, and seized-up car heater water mixing valves are sometimes encountered on older cars. Generally, the sturdy though somewhat noisy engine is tolerant of neglect and abuse, even forgiving those who ignore adjustment of tappet clearance or carburettor settings.

Most of the noise emanating from the power unit stems from excess clearance in the idler gear of the transmission , but it does not mean failure is imminent. Owners' neglect of their vehicles is a cause for concern; yet the 1100/1300 will still be driveable when the Hydrolastic suspension is depressurised or partially collapsed, when the gaiters on steering rack and constant-velocity outer joints are damaged, and when inner universal joints on the front-wheel drive are oil-sodden or loose. Periodic re-tightening of the steering pinion to steering column pinch bolt should be done by a franchised dealer.

Those who purchase a used car purchase its past maintenance history, which may not be readily apparent on casual inspection. This applies particularly to old 1100/1300 cars, which can vary greatly from one to another.

Specification of AA tested car

See p. 40

Make & model	AUSTIN/MORRIS 1100/1300
Production years	1968–present
Body alternatives	2-door Saloon, 4-door Saloon, Estate
Engine variants	1098cc OHV
	1275cc OHV
Data: AA test version	Austin 1300 Super, 2-door Saloon. 1971 model
Engine	In-line 4-cyl, watercooled, transverse front-mounted
	Bore 70.6mm, stroke 81.3mm, 1275cc. Comp ratio 8.8:1
Fuel system	1 SU semi-downdraught carburettor. Electric pump.
	8-gallon tank
Transmission	4-speed & reverse, synchromesh on all forward gears.
	Front-wheel drive.
	Diaphragm-spring clutch, $7\frac{1}{8}''$ diameter dry plate,
	hydraulically operated
Suspension front	Independent. Wishbone, Hydrolastic interconnected
Suspension rear	Independent. Trailing arm, Hydrolastic interconnected
Steering	Rack & pinion. $3\frac{1}{4}$ turns between full locks
	Turning circle $35\frac{1}{2}$ feet
Wheels	12" diameter, 4C rims
Tyres	5.50×12 cross-ply (Goodyear G8 fitted)
Brakes	Hydraulic, disc front/drum rear
Dimensions	Length 12'2$\frac{3}{4}$" Width 5'0$\frac{1}{4}$" Height 4'5" Wheelbase 7'9$\frac{1}{2}$"
(overall)	Ground clearance 6" Kerb weight (full tank) $16\frac{1}{2}$ cwts
Max speed (in gears)	First 28mph, second 47mph, third 74mph, top 87.3mph
Overdrive	Not applicable
Acceleration	0–60mph: 17.2 seconds; standing-$\frac{1}{4}$ mile: 20.7 seconds
Fuel consumption	overall: 36.5mpg
	steady 50mph: 45.4mpg (top gear)
	steady 70mph: 33.3mpg (top gear)
Fuel	Premium 4-star

What VISAR reveals

Legend: ■ Worse than average ▨ Average ▥ Better than average □ No data

All chart figures are percentages

	Age in years:	6–8	5–6	4–5	3–4	2–3	1–2
	Registration Suffix:	FG	H	J	K	L	M
Corroded front doors		20	14	10	6	4	9
Corroded rear doors		19	10	8	6	5	6
Corroded front wings		34	17	9	6	5	6
Corroded rear wings		18	11	9	6	2	3
Corroded front underwings		22	10	3	3	2	0
Corroded rear underwings		11	7	3	2	1	0
Corroded body sills		44	27	15	10	6	7
Corroded jacking points		28	15	9	4	5	3
Corroded floor		23	13	10	6	4	11
Corroded underbody frame members		29	16	13	8	5	3
Defective undersealing		36	23	17	16	12	12
Loose/misaligned driver's seat		12	15	14	13	7	15
Attend to engine mountings		10	6	5	3	2	3
Evidence of head gasket leaks		5	3	5	5	2	3
Noisy valve gear		21	25	24	24	20	38
Evidence of engine oil leaks		38	32	26	20	25	23
Attend to carburettor tuning		31	30	30	32	27	30
Evidence of fuel leaks		4	2	1	2	1	5
Final drive noise		9	4	5	4	2	3
Unsatisfactory gear change		17	19	18	15	3	3
Unsatisfactory auto gear change							
Clutch judder		11	11	11	11	14	13
Attend to front wheel bearings		31	17	13	7	5	6
Attend to steering box/rack		5	9	6	11	11	6
Attend to footbrake		10	8	7	6	6	15
Attend to handbrake		27	27	19	16	16	21
Corroded brake pipelines		37	27	24	13	6	8
Defective obligatory lights		26	23	21	11	8	2
Attend to charging system		4	4	3	2	1	5
Attend to horn		8	5	3	4	4	0

AUSTIN 1300 SUPER

From AA Road Test Report 239, 1971

Often imitated, still a favourite

 Since its debut, BMC's 1100 has had many imitators the 1300 option came with the Mark II version in 1967. Don't expect startling improvements in acceleration and top speed from the 1275cc engine. The idea was to achieve similar performance to the 1100, but with much less noise and fuss, particularly at motorway speeds. It works too, except that higher gearing has robbed the car of some of the 1100's low-speed flexibility (a sensible top-gear pullaway is about 25mph) so more gear changing is needed. One is rewarded with effortless cruising marred only by an irritating drone between 55mph and 65mph. Fuel consumption is excellent: 36½mpg overall, and 40mpg attainable with a little restraint. The clutch is rather heavy and abrupt, and there is some engine tremor on partial engagement. The testers were none too impressed by the springy, rubbery gear change either, especially into first at rest.

Although not sold on Hydrolastic suspension because of its vertical bounciness, its level glide over good surfaces and its ability to mop up bumps and ripples with no sway or pitch are admirable. Impressive stability, good tyre grip and an absence of roll enable even family motorists to scuttle rapidly round fast bends without drama, but beware of the tail-out twitch if it is necessary to throttle back suddenly in a tight bend. The brakes have improved in both weight and response, but the handbrake still can't cope with a 1-in-3 hill. Those who like to sit over the steering wheel will approve of the 1300's driving position, but more could be done to improve seat comfort and make the small pedals easier to work. All-round vision is fine, but screen cleaning could be improved by better wiper arcs and a bigger screenwasher reservoir. The ribbon speedometer is in clear view through the wheel and is flanked by minor controls which are just within reach if one sits right back. Safety features are none too numerous (why have tip-up front seats without safety catches on a four-door?), but the trimming has a pleasant unfussiness. Room in the back is outstanding considering the car's length and three-abreast seating is possible on the comfortably angled cushions. Trimming is conservative but equipment adequate. Front occupants are quite well served by the heater, but rear passengers receive little warmth at any time. Swivelling front quarter-lights keep the interior fresh in warm weather. The boot is restricted in height, but its width and depth are ample and there is no high rear sill.

Sound paintwork coats the attractive bodywork, and it is an easy car to clean, but undersealing is not standard. Major jobs are time consuming, but routine service work is easy with the rainshield removed. Although imitators have improved on BMC's design, many domestic users will prefer the practicality and security of buying the original. Any 1100 owners among them will certainly notice the improvements in the 1300.

Second thoughts – 3 years later

The Mark IIIs, which appeared in 1972, incorporated several useful changes and one or two less welcome ones. The carpets are plusher, the pedal pads larger and there are simple face-level vents on a new fascia which is hardly an improvement but is an easy Mark III identification. Revised front seats give improved support but they still tip forward unrestrained. Minor suspension changes permit a little more roll but convincingly stabilise cornering and a smaller wheel helps too. Outside and underbonnet there are more equipment deletions than improvements but on the whole the seating and suspension changes make a Mark III well worth preferring.

Morris 1800

AUSTIN/MORRIS 1800/2200
ENGINEERS' COMMENTS
Better than average – finally

When the 1800 series was launched in October 1964 it established new standards in terms of sensible space utilisation and level-ride quality for mass-produced family cars. It is a pity that it did not set equally high standards in terms of consistent quality right from the start. Initially, these roomy, unorthodox cars could have a number of irritating defects, mostly mechanical and costly to repair. They suffered from substantial oil leaks and there were legitimate complaints about excessive transmission noise and poor gear selection quality and clutch action. Some owners experienced rectifier troubles on early Lucas alternators too. The Hydrolastic suspension occasionally had faulty components. Horns, trafficator switches and lights did not always operate first time. Door opening mechanisms malfunctioned. Flexible engine mounts tended to need attention and renewal rather too frequently. In short, dealers and first owners felt let down.

The range achieved a high level of dependability and durability in later builds – the Mark II and III – however. It is unfortunate that this did not occur earlier.

Now, when the public has at long last come to associate the 1800 shape with better-than-average quality, a BLMC replacement is available.

Product modifications over the years have been steady and evolutionary rather than dramatic. Improvements in sealing and paint technology, and additional anti-rust protection have both reduced the likelihood of premature corrosion and retarded the spread and severity of rust deterioration of the body as the car ages.

Stone chipping of paint accounts for local rust spotting around headlamp units and front and rear wing ledges on F/G registration cars. Although these F/G cars are still better than average in terms of corrosion resistance, they are beginning to show rust 'bleeding' out of door seams and door edges. Body sills, particularly near their junction with front and rear wings, show localised paint blistering right up to J registration; there is a marked improvement thereafter. In common with other BLMC models, J registration paint tended to be rather more brittle than desirable, and local top coat damage could occur as a result. This paint system shortcoming has been remedied in subsequent builds and no longer presents a serious problem. If left untreated for only about 2 to 3 weeks, however, it could cause rust to spread beneath the colour coat, lifting it off in scabs.

The need to attend to lights, charging system or horn should alert owners to check for good earth returns and the absence of moisture. Adjustment of gear box linkages and engine idling speed can cure many poor auto change cases. It should be remembered that a number of design modifications were introduced to improve the ease of gear selection and general performance of the four-speed all-synchromesh manual gear box. Second gear ratio was changed from 2.217:1 to 2.06:1 in 1968 when the Mark II came out and the rod linkage system introduced in 1972 on the Mark II 1800 replaced the cumbersome and far-from-precise push-pull armoured-cable gear shift mechanism previously used. The more powerful 2200, also introduced in 1972, has always been equipped with the rod linkage system. It is not practicable to update the gear shift mechanism.

Valve gear noise can be reduced by an owner check and adjustment of valve tappet clearances, but the four-cylinder 1798cc engine is inherently noisy. The re-setting of these working clearances on the six-cylinder 2227cc OHC engine is beyond most do-it-yourselfers, but fortunately this engine, being of later design, is basically fairly quiet. The steering rack unit should be checked to ensure it is securely clamped to the subframes and that its gaiters are oil tight.

Those who need a large spacious family car could do worse than consider the purchase of a well looked after 1800 Mark II or III or a 2200.

Specification of AA tested car

See p. 44

Make & model	AUSTIN/MORRIS 1800/2200
Production years	1965–present
Body alternatives	4-door Saloon
Engine variants	1798cc OHV
	2227cc OHV
Data: AA test version	Austin 1800 Mk II, 4-door Saloon. 1970 model
Engine	In-line 4-cyl, watercooled, transverse front-mounted
	Bore 80.3mm, stroke 88.9mm 1798cc. Comp ratio 9:1
Fuel system	1 SU variable-jet carburettor. Mechanical pump.
	10.5-gallon tank
Transmission	4-speed & reverse, synchromesh on all forward
	gears. Front-wheel drive.
	Diaphragm-spring clutch, 8" diameter dry plate,
	hydraulically operated.
Suspension front	Independent. Transverse link, Hydrolastic interconnected
Suspension rear	Independent. Trailing arm, Hydrolastic interconnected
Steering	Rack & pinion. 3¾ turns between full locks
	Turning circle 40 feet
Wheels	14" diameter, 4½J rims
Tyres	165SR14 radial-ply (Dunlop SP68 fitted)
Brakes	Hydraulic, disc front/drum rear. Servo
Dimensions	Length 13'10" Width 5'7" Height 4'7½" Wheelbase 8'10"
(overall)	Ground clearance 6" Kerb weight (full tank) 22½ cwts
Max speed (in gears)	First 32mph, second 50mph, third 74mph, top 93mph
Overdrive	Not applicable
Acceleration	0–60mph: 16.0 seconds; standing-¼ mile: 20.0 seconds
Fuel consumption	overall: 28.0mpg
	steady 50mph: 34.2mpg (top gear)
	steady 70mph: 26.2mpg (top gear)
Fuel	Premium 4-star

What VISAR reveals

Worse than average | Average
Better than average | No data

All chart figures are percentages

	Age in years:	6–8	5–6	4–5	3–4	2–3	1–2
	Registration Suffix:	FG	H	J	K	L	M
Corroded front doors		8	7	6	3	2	0
Corroded rear doors		7	7	5	3	2	0
Corroded front wings		18	9	13	5	1	0
Corroded rear wings		9	9	14	4	2	0
Corroded front underwings		6	3	4	2	0	0
Corroded rear underwings		4	2	4	2	0	0
Corroded body sills		32	17	17	10	5	0
Corroded jacking points		9	5	7	3	0	0
Corroded floor		12	2	4	1	4	0
Corroded underbody frame members		12	8	5	3	1	0
Defective undersealing		25	22	11	12	20	14
Loose/misaligned driver's seat		2	8	7	7	2	0
Attend to engine mountings		10	6	2	3	0	2
Evidence of head gasket leaks		1	2	1	1	2	4
Noisy valve gear		40	24	31	31	30	34
Evidence of engine oil leaks		14	12	11	17	16	10
Attend to carburettor tuning		29	28	27	30	20	15
Evidence of fuel leaks		0	3	2	2	2	5
Final drive noise		8	3	6	8	11	0
Unsatisfactory gear change		4	1	2	3	0	0
Unsatisfactory auto gear change		4	13	7	0	0	0
Clutch judder		3	4	4	1	0	0
Attend to front wheel bearings		4	14	7	3	2	0
Attend to steering box/rack		14	8	10	15	12	0
Attend to footbrake		7	11	6	3	7	0
Attend to handbrake		7	7	5	9	6	4
Corroded brake pipelines		13	13	11	6	4	0
Defective obligatory lights		25	16	24	18	12	17
Attend to charging system		6	4	2	3	3	5
Attend to horn		9	10	10	9	0	0

AUSTIN/MORRIS 1800

From AA Road Test Report 230, 1970

The big car that isn't

With its blend of small-car agility, medium-car economy and big-car roominess, the 1800 is a rather unique cocktail that deserves its current success. Naturally the twin-carburettored S version shows its advantages when wound up through the gears, but most family motorists will probably be better served by the ordinary 1800's sweeter nature. It has low-speed affability and a steady idle, with first-time starting and a painless warm-up period. Although its exhaust and fan hum become obtrusive past 60mph, in most other respects the engine carries its years lightly. Certainly, no one should complain about fuel consumption and the test car achieved nearly 30mpg out of town. Oil consumption was disappointingly heavy, though.

The gear change is too notchy and quarrelsome about downchanges and the heavy clutch action can still provoke some engine wobble when pulling away from rest. The auto alternative is also inconvenient to control manually but is sufficiently smooth and sensitive to be worth serious consideration.

Manual steering

The testers prefer their 1800 with manual steering. Though weighty at walking speed, it avoids the unalterable lightness of the power system, which can be misinterpreted as loss of front-wheel grip.

When the going is potholed and bumpy, the interconnected suspension gives an extremely level ride without any lurch or pitch. However, there is a sort of tired damper feeling over mildly undulating surfaces and on certain bumpy bends the car sometimes nibbles its way round with an unwelcome diagonal jogging. On a well-surfaced motorway the big car sweeps along evenly with train-like steadiness even on a gusty day, and bends can be taken very fast. Road holding on both wet and dry roads is so impressively safe and steady that even an inexperienced driver can explore it without getting out of his depth.

The car strongly understeers when pressed with the power on, tucking into the bend when the driver lifts his foot. The brakes give easy, balanced stopping power without feeling over-servoed.

Good all-round vision

The controls are at full stretch, making inertia belts essential, and the upright steering angle makes one resort to a bus driver's hand shuffle when plenty of lock is called for. Deep glass areas give a good all-round view and the driving seat's support and legroom are good, even on long journeys.

Like others in the Longbridge family, inherent sizzles and rattles are induced by broken surfaces. Mechanical drones build up around 60mph and with transmission whine too, there is a veritable choir of activity.

Rear seat comfort is excellent, offering lounging spaciousness despite the model's compact length. Interior decor strikes an ideal balance between practicality and luxury. Compared with (or because of) interior room, the boot is adequate rather than cavernous. Heating still leaves much to be desired, although ventilation is much better on later cars. If it comes to the crunch, the immensely strong body is one of the safest cocoons to find oneself in and even a superficial look at the bodywork could not fail to impress. This is one of the few cars that will wear out its mechanicals before the body rots away.

Second thoughts – 4 years later

Nowadays, the testers would go for the 2200 six-cylinder version that provides the kind of smoothness and quietness that suits the model so well. Even today, the model's Granada spaciousness within Cortina dimensions continues to make it 'the big car that isn't'.

Chrysler 180

CHRYSLER 180/2 LITRE

ENGINEERS' COMMENTS

A quality car – almost

When Chrysler decided to produce a larger version of the Avenger to extend their European range of cars, they chose their French subsidiary to build it rather than a UK plant. The result is a car which has only a skin-deep affinity to its Coventry-designed and Coventry-built smaller brother; many of the mechanical parts are unmistakably Simca in concept. This car, which represents the top of the Chrysler Europe range, has not attracted a large following in the UK and thus the sample on which our findings are based is not extensive. Some basic trends can be detected, however.

The considerable improvements in anti-corrosion measures and paint technology undertaken since the car was launched in 1970 have borne fruit. Early cars suffered from the initial shortcomings of electrocoat primer paints which affected all major manufacturers in Europe and the UK at about that time. As a result, where sharp stones chip off small slivers of the top coat and the electrocoat primer, the way is opened for corrosion spots which can spread beneath the top coat and cause a sizeable but limited paint defect or paint

blister. If caught early on, this can be dealt with by very localised paint rectification; if ignored, it will needlessly mar the otherwise well-turned-out appearance of the car.

The car does not suffer from a structural corrosion problem or rust 'bleeding' out of welded joints, flange seams or doors, wings, boot and floor panels. In fact, apart from the marginal problem of incomplete coverage of underbody parts by bitumas-tic-type protection compounds, corrosion is not apparent in any important zone.

The engine no longer has even slight oil leaks, and attention to the latest-type carburettor is routine in nature, mostly a matter of idling speed adjustment. There are no engine overheating problems.

For a time it seemed that the aggravating problem of valve clatter, usually difficult to rectify, had been finally resolved. Such defects have an uncanny habit of re-appearing from time to time, however. It is possible to overtax conventional engine oil and the relatively thin, hardened skin on rocker and camshaft lobes; they then wear. Repairs can be quite costly. This is essentially a metallurgical problem and can be resolved only by changes in process control during manufacture. Switching to another oil will have little effect. Once wear has penetrated the hard skin of these sliding surfaces – the skin is too thin for the duty it is called upon to perform – the components wear out in a very short time. The only way to make sure that this rapid-wear process has not already started is to take off the rocker cover and inspect the cam shapes. It pays to seek the assistance of a qualified engineer to carry out this check before the purchase of a used 180 or 2 litre is finalised. When the footbrake is applied the braking system gives a very effective response due to its all-disc design, but this arrangement tends to be disappointing as far as effectiveness and the need for attention to the handbrake are concerned. There is little that the owner can do about it, apart from adjusting the mechanism to compensate for wear.

Any doubts on wheel bearing clearances can be resolved by a franchised dealer. He has the information and means for checking not only bearing play but also safe tolerance on MacPherson suspension, steering joint wear, and imbalance of wheels and tyres – all of which interact. Some owners have complained of niggling, recurring problems with switches and relays, water ingress into light units, squeaking windscreen wiper motors, low quality locks and handles, and stalling of the engine due to carburettor shortcomings. Such irritations tend to detract from the image of quality and durability which the car tries hard to present.

By now the 180/2 litre ought to be an utterly dependable range of cars, but this goal has not yet been reached. It is a pity, for with just a little more effort the manufacturer could achieve a high level of quality and durability.

Specification of AA tested car

See p. 48

Make & model	CHRYSLER 180
Production years	1971–present
Body alternatives	4-door Saloon
Engine variants	1812cc OHC
	1981cc OHC
Data: AA test version	Chrysler 180, 4-door Saloon. 1971 model
Engine	In-line 4-cyl OHC watercooled, front-mounted
	Bore 87.7mm, stroke 75mm, 1812cc. Comp ratio 9.2:1
Fuel system	1 Weber twin-choke carburettor. Mechanical pump. 14.3-gallon tank
Transmission	4-speed & reverse, synchromesh on all forward gears. Rear-wheel drive.
	Diaphragm-spring clutch, $8\frac{1}{2}''$ diameter dry plate, hydraulically operated
Suspension front	Independent. Coil spring, MacPherson strut, anti-roll bar
Suspension rear	Coil-sprung live axle, trailing link, telescopic damper
Steering	Rack & pinion. $4\frac{1}{4}$ turns between full locks
	Turning circle 36 feet
Wheels	13″ diameter, 5J rims
Tyres	165SR13 radial-ply (Michelin ZX fitted)
Brakes	Hydraulic, disc front/disc rear. Servo
Dimensions	Length 14′8″ Width 5′8″ Height 4′8″ Wheelbase 8′7″
(overall)	Ground clearance $4\frac{3}{4}''$ Kerb weight (full tank) $21\frac{1}{2}$ cwts
Max speed (in gears)	First 32mph, second 52mph, third 80mph, top 101.3mph
Overdrive	Not applicable
Acceleration	0–60mph: 12.0 seconds; standing-$\frac{1}{4}$ mile: 18.5 seconds
Fuel consumption	overall: 27.0mpg
	steady 50mph: 30.8mpg (top gear)
	steady 70mph: 26.5mpg (top gear)
Fuel	Premium 4-star

What VISAR reveals

Worse than average   Average   Better than average   No data

All chart figures are percentages

	Age in years:	6–8	5–6	4–5	3–4	2–3	1–2
	Registration Suffix:	FG	H	J	K	L	M
Corroded front doors				16	5	0	0
Corroded rear doors				12	3	1	0
Corroded front wings				0	0	0	0
Corroded rear wings				0	0	3	0
Corroded front underwings				8	0	0	0
Corroded rear underwings				0	0	0	0
Corroded body sills				0	8	0	0
Corroded jacking points		N	N	0	4	0	0
Corroded floor		O	O	0	0	0	0
Corroded underbody frame members		–	–	0	2	0	0
Defective undersealing		T	T	25	11	4	8
Loose/misaligned driver's seat		C	C	0	0	0	0
Attend to engine mountings		U	U	0	0	0	0
Evidence of head gasket leaks		D	D	0	0	0	0
Noisy valve gear		O	O	58	44	20	34
Evidence of engine oil leaks		R	R	50	18	23	24
Attend to carburettor tuning		P	P	17	29	28	24
Evidence of fuel leaks				0	0	4	0
Final drive noise		N	N	0	0	0	0
Unsatisfactory gear change		–	–	8	0	0	0
Unsatisfactory auto gear change							
Clutch judder		T	T	0	0	0	0
Attend to front wheel bearings		O	O	8	10	22	0
Attend to steering box/rack		N	N	0	3	9	8
Attend to footbrake				0	8	3	0
Attend to handbrake				27	29	21	17
Corroded brake pipelines				8	11	3	0
Defective obligatory lights				11	34	3	8
Attend to charging system				8	0	0	0
Attend to horn				0	0	3	0

A sensible compromise for some

This largest of the Chrysler range is an amalgam of Anglo/French design, although built exclusively at the Simca plant. Its size, capacity, and price put it midway between volume sellers like the Cortina, and 2-litre prestige offerings. Is it a sensible compromise?

The 1812cc engine produces enough power and performance to match most 2-litre rivals but it is not without its quirks of temperament, with some hesitancy and misfiring at times. It is inflexible in top gear too, and prefers a diet of free revs to give of its best. Unfortunately, it sounds frenzied as 6,000rpm approach and is not particularly quiet on the motorway. The gear change is poor, feeling springy and imprecise, making town driving a chore. Fuel consumption is respectable, however, with over 30mpg possible out of town, although the test car produced some pinking on 97octane 4-star petrol.

The 180's cornering is better than it first appears. Pronounced roll and vague steering response detract from its basically stable handling. The wheel remains acceptably light even when parking, however, and stability along ridges is steady, although the car dithers in a cross wind. Likewise, the ride becomes more creditable as conditions become more brutal. Although no match for a Peugeot 504, the 180 rides better than most other live-axled cars the testers know.

The brakes have too much servo assistance, but a firm pedal gives reassuring stopping. There is some fade under duress but the crash stop is powerful.

The interior is comfortable and well equipped, with good seating and a driving seat which will prove generally acceptable to family motorists. The fascia is more agreeable than most French creations and the wipers and deep screen give a commanding view forward but it is much harder to see out when reversing.

Ventilation arrangements are comprehensive and a match for all weathers, but the crude water-valved heater is disappointing to those familiar with the sensitive Hunter system. Rear seat comfort is well planned, although getting in can be tricky because of the sweeping door-frames and weak door checks. Oddments space is restricted, but the boot is extremely generous, although the loading sill is too high for comfort.

The 180 is well painted and bitumastic sealer is used on the floor pan, but is too skimpy on some vital areas to be convincing. The car's mechanical orthodoxy keeps routine maintenance easy, but the handbook is less informative than the Hillman's, for example.

The 180 certainly offers high standards of roominess, performance and economy, but one may wonder if too much mechanical affability has been sacrificed in the process. Its indifferent gear change and sloppy handling dampened the testers' driver enthusiasm and the car's appeal lay rather in its generous creature comforts and a straightforward design. Compared with the Cortina and cars of that ilk, it looks good, but costs more. Against the more distinguished 2-litre prestige saloons, it is struggling, but costs less. For some, it could be a sensible compromise.

Second thoughts – 3 years later

The 180's engine was enlarged to 1981cc for the automatic version now on sale in the UK. This really is a superb box – made in the US – and prompts the testers to up-rate the model for those who are set on having an automatic saloon. Interior design is even more attractive, with a splendid driving seat to match rear comfort. While it still lacks mechanical quietness, the bigger engine seems less temperamental. The testers found the 2-litre had some significant advantages that too few seem to know about, the most important of these being its auto transmission.

Citroën GS Club

CITROËN GS
ENGINEERS' COMMENTS
Novel, but complex

When Citroën launched their GS it received worldwide acclaim for its engineering ingenuity, but regrettably some of the very features which were praised proved not nearly as well-engineered or durable as Citroëns – component-wise and as a whole – generally are. On early-built cars a substantial number of engines and transmissions leave a good deal to be desired. Despite original claims, these could not be ranked as long-lasting or trouble-free. It is surprising that some of the troubles and customer complaints were not anticipated.

Those contemplating the purchase of a GS should remember that the car is a French breed, and thus designed for reaching fast cruising speed by taking advantage of the gear box and free revving of the engine. Driven in such a manner, it will be responsive and offer sensible fuel economy. But it is not designed to be a top-gear, low-speed town car.

Because it was needed to fill a gap in the Citroën range, the car was offered with some problems unresolved; it relied on the Company's good reputation and its array of novel features to carry the day. The car attempted too much in a highly sophisticated way; some of its components and assemblies were lacking in reliability and quality. For instance, camshaft lobe and rocker wear was high due to manufacturing shortcomings.

Design and manufacturing changes introduced in September 1972 – not least among them a change of second gear ratio on all manual gear boxes and a more powerful engine – have improved the car greatly. The 1220cc engine, an alternative to the original 1015cc power unit, also has a different final drive ratio to improve the car's flexibility on undulating roads. Since these front-wheel-drive power units are shoehorned into the very crowded front compartment which also houses the complex hydropneumatic suspension 'mechanism', it is not surprising that repair bills can be substantial if anything does go wrong. Being of air-cooled design, the car has no cylinder head gaskets – in the conventional sense – in the very ingenious but also complex flat-four opposed-cylinder units. The data under this heading on the VISAR table refer to manufacturing shortcomings which were overcome on the power units of post-September 1972 builds.

Mechanical and hydraulic complexity account for the disenchantment of owners who have attempted to do their own servicing. It simply is not a car for DIY enthusiasts. Even some dealers have found the carburettor setting and minor electric fault tracing a little unusual – for they have failed to make a success of routine adjustment while the car was still under warranty, as the M-registration percentages indicate. The carburettors are precision set at the factory. Attempts to improve on fuel economy by 'tinkering' with mixture strength are to be discouraged. Only idling speed should be adjusted. The all-disc power brakes can be a bit of a disappointment too. Pads wear out quickly and if not renewed in time, quickly score

the discs. The handbrake works on the front discs, but requires frequent adjustment to compensate for brake pad wear. Hydropneumatic suspension is basically similar to the one which Citroën have been using on their D series since 1955, but all layout and mechanical and hydraulic components are different. As in the case of the larger Citroëns (D series) it is an all-or-nothing system concept, as the car relies on high-pressure hydraulics for suspension and brakes; it is basically reliable, however.

Structurally it is a very sound car, and the initial minor paint and underbody protection adhesion problems have been resolved on L and M registration cars. In fact, after a disappointing 18 months the car is now as good as it ought to have been right from the start.

Specification of AA tested car

See p. 52

Make & model	CITROËN GS
Production years	1971–present
Body alternatives	4-door Saloon, 4-door Estate
Engine variants	1015cc OHC (1971–present)
	1222cc OHC (1972–present)
Data: AA test version	GS Club 1015cc, 4-door Saloon. 1972 model
Engine	Flat 4-cyl, aircooled, front-mounted
	Bore 74.4mm, stroke 58.9mm 1015cc. Comp ratio 9:1
Fuel system	1 Solex twin-choke downdraught carburettor.
	Mechanical pump. 9.75-gallon tank
Transmission	4-speed & reverse, synchromesh on all forward
	gears. Front-wheel drive.
	Diaphragm-spring clutch, 7.1" diameter dry plate,
	cable operated
Suspension front	Independent. Self-levelling hydropneumatic strut
Suspension rear	Independent. Trailing arm, hydropneumatic strut
Steering	Rack & pinion. $3\frac{3}{4}$ turns between full locks
	Turning circle $33\frac{1}{2}$ feet
Wheels	15" diameter, $4\frac{1}{2}$J rims
Tyres	145×15 radial-ply (Michelin ZX fitted)
Brakes	Hydraulic, all disc, independent dual circuit. Servo
Dimensions	Length 13'6¼" Width 5'3¾" Height 4'5¼" Wheelbase 8'4½"
(overall)	Ground clearance 6"–9½" Kerb weight (full tank) 18 cwts
Max speed (in gears)	First 27mph, second 43mph, third 68mph, top 91mph
Overdrive	Not applicable
Acceleration	0–60mph: 18.0 seconds; standing-¼ mile: 21.6 seconds
Fuel consumption	overall: 29.2mpg
	steady 50mph: 36.6mpg (top gear)
	steady 70mph: 27.4mpg (top gear)
Fuel	Premium 4-star

What VISAR reveals

Legend: ▓ Worse than average · ░ Average · ▨ Better than average · □ No data

All chart figures are percentages

	Age in years:	6–8	5–6	4–5	3–4	2–3	1–2
	Registration Suffix:	FG	H	J	K	L	M
Corroded front doors					7	2	0
Corroded rear doors					7	1	0
Corroded front wings					3	0	2
Corroded rear wings					3	0	0
Corroded front underwings					4	0	0
Corroded rear underwings					2	0	0
Corroded body sills					4	0	0
Corroded jacking points		N	N		2	0	0
Corroded floor		O	O		0	0	0
Corroded underbody frame members		–	–		2	2	0
Defective undersealing		T	T		14	16	0
Loose/misaligned driver's seat		C	C		2	0	0
Attend to engine mountings		U	U		0	0	0
Evidence of head gasket leaks		D	D		9	0	0
Noisy valve gear		O	O		18	15	4
Evidence of engine oil leaks		R	R		24	19	15
Attend to carburettor tuning		P	P		25	23	32
Evidence of fuel leaks					2	0	0
Final drive noise		N	N		6	2	0
Unsatisfactory gear change		–	–		2	0	0
Unsatisfactory auto gear change							
Clutch judder		T	T		0	0	0
Attend to front wheel bearings		O	O		0	0	0
Attend to steering box/rack		N	N		6	2	4
Attend to footbrake					2	4	0
Attend to handbrake					13	9	0
Corroded brake pipelines					2	4	0
Defective obligatory lights					39	18	12
Attend to charging system					0	8	0
Attend to horn					4	4	8

(The FG and H columns read vertically: NOT IN PRODUCTION)

CITROËN GS CLUB (1015cc)
From AA Road Test Report 267, 1972

Could be a winner – later

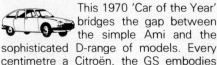

This 1970 'Car of the Year' bridges the gap between the simple Ami and the sophisticated D-range of models. Every centimetre a Citroën, the GS embodies striking styling and a unique technical specification. But what is it like on the road?

Well, for a start, the GS feels decidedly underpowered, for although it achieves an astonishing top speed of 91mph and proves quite lively when revved hard, it feels flat unless one works hard on the gear box. Throttle response is sluggish, too, resulting in a lethargic low-speed pullaway. The test car's overall fuel consumption of 29¼mpg is no match for a Simca 1100 or a Fiat 128, although 35mpg is possible with the GS, driven gently. Considering its short linkage, the gear change is disappointingly notchy and lumpy, and the low ratios (protected by strong synchromesh when the oil is warm) are rather whiney. But thanks to Autoroute breeding, the GS is smooth and quiet at high cruising speeds. The GS's soft hydropneumatic suspension is almost always unobtrusive, yet even the generally impeccable marshmallow ride is spoilt by cat's eyes and road humps which send a sudden quiver through the body. The testers can't fault either the steering or the handling, however, both of which make many so-called sports cars look rather silly. Despite their lightness, the brakes are not especially effective, but the curious-looking handbrake in the centre of the fascia is exceptionally powerful.

Initially the reclining front seats look and feel sumptuous, but they prove to be just too soft for comfort; backaches soon result. The wheel and pedals are well arranged though, and big windows and sensible wiper sweeps provide a clear outlook. GSs for the British market have a neat clear dash, with stalk switches on the column and fascia-mounted push-buttons working the minor controls.

Although one sits fairly erect in the back, there is ample room for three and even six-footers don't feel cramped. There is not much foot space though, and watch out for the hard-bar at shin level. The GS can't boast a host of interior appointments, but there are three ashtrays, a cigarette lighter, a central roof light and a clock. On the safety side the steering wheel is connected to the well-protected rack by a double-jointed column and anti-burst, childproof door catches are standard. Like most cars with air-cooled engines, the GS's heater is more of a fair-weather friend. Dependant on engine temperature and revs, it's very much an all-or-nothing affair. The Citroën's output is feeble, but the 'eyeball' fresh-air vents at each end of the fascia work very well.

Stowage space in the GS is restricted, but boot space is marvellous. Vast, square, and flat, it provides splendid load space within its carpet-lined, illuminated depths, and its bumper-height floor makes loading simple. The body, boasting a windcheating shape, seems light in construction and the testers were none too impressed by the quality of the chrome. Thin Tectyl underbody spray appears comprehensively applied, however, and there are no serious underwing mud traps. If there was a 'Wooden Spoon Award' for engine access the GS would get the testers' vote; the distributor points and tappets are nightmarish to get at.

In 1015cc form the GS is a car which just misses the mark. If Citroën would give it more power, better seats, improved heating and less fragile fittings it would be a world beater.

Second thoughts – 2 years later

Thanks to the new 1220cc engine, the GS is a lot more lively and its fuel consumption is more competitive at touring speeds. On the latest test car the camshaft drive didn't strip and armrest and ashtrays all stayed intact. There are still too many trim creaks and rattles though.

Daf 44

DAF 33/44

ENGINEERS' COMMENTS
A different breed of car

This car has several features which set it apart from all others in its class. One is its unique infinitely variable ratio gear box, which precludes a clashing of gears due to wear of synchromesh, badly spaced gear ratios, or even jerky automatic gear shifts. Since Daf's share in the UK market is still quite small, with a correspondingly small sample size, it would be misleading to form definite conclusions on all the items listed in the data table.

Until October 1973, all Daf cars were produced in the traditional method, whereby primer paint was sprayed all over the body. While the latest metal pre-treatment and electrocoat paint give the cars much improved anti-corrosion protection, particularly to hollow and partly closed sections, the quality of protection and paint finish, even on early Dafs, is good.

Corrosion on the front doors is confined to the lower door edges and an area behind the weather strip. There may also be some localised stone-chip damage to the front wings and the sills. In addition, mud trapping may lead to some underwing corrosion around the headlamp units and the upper location of the suspension's telescopic damper. As in the case of the body sills, however, corrosion is slow to progress. Moisture ingress into the headlamp units and into the passenger compartment accounts for the high proportion of obligatory lights requiring attention and for some rusting of the floor panels in F/G registration cars.

The shortcomings of factory-applied sealants and inadequate paint protection of the underbody frame members have been overcome by improvements in manufacturing specifications on cars produced after H registration. Daf models have been systematically improved, in fact. Factory-applied underbody protection is now of the solvent-based bitumastic type and from J registration onwards underfloor pressing corrosion has virtually disappeared. The brake pipelines, which suffer from a high incidence of corrosion on early models, have been given extra protection in the form of a very thin chromate film on top of their anti-rust zinc coating. Any corrosion which does occur is slight.

The attention required to the periodic problem of the footbrake column should not cause undue concern. Water ingress

➧

into the brake drums has been remedied. Brake adjustment is unusual. If the conventional procedure of adjustment is adopted to compensate for brake shoe lining wear, a pull to one side or the other almost inevitably occurs during hard braking. If in doubt, consult a Daf dealer.

The quality of the power transmission to the rear wheels has been improved. Up to H registration, some inherent pivot-pin stickiness affected the quality of take-up and disengagement of the centrifugal clutch. Owing to gear cutting inaccuracies, some Variomatics produced during the H and J registration period tend to be noisy; they rarely fail, however. Another source of noise is the two-cylinder air-cooled engine, which sounds clattery but is nonetheless very sturdy.

A Daf peculiarity is that of having to engage either forward or reverse before starting the engine, holding the car on the brake, preferably the footbrake. Some drivers tend to send the car darting forward or backward, depending on the gear selected, when they start the engine with the choke fully pulled out and the engine revving well above the clutch automatic engagement speed. In the F/G and H registration cars inspected, a particularly high incidence of slight accident damage to the rear bumpers and bumper valance was found. Poorly executed repair of such damage resulted in some unsightly surface corrosion. Better driver familiarisation with the peculiarities of this car would have prevented much disappointment.

Attention to front wheel bearings also implies a check for wear and smooth functioning of the steering joints. On extreme lock, in particular, the very direct acting rack and pinion steering tends to rattle a bit if lubricant leaks past the gaiter are left unattended.

Specification of AA tested car

See p. 56

Make & model	DAF 33/44
Production years	1967–present
Body alternatives	2-door Saloon, 2-door Estate
Engine variants	844cc OHV
Data: AA test version	Daf 44, 2-door Estate. 1973 model
Engine	Horizontally-opposed twin-cyl, air-cooled, front-mounted Bore 85.5mm, stroke 73.5mm, 844cc. Comp ratio 7.5:1
Fuel system	1 Solex downdraught carburettor. Mechanical pump. 8.5-gallon tank
Transmission	Variomatic automatic, infinitely variable ratios Transmission by twin belts to rear wheels. Centrifugal type clutch
Suspension front	Independent. Transverse leaf spring, telescopic damper
Suspension rear	Independent. Coil-sprung semi-trailing arm, telescopic damper
Steering	Rack & pinion. 3 turns between full locks Turning circle 31 feet
Wheels	14″ diameter, 4B rims
Tyres	135SR14 radial-ply (Michelin ZX fitted)
Brakes	Hydraulic dual circuit, drum front/drum rear.
Dimensions (overall)	Length 12′7½″ Width 5′0½″ Height 4′8″ Wheelbase 7′4½″ Ground clearance 7″ Kerb weight (full tank) 14 cwts
Max speed (in gears)	Not applicable this transmission. Max speed 72mph
Overdrive	Not applicable
Acceleration	0–60mph: 32.3 seconds; standing-¼ mile: 24.2 seconds
Fuel consumption	overall: 35.0mpg steady 50mph: 43.9mpg (top gear) steady 70mph: N/Rmpg (top gear)
Fuel	2-star

What VISAR reveals

Legend: ■ Worse than average ▨ Better than average ▦ Average □ No data

All chart figures are percentages

	6–8	5–6	4–5	3–4	2–3	1–2
Age in years / Registration Suffix:	FG	H	J	K	L	M
Corroded front doors	36	21	10	3	0	
Corroded rear doors						
Corroded front wings	27	29	6	0	0	
Corroded rear wings	15	8	5	2	3	
Corroded front underwings	17	30	0	0	5	
Corroded rear underwings	8	12	0	0	0	
Corroded body sills	30	25	13	3	0	
Corroded jacking points	8	7	13	0	5	
Corroded floor	33	11	0	0	0	
Corroded underbody frame members	18	24	0	0	0	
Defective undersealing	30	41	5	5	14	
Loose/misaligned driver's seat	15	6	0	0	9	
Attend to engine mountings	8	0	0	0	0	
Evidence of head gasket leaks	0	0	0	0	0	
Noisy valve gear	0	21	25	13	20	
Evidence of engine oil leaks	8	7	18	10	10	
Attend to carburettor tuning	8	31	29	15	5	
Evidence of fuel leaks	0	0	4	0	5	
Final drive noise	9	47	9	5	5	
Unsatisfactory gear change						
Unsatisfactory auto gear change	10	0	0	8	0	
Clutch judder	10	0	0	0	8	
Attend to front wheel bearings	0	18	8	8	14	
Attend to steering box/rack	0	12	8	0	5	
Attend to footbrake	17	12	4	2	5	
Attend to handbrake	8	12	4	15	10	
Corroded brake pipelines	46	19	12	5	14	
Defective obligatory lights	75	20	39	13	29	
Attend to charging system	0	0	0	0	0	
Attend to horn	0	0	0	2	0	

DAF 44 ESTATE

From AA Road Test Report 319, 1973

Nice at a price

Dutch Dafs offer power units from 750cc to 1300cc. The 44 is just one step up from the flyweight 33; although powered by a longer stroke, air-cooled, flat twin engine (and, of course, the ingenious Variomatic transmission), it shares the roomier body of the more sophisticated 66 and Marathon models.

The 44's acceleration is nothing to get excited about; 0–60mph in 32 seconds is way behind the times – especially at the price. Still, ease of driving is important and provided one drives with sufficient brio it is possible to keep pace with brisk city traffic. After a sluggish take-off, it scuttles along smoothly and briskly, pulling quite strongly from 25mph; overtaking above 45mph demands care, however. Around-town fuel consumptions are in the mediocre mid-twenties, but the test car managed 41 with gentle driving.

Driving is simplicity itself. Just select either forward or reverse, press either the stop or go pedal, and steer – belts, pulleys, vacuums and bob-weights do all the 'gear changing' in a smooth, stepless manner. The transmission is a little jerky as the centrifugal clutch engages, however, and the driver has no instant override control so the brakes have to work that much harder if one drives fast.

By small car standards the suspension provides adequate ride comfort, although it becomes more bobbly and disturbed on rutted surfaces – no match for an Escort or Viva in this department, nor with regard to road holding and handling either. Although the Daf suffers from twitchy tail-wag if one throttles back suddenly in mid-bend, however, it is graceful and virtually self-correcting. The steering helps; its lightness, precision and feel make it one of the car's highlights. The brakes are impressive too – they are heavy, but provide powerful all-square stops and clamp tight on a 1-in-3 hill.

The firm reclining front seats please occupants of almost all sizes and instrumentation is simple though adequate, but the testers disliked the offset pedals which make two-foot pedalling virtually essential. Vision is excellent, but the wipers leave bad blind spots. Easy-to-reach rockers work the minor switchgear, but the steering wheel spokes hide those for lights and wipers. With the front seats tipped forward rear entry is easy, but accommodation is not as roomy as that of rival estates from Austin/Morris or Fiat. Nevertheless, the backrest is nicely angled and there's room for a slender threesome, but creature comforts do not abound.

The headlining is carefully applied and the rubber-covered floor makes sense in an estate car. Boot space, already quite roomy, opens up to a spacious cargo area by the usual seat-folding arrangement, but loading is hampered by the tricky backrest catches and an awkward rear sill. The side-trims will soon show scratch marks too. The 44's heating doesn't work as well as the VW Beetle's, but the under-fascia vents push out really hot air at quite low engine revs. The faster one goes, the hotter it gets, so one simply feeds in cold air as required; the arrangement is rather like shower taps. Rather feeble fresh-air vents are provided in the fascia.

The 44's paintwork and finish are well up to class par, but underbody protection cannot match the Viva's. Nevertheless, most of the brightwork is of stainless material and there is little additional trim to harbour moisture. With the spare wheel and air cleaner removed it's easy to get at practically all service items under the bonnet.

It is a pity that the 44 is so expensive, because it is an appealing automatic possessing both character and charm. Unfortunately, one can find several congenial manual rivals offering the bonus of roomier accommodation and luggage space, heating and ventilation and more performance at the price.

Fiat 850 Saloon

FIAT 850

ENGINEERS' COMMENTS

Check for body rot

Compared with many other small cars of older design, the bodywork of a large number of Fiat 850s is badly affected by corrosion. As a result, these vehicles look unsightly quite prematurely. The root cause lies in the car's obsolescent factory-applied anti-rust treatment, and in a paint system which is more suited to a dry Continental climate than the damp weather of Britain.

Deposits from winter road salting and year-round industrial pollution induce corrosion at a rate which can seriously affect the structural strength of some cars over 5 to 6 years old. In the case of doors, rust deterioration begins at the joints of the outer-skin panels and their frames. Early rusting occurs on the surface of the wings, and may be followed eventually by rust from the inside out. The cause may be stone and grit bombardment, which erodes the none-too-effective thin protective paint layers, laying the metal bare to the corrosion-promoting acids contained in road salt and dirt. Corrosion is further aided by mud traps under the wings.

As a result of inadequate factory-applied underwing and underbody protection, some weakening by corrosion of the underbody structure can occur after only 3 to 4 years. Regular washing with a high-pressure hose, however, can dislodge and drastically dilute the underbody deposits which cause sheet metal decay. The rusting of enclosed hollow sections, such as body sills, starts from both the outside – where gravel rash penetrates through top coat and primer – and more significantly from the inside – where it can eat into the metal unobserved and unchecked. The result, after all too few years, is perforation, indicating serious deterioration. In cars over 6 years old, floor weakening is not uncommon, particularly where floor panels join the sill. Jacking points are also affected by rust, but owing to substantial local reinforcement there is little danger of them breaking away from the car body during a wheel change. Serious corrosion of the rear underwings usually does not manifest itself until cars are over 5 years old, but thereafter it increases at a fast rate.

Engine oil leakage is a frequent source of complaint and often has its roots in the sump or timing cover areas. Although not a

➧

57

common fault, some cases of seepage from fuel-pipe unions and plastic feed pipes have been noted. Gear box synchromesh action is satisfactory in the early life of the car, but occasionally deteriorates after a few years' service, the result of an inherent design limitation. Play in the front wheel bearings may require attention, although it should not be confused with wear in the steering swivel joints, which can be a problem on these vehicles. If in doubt, consult a Fiat dealer.

Both footbrake and handbrake tend to develop excessive free travel on pedal or lever. In the case of the handbrake, this is often due to the stretching of the cable, which may need periodic replacement. In general, regular maintenance and adjustment will in most cases restore full effectiveness. Brake pipe corrosion stems from the underbody layout; the pipes are clipped to the adjacent floorpan and underbody frame members, and corrosion of the latter spreads rapidly to the brake lines themselves.

Some 850s have a relatively high deterioration rate of headlamp reflectors, which usually stems from poor weatherproofing and resultant water ingress. Clutch judder on old cars can be due to oil seepage past the crankshaft seal. Engine mountings can occasionally give trouble, due to local rusting.

Older cars on which general corrosion is gaining a hold should be carefully checked with regard to structural soundness. Before replacing the horn, it pays to check that both electrical supply and earth return and their contacts are sound and rust-free. Anyone contemplating purchasing an old 850 should have it thoroughly inspected for body rot, largely a consequence of lack of care and maintenance on the part of the previous owner.

Specification of AA tested car

See p. 60

Make & model	FIAT 850
Production years	1964–1972
Body alternatives	2-door Saloon, Fixed Head Coupé, 2-seater Spider
Engine variants	843cc OHV, 903cc OHV
Data: AA test version	850 Special, 2-door Saloon. 1970 model
Engine	In-line 4-cyl, watercooled, rear-mounted
	Bore 65mm, stroke 63.5mm, 843cc. Comp ratio 9.3:1
Fuel system	1 Weber single-choke carburettor. Mechanical pump. 6.6-gallon tank
Transmission	4-speed & reverse with synchromesh on all forward gears. Rear-wheel drive
	Diaphragm-spring clutch, $6\frac{1}{2}$" diameter dry plate, cable operated
Suspension front	Independent. Transverse leaf-spring, telescopic damper
Suspension rear	Independent. Coil spring, semi-trailing arm, damper
Steering	Worm & sector. $3\frac{3}{4}$ turns between full locks
	Turning circle $33\frac{1}{2}$ feet
Wheels	13" diameter, $4\frac{1}{2}$J rims
Tyres	145SR13 radial-ply (Ceat "Drive" fitted)
Brakes	Hydraulic, disc front/drum rear
Dimensions (overall)	Length 11'8¾" Width 4'8½" Height 4'6½" Wheelbase 6'7¾"
	Ground clearance 5" Kerb weight (full tank) 14 cwts
Max speed (in gears)	First 23mph, second 40mph, third 58mph, top 83mph
Overdrive	Not applicable
Acceleration	0–60mph: 19.1 seconds; standing-¼ mile: 21.8 seconds
Fuel consumption	overall: 33.7mpg
	steady 50mph: 42.9mpg (top gear)
	steady 70mph: 31.7mpg (top gear)
Fuel	Premium 4-star

What VISAR reveals

Legend: ■ Worse than average ▨ Average ▨ Better than average □ No data

All chart figures are percentages

	6–8	5–6	4–5	3–4	2–3	1–2
Age in years: Registration Suffix:	FG	H	J	K	L	M
Corroded front doors	30	39	23	17		
Corroded rear doors						
Corroded front wings	40	32	17	9		
Corroded rear wings	39	36	13	5		
Corroded front underwings	32	22	6	2		
Corroded rear underwings	24	16	5	0		
Corroded body sills	53	49	36	34		
Corroded jacking points	30	21	15	8	N	
Corroded floor	31	10	7	0	O	
Corroded underbody frame members	50	29	18	12	I	
Defective undersealing	50	30	37	17	T	
Loose/misaligned driver's seat	0	0	0	0	C	
Attend to engine mountings	8	0	6	2	U	
Evidence of head gasket leaks	2	3	4	4	D	
Noisy valve gear	19	28	18	20	O	
Evidence of engine oil leaks	44	49	36	50	R	
Attend to carburettor tuning	30	26	37	19	P	
Evidence of fuel leaks	4	0	8	4		
Final drive noise	7	5	4	8	F	
Unsatisfactory gear change	15	13	8	4	O	
Unsatisfactory auto gear change						
Clutch judder	6	0	0	0	T	
Attend to front wheel bearings	37	30	17	28	U	
Attend to steering box/rack	8	3	16	7	O	
Attend to footbrake	26	21	31	47		
Attend to handbrake	32	20	21	36		
Corroded brake pipelines	36	22	12	29		
Defective obligatory lights	35	42	29	37		
Attend to charging system	0	3	4	0		
Attend to horn	4	5	6	7		

FIAT 850

From AA Road Test Report 126, 1966

Tough and likable little car

Judging by current trends, the days of the rear-engine car are numbered, although there are still eight large manufacturers producing them. They are mainly in the mini-to-medium class and thus represent competitive alternatives to the Imp. The Fiat 850 is one example.

Smooth changes

Cold starting in the 850 is instantaneous, and thanks to a rapid warm-up the heater works fast. Clever installation eliminates vibrations from the seemingly dated engine which spins with the smoothness of a modern five-bearing motor. Hard driving has no effect on the vigorous engine, although full throttle driving induces a lot of booming and drumming. The light, long-travel clutch engages smoothly, and the gearbox ratios are well chosen. Although difficulty is occasionally experienced in finding first gear, changes are usually smooth. Average fuel consumption is an impressive 41¾mpg. Town driving reduces this figure to the upper 30's, but up to 45mpg is possible on quiet cruising.

Light steering

Firm suspension gives the Fiat 850 a taut ride, with some pitch but little roll. Generally the steering is light and responsive, but becomes less effective with little self-centreing action. At higher speeds the car can be cornered tightly and quickly with no problems, but care is needed if one has to throttle back suddenly on a tight, wet bend – a tail slide could result. Normally, tyre grip is excellent and evasive action and tight turns are easily accomplished thanks to the light and easy steering. Drum brakes are entirely satisfactory in normal use, but proved less efficient during a harsh fade test. The handbrake holds the car easily on a 1-in-3 hill.

The front seats are too close together for comfort, giving a confined driving position that restricts elbow room. However, generous adjustment and reclining squabs enable most drivers to select a suitable driving position. The fact that the pedals are set on different planes is rather irritating.

Thick pillars

Excellent all-round vision is spoilt only by thick screen pillars, and allowance must be made for the hidden tail when reversing. The wipers cover a generous area, leaving only small unswept corners of the screen. All the dials and warning lights are visible through the steering wheel and the three confusingly similar switches to the right are easy to flip.

The interior is drab-painted metal, rubber floor mats and plain PVC. However, hidden features such as anti-burst locks and a sealed-off petrol tank give reassurance to the safety conscious. The back seat is comfortable, but is strictly for two and lacks legroom. Headroom is generous though, and items such as ashtrays and grab handles are standard. Various shutters control the heater, which is complex but works well. Fascia vents waft cool air through the de-mister ducts when the temperature control is cut off. Swivelling quarter-lights can be opened without adding too much to the noise level.

Good paintwork

Luggage must be lifted high to clear the front wings, but two medium-size cases and a couple of soft bags can be stowed. The paintwork is excellent, and sensibly, most of the brightwork is of non-corrosive material. It is a pity that the engine cover restricts access to what is otherwise a very handy power unit, but the back body panel can be removed if necessary.

The 850 is a tough, likable little car. Its performance and handling make it nimble and manoeuvrable and its fuel economy is excellent. Interior trimming is spartan, but it is nice to know one is cocooned in a safe bodyshell. It may never win a 'Car of the Year' award, but Fiat's know-how should assure their 850 of a sound and relatively trouble-free life.

Fiat 127

FIAT 127
ENGINEERS' COMMENTS
A car which has gained friends

Given the relatively recent introduction of this model and thus the small sample size involved in this survey, comment will be in the nature of general guidance since it is too early to discern lasting trends, particularly in those major components and structures which it did not inherit or borrow from other Fiat models. Many of the comments on the 128's paint system and corrosion resistance also apply to its smaller brother, the 127.

Rust staining

Occasional instances of slight rusting around the door seams have been noted, which suggests that a careful check should be made of these areas. The lower sections of the rear wings are somewhat vulnerable to rust as a result of stone chipping, which also applies – to a limited extent – to the rear underwings. Good factory-applied underbody protective coatings were only introduced in 1973, so some cases of underframe external corrosion which have been noted may be associated with the poor application of some compounds. The absence of floor corrosion beneath floor coverings indicates that a high standard of sealing against water ingress has been achieved in the passenger compartment. Some water leaks on K registration cars produced rust staining of the boot but no structural weakening.

Not a bad record

The apparent high incidence of cylinder-head gasket leakage should not cause undue alarm. The 127's engine unit is basically similar to that previously fitted to the 850 Sport, and the latter unit has not had a bad record in terms of engine reliability.

Pronounced valve gear noise occurs relatively frequently, although this is usually reduced to an acceptable level by tappet clearance adjustments. A degree of noise is characteristic of the engine, however, and it would be impractical to attempt to eliminate it altogether. In common with many vehicles using the transverse layout, some general transmission whine is also a peculiarity of this model. Universal joints tend to require more attention in such a front-wheel-drive layout than in a conventional drive arrangement.

Synchromesh action is generally acceptable, although some cases of weakness in ➧

61

the first gear action have been experienced. The 127 shares front-wheel maintenance problems with the Fiat 850. Attention is occasionally necessary to front wheel bearings in order to eliminate excessive play; it is best left to a Fiat dealer to diagnose and rectify.

Braking efficient, but...

While generally efficient, the braking operation is frequently marred by excessive travel on the footbrake and handbrake mechanisms. Regular routine maintenance and adjustment will generally restore full effectiveness, but an occasional handbrake cable replacement may be required where excessive stretching has occurred.

The 127 is the successor to the 850, which is now manufactured in Spain by SEAT. The 127, however, incorporates many of the structural improvements introduced in Fiat's small car range over recent years. It is a car which is likely to gain some new

friends and still please those who found the 850 a congenial small run-about town car which is also eminently suitable for country jaunts. It does, of course, incorporate many safety-orientated design and manufacturing concepts recently introduced into the Fiat range. Not the least of these is a strong impact-resistant passenger compartment and a steering wheel which collapses readily if struck by the driver in the event of a frontal collision.

The sample of M registration cars follows the general pattern but is too small to qualify as above average, below average or average.

Specification of AA tested car

See p. 64

Make & model	FIAT 127
Production years	1971–present
Body alternatives	2-door Saloon, 3-door Saloon
Engine variants	903cc OHV
Data: AA test version	2-door Saloon. 1972 model
Engine	In-line 4-cyl, watercooled, transverse, front-mounted Bore 65mm, stroke 68mm, 903cc. Comp ratio 9:1
Fuel system	1 Weber single-choke carburettor. Mechanical pump. 6.5-gallon tank
Transmission	4-speed & reverse, with synchromesh on all forward gears. Front-wheel drive Diaphragm-spring clutch, $6\frac{1}{4}''$ diameter dry plate, cable operated
Suspension front	Independent. MacPherson strut, coil spring, anti-roll bar
Suspension rear	Independent. Telescopic strut, transverse spring
Steering	Rack & pinion. $3\frac{1}{2}$ turns between full locks Turning circle $31\frac{1}{4}$ feet
Wheels	13" diameter, 4J rims
Tyres	135SR13 radial-ply (Cinturato CN 54 fitted)
Brakes	Hydraulic, dual-circuit, disc front/drum rear
Dimensions (overall)	Length 11'0" Width 5'0" Height 4'6" Wheelbase 7'3½" Ground clearance 5" Kerb weight (full tank) 14 cwts
Max speed (in gears)	First 24mph, second 42mph, third 64mph, top 80mph
Overdrive	Not applicable
Acceleration	0–60mph: 15.9 seconds; standing-$\frac{1}{4}$ mile: 20.2 seconds
Fuel consumption	overall: 36.25mpg steady 50mph: 43.4mpg (top gear) steady 70mph: 31.4mpg (top gear)
Fuel	Premium 4-star

What VISAR reveals

		Worse than average			Average
		Better than average			No data

All chart figures are percentages

Age in years:	6–8	5–6	4–5	3–4	2–3	1–2
Registration Suffix:	FG	H	J	K	L	M*
Corroded front doors				9	9	0
Corroded rear doors						
Corroded front wings				3	4	0
Corroded rear wings				13	8	0
Corroded front underwings				3	0	0
Corroded rear underwings				5	0	0
Corroded body sills				12	5	0
Corroded jacking points	N	N		6	0	0
Corroded floor	O	O		0	0	0
Corroded underbody frame members	–	–		10	0	0
Defective undersealing	T	T		22	5	0
Loose/misaligned driver's seat	C	C		3	0	0
Attend to engine mountings	U	U		3	0	0
Evidence of head gasket leaks	D	D		0	8	0
Noisy valve gear	O	O		36	45	20
Evidence of engine oil leaks	R	R		28	25	20
Attend to carburettor tuning	P	P		19	24	10
Evidence of fuel leaks				0	0	0
Final drive noise	N	N		9	0	0
Unsatisfactory gear change	–	–		11	3	0
Unsatisfactory auto gear change						
Clutch judder	T	T		0	0	0
Attend to front wheel bearings	O	O		26	13	10
Attend to steering box/rack	N	N		9	8	10
Attend to footbrake				29	18	20
Attend to handbrake				17	13	0
Corroded brake pipelines				6	3	0
Defective obligatory lights				9	11	0
Attend to charging system				0	0	0
Attend to horn				5	5	0

(The FG and H columns read vertically: "NOT IN PRODUCTION")

* See Engineers' Comments, p.62

Roomy and raucously eager

Based on a subtle mixture of already established Fiat components, the 127 emulates the front-drive, transverse layout of the Mini and the 1100 and abandons the rear-engine configuration of the 850 which it replaces in the Fiat range. The power unit, in fact, comes from the old 850 and it propels the 127 with outstanding liveliness. Low-speed response is particularly impressive, with a clean pull away from 20mph in top. Its low gearing, however, creates increased frenzy as 70mph approaches. The power unit sounds very busy when wound up through the gears and is less congenial mechanically than the more advanced 128 unit. Nevertheless, starting and idling are always reliable, with a quick warm-up aided by its thermostatic cooling fan. Gear ratios are well spaced, but shift quality is springy and imprecise, making town driving a bit of a chore. A creaky clutch action does not help matters, either.

Average fuel consumption is satisfactory for the performance, but even with restrained driving it cannot match the frugality of a Mini. Tank range is limited and the low-level lamp is a good idea, although it cried 'wolf' on the test car.

MacPherson struts at both ends – similar to the 128 – give agile cornering, permitting one to hurtle into bends with great confidence in most situations. On wet corners, however, the normally helpful 'tuck-in' caused by cutting power can turn into rear-end breakaway. Fortunately, the sensitive steering greatly helps control and gives an unmistakeable feel about the state of front-wheel grip.

Like the 128, the ride is taut and absorbs the discomfort of bumps well, especially at lower speeds. As speed or the severity of the bumps increases, however, it becomes more jittery. The brake pedal's unnerving long travel and lack of initial progression do not give a fair picture of the brakes' overall efficiency. They show impressive stopping power, especially in the wet, and they do resist fade.

It is easy to step in and out of the front, but the driving position seems good for only an hour or so because one lacks spinal support. The wheel is too high and the pedals too close – a common malady of Italian cars. Instrumentation is neat and forward vision reasonable. The rear view is more difficult and a bigger interior mirror would help here.

Although its engine size and kerb space make the 127 comparable to small cars like the Mini Clubman and Datsun Cherry, its space for people and luggage is superior to any car in this group. Rear passengers, in particular, are treated to remarkably generous legroom and seat support. Yet a sense of austerity seems to pervade the look and feel of the interior, which does less than justice to its comfort and equipment.

Boot space is very generous by small car standards; its good height and regular shape make it a match for serious luggage. The heater is quite generous to front occupants, but insufficient at foot level behind. A stuffy feeling may encourage one to lower a side window, but then fumes are drawn in through the rear extractors working in reverse, which may result in headaches and sore throats. To make life more difficult, the face-level vents cannot deliver cold air when the heater is on.

Easier for DIY

The mechanical thoroughness of such a small car is impressive. It is a lot easier to work on than the 128 for routine maintenance. Despite its greater roominess, however, the 127 still feels like a Mini – eager rather than sedate, with a raucous engine and quicksilver cornering response. These characteristics will recommend it less to steady family-saloon types who like their home comforts.

Fiat 128

FIAT 128
ENGINEERS' COMMENTS
Anti-rust...too early to judge

In common with other Fiat cars, the 128 shows the various stages in the development of better metal pre-treatment and paint system aimed at combatting the principal enemy of long body life – rust. Early models suffered from the initial shortcomings of the electrocoat primer paint and limited coverage by paint of the inside of hollow sections. Stone and grit bombardment could cause cracking of the outer colour coat on these early cars. Once chipped, a local surface blemish could spread underneath the top paint coat and cause unsightly rusting.

New process
The front doors of this model are prone to surface corrosion due to stone damage, as are the four wings on the generous flange areas of the wheel arches. This creeping rust, if untreated when it first appears, can be costly to cure. The post-1973 production vehicles have been treated with the much-advertised 'new' anti-rust process used by most European and Japanese car makers for a number of years. It is too early to confirm whether this has had the marked beneficial effect on the rate of deterioration which Fiat claim. It will take

some 4 years at least before a meaningful judgement can be passed.

Paint problems
The 128's underwings are not seriously affected by corrosion, because they receive better factory-applied anti-rust protection than most cars. The higher percentage of corrosion displayed by H registration vehicles is probably due to paint and production problems which other European manufacturers also experienced about the same time.

Body sill corrosion is generally due to attack by stones, corrosive salt, and trapping of slush and dirt behind the sill bright strip embellisher, where fitted. On a happier note, the absence of any instances of visible floor corrosion beneath the floor covering suggests a high standard of watersealing of bulkhead joints, doors, windows and windscreen. There is still room for improvement in the type and placement of the factory-applied underbody compound; some cars occasionally show untreated patches.

Valve-gear noise
The apparent sudden increase on recent models of excessive valve-gear noise does

not indicate a deterioration of standards. Rather, this is a reflection of the fact that some of the cars inspected were in need of attention to tappet adjustment. In some cases, the vehicles were still covered by the manufacturer's warranty, and were brought for examination by individuals in dispute with their garage.

Engine oil seepage is not a frequent complaint on the 128. The Weber carburettor fitted on this model seldom gives cause for concern. Its main requirement is one of idling adjustment. Some cases of weak synchromesh have been noted, but a more common complaint is a lack of ease of gear selection, a characteristic of many vehicles with a transverse engine installation.

Earlier final drive assemblies

Universal joints should be inspected, as they tend to need replacing on older cars. The steering rack, normally a reliable unit, occasionally suffers from oil seepage past the gaiters. If these are damaged or split in the process, they will need to be replaced. The assembly must then be refilled with the factory-approved lubricant. Some early models may also show signs of noise and wear on the final drive assembly.

The brakes suffer fairly frequently from excessive free travel on the foot pedal and to a lesser degree on the handbrake linkages. Brake adjustment and replacement of disc pads usually restores full effectiveness.

Obligatory lights, in common with other Fiats, still tend to suffer from poor electrical contacts and an above-average failure rate for bulbs. On early models it pays to look for cases of deterioration of headlamp reflectors. The location of the light unit tends to promote moisture ingress due to salt spray and road slush.

Specification of AA tested car

Make & model	FIAT 128	See p. 68
Production years	1970–present	
Body alternatives	2-door Saloon, 4-door Saloon, fixed head Coupé, Estate	
Engine variants	1116cc OHC, 1290cc OHC	
Data: AA test version	4-door Saloon. 1973 model	
Engine	In-line 4-cyl, watercooled, transverse, front-mounted Bore 80mm, stroke 55.5mm, 1116cc. Comp ratio 8.8:1	
Fuel system	1 Weber single-choke carburettor. Mechanical pump. 8.3-gallon tank. Low-level warning	
Transmission	4-speed & reverse, synchromesh on all forward gears. Front-wheel drive. Diaphragm-spring clutch, 7″ diameter dry plate, cable operated	
Suspension front	Independent. MacPherson strut/coil spring, anti-roll bar	
Suspension rear	Independent. Telescopic strut, transverse spring	
Steering	Rack & pinion. $3\frac{1}{2}$ turns between full locks Turning circle 36 feet	
Wheels	13″ diameter, $4\frac{1}{2}$J rims	
Tyres	145SR13 radial-ply (Cinturato CN 54 fitted)	
Brakes	Hydraulic, dual-line, disc front/drum rear. Servo	
Dimensions (overall)	Length 12′7$\frac{3}{4}$″ Width 5′2$\frac{3}{4}$″ Height 4′8″ Wheelbase 8′0$\frac{1}{2}$″ Ground clearance 5$\frac{3}{4}$″ Kerb weight (full tank) 16$\frac{3}{4}$ cwts	
Max speed (in gears)	First 30mph, second 48mph, third 73mph, top 86mph	
Overdrive	Not applicable	
Acceleration	0–60mph: 15.5 seconds; standing-$\frac{1}{4}$ mile: 21.0 seconds	
Fuel consumption	overall: 34.0mpg steady 50mph: 38.4mpg (top gear) steady 70mph: 29.0mpg (top gear)	
Fuel	Premium 4-star	

What VISAR reveals

All chart figures are percentages

	Age in years: 6–8	5–6	4–5	3–4	2–3	1–2
Registration Suffix:	FG	H	J	K	L	M
Corroded front doors		19	14	9	4	0
Corroded rear doors		10	8	10	4	0
Corroded front wings		34	24	12	6	0
Corroded rear wings		29	19	12	6	0
Corroded front underwings		0	12	1	0	0
Corroded rear underwings		0	12	0	0	0
Corroded body sills		34	31	13	5	0
Corroded jacking points	Z	10	4	6	0	0
Corroded floor	O	0	0	0	0	0
Corroded underbody frame members	—	5	7	2	1	0
Defective undersealing	T	18	14	15	15	9
Loose/misaligned driver's seat	C	0	0	5	2	0
Attend to engine mountings	U	0	0	0	0	0
Evidence of head gasket leaks	D	0	2	0	2	0
Noisy valve gear	O	10	6	18	16	26
Evidence of engine oil leaks	R	16	14	18	13	13
Attend to carburettor tuning	P	10	20	23	21	22
Evidence of fuel leaks		0	0	0	0	4
Final drive noise	N	10	4	3	4	0
Unsatisfactory gear change	—	10	8	6	2	5
Unsatisfactory auto gear change						
Clutch judder	T	0	0	2	0	0
Attend to front wheel bearings	O	5	10	26	14	4
Attend to steering box/rack	N	14	0	6	8	13
Attend to footbrake		5	20	26	17	4
Attend to handbrake		5	30	31	5	0
Corroded brake pipelines		5	6	11	3	0
Defective obligatory lights		10	37	21	23	16
Attend to charging system		0	0	0	0	4
Attend to horn		0	0	1	2	0

FIAT 128

From AA Road Test Report 320, 1973

Roomy, refined and vivacious

The front-wheel-drive 128 was Fiat's first attempt at the layout popularised by the Mini/1100. Since its introduction and a 'Car of the Year' award, it has had to face competition first from the Renault 12 and now from the Allegro.

In spite of its perky nature and low overall gearing, the 128 manages to be one of the smoothest, quietest, and best insulated saloons in its class. It starts easily and is flexible, pulling cleanly from around 20mph in top. With restraint, 41mpg is possible in subdued country motoring, but harder use lowers consumption to 27mpg. Assessed against its competitors, the 128's thirst is very respectable. Compared with, say, an Escort or Avenger, the gearshift offers nothing to get excited about, although it is better than average alongside most transverse layouts. Its good synchromesh is generally unobstructive and despite some springiness, the lever moves with a reasonably defined action. The test car's clutch tended to slip during arduous use, but normally performed impeccably.

Progressive, fail-safe handling puts the 128 ahead of practically all its front-wheel-drive rivals. Ultimately the front runs wide under power, but sudden deceleration merely causes it to tighten gently into the turn. The light, smooth steering provides excellent feel, and straight-line running in side winds is impeccable. Below 40mph no-nonsense tautness allows minor disturbances to reach the interior, but this restlessness diminishes as the pace quickens. Compared with domestic offerings, it matches their better qualities in ride and handling without their attendant shortcomings. The 'suddenness' of the brakes can be disappointing if one feels progressiveness is more important than standing the car on its nose. Fade and water resistance are good, and the handbrake works well.

Cloth-trimmed seats with their excellent rake adjustment offer adequate support and location, but the pedals are too high.

Thanks to big, deep windows, vision is excellent, with all four corners in clear view and wipers (with a useful 5-second delay sweep) positioned to avoid blind spots. Two bold and neatly calibrated dials are in clear view through the steering wheel, but the warning lights between them can dazzle at night. Most minor controls are within easy reach, although the choke, hand throttle and heater controls are exceptions; so too is the laborious screenwasher bulb. Column stalks work the lights and wipers.

Seat comfort and exceptional roominess become obvious when one steps into the car. Foot entry space is restricted, but rear seat legroom proves surprisingly similar to an Austin 1300. The headlining looks rather sombre, but the fit and finish of the fascia and fittings are impressive. Childproof locks are a serious omission on the back doors, but the 128's safety features are numerous. The heater is both efficient and sensitive to adjustment, but the direction of air is dependant on a hinged flap under the fascia. Fresh-air ventilation arrangements work well, and swivelling front quarter-lights help. Boot space is generous and despite a high rear sill, it isn't too difficult to load.

Beneath the glossy paint finish there were several gaps in the test car's corrosion resistance, especially on underbody sealant, which was scantily applied. Since the test car was produced, however, Fiat have made a determined effort to improve their anti-rust manufacturing techniques.

Even with the spare wheel and air cleaner removed, access to the engine is awkward. One may well dread the prospect of even adjusting the alternator drive belt, and valve adjustment is also difficult to accomplish oneself.

The 128's mixture of practicality, refinement and sheer vivacity present a powerful argument, especially as this last quality is so depressingly absent in most of the competition.

Fiat 124 Special T

FIAT 124

ENGINEERS' COMMENTS

Rugged car, quicker deterioration

The 124, in common with others in the old-style Fiat range, suffers from the early appearance of corrosion on door seams, wheel arches, body sills and underwings. This corrosion, which tends to spread beneath the paint film and leads to rapid deterioration in appearance, is basically the result of an obsolescent anti-rust metal pre-treatment and paint system. Cars produced from C up to about H registration are noted for this. The latest Fiat cars are as corrosion-resistant as most, since the recent, much-advertised 'new' anti-rusting measures adopted reflect the technology already proven by Fiat's major European competitors. The low incidence of internal floor corrosion indicates that the sealing of panel seams, windscreen, sliding windows and doors against water ingress is of a high quality.

Some structurally significant corrosion of the underbody frame members first manifests itself in about the fourth year of the car's life. Its subsequent rate of increase, however, is higher than average but the passenger compartment is so strong initially that this does not endanger the occupants in the event of a crash. Brake pipelines often suffer from corrosion as a result of mud packing around them and the rusting of underbody panels to which they are attached.

The above-average need to attend to front seat mountings and adjustments often demands no more of the car owner than a timely re-tightening of the attachment fasteners and periodic checks thereafter. A frequently encountered complaint on this model is excessive valve gear noise from both the rockers and the single-roller timing chain. This is inherent in the engine design and not indicative of imminent failure, but it can become very obtrusive unless adjustment correction is carried out. Engine oil leaks are more in the nature of seepage from around the sump and timing cover seals and gaskets than a significant loss. The carburettor frequently requires attention to tuning and external linkage to eliminate over-richness and erratic idling. If neglected, high fuel consumption can result. The engine, clutch and gear box are basically reliable units. The noise from the final-drive unit, while annoying, is rarely excessive and not indicative of the need for a costly repair.

Wheel bearing attention

The front wheel bearings call for more frequent attention than those of some other cars, but this does not imply that they are liable to collapse under normal motoring conditions. The complex procedure for checking and adjusting free play is best left to the manufacturer's accredited dealers. This is particularly so, as any wheel rock found can easily be due to wear in the upper swivel joints. Such wear increases with age and is readily confused with wheel bearing rock.

The all-round disc system, which normally gives little cause for concern, can suffer from excessive free-pedal movement if regular replacement of brake pads is delayed. The self-adjusting handbrake, in common with others of its type, experiences occasional seizure of the caliper mechanism. As far as steering is concerned, attention should be directed towards oil leaks and linkage joint wear.

Poor lighting

Inadequate weather sealing, allowing ingress of moisture resulting in deterioration of headlamp reflectors, and bad earth-return due to rusting account for the poor showing of the obligatory lights. While there is a general tendency to relate such defects to the age of the vehicle, the Fiat 124 deteriorates in this respect more than average once it is over 4 years old, but this need not imply costly repairs if caught in time. The model which is now being built under licence in a number of countries is basically a rugged, well-proven European design.

The sample of M registration cars follows the general pattern but is too small to qualify as above average, below average or average.

Specification of AA tested car

Make & model	FIAT 124	*See p. 72*
Production years	1966–present	
Body alternatives	4-door Saloon, Estate, Coupé (124 Sport), Spider	
Engine variants	1197cc OHV, 1438cc OHV, 1438cc OHC (Special T & Sport)	
	1592cc OHC, 1608cc OHC, 1756cc OHC	
Data: AA test version	124 Special, 4-door Saloon, 1438cc OHV. 1969 model	
Engine	In-line 4-cyl, watercooled, front-mounted	
	Bore 80mm, stroke 71.5mm, 1438cc. Comp ratio 9:1	
Fuel system	1 Weber twin-choke carburettor. Mechanical pump.	
	8.5-gallon tank. Low-level warning	
Transmission	4-speed & reverse, synchromesh on all forward	
	gears. Rear-wheel drive	
	Diaphragm-spring clutch, 7.2″ diameter dry plate,	
	cable operated	
Suspension front	Independent. Coil spring, telescopic damper, anti-roll bar	
Suspension rear	Coil-sprung live axle, Panhard rod, telescopic damper	
Steering	Worm & roller. 3 turns between full locks	
	Turning circle 37 feet	
Wheels	13″ diameter, 4½J rims	
Tyres	150SR13 radial-ply (Cinturato fitted)	
Brakes	Hydraulic, disc front/disc rear. Servo	
Dimensions	Length 13′3½″ Width 5′3½″ Height 4′4¼″ Wheelbase 7′11½″	
(overall)	Ground clearance 4¾″ Kerb weight (full tank) 18¼ cwts	
Max speed (in gears)	First 26mph, second 45mph, third 69mph, top 92mph	
Overdrive	Not applicable	
Acceleration	0–60mph: 14.1 seconds; standing-¼ mile: 19.5 seconds	
Fuel consumption	overall: 27.5mpg	
	steady 50mph: 34.5mpg (top gear)	
	steady 70mph: 26.9mpg (top gear)	
Fuel	Premium 4-star	

What VISAR reveals

Legend: ■ Worse than average | ▒ Average | ▨ Better than average | □ No data

All chart figures are percentages

	Age in years: 6–8	5–6	4–5	3–4	2–3	1–2
Registration Suffix:	FG	H	J	K	L	M*
Corroded front doors	35	19	32	10	12	0
Corroded rear doors	49	21	24	14	8	0
Corroded front wings	51	41	26	8	7	5
Corroded rear wings	40	34	28	15	5	0
Corroded front underwings	34	19	10	2	3	0
Corroded rear underwings	21	11	7	1	0	0
Corroded body sills	62	48	37	21	4	5
Corroded jacking points	33	25	16	12	3	0
Corroded floor	16	0	7	0	0	0
Corroded underbody frame members	33	15	19	3	0	0
Defective undersealing	56	27	23	10	8	10
Loose/misaligned driver's seat	7	9	9	6	5	0
Attend to engine mountings	2	1	0	1	1	0
Evidence of head gasket leaks	0	2	7	2	0	0
Noisy valve gear	30	42	38	19	23	20
Evidence of engine oil leaks	35	33	32	30	13	20
Attend to carburettor tuning	48	42	48	40	15	20
Evidence of fuel leaks	3	0	2	1	0	0
Final drive noise	5	7	0	1	3	0
Unsatisfactory gear change	2	0	0	2	0	0
Unsatisfactory auto gear change						
Clutch judder	2	0	0	1	0	0
Attend to front wheel bearings	28	24	17	19	18	10
Attend to steering box/rack	10	7	5	7	12	0
Attend to footbrake	34	21	28	12	12	10
Attend to handbrake	24	19	31	22	20	20
Corroded brake pipelines	35	23	20	8	7	0
Defective obligatory lights	37	31	53	20	9	0
Attend to charging system	2	0	0	1	0	0
Attend to horn	4	9	2	6	2	0

* See Engineers' Comments, p.70

FIAT 124 SPECIAL

From AA Road Test Reports 313, 1973
and 214, 1970

Family saloon with 'vivace'

Its eager performance and easy handling made the conventional Fiat 124 Saloon a 'natural' for the GT treatment. Fiat soon obliged with this 1438cc Special, which improved an already lively performer. The car thrives on high revs, and its thrumming smoothness makes it ideal for the man who enjoys driving and likes his car to sound as if it is enjoying the experience too. The price paid is a mild unwillingness to start first time and some signs of raggedness after too much top-gear trundling. The gear shift is a bold lever with a big knob, but its short, clean movements require none of the strong-arm effort its appearance suggests. It may, however, send one staggering away from rest in third by mistake until accustomed to its spring bias.

Fuel consumption on the model is nothing special but it is hard to discipline oneself into leisurely driving! The 1200 version managed 32mpg in a later test and quiet driving makes this feasible in the Special too. Tank range is a poor 200 miles with an 'alarmist' low-level lamp to add to one's confusion.

Exhilarating suspension

Like its eager engine, the car's perfectly orthodox coil-sprung suspension also proves exhilarating. The 124's verve brings back real 'vivace' to family-saloon motoring.

On smooth roads, the 124's cornering is sure-footed and enormous fun, while the sensitive steering gives one lots of confidence. The ride itself is less impressive, however. Although the shuddering and jolting are removed, there is unwanted bobbing and bouncing at times. When the bumps and bends come together, stability can be affected. The all-disc braking on the test car suffered from undue effort and a spongy pedal action. Later cars with a servo are much better, however.

Inaccurate dials

All, except shorter people, will wish they had longer arms and shorter legs when driving the 124. Adjustable seat backrests help offset this, but the mechanism is not as helpful as the 128's. The Special has a neater set of dials, but they tend to be inaccurate. The box-like body shape pays dividends in rearward vision and the rear extremities are just in view to the driver. Escort-type screen vents give good ventilation in summer but their temperature setting is tied to the heater so the interior gets stuffy in winter. The floor heat is generous but is regulated by a crude flap arrangement. Quarter-lights open to relieve stuffiness, but at the cost of some wind noise.

Good safety features

The rear seat is well designed, but legroom is only just adequate and some may find it difficult to negotiate the door sills and intrusive belt reels. Trim was plain, but pleasing in the Special tested, and carpets and cloth seats were featured in later versions. Oddments space is limited but the boot is very deep and roomy, with lighting. Safety is seriously heeded in interior design, with secure seat mounts and reasonable padding as well as progressive deformation of the main structure.

Scanty undersealing

Standards of construction and rust protection are less thorough than superficial examination suggests – the underbody seal is scanty and paint is too prone to blister and lift. On the other hand, the technical specification is very comprehensive and the under-bonnet layout reasonably accessible, although the handbook makes some items appear easier to get at than is really the case.

The 124's best asset is undoubtedly the fact that it remains such fun to drive, despite its orthodox design. Its chunky styling doesn't date either, and the Special will please the man who wants something sporty but whose circumstances demand something more practical.

Ford Capri 1300

FORD CAPRI MARK I
ENGINEERS' COMMENTS
Attractive styling induces rust

The incidence of corrosion on this car naturally increases with age, but in addition it is affected by developments in paint technology. Earlier models, for example, suffered from some paint intercoat adhesion shortcomings. The Capri is not an easy car to give good protection. As it is performance orientated, it will often be driven harder than other cars. Furthermore, the body styling exposes the sills, in particular, to bombardment by stones and road grit thrown up by the front wheels. It is thus not surprising that the sills suffer more from a certain amount of surface corrosion than the all-makes average.

Strength not affected

Body design also plays a role in the corrosion of the front wings, which curve low down behind the wheels and become readily packed with mud, corrosion-promoting salts, and slush. As a result of this styling, the wing flanges, which tuck under, are vulnerable to stone damage and resultant surface corrosion. Most of the rusting occurs on the outside and hence does not affect the car's structural strength, which relies heavily on the hollow, closed body sills.

Such corrosion as does occur at the internal junction of the boot, rear wing arch and rear-seat structure generally progresses slowly. Unfortunately, metal pre-treatment and electrocoat primer paint, which can give optimum anti-corrosion protection, penetrate this zone of the car only with particular difficulty. There is an above-average tendency for water to leak into the boot in F/G registration cars and as a result, rust signs are noticeable on some cars. The front underwings suffer worse-than-average corrosion, which is caused by the accumulation and trapping of road salts, spray and mud around the MacPherson strut mountings. The rear underwings can suffer stone damage and mud packing, particularly in the lower area forward of the rear wheels.

Older cars in this range often have poor weatherproofing. As a result, water collects on the floor under the carpeting, producing surface corrosion. Recent models of the Capri have received partial underbody protection at the time of manufacture. The benefit of this bitumastic treatment is noticeable on cars of K, L and M registration.

73

The driver's seat and runners on this car tend to work loose. In addition, there is frequently some movement of the back rest in relation to the seat, owing to the fact that the back rest hinges forward in order to permit access to the rear seat. A front seat with undue movement and sagging upholstery is a sign of a well-used car.

Gear box, clutch and final drive – consistently good features of the model range – are highly reliable. The engine is relatively free of oil leaks and requires little attention, apart from routine maintenance, to keep it turning sweetly. Tappet clearance adjustment, of course, is a component of such maintenance.

The direction indicator lamps on the earlier models tend to fill with water, and the positioning of the rear number plate lamp makes it vulnerable to accidental damage.

Headlamps

Water ingress into the oblong headlamps leads to shorter bulb life. The effective sealing of these lights has been a problem on most cars which have adopted this styling feature.

A not uncommon fault in the Capri range is the tendency for the car to pull to one side when it is brought to a sudden stop from speed by braking hard. A Ford dealer can sort this problem out better than the average DIY man.

Specification of AA tested car

See p.76

Make & model	FORD CAPRI
Production years	1969–1974
Body alternatives	2-door Saloon Fastback, Saloon Hatchback (Mark II)
Engine variants	1298cc OHV, 1599cc, 1996cc, 2994cc, 3093cc OHV 1593cc OHC, 1993cc OHC
Data: AA test version	Capri GT, 1593cc OHC. 1973 model
Engine	In-line 4-cyl, watercooled, front-mounted Bore 90.6mm, stroke 66mm, 1593cc. Comp ratio 9.2:1
Fuel system	1 Weber twin-choke carburettor. Mechanical pump. 10.5 gallon tank
Transmission	4-speed & reverse, synchromesh on all forward gears. Rear-wheel drive. Diaphragm-spring clutch, 8½" diameter dry plate, cable operated
Suspension front	Independent. MacPherson strut, coil spring, anti-roll bar
Suspension rear	Leaf-sprung live axle, anti-roll bar, telescopic dampers
Steering	Rack & pinion. 3¾ turns between full locks Turning circle 32 feet
Wheels	13" diameter, 5J rims
Tyres	165SR13 radial-ply (Michelin ZX fitted)
Brakes	Hydraulic, dual-line, disc front/drum rear. Servo
Dimensions (overall)	Length 13'11¾" Width 5'4¾" Height 4'2¾" Wheelbase 8'4¾" Ground clearance 4½" Kerb weight (full tank) 18 cwts
Max speed (in gears)	First 39mph, second 57mph, third 82mph, top 100mph
Overdrive	Not applicable
Acceleration	0–60mph: 11.5 seconds; standing-¼ mile: 19.0 seconds
Fuel consumption	overall: 29.5mpg steady 50mph: 40.3mpg (top gear) steady 70mph: 30.2mpg (top gear)
Fuel	Premium 4-star

What VISAR reveals

Worse than average ■   Average ▨

Better than average ▧   No data ☐

All chart figures are percentages

	Age in years: 6–8	5–6	4–5	3–4	2–3	1–2
Registration Suffix:	FG	H	J	K	L	M
Corroded front doors	20	12	12	6	4	2
Corroded rear doors						
Corroded front wings	35	25	17	8	4	0
Corroded rear wings	20	11	11	7	3	2
Corroded front underwings	18	9	6	2	1	0
Corroded rear underwings	14	8	4	2	1	0
Corroded body sills	26	26	24	14	6	2
Corroded jacking points	14	13	10	5	2	2
Corroded floor	5	12	13	1	0	0
Corroded underbody frame members	20	11	10	4	2	1
Defective undersealing	13	15	8	11	21	0
Loose/misaligned driver's seat	5	18	5	5	11	12
Attend to engine mountings	3	0	0	0	0	0
Evidence of head gasket leaks	0	3	1	1	1	0
Noisy valve gear	31	18	17	21	17	13
Evidence of engine oil leaks	33	32	20	21	25	19
Attend to carburettor tuning	34	48	29	32	27	23
Evidence of fuel leaks	2	1	1	1	2	0
Final drive noise	3	4	7	3	3	4
Unsatisfactory gear change	0	4	7	2	3	0
Unsatisfactory auto gear change						
Clutch judder	5	2	2	2	2	7
Attend to front wheel bearings	14	8	15	12	24	14
Attend to steering box/rack	16	8	11	9	6	0
Attend to footbrake	19	15	23	13	12	18
Attend to handbrake	21	12	13	12	7	12
Corroded brake pipelines	18	15	15	4	2	2
Defective obligatory lights	37	26	29	23	13	10
Attend to charging system	13	4	2	3	2	0
Attend to horn	12	3	2	3	1	2

FORD CAPRI 1600 GT

From AA Road Test Report 304, 1973

Updated, uprated – but better?

 The first Capri's firm, no-nonsense ride and trim handling, combined with good performance, fully justified its sporting pretentions. Now the range has been revised and rationalised. Minor styling changes have also been introduced, but more significantly the suspension has been softened and an overhead camshaft engine now provides the power.

Acceleration through the gears is faster, as is top speed, but it is a poor slogger in top. An efficient automatic choke gives first-time starts and the new car's ability to cruise at up to 70mph without fuss is a real improvement. Fuel consumption is also better, 29½mpg overall being very satisfactory. Normally one can expect 25 to 34mpg and a range of about 270 miles on a tankful. The gear lever is well positioned and its light but precise feel makes gear changing a pleasure. Sensible ratios do much to disguise the engine's torque deficiencies, but a 1-in-4 hill start is the best attainable.

Tidy, predictable cornering

Cornering proves tidy and predictable right to its quite high limits, yet the test car's handling was found to be less precise and pleasing in normal spirited use. When pressed, it imparts a feeling of sloppiness and vagueness that dampens enthusiasts' ardour. It should be conceded, however, that the less demanding family man will probably go for the softer ride and lighter steering, discounting the rest. The brakes are fine in normal circumstances, but caused the test car to slew when applied really hard. A non-intrusive servo eases the pedal load, and both fade and water resistance are good.

The front seats are very comfortable, but tall drivers could use a little more legroom. Vision will be marred for some by the inability to see the nearside front wing tip (aggravated by the way the wipers park), and by blind spots to the rear. The new instruments are bolder and much more legible than those of their predecessor, but the push buttons for wipers and lights are closely grouped and are confusingly similar.

Pleasing interior

Subtle revisions have marginally improved rear legroom and increased oddments space, yet things remain cramped for rear occupants unless they are short. Low doorframes, restricted foot entry and front seat squabs that fall back on the unwary are features to contend with, although entry and exit are not difficult by sports coupé standards. The car's low-cost optional cloth trim is a pleasing feature. The neat fit of the carpeting is appreciated, as are the interior fittings, which include a glove-box, centre console tray, clock and lidded compartment between the front seats.

The Capri's excellent ventilation system offers plenty of finely controllable ram flow through the swivelling 'eyeball' fascia vents; the two-speed booster fan is very quiet and efficient, even on slow. The heating arrangements are equally well thought out, with a temperature slide that instantly obeys. The ability to waft cool air to the screen while enveloping the floor with warmth is very welcome.

Cosmetic exterior changes

Apart from bigger headlamps, exterior changes are cosmetic and nothing appears to have changed in terms of construction and finish. Ford's undersealing is just too scanty to contend with gravel and saline attack, and there are some bad mud traps under the wings. The orthodox power train makes maintenance easy, and access to the engine is generally good.

In spite of the Capri's undeniable improvements in fuel economy, quieter cruising, seating and instrumentation, the handling precision in what purports to be a sporting coupé has suffered. The model has lost a lot of its strength of character. Ford may be correct in their marketing philosophy, but take a cool look before making a commitment to this Capri – things aren't all they appear to be.

Ford Corsair V4 De Luxe

FORD CORSAIR

ENGINEERS' COMMENTS

DIY may not be enough

The paint system – early electrocoat primer – and the anti-rust protection which the Corsair received are as good as those on cars of similar vintage and price. Some cars, however, show signs of rust emanating from welded joints on wings and doors. If the car has not been regularly washed, and deposits of mud and road grit have not been removed from the car's underside, a number of sheet-metal zones may be wafer thin. Such underbody deposits are rich in chemicals and salts which, over a period of time, can eat through most protective paint systems to the metal beneath.

Rust traps

Bright trim fixings can lose their thin anti-corrosion layers after a few years and thus be the starting point for the spread of rust. Where the underwing and underbody frame members join the larger, flatter metal panels, corrosion can be most rife. These undisturbed, frequently unnoticed mud and dirt entrapment zones are often slightly wet and are thus maintained in a state of corrosion 'animation'.

Wing mirrors and radio aerials – as extras – are fitted after manufacture and necessi-

tate the drilling of holes, the edges of which are not adequately rustproofed. Drain holes in doors and sills are all too often found to be partly or totally blocked by caked dirt, which together with moisture generates slow-acting corrosion that gnaws away at the inside of the door panels.

Internal corrosion of such longitudinal members as the body sills and rear wheel arch reinforcement, however, is more serious. The body sills of F/G registration cars show a high degree of rust erosion. This stems from their position on the car, as a result of which the closed, hollow structures are subjected to extensive external bombardment by road salt and grit and to the internal splash of a corrosively-active dispersed spray. A neatly painted, dull black body sill, or any area which differs slightly in colour, may indicate an attempt to disguise extensive surface rusting. A simple magnet can be used to determine whether there is filler or sound sheet metal beneath the sill's paint; only sound steel will attract and hold such a magnet. If in doubt, call in an expert.

The MacPherson strut mountings are another item to check. Some surface

◢

corrosion and rust 'bleeding' around the top mount and its structural reinforcement is to be expected and is not an indication of imminent failure. On the other hand, a cleverly patched and locally oversprayed area surrounding the upper MacPherson mount demands an explanation from the seller. Internal corrosion of the floor panels should generally be quite slight and superficial. It is advisable to lift the carpets and underlay to check the extent and severity of any existing corrosion.

Watch out for 'bargains'

Some clutch judder and an above-average need for attention to the handbrake mechanism – features of a few older Corsairs – may be a price worth paying if one is bargain-hunting. However, if a thin screwdriver can be pushed without undue force through the surface rust of underbody frame members right into the hollow sections, the car could prove a very costly 'bargain'.

Poor connections, premature bulb failure, or flickering lights may be the result of water ingress past seals. The horn in particular should have a good earth connection and a functioning electric supply. Horn ring problems are not uncommon on early Corsairs, but it is well to remember that a fully operational horn is a legal requirement.

Dampers have a limited life. The degree of their effectiveness lessens as wear increases on the rubber element which joins them to the main body structure. Wear and deterioration of the anti-roll bar rubber bush connection – part of the lower linkage on the MacPherson front suspension – are a common feature of ageing cars. Replacement is not expensive, and improves ride, comfort and road handling.

Specification of AA tested car

See p. 80

Make & model	FORD CORSAIR
Production years	1963–1970
Body alternatives	4-door Saloon, Estate
Engine variants	1498cc OHV, 1662cc OHV, 1996cc OHV (V4-cyl arrangement on 1662cc & 1996cc)
Data: AA test version	Corsair 2000E 4-door Saloon, 1969 model
Engine	V4, 60° inclined, watercooled, front-mounted Bore 93.7mm, stroke 72.4mm, 1996cc. Comp ratio 8.9:1
Fuel system	1 Weber twin-choke carburettor. Mechanical pump. 10-gallon tank
Transmission	4-speed & reverse, synchromesh on all forward gears. Rear-wheel drive. Diaphragm-spring clutch, 8" diameter dry plate, hydraulically operated
Suspension front	Independent. MacPherson strut, coil spring, anti-roll bar
Suspension rear	Leaf-sprung live axle, telescopic dampers
Steering	Recirculating ball. $4\frac{1}{2}$ turns between full locks Turning circle $36\frac{1}{2}$ feet
Wheels	13" diameter, $4\frac{1}{2}$J rims
Tyres	165SR13 radial-ply (Goodyear G800 fitted)
Brakes	Hydraulic, disc front/drum rear. Servo
Dimensions (overall)	Length 14'8½" Width 5'3½" Height 4'7½" Wheelbase 8'5" Ground clearance 6" Kerb weight (full tank) $21\frac{1}{4}$ cwts
Max speed (in gears)	First 35mph, second 52mph, third 74mph, top 96mph
Overdrive	Not applicable
Acceleration	0–60mph: 11.3 seconds; standing-$\frac{1}{4}$ mile: 18.1 seconds
Fuel consumption	overall: 26.5mpg steady 50mph: 33.3mpg (top gear) steady 70mph: 25.3mpg (top gear)
Fuel	Premium 4-star

What VISAR reveals

Legend: ■ Worse than average ▨ Average ▨ Better than average ☐ No data

All chart figures are percentages

	Age in years: 6–8	5–6	4–5	3–4	2–3	1–2
Registration Suffix:	FG	H	J	K	L	M
Corroded front doors	22	12				
Corroded rear doors	24	14				
Corroded front wings	26	16				
Corroded rear wings	28	7				
Corroded front underwings	17	21				
Corroded rear underwings	11	15				
Corroded body sills	45	26				
Corroded jacking points	13	12	N	N	N	N
Corroded floor	11	0	O	O	O	O
Corroded underbody frame members	30	25	–	–	–	–
Defective undersealing	44	20	T	T	T	T
Loose/misaligned driver's seat	3	0	C	C	C	C
Attend to engine mountings	0	3	U	U	U	U
Evidence of head gasket leaks	0	0	D	D	D	D
Noisy valve gear	25	22	O	O	O	O
Evidence of engine oil leaks	34	34	R	R	R	R
Attend to carburettor tuning	33	44	P	P	P	P
Evidence of fuel leaks	3	3				
Final drive noise	7	3	F	F	F	F
Unsatisfactory gear change	0	0	O	O	O	O
Unsatisfactory auto gear change						
Clutch judder	8	3	T	T	T	T
Attend to front wheel bearings	17	15	U	U	U	U
Attend to steering box/rack	8	9	O	O	O	O
Attend to footbrake	18	10				
Attend to handbrake	37	13				
Corroded brake pipelines	12	16				
Defective obligatory lights	36	43				
Attend to charging system	8	3				
Attend to horn	30	12				

FORD CORSAIR 2000E

From AA Road Test Report 206, 1970

Showroom appeal...but

 The success of the prestige 2000s from Rover and Triumph has forced volume producers like Ford to present alternatives to their traditional big 'sixes' at a similar price. The earlier Corsair used the Classic's 1500 in-line engine but V-4s were introduced in late 1965. Although advertised as 'the car that is seen but not heard', the rumbling harshness of the power unit contradicts that claim. Acceleration is excellent, however, and it pulls well from low speed in top gear. The clamour is worse than that of the Zephyr and Capri using the same engine, confirming the afterthought nature of this installation. The gear change merits high praise, however, with slick, slicing movements through a well-chosen set of ratios. The testers' only grouse concerns the centre console lid, which can bang the driver's elbow as he changes gear with a flourish. Fuel consumption compares well with some other 2-litre cars of inferior performance; the test car managed 30mpg in leisurely driving. The range between fill-ups is only 225 miles, however.

The taut suspension of the Cortina 1600E contrasts sharply with the Corsair's gentle damping and soft springing. The suspension of the 2000E enables it to deal easily with broken surfaces, but there's too much pitching and heaving over undulations. This also detracts from its cornering manners, for despite grippy road holding, its kangaroo pitching on uneven bends can be unnerving. The steering, made lower-geared for the V-4, also feels unsporting with woolly free movement from straight ahead. It does manage to keep parking effort reasonable, however. The brakes, on the other hand, are a good match for the car's performance.

Aimed at those who could afford to run a grander car but see little point in doing so, the 2000E pays much attention to comfort and control. Its furnishings are lavish with a good set of instruments and extremely comfortable seats. The back seat, with its generous shaping and proper cushion support, is a notable improvement on previous Corsairs. Legroom is tight behind the taller driver (who might also seek more rearward movement), but things are better on the passenger's side. Vision is good to the rear but the whereabouts of the pointed bonnet is mostly left to intelligent guesswork. Headlights are well up to the car's performance and bright automatic reversing lamps operate even with the ignition off.

Interior ventilation is to the usual high Ford standard, equal to the best and better than most. The heater's output on 'full' is volcanic, although the air blender on the test car dispensed separate draughts of cold and hot when the temperature setting was reduced. Trim standards are high, with a glossy wood fascia, snugly fitting pile carpet, and clever imitation leather upholstery. The large luggage boot, fully trimmed and carpeted, is more luxurious than the inside of many family saloons! Luggage must be heaved over a prominent sill, however, and the enforced security of key-only boot opening is a nuisance sometimes. Special 2000E features include a standard pushbutton radio and a vinyl-covered outside roof.

Under-bonnet length is less than half filled by the short V-4 block, yet access to plugs and some ancillaries is cramped because of the engine's width and intruding strut mountings. Fusing is improved but a DC dynamo is retained. There are no grease nipples and the test car creaked on full lock as if to question this simplification.

The Executive Corsair justifies its pretentions to grandeur in terms of equipment and appointment, but its noise and indifferent ride and handling blur the image when one goes motoring with it. Motoring priorities should be sorted out before allowing the Corsair to bewitch with its considerable showroom appeal.

Ford Cortina Mark II Super

FORD CORTINA MARK II

ENGINEERS' COMMENTS

Popular with fleet operators

When Ford introduced the Cortina Mark I in 1962, they departed from many hitherto unchallenged concepts of design and production of a light-weight, cheap-to-produce, medium-sized family car. The Mark II is a restyled continuation of the Mark I.

In 1962, the Cortina – with its MacPherson strut front suspension and a very orthodox live axle – was a trendsetter. Imitation is the sincerest form of flattery; Alfa Romeo, Fiat, Chrysler UK, BMW, VW, Peugeot, Honda, Mazda, Datsun and Toyota have all followed suit in one model or another. The simple solution of taking a telescopic hydraulic damper, surrounding it with a coil spring, holding the lower end with a link and an anti-roll bar, and locating the top end in the reinforced front wing area – with a controlled amount of flexibility or 'compliance' – is still a system with a future. It can, however, deteriorate through wear and age during its useful service life. For one thing, this system is sensitive to wheel balance and prone to deterioration of the upper rubber mounting assembly. Because it is difficult to obtain perfect anti-corrosion paint protection between the flat steel

reinforcing plate and the sheet steel bracket joined to the wing structure, some progressive rusting does occur. The suspension assembly becomes readily packed with salt-laden slush, mud and dirt, but structural failure – usually easily detected during compulsory annual DoE tests of old cars – is quite rare. Front wings, however, tend to rust through from the inside outwards unless the underside is washed regularly with a pressure hose. Underwing protection compound was not applied to the Cortinas at the time of manufacture.

Vulnerable sills

Slipper-dip priming, which was the process of anti-rust treatment employed on the Mark II and is still the standard process on a number of volume-produced vehicles, does not provide for a consistent protective paint film inside the box sections of sill and underbody reinforcement. There may be some rust staining at the sill-to-wing joints, for instance. Should underfloor corrosion and substantial rusting of the structurally important underbody members – including the longitudinal frame to which the rear springs are anchored – be detected on older cars, check the sills. If they appear to be rust-free, plastic filler and a quick overspray may be the explanation. The Mark II can be a good buy, but beware the glossing over of a corrosion problem, rust pinholing for example, which started from the inside of door sill panels.

Good weatherproofing of the passenger compartment means that little or no moisture is trapped under the floor covering. This feature accounts for the above–average appearance of the floor panels when carpet, felt or rubber are lifted. Nonetheless, 16% of F/G registration cars had received underfloor repairs. Although it is possible to weld in new sections, provided the adjoining ones are sound metal, this is not a DIY job and it could be a costly one. The procedure for checking the structural strength of a car – outlined in the engineers' comments on the Corsair – is recommended.

Shorter tyre life?

Both wheel-bearing play and age-induced deterioration of the MacPherson steering suspension and damper elements can lead to a lowering of ride comfort and handling precision as well as unnecessarily short front-wheel tyre life. A Ford dealer can carry out the necessary checks and restore the assemblies to their designed performance limits. Be sure to seek advice about the likely costs of any restoration work involved.

Some water ingress into light units can result in a shortening of bulb life.

Based on its overall performance the Cortina Mark II proved to be a car with a marked customer appeal, and many fleet operators regretted its phasing out in favour of the Mark III which is radically different in terms of size, style, engineering specification and manufacturing processes.

Specification of AA tested car

Make & model	FORD CORTINA MK II	See p. 84
Production years	Mk II 1966–1970	
Body alternatives	2-door Saloon, 4-door Saloon, Estate	
Engine variants	1298cc OHV, 1599cc OHV, 1558cc OHC	
Data: AA test version	1300cc 2-door Saloon de luxe. 1970 model	
Engine	In-line 4-cyl, watercooled, front-mounted	
	Bore 81mm, stroke 63mm, 1298cc. Comp ratio 9:1	
Fuel system	1 single-choke Autolite carburettor. Mechanical pump. 10-gallon tank	
Transmission	4-speed & reverse, synchromesh on all forward gears. Rear-wheel drive	
	Diaphragm-spring clutch, $7\frac{1}{2}''$ diameter dry plate, hydraulically operated	
Suspension front	Independent. MacPherson strut, coil spring, anti-roll bar	
Suspension rear	Leaf-sprung live axle, telescopic dampers	
Steering	Recirculating ball. $4\frac{1}{2}$ turns between full locks	
	Turning circle $30\frac{1}{4}$ feet	
Wheels	13" diameter, $4\frac{1}{2}$J rims	
Tyres	165SR13 radial-ply (Cinturato fitted)	
Brakes	Hydraulic, disc front/drum rear	
Dimensions (overall)	Length 14'0" Width 5'5" Height 4'7" Wheelbase 8'2"	
	Ground clearance 7" Kerb weight (full tank) $17\frac{1}{4}$ cwts	
Max speed (in gears)	First 27mph, second 41mph, third 68mph, top 88mph	
Overdrive	Not applicable	
Acceleration	0–60mph: 18.8 seconds; standing-$\frac{1}{4}$ mile: 21.2 seconds	
Fuel consumption	overall: 31.0mpg	
	steady 50mph: 42.9mpg (top gear)	
	steady 70mph: 27.5mpg (top gear)	
Fuel	Premium 4-star	

What VISAR reveals

Legend: ▓ Worse than average ░ Average ╱ Better than average ☐ No data

All chart figures are percentages

	Age in years: 6–8	5–6	4–5	3–4	2–3	1–2
Registration Suffix:	FG	H	J	K	L	M
Corroded front doors	15	10				
Corroded rear doors	12	10				
Corroded front wings	30	24				
Corroded rear wings	28	17				
Corroded front underwings	18	12				
Corroded rear underwings	14	14				
Corroded body sills	35	24				
Corroded jacking points	14	11	N	N	N	N
Corroded floor	7	3	O	O	O	O
Corroded underbody frame members	24	16	—	—	—	—
Defective undersealing	27	15	T	T	T	T
Loose/misaligned driver's seat	5	8	U	U	U	U
Attend to engine mountings	3	1	U	U	U	U
Evidence of head gasket leaks	4	1	D	D	D	D
Noisy valve gear	31	31	O	O	O	O
Evidence of engine oil leaks	45	31	R	R	R	R
Attend to carburettor tuning	34	27	P	P	P	P
Evidence of fuel leaks	4	3				
Final drive noise	6	4	F	F	F	F
Unsatisfactory gear change	2	7	O	O	O	O
Unsatisfactory auto gear change						
Clutch judder	4	7	T	T	T	T
Attend to front wheel bearings	17	14	U	U	U	U
Attend to steering box/rack	14	15	O	O	O	O
Attend to footbrake	21	16				
Attend to handbrake	24	14				
Corroded brake pipelines	17	10				
Defective obligatory lights	34	38				
Attend to charging system	6	4				
Attend to horn	9	2				

FORD CORTINA MARK II

From AA Road Test Reports 218, 1970
and 212, 1970

Obsolete but not outmoded

The Mark II Cortinas were introduced in late 1966 and like their predecessors offered a lot of car for the money, with a range of engine and trim options in saloon or estate car guise.

The cross-flow 1300 and 1600 engines both have five main bearings and an excellent reputation for durability, unlike the earlier 1200 Mark I. They feel similar on the road too with 0–60mph times varying from 18.8 seconds for the 1300 saloon to 16.0 seconds on the 1600 saloon; 1600 Es and GTs are even quicker at 13.3 seconds. The 'Kent' engine is not very refined at its slowest and fastest speeds, with vibration below 30mph and a resonant boom past 70mph – there are lesser harsh periods in between too. With careful driving in the 1300 40mpg is possible and normal mixed use results in a typical 31mpg on all versions. On the whole, the 1600 manual saloon is the best all-rounder. Oil consumption tends to be non-existent.

Surprisingly wieldy

Given the right set of 4½J wheels and radials, the Cortina II is surprisingly wieldy, possessing steady road holding right to remarkably high limits. The leaf-sprung live axle is commendably 'tame' and in terms of ride comfort, too, the car is good over bad surfaces, with only bigger potholes causing the rear axle to flutter – the overall impression is better than the Hunter or Marina. The 1600E has stiffer suspension for tauter cornering, but for family use the standard springing feels the nicest compromise.

The brakes are progressive and powerful but non-servoed versions need a firm pressure to attain their commendable crash stop. Nose dip is quite pronounced and although fade resistance is good, the brakes take a long while to get over flooding. Like the pedal, the handbrake is weighty but powerful and easily tackles a 1-in-3 slope.

The driver's comfort depends on which version he is sitting in. The Super models were much more comfortable than the ordinary de luxe cars. The controls are superbly placed and the remote gear shift on the Supers and GTs is above average even by today's standards, although the low second gear ratio is irritating. The steering wheel feels too high for some, especially as it is heavily dished and close to the driver. All-round vision is very good and on later versions the instruments are attractively inset in a black PVC covered surround.

Pioneer ventilation

With its pioneer face-level ventilation system and efficient heater, the Cortina II feels ahead of its time and some people say the Mark III system isn't half as good. Wind noise is still apparent, despite being able to get plenty of fresh air without lowering a door glass. Engine noise comes and goes in waves so one tends to choose an acoustic trough for cruising. On the whole, noise suppression is not as good as the Capri or Escort.

Rear entry is easy on four-door cars but the two-door versions are best in de luxe form, because the entire seat tilts forward to ease one's passage. Once settled, the two-door's cushion gives better support and the absence of door armrests improves its width too but rear legroom is very restrictive. Perhaps the gigantic boot will be some consolation, and oddments space, with fascia box and shelves, is reasonable too.

Mechanically orthodox

The Cortina's mechanical orthodoxy makes it extremely popular, as under-bonnet access for servicing is excellent.

The Cortina II was a careful refinement on the Mark I, producing results that were far better than in theory they should have been. True, some people would have wished for more rear passenger comfort rather than boot space, but overall it proved a most agreeable performer, with plenty of creature comforts thrown in.

Ford Cortina 1300L

FORD CORTINA MARK III
ENGINEERS' COMMENTS
Better anti-corrosion process

The Ford Motor Company pioneered the electrocoat primer process of anti-rust treatment in which the whole bodyshell of the car is immersed in a large tank containing a solution of water, pigment and resin. The bodyshell is electrically charged to attract the pigment and resin, which are deposited as a thin, uniform primer paint layer all over the sheet steel, penetrating into hollow sections and even into spot-welded joints and close-fitting junctions. It is claimed that this process achieves better anti-corrosion protection than any previous mass-production method. Generally, our statistics support Ford's claim to have achieved remarkably good protection, although there were some early setbacks in production control at the factory and disappointments in paint formulation.

Before top coat
The New Cortina can be rated among the successes of this process, which is carried out before application of the colour top coat by conventional paint spraying. There are few internal and closed sections in which the process does not give good anti-corrosion protection. Initially, however, the intercoat adhesion primer to phosphate substrata or primer to top coat was not always adequate and localised splintering off of this anti-rust layer resulted. Where such slight surface blemishes do occur, the appearance can be easily restored by using a small brush and a tin of the appropriate colour coat, which can be found in most car accessory shops. It is usually necessary only to touch in such chips on door, wing, valance and sill panels.

Improved steering
The rack-and-pinion steering is generally trouble-free and a great improvement on the recirculating-ball type of earlier Cortina models. Ride and handling were much improved by the introduction of anti-roll bars in front and rear on the 1974 series. In contrast to the Cortina Mark I and II, the New Cortina (Mark III) does not suffer from the occasional adverse build-up of tolerances in the manufacture and assembly of its front suspension, wheel bearings, and wheels and tyres, which made itself felt as vibration and steering tremor. The MacPherson strut assembly has been discarded in favour of the more orthodox double wishbone. This, of course, has no

◆

upper anchorage location in the reinforced underwing area, and suffers less from age-induced deterioration of steering and suspension joints.

Back-axle noise

Gear-box and clutch operation are good and do not measurably deteriorate with age. The incidence of back-axle noise has been of some concern to the manufacturers, but it is more a source of customer annoyance than a warning of the likelihood of imminent mechanical failure. The overhead camshaft engine with its cog-belt camshaft drive is generally quieter than the tappet and push-rod operated one.

The layout of the handbrake mechanism is good, emergency braking at speed can produce a pull to one side. The problem of water ingress and poor electric contact or relatively short bulb life has also been largely overcome on the New Cortina.

Oil leaks not serious

Flexible engine mounts, never a bad feature on Cortinas, are very good. Engine oil leaks are rarely a serious problem, amounting to no more than a trace of general oiliness unless the filter seal is badly mangled during its routine cartridge renewal.

All in all, it is not surprising that the New Cortina has established itself so well – at the expense of the competition – in the middle-cost bracket of the popular car ranges in the UK.

Specification of AA tested car

See p. 88

Make & model	FORD CORTINA MK III
Production years	1970–present
Body alternatives	2-door Saloon, 4-door Saloon, Estate
Engine variants	1298cc OHV, 1599cc OHV
	1593cc OHC, 1993cc OHC
Data: AA test version	1593cc OHC, 4-door Saloon XL. 1974 model
Engine	In-line 4-cyl, watercooled, front-mounted
	Bore 87.7mm, stroke 66mm, 1593cc. Comp ratio 9.2:1
Fuel system	1 Ford multi-jet carburettor. Mechanical pump.
	11.9-gallon tank
Transmission	4-speed & reserve, synchromesh on all forward
	gears. Rear-wheel drive.
	Diaphragm-spring clutch, $7\frac{1}{2}$" diameter dry plate,
	cable operated
Suspension front	Independent. Coil spring, double wishbone, damper
Suspension rear	Coil-sprung live axle, trailing link, telescopic damper
Steering	Rack & pinion. $3\frac{3}{4}$ turns between full locks
	Turning circle $33\frac{1}{2}$ feet
Wheels	13" diameter, $4\frac{1}{2}$J rims
Tyres	165SR13 radial-ply (Cinturato fitted)
Brakes	Hydraulic. Dual circuit, disc front/drum rear. Servo
Dimensions	Length 14'0" Width 5'8" Height 4'6" Wheelbase 8'$5\frac{1}{2}$"
(overall)	Ground clearance 5" Kerb weight (full tank) $20\frac{1}{2}$ cwts
Max speed (in gears)	First 29mph, second 51mph, third 73mph, top 95mph
Overdrive	Not applicable
Acceleration	0–60mph: 15.1 seconds; standing-$\frac{1}{4}$ mile: 20.9 seconds
Fuel consumption	overall: 27.0mpg
	steady 50mph: 37.3mpg (top gear)
	steady 70mph: 27.3mpg (top gear)
Fuel	Premium 4-star

What VISAR reveals

Legend: Worse than average / Average / Better than average / No data

All chart figures are percentages

	Age in years: 6–8	5–6	4–5	3–4	2–3	1–2
Registration Suffix:	FG	H	J	K	L	M
Corroded front doors			11	7	4	3
Corroded rear doors			13	7	5	4
Corroded front wings			16	8	5	3
Corroded rear wings			12	6	5	4
Corroded front underwings			8	1	1	1
Corroded rear underwings			5	1	1	1
Corroded body sills			24	12	6	6
Corroded jacking points	N	N	8	4	3	4
Corroded floor	O	O	2	0	0	0
Corroded underbody frame members	–	–	8	4	3	1
Defective undersealing	T	T	18	13	13	7
Loose/misaligned driver's seat	C	C	6	6	4	2
Attend to engine mountings	U	U	1	0	0	0
Evidence of head gasket leaks	D	D	2	2	1	1
Noisy valve gear	O	O	22	19	15	15
Evidence of engine oil leaks	R	R	31	29	21	28
Attend to carburettor tuning	P	P	29	30	23	22
Evidence of fuel leaks			0	2	1	3
Final drive noise	N	N	13	15	14	8
Unsatisfactory gear change	–	–	7	2	0	0
Unsatisfactory auto gear change						
Clutch judder	T	T	2	4	4	2
Attend to front wheel bearings	O	O	17	13	12	11
Attend to steering box/rack	N	N	10	3	3	4
Attend to footbrake			17	16	12	14
Attend to handbrake			10	11	10	5
Corroded brake pipelines			6	5	2	1
Defective obligatory lights			33	17	14	11
Attend to charging system			2	3	2	2
Attend to horn			2	3	1	0

FORD CORTINA 1600XL

From AA Road Test Report 323, 1973

Improved best seller

 The current Cortina has certainly been an unqualified marketing success. However, the testers were disenchanted with the road-going manners of earlier versions as well as their unpleasant fascias and disappointing ventilation. Ford have introduced significant revisions for 1974 models, embracing all these aspects and giving the popular 1600XL the overhead camshaft engine for the first time. The 1600XL is actually smoother than the 2000 now, particularly in terms of the drumming and drive-line quiver which may still seriously disenchant one with the bigger car. Surprising though it may seem, most people will probably find the 2000 gives them better fuel consumption, particularly if they do not use all of its considerably livelier acceleration. Both have superb gear changes, though the 1600 now has a bias towards the right, after the German fashion. This apart, they both move with a sweet and easy action that could hardly be bettered.

With its revised springing and added anti-roll bar, the '74 series Cortina is a vast improvement over previous Mark IIIs. Whether it now measures up to its market rivals is another matter. The recalcitrant steering and corkscrewing body motion, especially evident on bumpy corners, have now been tamed so that one feels happy to explore the underlying roadholding and predictable breakaway characteristics that have always been impeccable. There is still some wriggling and wavering, but the lighter, more precise steering makes correction much easier, although road feel could still be improved.

Likewise, its straight-line ride feels better damped than previous series, with supple reaction to single potholes, for example. More exacting conditions betray an unyielding firmness that feels second-best to the Victor, let alone sophisticated models like the Maxi and Renault 16. The brakes work very well.

The new fascia is attractive both at first sight and 1,000 miles later. It is a pity that the light and indicator stalks have to be on the wrong side and work upside down, though! Getting into the driver's seat is complicated by the low door-frame and sloping screen, but the seat is comfortable and the relationship between seat, wheel and pedals is a good one. After a longer drive, however, shorter drivers complain of too much thigh support and not enough in the small of the back. At the rear, there are few complaints. The increased rear-seat comfort was a Mark III superiority praised from the start and its longer wheel base has given those extra inches of legroom that make all the difference. Getting out, however, can be tricky for the less agile.

Boot space is adequate rather than generous and the spare wheel is inconveniently stowed flat under a flimsy rubber mat; oddments space is just about sufficient. The revised ventilation system amounts to a resurrection of the old Mark II arrangement, which is quite good enough. The heater is an efficient air-blending type that gives good variations of heat instantly but there is a tendency, after a pause in traffic, for fumes to filter into the interior. The Cortina's preoccupation with curvacious styling gives the lower panelwork a hard time with grit and spray thrown up from the wheels. Underbody corrosion protection is pathetically half-hearted and paintwork and general finish outside leave a lot to be desired, but interior trim is of an impressive standard.

Easy servicing has always been a characteristic of the model, and mechanically the new OHC engine room remains an undemanding prospect, even for home mechanics.

Compared with other conventional family saloons, the latest Cortina is now pleasant enough, but devotees of advanced engineering will remain unimpressed. The Cortina has improved but one still wonders whether it is as good as it should be.

Ford Escort 1300XL

FORD ESCORT
ENGINEERS' COMMENTS
Body protection problems

The Escort, that big 'little car' from the Halewood Plant, has been one of the most versatile automobiles produced by Ford. It can be extremely utilitarian, or the roar-iest of rally cars. The power units, final drive, and some suspension elements do differ, of course, but it is all housed within the same basic bodyshell and that has changed remarkably little through the 6½ years of the model's run.

The rather rapid deterioration of Escorts more than 5 years old – as seen from the data table – is not likely to be so severe for cars produced after late 1970. Changes in the manufacture of the electrocoated bodyshell have eliminated some, though not all, of the inherent weaknesses.

Anti-rust protection

Partial underbody treatment with a water-based bituminous compound was introduced to give extra protection to the underwings and the floor panels most exposed to erosion by grit bombardment. In addition to providing semi-resilient external anti-rust protection, the compound acts as a sound deadener. Not the best of materials, it is frequently poorly applied at the factory. The compound eventually cracks with age, forming pockets in which corrosion-promoting mud, grit, road salt and slush are held.

Some, but by no means all, cars of the early production years had intercoat paint adhesion problems. As a result, stones flung up by the front tyres and by passing traffic could produce a rash of chipped paint, and thus a starting point for local surface corrosion.

Early owner attention in the form of re-priming the bare metal after removal of the rust spots and touching-in usually brings cars so affected back to a good standard of appearance. Occasionally a partial re-treatment and re-spraying of badly affected panels by a Ford franchised dealer is necessary. Sealing against water ingress past the front bulkhead in particular, and from there under the floor covering of the passenger compartment was not fully effective on early cars. This problem has since been cured, however. In addition, the sealing of boot panels to rear wings and rear-seat support structures allowed some road splash to penetrate the boot and be retained there. Rusting inevitably followed in due course.

Engine oil leaks produce a messy general oiliness on older cars. The effectiveness of crankshaft oil seals decreases with age, but there has been a change in specification and a significant improvement since the 1967–9 cars. During the same period, numerous instances of partial seizure of the handbrake cable in its nylon sheath gave rise to above-average need for handbrake attention. Changes in specification largely solved the problem.

Uprated engine

An uprating of the engine, which is also used on other cars in the current Ford range, has resulted in a more generously dimensioned tappet or cam follower and change in cam form. These have significantly extended durability and reduced the need for tappet adjustment to combat noise and restore optimum engine perfor-

mance. A good-quality gear change and reliable clutch have been an Escort 'plus' throughout. The car does not always pull up squarely from an emergency stop, however, and the brakes thus tend to require an above-average amount of routine service attention – particularly the all-drum version – if it is regularly driven hard.

Deterioration with age and usage of the MacPherson strut and its anchorages is commented on in sections covering the Ford Cortina Mark II, the Corsair, and the Capri. It is a common feature of these cars and many a casual inspection has diagnosed the need for wheel bearing adjustment when the problem was essentially one of progressive suspension deterioration or lack of dynamic balance of the front wheels.

Specification of AA tested car

See p. 92

Make & model	FORD ESCORT
Production years	1968–present
Body alternatives	2-door Saloon, 4-door Saloon, Estate (2 & 4 door)
Engine variants	1098cc OHV, 1299cc OHV, 1599cc OHV
	1558cc 2xOHC, 1601cc OHC, 1993cc OHC
Data: AA test version	Escort 1100L, 2-door Saloon. 1973 model
Engine	In-line 4-cyl, watercooled, front-mounted
	Bore 81mm, stroke 53.3mm, 1098cc. Comp ratio 9:1
Fuel system	1 Autolite carburettor. Mechanical pump.
	9-gallon tank
Transmission	4-speed & reverse, synchromesh on all forward
	gears. Rear-wheel drive
	Diaphragm-spring clutch, $6\frac{1}{2}''$ diameter dry plate,
	cable operated
Suspension front	Independent. MacPherson strut, coil spring, anti-roll bar
Suspension rear	Leaf-sprung live axle, telescopic dampers
Steering	Rack & pinion. $3\frac{1}{2}$ turns between full locks
	Turning circle 30 feet
Wheels	12″ diameter, $4\frac{1}{2}$J rims
Tyres	5.50×12 cross-ply (Firestone radials fitted)
Brakes	Hydraulic. Disc front/drum rear. Optional servo
Dimensions	Length 13′4$\frac{3}{4}$″ Width 5′1$\frac{3}{4}$″ Height 4′6″ Wheelbase 7′10$\frac{1}{2}$″
(overall)	Ground clearance 5″ Kerb weight (full tank) 16$\frac{1}{4}$ cwts
Max speed (in gears)	First 26mph, second 45mph, third 68mph, top 80mph
Overdrive	Not applicable
Acceleration	0–60mph: 20.6 seconds; standing-$\frac{1}{4}$ mile: 22.3 seconds
Fuel consumption	overall: 34.0mpg
	steady 50mph: 41.6mpg (top gear)
	steady 70mph: 26.0mpg (top gear)
Fuel	Premium 4-star

What VISAR reveals

Worse than average | Average | Better than average | No data

All chart figures are percentages

	Age in years: 6–8	5–6	4–5	3–4	2–3	1–2
Registration Suffix:	FG	H	J	K	L	M
Corroded front doors	20	17	14	6	3	2
Corroded rear doors						
Corroded front wings	29	27	20	6	3	1
Corroded rear wings	20	16	14	6	3	1
Corroded front underwings	20	11	10	3	2	0
Corroded rear underwings	8	7	7	2	1	0
Corroded body sills	33	31	23	10	4	3
Corroded jacking points	10	9	12	6	2	1
Corroded floor	22	29	17	8	4	7
Corroded underbody frame members	16	14	11	6	4	0
Defective undersealing	40	15	24	19	19	14
Loose/misaligned driver's seat	5	3	3	2	4	4
Attend to engine mountings	3	2	1	0	0	0
Evidence of head gasket leaks	3	1	2	1	1	0
Noisy valve gear	27	24	23	17	17	18
Evidence of engine oil leaks	46	35	26	23	15	18
Attend to carburettor tuning	31	25	26	28	21	18
Evidence of fuel leaks	4	3	2	1	1	0
Final drive noise	9	5	6	5	3	1
Unsatisfactory gear change	1	3	4	1	0	0
Unsatisfactory auto gear change						
Clutch judder	5	4	3	2	2	4
Attend to front wheel bearings	18	22	16	13	16	12
Attend to steering box/rack	12	11	7	5	5	8
Attend to footbrake	22	23	18	18	14	13
Attend to handbrake	27	18	17	13	10	13
Corroded brake pipelines	9	11	10	7	2	1
Defective obligatory lights	25	19	22	23	16	2
Attend to charging system	4	3	3	1	1	0
Attend to horn	5	2	2	2	1	1

FORD ESCORT 1100L

From AA Road Test Report 292, 1972
and Road Impression 90, 1973

Appealing, but the 1300 is better

The Escort – *'the small car that isn't'* – was introduced in 1968 as an 1100 replacement for the Anglia. Since then its range and scope have been greatly increased, but for this test it's back to basics.

Despite dismal weather conditions the figures achieved were representative. This Escort does not excel in either acceleration or economy. It performs like an Austin/Morris 1100 – a little quicker through the gears, a little slower in top. Sadly, neither model can match the verve of practically any continental 1100. Starting and idling are both reliable, and peaceful cruising extends to 65mph. Beyond this speed a resonance develops, which becomes an unpleasant drone by 70mph.

Gear changing . . . full marks!

The gear change is one of the best in the business, with unbeatable synchromesh and an unbiased short movement making fast shifts easy. Clutch action is short and light, but abrupt – learners be warned! The test car's overall fuel consumption was 34mpg, but gentle cruising will give just under 40mpg with a low of 29mpg if the car is driven really hard.

The Escort proves what can be achieved with a relatively simple suspension. Despite the crude back axle location, the rear end feels remarkably well tamed until a pothole is met in mid-bend. Springing is set up on the firm side but provides a level, well-damped ride although it lacks the super-absorbency of a Renault or Simca. There is more than a hint of sportiness about the Escort's manners which is reflected in the trim, quick, and precise handling. The 1100's performance is placid, however, which may tend to limit one's enthusiasm. Despite trying hard it is difficult to create a tail slide, even in the wet. Credit is due here to the tenacious Firestone F100 radial tyres, which, like front-disc brakes and a servo, are optional extras. Some may feel the brakes are rather too light, but they certainly stop the car well. They are fade and water resistant, and the handbrake copes easily with a 1-in-3 hill.

Comfort at the wheel is spoilt by swing-link seat adjusters which enforce an upright posture for tall drivers. There is not much thigh and lumbar support either. The driver has a clear view of the simple instrumentation through the wheel, and the fascia rocker switches and multi-purpose column stalk are all within easy reach. The pedals are sensibly spaced too. All-round outlook is fair. There is a wide interior mirror and the wipers sweep useful arcs, but there are blind spots three-quarters to the rear and the tail isn't visible when reversing.

Unless front occupants sit forward a little, those behind will find both kneeroom and legroom are pinched. Trimming is in spartan PVC and under-fascia shelves must cope with the family's oddments. Boot space is roomy for a compact car. The Escort features that put most competition in the shade are the excellent heating and ventilation arrangements. Rotary fascia outlets deliver plenty of air, and a discreet booster fan combines with an effective extraction system to provide a comfortable atmosphere. The heating system rates as one of the best available. Its air-blender mixes very efficiently and even rear passengers' feet benefit.

Improved paintwork

The paintwork on the new test car was better than on other Escorts met, but there is nothing special about the body's under-protection. No undersealing is applied, and underwing mud traps abound. With a brake servo fitted, working on the distributor is tricky, but otherwise, access to engine components is uncomplicated. Despite its obvious appeal, it can be a false economy to buy the 1100 Escort. One may save £35, but performance is decidedly inferior compared with the 1300, meaning more gear changing with fuel consumption only marginally better.

Ford Granada

FORD GRANADA/CONSUL

ENGINEERS' COMMENTS

Owners more blemish-conscious

The range of cars being produced in the modernised Dagenham Plant has relatively few bad remarks stacked up against it. The corrosion that has been found is almost always on the surface of panels exposed to stone-chipping damage and it can be dealt with relatively easily by DIY touching-in of the odd spot, provided that the top coat is of the solid colour variety. If the greater visual appeal of metallic paint is desired, then it is not so easy for the owner to blend in a distinct chip with a tin of touch-up paint. The chips rarely penetrate through to the bare metal, however.

The figures with regard to door corrosion on M registration cars may in part be explained by two factors. The sample size was relatively small and in addition many of the cars submitted for inspection were subject to dispute on warranted quality of what, at least in the minds of the owners, is an above-average-price motor car. These cars were sometimes submitted not because they were defective but rather because it was felt that they had been presented by the dealer at a standard of quality incommensurate with their price tag.

Improved paintwork

First owners of prestige cars tend to be rather more conscious of minor surface blemishes than those of rather more everyday cars. Nonetheless, it would appear that some chipping down to the fairly corrosion-resistant electrocoat primer was encountered on M registration cars. This is a production control problem and partly due to a decision that some top coat splintering is more acceptable than chipping right through to the bare metal. It is difficult to achieve both desirable properties at the same time. Until recently the chip size was kept small, and the rust which formed in these little pits spread under the top coat of paint. This form of visual deterioration, known as filiform corrosion, has been virtually eradicated by improved painting technology. The wing panel flanges around the wheel arches are the most likely places for this largely cosmetic and minor-scale damage to be found, and a check round the bright trim might show that it has not been fitted without some damage to the adjoining painted areas of wing, door and sill.

The partial underbody protection which the

car receives at the factory could be of better quality and more carefully applied to cover a larger proportion of the vehicle's underside.

Final drive noise

Some of the early K registration cars were inclined to have a noisy valve gear train, but this does not imply a risk of imminent engine failure. Final drive noise on M registration cars, while an occasional complaint, is not indicative of any inherent problem. It can be attributed principally to three factors. One is the fact that the single floor pressing, so beneficial in the fight against corrosion, also acts as a tight kettle-drum skin or the back of a violin, acoustically magnifying any small mechanical excitation or disturbance.

The second factor is the fact that volume-produced cars have a cut but not ground hypoid pinion and crown wheel. Although lapped together as a pair, they may initially evince a growl or a whine which can both irritate and frighten owners. It takes time for the hard spots to be rubbed off in actual service.

The third factor is the dynamic balance of prop shaft and the rear wheels, which is critical.

Easily-dealt-with leaks

Leaks past the gaiters of the rack-and-pinion steering box are a problem which can be fairly easily dealt with. The 2494cc engine is noted for its clattering valve gear, but will soldier on without much fuss. The roomy car can stand a considerable amount of harsh indifferent treatment and still come up bright and shiny after a good 'wash and brush up' – both inside and out.

Specification of AA tested car

See p. 96

Make & model	FORD GRANADA
Production years	1972–present
Body alternatives	4-door Saloon, Estate
Engine variants	2494cc OHV V-6
	2994cc OHV V-6
Data: AA test version	Granada 3000 GXL, Automatic. 1972 model
Engine	V6-cyl, 60˚ inclined, watercooled, front-mounted
	Bore 93.7mm, stroke 72.4mm, 2994cc. Comp ratio 8.9:1
Fuel system	1 Weber twin-choke carburettor. Mechanical pump. 14.25-gallon tank
Transmission	Automatic. Torque convertor. 3-speed & reverse. Rear-wheel drive.
Suspension front	Independent. Coil spring, wishbones, anti-roll bar
Suspension rear	Independent. Coil spring, semi-trailing arm
Steering	Rack & pinion. Power-assisted. $3\frac{1}{2}$ turns between full locks. Turning circle 34 feet
Wheels	14" diameter, 6J rims
Tyres	185SR14 radial-ply (Michelin ZX fitted)
Brakes	Hydraulic, dual circuit, disc front/drum rear. Servo
Dimen mensions (overall)	Length 15'3½" Width 5'10½" Height 4'7½" Wheelbase 9'1" Ground clearance 5" Kerb weight (full tank) 28 cwts
Max speed (in gears)	Low 49mph, Intermediate 82mph, top 108mph
Overdrive	Not applicable
Acceleration	0–60mph: 11.7 seconds; standing-¼ mile: 18.9 seconds
Fuel consumption	overall: 21.0mpg
	steady 50mph: 30.8mpg (top gear)
	steady 70mph: 22.5mpg (top gear)
Fuel	Premium 4-star

What VISAR reveals

Legend: ▩ Worse than average ▨ Average ▤ Better than average ☐ No data

All chart figures are percentages

	Age in years: 6–8	5–6	4–5	3–4	2–3	1–2
Registration Suffix:	FG	H	J	K	L	M*
Corroded front doors				6	6	5
Corroded rear doors				6	6	5
Corroded front wings				5	5	0
Corroded rear wings				5	4	0
Corroded front underwings				2	2	0
Corroded rear underwings				2	1	0
Corroded body sills				12	10	0
Corroded jacking points	N	N	N	11	2	0
Corroded floor	O	O	O	0	0	0
Corroded underbody frame members	–	–	–	6	1	0
Defective undersealing	T	T	T	18	18	20
Loose/misaligned driver's seat	C	C	C	4	4	0
Attend to engine mountings	U	U	U	0	0	0
Evidence of head gasket leaks	D	D	D	0	1	0
Noisy valve gear	O	O	O	25	16	5
Evidence of engine oil leaks	R	R	R	27	32	20
Attend to carburettor tuning	P	P	P	22	23	5
Evidence of fuel leaks				0	1	0
Final drive noise	N	N	N	5	9	10
Unsatisfactory gear change	–	–	–	4	0	0
Unsatisfactory auto gear change				0	3	0
Clutch judder	T	T	T	5	5	0
Attend to front wheel bearings	O	O	O	8	2	0
Attend to steering box/rack	N	N	N	11	3	5
Attend to footbrake				7	11	0
Attend to handbrake				4	5	0
Corroded brake pipelines				5	1	0
Defective obligatory lights				38	28	5
Attend to charging system				0	4	5
Attend to horn				5	3	5

See Engineers' Comments, p.93

FORD GRANADA 3000GXL

From AA Road Test Report 282, 1972

Opulent yet practical package

The Granada, which replaces the Mark IV Zephyr/Zodiac, is available with three engine sizes and various trim and body variations. Ford's 3-litre V-6 (there's also a 2.5 version) adapts well to Granada with reasonable refinement and a surprising willingness to rev. The automatic loses on performance – a 2.5 Consul with manual transmission is quicker – but the transmission's behaviour is generally delightful. Two strong points are good down-change sensitivity, and the delay of up-changes to give optimum acceleration by just flooring the accelerator. The selector quadrant could be smoother, however. Starting is not instantaneous, and stalling can occur immediately afterwards. Fuel consumption figures range from 18 to 25mpg depending on the traffic and how much one hurries. The last gallon slowly gurgles into the tank, but a range of 250 miles is possible without it.

Those who last owned a Mark IV will be pleased with both the Granada's ride and handling, although some 2-litre saloons still do better. Its low-speed ride is outstanding, but its long-distance motoring manners are spoilt by too much heaving and tossing, barouche-style, at higher speeds. Proper semi-trailing arms with less geometry changes have tamed cornering behaviour compared with the precipitous Mark IV Zodiac. Normally the tail begins to move out at still modest speeds, but this behaviour is much more gentle than before and the higher-geared, power-assisted steering is ideally weighted, even though the 'feel' is artificial.

Comfort in the driving position depends on one's size, as it favours larger people and there is insufficient adjustment to suit everybody – the wheel is fixed, for instance. Rear vision is poor, whatever one's size, and the mirror makes things worse. However, there is a good forward view and comprehensive instrumentation, but the gimmicky push-button minor switches are difficult to find in the dark. The ventilation system proved inadequate on the test car, and although there has been an improvement on later cars, output is still uneven and uncertain. One may find the headlamp main beam inadequate too, but horns and reverse lamps work well. The Granada is quieter than the 2.5 Consul tested, and it is a very easy cruiser. Rear passenger room is generous, although not to the extent of its predecessor's surfeit of space. All the seats would be better with more firmness of support. Boot space is generous, but the thin rubber mat and dim illumination from rear lamps are what one would expect on a less expensive car. Oddments space is good, although the front console box is like a hot cupboard with the heater on. Ducted rear footwell heating is less successful than one would expect and the driver gets less than his passenger at the front. Trim and equipment are luxurious, but there is more than a hint of flamboyance with glossy plastic wood and jazzy door trims. Inertia reel belts are standard and safety padding is wisely designed to prevent serious injury rather than minor bruising.

Good Under-Bonnet access

The owner will welcome the bolt-on wings when the rust bug gets to work in their dreadful mud traps. The skimpy undersealing is thick in some places but completely missing elsewhere, and the body is decorated with moisture-harbouring brightwork. Under-bonnet access seems better than the Mark IV's and the handbook is very helpful. The spare wheel can be tricky to remove from the boot, however. The Granada is an improved and more practical proposition than its predecessor, although it looks more compact than it really is. Yet we think it betrays mean economies at the price and lacks driver enthusiast appeal. It is more suited to the man who likes his creature comfort in an opulent yet practical package.

Ford Zodiac

FORD ZODIAC/ZEPHYR 6

ENGINEERS' COMMENTS

Inspect underbody thoroughly

This car never quite caught the public imagination. It had an unusually short production run, yielding to the better engineered Granada/Consul. In good condition it can be a good buy – if one does not mind its fairly healthy thirst for petrol. The strangest feature is its all-independent suspension, in which front and rear all too often fight each other when the car is driven brusquely along the typical, winding British country road. Happily, this oddity has not been passed on to the Granada/Consul. The MacPherson strut front and semi-trailing rear suspension could, on many a road, produce a side shuffle movement due to camber changes, imposing an unexpected strain on tyres, linkages, and the driver's skill.

Owner maintenance?

If the car pulls to one side when full braking power is applied, it may be the result of the previous owner's lack of maintenance of the all-disc system, ie the failure to replace pads in time and attend to the handbrake mechanism. The swinging calipers on the rear, which are also operated by the handbrake, tend to seize up. Before completing the purchase of one of the F/G registration cars, it pays to check the following items. Be sure the horn ring on the steering column and the earth return are fully effective, even on extreme lock, that the steering column gear change linkage gives a precise, clean change and that the alternator and its associated control box will maintain the charging of the battery with all lights working and the engine running at no more than about one-quarter of full throttle.

Design modifications

Cylinder head gasket failure was a feature of the early V–6 engines, a problem largely eliminated by the introduction of modified gaskets. Similarly, design modifications have reduced valve gear noise on engines built after 1970. The high incidence of noise from final drive gears on early models was reduced on later ones by the more liberal use of rubber in the final drive mounts. A high proportion of J registration cars inspected had automatic gear boxes, hence the incidence of poor auto changes. Attention to front wheel bearings does not imply wear or costly replacement. They are of the taper roller type and have an in-built clearance which can easily be mistaken for ▶

undue rock and end float. Steering joints, however, may show wear on older cars. Dynamic balancing of wheels and tyres does improve ride and road holding.

Some moisture ingress, particularly on F/G registration cars, is a feature of the model's light units. This accounts for the above-average need to replace bulbs. Stone chips or slight bumps induced some local rusting of the front and rear bumper valances on one-third of F/G registration cars.

Underbody rust

The underside of those cars which were given no additional underbody protection suffers from general rusting more than the all-makes average. This includes under-floor pressings, front underwings, under-body frame members and rear under-wings. The underside of F/G registration cars can look quite rusty, for only about one car in three had underbody protection treatment applied by a specialist firm or the Ford dealer. Rusting of the underside, however, has rarely advanced to the point of irreversible structural weakening. By scraping all rust off, applying etch primer paint to the bare metal and overspraying with a protective coating, the car's useful life can be extended. This is a tedious and messy job, best left to a specialist who has the equipment to steamclean or high-pressure hot-water clean, and shot blast away or otherwise remove all traces of rust before painting and finally sealing the steel sections. If underbody rust is neglected for too long a time, it is hardly worth the considerable expense of welding in new panels.

Before purchasing a Zodiac/Zephyr, get the seller to put it on a hoist. Then inspect its 'belly' thoroughly, ensuring that the point of a screwdriver does not penetrate the underside when tapped against it.

Specification of AA tested car

See p. 100

Make & model	FORD ZODIAC MK IV
Production years	1966–1971
Body alternatives	4-door Saloon, Estate
Engine variants	2994cc V-6 OHV

Data: AA test version	Zodiac Mk IV, 4-door Saloon. 1966 model
Engine	V6-cyl, 60° inclined, watercooled, front-mounted
	Bore 93.7mm, stroke 72.4mm, 2994cc. Comp ratio 8.9:1
Fuel system	1 Weber twin-choke carburettor. Mechanical pump.
	15-gallon tank
Transmission	4-speed & reverse, synchromesh on all forward
	gears. Rear-wheel drive
	Diaphragm-spring clutch, 9″ diameter dry plate,
	hydraulically operated
Suspension front	Independent. MacPherson strut, coil spring, anti-roll bar
Suspension rear	Independent. Coil spring, semi-trailing, wishbone
Steering	Recirculating ball. 5 turns between full locks
	Turning circle 36 feet
Wheels	13″ diameter, 4½J rims
Tyres	6.70×13 cross-ply (tubeless tyres fitted)
Brakes	Hydraulic, disc front/disc rear. Servo
Dimensions	Length 15′5¾″ Width 5′11¼″ Height 4′10″ Wheelbase 9′7″
(overall)	Ground clearance 6½″ Kerb weight (full tank) 26⅞ cwts
Max speed (in gears)	First 34mph, second 48mph, third 76mph, top 101mph
Overdrive	Not applicable
Acceleration	0–60mph: 11.9 seconds; standing-¼ mile: 18.1 seconds
Fuel consumption	overall: 19.3mpg
	steady 50mph: 24.7mpg (top gear)
	steady 70mph: 20.7mpg (top gear)
Fuel	Premium 4-star

What VISAR reveals

Legend: Worse than average · Average · Better than average · No data

All chart figures are percentages

	Age in years:	6–8	5–6	4–5	3–4	2–3	1–2
	Registration Suffix:	FG	H	J	K	L	M
Corroded front doors		9	9	4	7		
Corroded rear doors		8	10	4	6		
Corroded front wings		34	13	7	3		
Corroded rear wings		25	11	5	7		
Corroded front underwings		18	18	7	9		
Corroded rear underwings		5	12	7	9		
Corroded body sills		27	20	11	9		
Corroded jacking points		21	14	6	8	Z	Z
Corroded floor		15	0	0	0	O	O
Corroded underbody frame members		21	17	7	5	–	–
Defective undersealing		8	60	33	14	T	T
Loose/misaligned driver's seat		3	3	3	0	C	C
Attend to engine mountings		0	3	4	3	U	U
Evidence of head gasket leaks		6	10	6	3	D	D
Noisy valve gear		39	15	19	12	O	O
Evidence of engine oil leaks		58	39	39	21	R	R
Attend to carburettor tuning		29	30	31	12	P	P
Evidence of fuel leaks		5	0	6	0		
Final drive noise		24	10	3	3	F	F
Unsatisfactory gear change		7	0	0	0	O	O
Unsatisfactory auto gear change		0	0	6	0		
Clutch judder		7	7	0	3	T	T
Attend to front wheel bearings		25	16	11	25	U	U
Attend to steering box/rack		14	7	19	9	O	O
Attend to footbrake		22	13	6	0		
Attend to handbrake		27	13	9	12		
Corroded brake pipelines		20	9	8	3		
Defective obligatory lights		45	28	31	30		
Attend to charging system		15	3	3	3		
Attend to horn		15	3	5	3		

From AA Road Test Reports 143, 1967 and 186, 1969

A smooth, flexible lot of car

The designers laid out an entirely new design after the Mark III, discarding the old 'straight six' in favour of a 'V' engine layout, for example. Maximum speed is not outstanding, but acceleration is surprising for so big and roomy a saloon. The car can cruise between 80 and 90mph effortlessly and quietly and yet can accelerate in top from as low as 12mph. Unfortunately, the clutch can be jerky in town driving, although it has ample grip for more arduous use, and a 1-in-3 hill start causes no trouble at all. The floor gear change has a longer, heavier movement than later Fords. It suits this car well enough once one is used to the bias to the right and the slight obstructiveness into lower gears. A column shift and bench seat are also available.

Longer range tank

The test car's excellent performance was fully exploited and 19¼mpg seemed fair enough; something between this and 23mpg seems likely given more restrained use. The bigger, 15-gallon tank is appreciated on this heavier car.

The Mark IV range are the first Fords to use independent rear suspension. So long as the car is fitted with revised radials on wider rims, initial cornering is grippy and neutral handling, despite pronounced roll which is visually amplified by the tilt of the enormous bonnet. Breakaway is reached at quite modest speeds, however, occurring in a rushed and ragged manner. Perhaps the very low-geared steering makes matters worse. The optional power assistance is no help either, for it only reduces wheel turns by half a revolution and is completely devoid of feel. The suspension deals quite well with most surfaces, however, and is generally more acceptable under duress than the car's cornering behaviour.

Brakes are disappointing in a crash stop because the rear brakes slew the car sideways prematurely. Perhaps the all-disc system gives the rear braking too much to do. Check braking is smooth and effortless, however, and the fascia handbrake can manage a 1-in-3 hill.

Vision impressive, but forward only

With its gargantuan bonnet but impressive forward vision and good wipers, the Zodiac is ideal for the driver who likes 'a big motor'. The rear wings, while short, are out of sight, however, and blind rear quarters are also a problem. Minor controls are all illuminated at night and the bucket front seats give good support except when cornering roll builds up. The ventilation system provides cold or warmed air, and the heater is powerful, although a lot of practice is required to get best results.

Getting in and out is easy, with widely opening doors and good foot entry. Inside, too, seating is very roomy and comfortable. There is generous legroom in the rear, even behind the lanky driver who needs the seat right back. With the centre armrest folded away, the rear seat can accommodate three adults.

Trimming is very luxurious and good safety padding is provided too, although the seat-belt buckles sit too high when fastened. Interior oddments stowage is not very generous, but the boot is vast and can be opened without the key if one wishes. The spare wheel and tools are all stowed at the front end, where the engine cowers behind the wheel. The paint shows some imperfections, and the underside has no additional protection beyond paint and primer.

Comfortable and quiet

The Mark IV range, like the Austin 1800, offers outstanding accommodation, but in a radically different way. The Zodiac's comfort and quietness must be set against its thirst and precipitous handling when pressed. Nevertheless, it is a lot of car for the money.

Hillman Avenger 2 Door Grand Luxe

HILLMAN AVENGER
ENGINEERS' COMMENTS
Anti-rust features

The Avenger was designed and built featuring an anti-corrosion treatment process based on electrocoat primer paint. The intention was to give a durable paint system with good visual appearance and, most important, better anti-corrosion protection in hollow sections than is normally achieved by the slipper-dip method of application of primer paints.

The incidence of underbody corrosion is low for a volume-produced car. In addition, thanks to good process plant control, there is little evidence of serious internal corrosion in such closed sections as body sills and underbody stiffening members.

During 1970–1 production, the paint system was rather more brittle than desirable. Stones flung up by the front wheels and by passing traffic can chip paint off down to the sheet steel, or at least down to the first anti-rust layer, on the lower portions of doors, wings and particularly body sills. If not dealt with promptly, such localised surface damage can allow corrosion to creep under the top coat, necessitating a more extensive paint touch-up job later on. The solution is to strip down to the bare metal in the affected area

and apply an etch primer or zinc-based aerosol, a filler surfacer coat and then the proper shade of colour top coat.

On some M registration cars the top coat of paint can flake off in small chips when sharp objects strike it, or when in contact with doors, pillars or other obstructions in confined spaces. This may be diagnosed as corrosion, but it generally is not, as the essential anti-rust layers of phosphate metal treatment and primer paint are usually unaffected. Small-brush application of the colour coat within 2 weeks of superficial damage will generally prevent subsequent rusting and marring of the visual appeal.

The underwing areas are treated with a good quality solvent-based bitumastic layer, which is superior to the more commonly used water-based type. It acts both as a sound deadener and an overlay to combat abrasion and grit impact. The remainder of the underbody is not specially protected during manufacture and relatively few owners have had underbody compounds subsequently applied by dealers. The performance of the compounds applied after sale has not been as good as one might hope, largely because they have not all been fully compatible with the partial underbody protection applied at the factory. Even so, with the exception of some cars produced in 1970–1, the incidence of underfloor corrosion is below average throughout the range of the survey. Equally good is the waterproofing of the interior passenger compartment. Some early-production Avengers may show signs of water ingress into the boot and yet be free of corrosion.

The noise level of the push-rod engine's valve gear can be reduced by adjusting the tappet clearance. The engine suffers a slight seepage of oil past the crankshaft seals, as well as seepage past the seal at the flywheel end, the latter occasionally producing clutch judder.

Some early models had pronounced axle whine, which has been remedied in subsequent production runs. Any carburettor tuning requirements are usually confined to simple adjustments. When checking the taper wheel bearings – which are designed with some end float – for play and rock, the upper location of the MacPherson strut should also be examined for wear. Dynamic wheel re-balancing can also be particularly beneficial.

In common with other users of non-circular lights, problems in headlamp sealing against moisture ingress were experienced in the first 3 years of production.

The third gear synchromesh is prone to premature wear, a persistent problem in an otherwise robust gear box. Where such deterioration does occur, however, it is largely due to bad driving habits. Hillman cars, particularly the sportier versions, tend to get noisier with age and mileage, but they soldier on even after having suffered considerable abuse and neglect at the hands of indifferent drivers.

Specification of AA tested car

See p. 104

Make & model	HILLMAN AVENGER
Production years	1970–present
Body alternatives	2-door Saloon, 4-door Saloon, Estate
Engine variants	1248cc OHV, 1498cc OHV
	1295cc OHV, 1600cc OHV
Data: AA test version	Avenger 1500GL, 4-door Saloon. 1970 model
Engine	In-line 4-cyl, watercooled, front-mounted
	Bore 86.1mm, stroke 64.3mm, 1498cc. Comp ratio 9.2:1
Fuel system	1 Zenith Stromberg sidedraught carburettor. Mechanical pump. 9-gallon tank
Transmission	4-speed & reverse, synchromesh on all forward gears. Rear-wheel drive
	Diaphragm-spring clutch, $7\frac{1}{2}''$ diameter dry plate, cable operated
Suspension front	Independent. MacPherson strut, coil spring, anti-roll bar
Suspension rear	Coil-sprung live axle, upper/lower locating arms
Steering	Rack & pinion. $3\frac{3}{4}$ turns between full locks
	Turning circle 34 feet
Wheels	13″ diameter, $4\frac{1}{2}$J rims
Tyres	5.60×13 cross-ply (Dunlop C41 fitted)
Brakes	Hydraulic, disc front/drum rear. Optional servo fitted
Dimensions	Length 13′5½″ Width 5′2½″ Height 4′8″ Wheelbase 8′2″
(overall)	Ground clearance $5\frac{1}{2}''$ Kerb weight (full tank) 17 cwts
Max speed (in gears)	First 31mph, second 51mph, third 76mph, top 84mph
Overdrive	Not applicable
Acceleration	0–60mph: 17.4 seconds; standing-$\frac{1}{4}$ mile: 20.4 seconds
Fuel consumption	overall: 29.3mpg
	steady 50mph: 35.6mpg (top gear)
	steady 70mph: 26.6mpg (top gear)
Fuel	Premium 4-star

What VISAR reveals

Legend: ▓ Worse than average | ░ Average | ▨ Better than average | ☐ No data

All chart figures are percentages

	Age in years:	6–8	5–6	4–5	3–4	2–3	1–2
	Registration Suffix:	FG	H	J	K	L	M
Corroded front doors			14	11	4	3	6
Corroded rear doors			10	11	4	2	9
Corroded front wings			13	14	4	2	2
Corroded rear wings			12	14	4	2	1
Corroded front underwings			0	3	2	1	2
Corroded rear underwings			0	3	2	1	2
Corroded body sills			19	22	9	5	2
Corroded jacking points		N	6	7	2	2	1
Corroded floor		O	0	2	2	1	0
Corroded underbody frame members		I	5	7	4	3	6
Defective undersealing		T	16	12	14	11	19
Loose/misaligned driver's seat		C	0	1	0	0	2
Attend to engine mountings		U	2	1	1	1	1
Evidence of head gasket leaks		D	3	5	3	0	0
Noisy valve gear		O	18	32	29	22	16
Evidence of engine oil leaks		R	46	44	29	21	34
Attend to carburettor tuning		P	35	32	26	21	29
Evidence of fuel leaks			1	2	2	1	2
Final drive noise		N	10	6	12	4	5
Unsatisfactory gear change		I	12	7	7	6	7
Unsatisfactory auto gear change							
Clutch judder		T	11	4	4	2	3
Attend to front wheel bearings		O	22	19	12	13	8
Attend to steering box/rack		N	10	9	4	6	9
Attend to footbrake			12	5	2	3	5
Attend to handbrake			10	10	9	6	2
Corroded brake pipelines			6	10	11	4	2
Defective obligatory lights			36	33	28	14	6
Attend to charging system			3	3	1	1	2
Attend to horn			0	4	3	5	6

Safe, staid and uninspiring

Cost-cutting, weight-paring, and ease of manufacture were uppermost in the minds of the Avenger's designers, so advanced engineering was out of the question. The push-rod engine has few features of merit, but it performs with reasonable restraint to give adequate performance in 1500 form. The 1250, however, seems very spiritless. Fuel consumption is mediocre in normal give-and-take use, but does improve with throttle restraint. Starting and idling are reliable, however, and the gear change and clutch are very light and pleasing to use, making the Avenger an easy car to drive smoothly in traffic.

The familiar mixture of independent front suspension with a coil-sprung live rear axle gives an adequate ride and has dependable cornering manners. The model is a reasonable compromise, dealing with bigger bumps better than most of its type, but feeling rather jittery over minor surface faults. It certainly lacks the levelness of its French cousin, the Simca. Gentle nose drift is the predominant cornering characteristic and the steering is light and helpful, especially on a bumpy corner when the tail can shrug off course. The model brakes well without needing the optional servo – pedal loads are still modest and fade-resistant without it. The handbrake holds securely on a 1-in-3 hill but the car will not restart on this gradient.

The GL's cloth seats give good grip and adequate support with every adjustment. The positions of wheel and pedals are just right and everything works with flattering ease. A pair of turret switches on the column are used to operate lights and wash-wipe facilities. The layout's weakest aspect is the cheap and nasty look of the instruments, which, in addition, are obscured by the driver's hands.

With good wind-sealing and freedom from resonance, the GL can be cruised at any legal speed without strain. Rear space and seat support are better than any live-axled rival. The heating and ventilation systems are good too, except that the temperature changes from hot to cold with less than one-quarter inch of movement of the control slide. The fascia ventilators do not keep door glasses clear, but manage their main task well. Trim on the GL is a clever blend of plastic and cloth, well fitted and durable. Excellent door oddments boxes are useful and the boot is very roomy. Safety padding is fair but the static belts can be inconvenient to adjust.

Underbody sealer is only applied to the wheel arches, but it is done properly. This is just as well, for there are some nasty mud-harbouring cavities at the front. The lightweight panelling flexes in the most extraordinary places and the fuel tank seems vulnerable to weathering.

The underbonnet layout is one of the tidiest there is, but the test car seemed prone to oil leaks and fan belt skidding. Some items of electrical equipment seem near the limit of their capacity – fuses, dynamos, and battery, for example. Routine maintenance is simple and the handbook is a great help.

Second thoughts – 4 years later

There have been useful improvements in detail over the years – proper fuses, an alternator, and a pre-engaging starter have been added, for example. Most important, 1300 and 1600 engines with better breathing have enhanced performance without impairing economy. Though hardly a ball of fire, the 1300 is worthier now. Of course, the Marina's advent made the Avenger design look almost avant-garde! In fact, they both share the merits of easy maintenance and capacity for four adults with luggage.

The Avenger does not excel at anything in particular, yet for those seeking a family transporter rather than a new motoring experience, it could fit the bill well.

Hillman Hunter GL

HILLMAN HUNTER
ENGINEERS' COMMENTS
Reliable, but prone to rust

As paint is chipped from the Hunter's front and rear doors, through bombardment by flying stones and road grit or contact with walls, posts and other cars, corrosion gains a foothold. Early application of an etch primer or zinc aerosol touch-in to the bared metal, followed by a filler coat and the correct shade of top-coat paint, can slow rust and paint blistering.

In cars over 6 years old, the lower 3 to 4 inches of the doors and parts of the door bottoms often show signs of rusting from the inside outwards. DIY repairs to disguise this corrosion can soon become unsightly and are rarely effective. The answer is to keep all drain holes free. Panel replacement provides a permanent, but costly, solution.

Rusting behind the bright trim is a feature of older cars in the Hunter range which have rubbing strips fitted with steel clips. The packing of mud, road salt and grit in the underwing zones can be a problem, unless these areas are regularly washed with a pressure hose. If this has not been done, wing areas close to the upper mounting of the MacPherson suspension leg and around the headlamps can be badly affected by rust. After 6 to 7 years, despite a continuous film of paint on the outside, the wing metal may be wafer thin.

It is difficult to obtain good anti-corrosion metal pre-treatment and primer paint coverage on both the external and internal surfaces of the sills, particularly at the points where they join the front and rear wing. This is illustrated by the development of ungainly sill rust fairly early in the life of F/G and H registration cars. Owing to a production problem, paint drippings ran from the doors onto the sills at the time of manufacture. These paint runs were ground off, down to the bare metal, and then a thin top coat was applied to the sills. Cars of subsequent manufacture have received improved paint protection.

In older cars, inside-out corrosion is also a problem. This eventually results in the perforation of the sill. However, corrosion is rarely extensive enough in cars of the VISAR survey age group to make the body structure unsafe. The potential buyer should watch out for either extensive perforation of the sill or the attempt to disguise serious corrosion by the application of plastic filler.

Some corrosion of the boot due to water ingress is a feature of about one in eight of the F/G registration cars inspected. Floor corrosion on older cars is largely attributable to poor underbody protection which, with ageing, allows road salts and moisture to come in contact with the sheet metal. In addition, water ingress past door seals and under the interior floor covering can cause an irreversible weakening of the steel pressings.

The underframe strengthening members of cars over 6 years old show a rapid rise in corrosion and expert advice ought to be sought before DIY repairs are undertaken. The potential purchaser who finds serious underframe corrosion, floor rusting and perforation of sills should seriously consider whether it is economical to buy a car whose structural strength may be suspect. Restoration in such cases can be costly. Slight engine oil leaks are a regular source of irritation for Hunter owners, but they are not a cause for concern. Attention to linkages and idling speed adjustment will usually improve a poor-quality automatic gear change and tappet adjustment can cure valve gear noise to a large extent. Since the front suspensions of the Hunter and the Avenger are similar, the comments regarding front wheel bearing attention requirements which appear in the section on the Avenger apply equally to the Hunter. A car of sturdy, uncomplicated design and construction, the Hunter has been a favourite for many years with fleet operators who are concerned with overall car-operating costs and reliability. By and large, this car will require relatively little in expenditure on servicing, repair and parts replacement during the first 3 to 4 years of its life. Older cars, however, should be thoroughly inspected before purchase.

Specification of AA tested car

See p. 108

Make & model	HILLMAN HUNTER
Production years	1966–present
Body alternatives	4-door Saloon, 4-door Estate
Engine variants	1496cc OHV, 1725cc OHV
Data: AA test version	Hunter GL, 1725cc 4-door Saloon. 1971 model
Engine	In-line 4-cyl, watercooled, front-mounted
	Bore 81.5mm, stroke 82.6mm, 1725cc. Comp ratio 9.2:1
Fuel system	1 Stromberg variable-jet carburettor. Mechanical pump. 10-gallon tank
Transmission	4-speed & reverse, synchromesh on all forward gears. Rear-wheel drive.
	Diaphragm-spring clutch, $7\frac{1}{2}''$ diameter dry plate, hydraulically operated
Suspension front	Independent. MacPherson strut, coil spring, anti-roll bar
Suspension rear	Leaf-sprung live axle, telescopic dampers
Steering	Recirculating ball. 4 turns between full locks
	Turning circle 36 feet
Wheels	13″ diameter, $4\frac{1}{2}$J rims
Tyres	5.60×13 cross-ply (Dunlop C41 fitted)
Brakes	Hydraulic, disc front/drum rear. Servo
Dimensions	Length 14′0″ Width $5′3\frac{1}{2}''$ Height 4′6″ Wheelbase $8′2\frac{1}{2}''$
(overall)	Ground clearance $6\frac{1}{2}''$ Kerb weight (full tank) $18\frac{1}{4}$ cwts
Max speed (in gears)	First 31mph, second 47mph, third 72mph, top 86mph
Overdrive	Not applicable
Acceleration	0–60mph: 15.0 seconds; standing-$\frac{1}{4}$ mile: 20.0 seconds
Fuel consumption	overall: 28.7mpg
	steady 50mph: 37.0mpg (top gear)
	steady 70mph: 25.9mpg (top gear)
Fuel	Premium 4-star

What VISAR reveals

Legend:
- Worse than average
- Average
- Better than average
- No data

All chart figures are percentages

	6–8	5–6	4–5	3–4	2–3	1–2
Age in years: Registration Suffix:	FG	H	J	K	L	M
Corroded front doors	16	4	10	9	4	4
Corroded rear doors	12	4	9	8	4	6
Corroded front wings	37	13	15	8	3	2
Corroded rear wings	20	5	11	8	4	3
Corroded front underwings	14	0	5	2	1	0
Corroded rear underwings	10	0	4	2	1	0
Corroded body sills	42	22	21	15	7	4
Corroded jacking points	13	4	8	4	2	0
Corroded floor	31	5	0	3	2	6
Corroded underbody frame members	27	12	13	11	8	3
Defective undersealing	46	25	20	18	15	6
Loose/misaligned driver's seat	3	0	0	0	0	0
Attend to engine mountings	2	1	4	3	1	0
Evidence of head gasket leaks	1	0	1	0	0	0
Noisy valve gear	28	23	25	22	21	26
Evidence of engine oil leaks	63	57	60	49	36	33
Attend to carburettor tuning	48	49	39	35	32	45
Evidence of fuel leaks	7	1	2	2	0	0
Final drive noise	2	6	6	4	7	3
Unsatisfactory gear change	5	9	1	2	3	2
Unsatisfactory auto gear change	14	7	7	17	13	0
Clutch judder	1	6	2	1	2	0
Attend to front wheel bearings	16	23	31	22	30	16
Attend to steering box/rack	10	0	6	4	6	4
Attend to footbrake	11	14	12	6	10	15
Attend to handbrake	17	11	16	11	8	4
Corroded brake pipelines	20	6	11	6	3	0
Defective obligatory lights	36	22	20	16	10	2
Attend to charging system	3	3	2	0	1	2
Attend to horn	4	3	3	3	1	5

HILLMAN HUNTER GL

*From AA Road Test Report 234, 1971
and Road Impression 86, 1972*

Dated but worth consideration

The Hunter sticks to well-tried orthodoxy with periodic 'face lifts'. The range was introduced with names like Minx, Gazelle and Vogue to denote different stages of trim and tune, but now they are all 'Hunter' except the top-of-the-range Sceptre variant.

The GL uses an alloy head and 1725cc with a single carburettor. The DL and Super use less powerful versions. Performance is brisk but not electrifying and the engine feels rough below 30mph in top, with a rather jittery idle. It starts quite easily, but a baritone growl afflicts 60–70mph cruising unless the optional overdrive is fitted. The gear change is heavier than that of the flick-switch Avenger, but it is still cleanly precise. Although overall consumption is only average, the Hunter responds well to economy tactics, especially with overdrive, when 35mpg is to be expected out of town. The tank is dilatory about accepting the last gallon, but the gauge is accurate.

Although older-style recirculating ball steering is used, its effort and responsiveness, with good feel of the road, are most pleasing. During normal cornering, the car predictably understeers. If one tries only a little harder, however, the tail eases out readily, making things more entertaining. The driver who knows his car remains master of the situation, because the Hunter tends to lose its grip early and progressively, rather than later and malevolently. The ride evokes neither enthusiasm nor strong criticism. It smooths bumps and jolts well enough, but there is too much plunging at speed or unevenness around town for occupants to feel really at ease. The brake pedal felt spongy on every car tried and side-to-side unevenness afflicts the brakes when in arduous use.

Although the accelerator is too high and too offset, the Hunter looks and feels good for the driver. The instruments are cosily traditional, yet far more legible than on some vulgar, trendy designs. Vision is fine all round, but head movement is necessary when emerging from a side-turning at an angle. Circular 'eye ball' fresh air vents work powerfully and the air-blending heater is splendidly controllable – far more convenient than that of the Avenger!

Traditional British trim

When introduced, the Hunter was one of those rare family saloons that placed rear-seat comfort before boot space. There is sufficient space to provide anatomically correct seating with reasonable legroom, unless a passenger is behind a tall driver. The traditional interior trim is durable, well fitted, and very British. The boot would be fine if the spare wheel could live elsewhere. Best to put it on the roof when holiday time arrives.

Although the Hunter's clean lines are attractive, closer inspection reveals flaws beneath the make-up. The light-gauge metal makes thoughtful design and conscientious painting and protection essential, and regrettably neither are conspicuously evident. There are bad underwing cavities and rough welds, and the undersealing is absent in some vital stress areas.

Accessibility is the byword to describe the Hunter's mechanical layout. Despite its inclined block, the engine is easy to work on. The jacking points are located at front and rear rather than at the sides.

Second thoughts – 3 years later

Chrysler seem to make the Hunter more transatlantic every time they do a minor restyling. We think the 1971 car looked much nicer inside and out. There is a little more power now, but nothing basic has changed in 9 years and it is a model that now feels dated to those who fix their sights on a mechanical innovation. Yet with 'new' models like the Marina doing well, the Hunter must still be worth consideration.

Hillman Super Imp

HILLMAN IMP
ENGINEERS' COMMENTS
Corrosion trouble spots

Corrosion problems on some of the older Imps are mainly due to the limitations of production. A large number of relatively small sheet metal pressings and spot welds are used to form the body. The slight relative movements of these fabricated joints, over a period of years, remove much of the factory-applied anti-corrosion treatment and primer paint. In addition, paint runs on body sills are removed – in the paint rectification bay of the factory – to improve appearance, an operation which lessens the effectiveness of the anti-corrosion measures.

Rusting progresses with age, the rear wing areas in particular showing a marked increase of corrosion on those cars over 3 years old. Door and wing corrosion in the early life of the car is the result of damage to these panels, most commonly caused by stones and grit. In cars over 6 years old, some inside-out corrosion of the lower sections of the door panels can occur.

Underbody sealing compounds, which are not generally applied at the time of manufacture, show a surprising lack of effectiveness, even on late model cars. This is usually the result of unsuitable material and poor application. The material readily cracks after a relatively short life, allowing salt-laden moisture to be retained in the pockets thus formed.

Body sill problems

The high incidence of body sill corrosion is due to two factors. One is the bombardment of the body sill exterior by stones, grit, salt and slush which often results in an ungainly rust rash. The second is the difficulty of obtaining complete coverage of all internal surfaces of the three-part hollow sill section with anti-corrosion treatment and primer paint. Provided serious, flake-type internal rusting has not gotten a foothold, it is possible to extend the useful structural life of the car. A specialist firm can do this by spraying petroleum- or wax-based anti-corrosion compounds into these and other hollow sections. Such remedial measures are usually too late for cars more than 3 years old, however. The incidence of floor corrosion, on the other hand, is generally less than average, particularly with regard to older cars.

Seat runner adjustment

The seat runner adjustment mechanism, though improved over the years, is still poor and subject to wear, which sometimes necessitates its replacement on older cars.

Noisy engine

Owing to the positioning of the engine, its all-aluminium construction and the absence of refined sound insulation, the Imp is not a particularly quiet car. However, it does not suffer unduly from valve gear noise. In common with many other cars, the engine seals leave something to be desired. Although they result in oil fouling of the engine transmission casings, only rarely is more than the occasional drop of oil lost.

The freely revving engine requires frequent carburettor adjustment throughout its life. Early models had an above-average incidence of transmission and final-drive noise and some failures. If the filler cap gasket is dislodged, some fuel spillage is possible.

Regular maintenance and adjustment of the footbrake and handbrake are essential. The handbrake mechanism is exposed to road grit, which prejudices maintenance-free life. The very direct acting rack-and-pinion steering can suffer from failure of the rubber gaiter, which leads to undue rack-tooth wear.

Some end play is a design feature of taper roller bearings and is not an indication of excessive wear. Substantial camber changes due to the front-suspension and rear-wheel-drive layout tend to shorten tyre life compared with most conventional cars. This is particularly the case where owners have not observed the very marked differential in tyre pressure settings front to rear.

Specification of AA tested car

See p. 112

Make & model	HILLMAN IMP
Production years	1963–present
Body alternatives	2-door Saloon, 2-door Coupé, 2-door Estate
Engine variants	875cc OHC
Data: AA test version	Imp de luxe Saloon. 1971 model
Engine	In-line 4-cyl, watercooled, rear-mounted
	Bore 68.1mm, stroke 60.4mm, 875cc. Comp ratio 10:1
Fuel system	1 Solex carburettor. Mechanical pump.
	6-gallon front tank
Transmission	4-speed & reverse, synchromesh on all forward gears. Rear-wheel drive.
	Diaphragm-spring clutch, $6\frac{1}{4}$″ diameter dry plate, hydraulically operated
Suspension front	Independent. Coil spring, telescopic damper, swing axle
Suspension rear	Independent. Coil spring, telescopic damper, semi-trailing
Steering	Rack & pinion. $2\frac{3}{4}$ turns between full locks
	Turning circle $31\frac{1}{2}$ feet
Wheels	12″ diameter, $4\frac{1}{2}$J rims
Tyres	5.50×12 cross-ply (Goodyear G8 fitted)
Brakes	Hydraulic, drum front/drum rear
Dimensions	Length 11′7″ Width 5′0$\frac{1}{4}$″ Height 4′6$\frac{1}{2}$″ Wheelbase 6′10″
(overall)	Ground clearance 6″ Kerb weight (full tank) 14 cwts
Max speed (in gears)	First 23mph, second 42mph, third 67mph, top 78mph
Overdrive	Not applicable
Acceleration	0–60mph: 20.0 seconds; standing-$\frac{1}{4}$ mile: 20.6 seconds
Fuel consumption	overall: 36.0mpg
	steady 50mph: 47.6mpg (top gear)
	steady 70mph: 34.0mpg (top gear)
Fuel	Premium 4-star

What VISAR reveals

Worse than average | Average
Better than average | No data

All chart figures are percentages	Age in years:	6–8	5–6	4–5	3–4	2–3	1–2
	Registration Suffix:	FG	H	J	K	L	M
Corroded front doors		18	11	8	6	8	0
Corroded rear doors							
Corroded front wings		19	15	9	7	9	0
Corroded rear wings		20	15	12	3	2	0
Corroded front underwings		5	9	7	1	0	0
Corroded rear underwings		7	10	7	1	0	3
Corroded body sills		43	33	20	18	16	6
Corroded jacking points		15	5	4	5	2	8
Corroded floor		8	8	1	4	2	0
Corroded underbody frame members		19	10	12	4	4	0
Defective undersealing		32	27	21	19	15	27
Loose/misaligned driver's seat		2	7	9	4	1	6
Attend to engine mountings		6	7	5	4	0	3
Evidence of head gasket leaks		2	3	2	1	0	0
Noisy valve gear		11	9	6	9	8	12
Evidence of engine oil leaks		49	37	32	37	41	35
Attend to carburettor tuning		40	33	31	27	18	50
Evidence of fuel leaks		10	5	9	3	4	0
Final drive noise		9	10	2	3	6	0
Unsatisfactory gear change		8	7	2	0	0	0
Unsatisfactory auto gear change							
Clutch judder		4	6	3	2	0	0
Attend to front wheel bearings		19	28	25	24	23	18
Attend to steering box/rack		15	8	8	2	21	24
Attend to footbrake		31	26	20	23	14	41
Attend to handbrake		30	22	16	17	14	13
Corroded brake pipelines		20	9	13	8	10	0
Defective obligatory lights		27	14	15	24	15	31
Attend to charging system		5	7	3	4	1	0
Attend to horn		2	2	1	2	0	0

111

Cheap motoring with aplomb

Introduced in early 1963, the Imp missed the small-car boat and had to take second place behind the ubiquitous Mini. Like British Leyland's baby, there are several Imp variants, but here the next-to-basic de luxe will be examined.

A touchy choke, a long warm up, and jerky drive-shaft rubbers mean a jumpy start to the day, but once it is warmed up the engine really comes alive. By rights it should not perform so briskly on only 875cc or be so beautifully smooth to 7,000rpm. It's flexible too, trickling away in top from as low as 12mph. The engine is not quiet, though, shouting its presence on full throttle and letting forth a depressing boom between 60 and 70mph. Hard driving gives a low of 30mpg, but gentle drivers will record an easy 43mpg. The clutch proves disconcertingly 'quick' to newcomers, but it is light to work and a 1-in-3 hill start is just manageable.

Excellent on corners

On all but the smoothest roads, the Imp's ride is choppy and jerky. Cornering roll is minimal though, and cornering prowess is excellent by rear-engined standards. Abrupt oversteer is apparent only if one throttles back suddenly in mid-corner. The steering has almost 'go-kart' response, which is all right but for the fact that it suffers from kickback on rough roads. Light, fade-free drum brakes have an easy time in the dry. After 10 miles of motorway rain spray, however, those on the test car proved frighteningly inefficient on first application, then tweaked the car suddenly to the left on the second. The handbrake is excellent.

Seating improved but . . .

The small upright seats are disenchanting, but they are at least an improvement on the previous erect perches. Various mounting holes enable tall drivers to stretch and be less aware of the offset pedals. Large windows and well-placed wipers give almost uninterrupted vision, but corner windscreen blind spots are irritating. The latest fascia contains neat, round dialled instruments, while a single multi-purpose stalk replaces the former two levers on either side of the steering column. Minor controls are easily reached.

Heater's long warm-up time

Entry is easy with head ducked, but it takes a little more agility to reach the back seat. The generous cushion and squab offer adequate comfort for most people, but six-footers, unfortunately, have no head-room and their knees jam behind the front seats. 'De luxe' does not mean fancy trimmings: fibreboard lines the doors, the floor has only rubber mats, and painted metal abounds. There are two ashtrays, but it is necessary to pay extra for the heater's single-speed booster fan. The heater itself is not very impressive. It takes a long time to warm up, the water valve is slow to respond to adjustment, and the direction-control flap under the fascia is so remote that it is best worked by the driver's left foot. Hinged front quarter-lights make do in the absence of proper fresh-air fascia vents. Luggage space is normally restricted, but with the back seat folded forward, over a square yard of cargo space becomes available. Safety features do not abound. The door levers and window winders are particularly intrusive, but the fascia is reasonably padded, the sun visors pliable, and the steering wheel dished.

It is nice to find crevice-free wheel arches for a change, but couldn't the undersealing be more uniformly applied? Nonetheless, the Imp feels sturdily constructed, and both paint and chrome have a well-polished smoothness. Engine access makes life easy for DIY types, but a local Chrysler agent is a distinct advantage for major jobs. Despite its ride and handling drawbacks, the Imp is a nimble, entertaining car that offers cheap, versatile motoring with a dash of aplomb.

Jaguar XJ6L

JAGUAR XJ6
ENGINEERS' COMMENTS
More than a status symbol

The Jaguar XJ6 is a heavy, luxurious car whose clean, elegant lines neatly envelope the wheels and squat tyres, thus minimising the risk of stones being thrown along its flanks. Those who can afford the running of it are rightly proud of a car that is more than a status symbol. Owners and their passengers will be cossetted by its lush seats and well-appointed interior years after other cars already exhibit signs of age and wear.

The metal pre-treatment and the low-bake paint system give a good, durable and corrosion-resistant finish which persists through the years if the owner takes proper care of the car by washing and drying it regularly. Seven-year-old cars do tend to show some evidence of surface corrosion on edges of doors and adjacent body sill, the result of untreated chip damage. Cars of this age are usually no longer cared for by their first owners, having been acquired by others less inclined to deal with surface blemishes before they merge into small patches of rust. The corrosion which does occur, however, does not affect the structural strength of the body, the jacking points, or the brake lines.

Little underbody corrosion
Our statistics clearly demonstrate that lack of regular maintenance and service affects a quality car as much as any run-of-the-mill vehicle. In addition, the general ageing process ultimately leaves its mark. The factory-applied underbody protection compound, for example, begins to crack and allows road salt, slush and spray to come in contact with the paint and thereafter the sheet steel panels. The incidence of significant corrosion on the underside, even on 7-year-old cars, is very low, however. Some cars in this age group suffer water ingress past rubber seals on doors and the boot lid.

The carburettors demand more tuning than those of average family saloons. In addition, the automatic choke occasionally needs a mechanic's attention. Valve gear noise, largely due to the rattle of the long timing chain, increases with age and mileage. Adjustment of tappets and renewal of the timing chain are beyond the capability of most do-it-yourselfers.

Budget for refinements
Refinements introduce complications and the need to budget for extra attention,

▶

repair and replacement. It is all too common for drivers parking in confined spaces to strain the pump of the power-assisted steering when on full lock. This tends to produce squeaks, leaks and unnecessary wear on the pump drive belts. The Jaguar engine is inclined to use more oil than many others; this is a basic design factor and generally not due to excessive oil leaks past seals, rocker covers and other joints, although it pays to re-tighten these occasionally.

Fuel leaks may be due to slight spillage of petrol from the carburettor drip tube. An expert mechanic can cure this by lowering the float level slightly. The electric fuel pump, located in the boot, may require some attention after a year or two, and on older cars must be considered to be soon due for replacement.

Drivers exceed skill

The absence of owner maintenance shows itself in long pedal travel, poor, unbalanced brake performance, and scored discs. On older cars the effectiveness of the telescopic dampers and the rubber elements in their attachments should also be checked for wear and age deterioration.

Rear hub bearings and driveshafts occasionally require renewal after 2 years. The car is a steady, safe vehicle with precise road holding, but judging by the need for attention to accident damage, Jaguar drivers, more than most, tend at times to exceed their own skill. Some minor body repair work, generally well executed, was found in 50% of J, K and L registration cars. In cars over 7 years old, two out of three required some minor body repair because of accident damage.

The sample size for M registration cars is so small that it would be misleading to qualify the percentages as above average, below average, or average.

Specification of AA tested car

See p. 116

Make & model	JAGUAR XJ6
Production years	1968–present
Body alternatives	4-door Saloon, 2-door Coupé
Engine variants	2792cc OHC (1968–1973)
	4235cc OHC (1968–present)
Data: AA test version	XJ6 4.2 Automatic, 4-door Saloon. 1969 model
Engine	In-line 6-cyl, watercooled, front-mounted
	Bore 92.1mm, stroke 106mm, 4235cc. Comp ratio 9:1
Fuel system	2 SU variable-jet carburettors. 2 electric pumps.
	2 tanks, total capacity 23 gallons
Transmission	Automatic. Torque convertor. 3-speed & reverse
	Rear-wheel drive
Suspension front	Independent. Double wishbone, coil spring, damper
Suspension rear	Independent. Coil spring, telescopic dampers
Steering	Rack & pinion. Power-assisted. 3.33 turns between
	full locks. Turning circle 37 feet
Wheels	15" diameter, 6" rims
Tyres	E70VR15 radial-ply (Dunlop fitted)
Brakes	Hydraulic, dual circuit, disc front/disc rear. Servo
Dimensions	Length 15'9" Width 5'9" Height 4'4" Wheelbase 9'1"
(overall)	Ground clearance 6" Kerb weight (full tank) 33¼ cwts
Max speed (in gears)	Low 56mph, Intermediate 87mph, top 117mph
Overdrive	Not applicable
Acceleration	0–60mph: 10 seconds; standing-¼ mile: 17.3 seconds
Fuel consumption	overall: 16.75mpg
	steady 50mph: 22.0mpg (top gear)
	steady 70mph: 19.8mpg (top gear)
Fuel	Premium 4-star

What VISAR reveals

Legend: Worse than average | Average | Better than average | No data

All chart figures are percentages

	Age in years: 6–8	5–6	4–5	3–4	2–3	1–2
Registration Suffix:	FG	H	J	K	L	M*
Corroded front doors	22	4	6	4	0	0
Corroded rear doors	13	4	8	3	1	0
Corroded front wings	10	6	8	0	1	0
Corroded rear wings	7	9	5	4	0	0
Corroded front underwings	8	3	0	2	0	0
Corroded rear underwings	4	2	0	0	1	0
Corroded body sills	20	4	13	9	3	0
Corroded jacking points	19	0	5	2	0	0
Corroded floor	15	0	0	0	0	0
Corroded underbody frame members	2	0	6	0	0	0
Defective undersealing	10	4	4	6	6	8
Loose/misaligned driver's seat	7	6	5	2	0	0
Attend to engine mountings	0	1	1	0	0	0
Evidence of head gasket leaks	4	7	3	2	0	0
Noisy valve gear	44	25	25	29	15	15
Evidence of engine oil leaks	29	47	46	45	21	15
Attend to carburettor tuning	32	31	30	43	32	31
Evidence of fuel leaks	7	12	7	3	6	8
Final drive noise	4	6	4	0	6	8
Unsatisfactory gear change						
Unsatisfactory auto gear change	13	7	7	4	4	0
Clutch judder	5	0	4	2	0	0
Attend to front wheel bearings	22	8	19	17	6	8
Attend to steering box/rack	32	20	18	23	6	8
Attend to footbrake	23	4	10	19	6	8
Attend to handbrake	4	8	8	5	0	0
Corroded brake pipelines	0	0	5	5	0	0
Defective obligatory lights	29	21	25	21	18	15
Attend to charging system	0	6	0	2	6	0
Attend to horn	7	0	5	2	0	0

* See Engineers' Comments, p.114

JAGUAR XJ6 (SWB)

From AA Road Test Report 227, 1970

Fast, silent and thirsty

The XJ6 still has a waiting list of buyers and the admiration of the motoring press. It is interesting to compare it with cheaper alternatives to determine what one gets for the extra cost, apart from the prestige.

Even this 'old' six-cylinder version goes faster with more mechanical refinement. Resonance periods do not exist; only slight roughness at higher revs and heavy oil consumption betray its age. It idles with rock-steadiness and is happy in traffic, although a sudden accelerator action can cause surge away from rest. The automatic transmission is at its best in normal motoring, but feels more jerky and flustered when hastened.

Perhaps a buyer of this calibre does not worry about fuel costs. The best the test car managed was 20mpg; the XJ6 is not very responsive to economy techniques. However, the twin tanks give a splendid range of 375 miles.

To provide a 'boulevard' ride with tenacious cornering is no easy task, especially in a large saloon. The XJ6 is about the best attempt yet at doing this. In fact, cornering prowess has taken precedence, but the ride is of an extremely high order – only humps and waves cause the damping to reduce its grip. There is some radial knobbiness too, but above 40mph broken surfaces are coped with easily. Roadholding is excellent and the car will sweep round bends with the flat, quicksilver response of a Mini. Ultimately, though, the tail will ease out at higher cornering forces and cutting the power at this point makes the situation worse. The power steering prompted the testers' biggest reserva-

tions, for although it does all those light and easy things one expects around town, on open roads it feels as if one is driving on ice all the time. The test car's brakes tended to grab and pull to one side, but their normal powerful response to light loads is most reassuring.

The traditional Jaguar control layout concentrates on tidy symmetry. The grouping of minor switches is outmoded and embarrassing, although the clocks are fine. Some people miss being able to adjust the height of seat or wheel, but the reach can be altered. The driving position will keep most people happy even on long runs, because the seat concentrates on support rather than plushness. Wiper arcs and thick screen pillars create vision problems and the car's bulk makes it difficult to 'place' through gaps with confidence. The rear seat is surprisingly disappointing, with insufficient footroom or thigh support.

As well as its hushed engine, tyre noise is muted to a remarkable degree. Subdued wind hiss is the loudest noise on motorways, unless it is a warm day when the feeble ventilation system forces one to open a quarter-light. The heater serves front and rear footwells separately but constantly needs to be boosted by the fan in cold weather, and the temperature control is slow to respond. The boot is irregularly shaped, but oddments stowage inside is thoughtfully planned. Although one can get a better paint job for the price, body construction and underbody protection against rust are good. Access for routine attention is also good, making this Jaguar a more practical secondhand proposition than most.

Second thoughts – 4 years later

The XJ6 remains a remarkable car and the inadequate rear-seat comfort has now been improved in the current long-wheelbase version. The control layout and the ventilation system have been revised, although these have not yet been tried. The XJ12 has been tested and found even faster, quieter, and thirstier than the XJ6! Both models excel, not as lazy chauffeur-driven cars, but when driven in spirited fashion over a variety of roads.

MG Midget

MG MIDGET/AUSTIN SPRITE

ENGINEERS' COMMENTS

Improved body protection

This popular two-seater is, as the name implies, a small sports car in the traditional mould. Unlike the higher priced out-and-out sports car, it has a following who spend much of their time 'tinkering' with the engine. The very high proportion of cars in need of carburettor attention merely goes to prove that enthusiasm is no substitute for competence. Many youngsters would be better advised not to attempt quite so much, sticking simply to balancing the twin SU carburettors and adjusting the idling speed. Fuel leaks are often due to unions requiring tightening and an exessively high float level. Slight leaks on the slave cylinder of the hydraulically-operated clutch can cause judder.

Poor location tends to promote surface rusting of the brake pipelines, and hence gradual deterioration with age. The lack of owner maintenance largely accounts for the need to attend to footbrake and handbrake adjustments.

F/G registration cars did not have underwing or underbody compounds applied during manufacture and consequently show a fair amount of corrosion of underfloor pressings and frame members.

The garage-applied underbody protection coat on F/G and H registration cars is often cracked with age, allowing corrosive salts and moisture to gain access to the steel. The structure is rarely weakened to the point of imminent danger, however.

A loose driver's seat is generally the result of negligence rather than deficiencies in the basic design. On older models it is not uncommon to find the damper levers working loose on their bolted attachment and starting to leak. If not attended to promptly, this can develop into a relatively costly repair, quite apart from lowering the quality of the ride, which is on the hard side at the best of times.

It is interesting to note that when the electrocoat-painted body protection started in late 1970 a marked improvement in corrosion resistance was soon accomplished. Despite some initial problems with process control, the end result is a better protected and more durable car. This can best be seen in the significantly lower rate of corrosion of jacking points, body sills, both sides of the floor pressings, and the underbody frame members.

Pre-1970 cars were immersed in a solvent

117

based red primer which was allowed to find its way by gravity onto the previously prosphated surfaces. This process has three major drawbacks. First, protective primer paint cover on edges and corners can be so thin as to be almost non-existent. Second, in the drying process solvents wash off a fair amount of the primer coating on joints and internal closed sections, where paint protection is most important, and third, sags and runs of paint have to be removed by sanding down to bare metal. In the electrocoat process, by contrast, as the body is immersed, electrical attraction causes pigment and resin to be deposited as an even matt surface coating all over it. It pays to attend to a series of small stone chips before the paint is lifted off in scabs or blisters. The procedure outlined in the comments on the MGB applies.

Engine oil leaks can be greatly reduced by tightening the sump bolts, and obtaining a new sump gasket and a new rocker cover gasket. Overheating and some occasional cylinder head gasket failure are features of the 1275cc engine when it is driven too hard for long periods. The engine's proneness to valve gear clatter can never be completely eliminated, but tappet-clearance adjustment can reduce it significantly.

Deterioration with age occurs not only in the swivelling joints but also in the rubber bushes of the front suspension arm. The need for periodic adjustment to front wheel bearings is a feature of older cars. Checks for excessive bearing play and wear in steering and suspension joints are best undertaken by franchised dealers who can restore these to manufacturer's tolerances.

Specification of AA tested car

Make & model	MG MIDGET	See p. 120
Production years	Mk I, II, III 1962–present	
Body alternatives	Sports 2-door (soft-top & hard-top)	
Engine variants	1098cc OHV (1962–66)	
	1275cc OHV (1966–74)	
Data: AA test version	Midget Mk III, soft-top. 1970 model	
Engine	In-line 4-cyl, watercooled, front-mounted	
	Bore 70.6mm, stroke 81.3mm, 1275cc. Comp ratio 8.8:1	
Fuel system	2 SU variable-jet carburettors. Electric pump.	
	6-gallon tank	
Transmission	4-speed & reverse, synchromesh on 3 higher	
	gears. Rear-wheel drive.	
	Diaphragm-spring clutch, $6\frac{1}{2}''$ diameter dry plate,	
	hydraulically operated	
Suspension front	Independent. Coil spring, wishbone, lever damper	
Suspension rear	Leaf-sprung live axle, lever arm damper	
Steering	Rack & pinion. $2\frac{1}{4}$ turns between full locks	
	Turning circle 32 feet	
Wheels	13" diameter Rostyle, $3\frac{1}{2}$J rims	
Tyres	145SR13 radial-ply (Cinturato fitted)	
Brakes	Hydraulic, disc front/drum rear	
Dimensions	Length $11'5\frac{3}{8}''$ Width $4'6\frac{7}{8}''$ Height $4'0\frac{1}{2}''$ Wheelbase 6'8"	
(overall)	Ground clearance $4\frac{1}{2}''$ Kerb weight (full tank) 14 cwts	
Max speed (in gears)	First 30mph, second 57mph, third 80mph, top 93mph	
Overdrive	Not applicable	
Acceleration	0–60mph: 14.8 seconds; standing-$\frac{1}{4}$ mile: 19.8 seconds	
Fuel consumption	overall: 29.1mpg	
	steady 50mph: 39.2mpg (top gear)	
	steady 70mph: 30.3mpg (top gear)	
Fuel	Premium 4-star	

What VISAR reveals

Legend: ■ Worse than average ▨ Average ▨ Better than average □ No data

All chart figures are percentages

	6–8	5–6	4–5	3–4	2–3	1–2
Age in years: / Registration Suffix:	FG	H	J	K	L	M
Corroded front doors	22	20	13	5	5	
Corroded rear doors						
Corroded front wings	25	17	8	3	0	
Corroded rear wings	27	13	8	4	0	
Corroded front underwings	5	4	4	0	0	
Corroded rear underwings	7	4	0	0	0	
Corroded body sills	36	22	11	8	0	
Corroded jacking points	6	23	4	0	0	
Corroded floor	14	12	0	0	0	
Corroded underbody frame members	19	11	6	2	0	
Defective undersealing	42	17	19	3	4	
Loose/misaligned driver's seat	0	8	0	5	3	
Attend to engine mountings	3	2	4	3	0	
Evidence of head gasket leaks	0	3	4	5	3	
Noisy valve gear	11	3	27	18	4	
Evidence of engine oil leaks	30	13	37	54	41	
Attend to carburettor tuning	46	47	46	48	36	
Evidence of fuel leaks	0	10	0	2	0	
Final drive noise	5	12	9	10	4	
Unsatisfactory gear change	3	0	0	0	4	
Unsatisfactory auto gear change						
Clutch judder	3	7	0	10	7	
Attend to front wheel bearings	21	13	16	7	4	
Attend to steering box/rack	6	11	24	21	8	
Attend to footbrake	24	19	12	9	4	
Attend to handbrake	19	7	8	12	4	
Corroded brake pipelines	25	29	24	4	3	
Defective obligatory lights	13	6	27	10	21	
Attend to charging system	0	0	3	0	0	
Attend to horn	10	7	13	5	14	

Soundly built plus fun appeal

 The Midget used to be a de luxe Sprite, but both models are now identical except for their badges.

Powered by a de-tuned 1275 Cooper S engine, the Midget's acceleration and maximum speed are uncannily close to that of the rival Triumph Spitfire. The sturdy engine of the Mark III revs freely and combines willingness with outstanding flexibility, but the one tested came near to boiling in heavy traffic. Town driving averages 24mpg, but 35mpg is possible on quiet open roads. Refuelling stops are frequently needed, however, because the tank is ridiculously small.

The clutch has a smooth, firm bite with plenty of grip, and noise apart, the gearbox is excellent. Unsynchronised first gear occasionally balks, but usually the stubby lever can be snapped to and fro easily. Pothole dodging is strongly recommended because the stiff, firmly damped suspension creates a good deal of choppiness and bumping, but despite the crudity of its springing the Midget handles extremely well. It speeds round corners with very little roll, and although a bump will make the tail hop out of line in a corner, the steering is so quick and positive that any waywardness is quickly checked. Powerful braking is available with modest pedal pressure but some fade was evident in hard use, and four firm applications were needed to dry the brakes after a watersplash soaking. The handbrake is unusually powerful.

Getting in and out requires some agility, but once inside, one appreciates the new, smoothly contoured seats equipped with reclining squabs which lack only shoulder support. Nevertheless, anyone over 5 feet 10 inches will be cramped behind the wheel, for rearward seat adjustment is restricted by the small luggage deck behind. The pedals are slightly offset, but toe-and-heeling is easy.

There is a clear view of the road ahead through the slot-like windscreen, except in wet weather when the wipers leave bad unswept triangles. Three flexible windows in the hood eliminate serious blind spots, and the dipping interior mirror is a sensible size. An attractive set of informative instruments is set in a fascia of black-crackle finish, but the steering wheel's broad spokes stupidly mask the lower third of the speedometer and tachometer and their built-in warning lights. Various switches, including the multi-purpose column stalk, are all easily reached.

There is quite a sumptuous appearance to the interior, with embossed PVC seat trim, foam-backed side panels and black-and-chrome fittings as well as nicely fitted carpeting. Wind-up windows, opening front quarter-lights and a simple all-or-nothing heater are also standard. Boot space is cramped, but there is a little extra available space behind the seats.

The Midget's latest hood is a sleeker looking integral one which is easy to pull over one's head in a sudden downpour. Snap fasteners complete the job, making the interior snug, rattle-free and almost rainproof. However, wind noise reaches almost deafening proportions at high speeds.

The test car's smooth white paintwork had an impressive finish and its minimal brightwork reduces the number of water traps. Full undersealing is standard and a commendable feature at the price. If the bonnet could be raised higher, accessibility would be excellent except for the distributor and battery, which are rather awkwardly placed.

Over the years, the Midget has never overreached itself and become too sophisticated. That is why it is still noisy, rather cramped and harshly sprung, but it has so many plus factors that anyone in the market for a soundly made, reasonably priced, wind-in-the-face sports car with lots of fun appeal would find their search over.

MGB

MGB
ENGINEERS' COMMENTS
Improved production technology

This car has a faithful following in the UK and North America. Though little modified in engineering specification over many years, it has nonetheless undergone some significant changes in production technology, mainly in better anti-corrosion treatment and paint systems. Underbody and underwing areas have had a coating applied at the factory, but not all the hoped for improvements have materialised. For although the tyres are well shrouded by the wheel arches, stone chipping of the body sills has been a problem in the past. Also affected have been the lower parts of the wings, both front and rear, and the doors. All these panels are liable to be spattered with gravel, salt and grit due to the low ground clearance, with a surface corrosion rash developing as a result. Rust staining behind the bright trim can be an annoying feature, particularly on light-coloured cars. The underwings have some ready-made mud traps where aggressive elements can form pockets. If not dislodged by a powerful jet of water, these will cost the neglectful owner dearly.

In F/G registration cars, rust damage – mainly of the surface attack variety rather than the destructive type – is particularly bad. Body sill, wing and door areas, and even the generally watertight boot suffer from rust damage much more than the all-makes average.

The paint system employed is the early electrocoat, which disappointed all concerned. It did not live up to its claims of better anti-corrosion protection than the traditional BMC method. H registration cars generally gave better paint adhesion but another batch of brittle paint systems was released with the production of J registration cars. Whereas F/G registration cars suffer from scab blistering – the dislodging of paint flakes up to $\frac{1}{2}$ inch in diameter following stone damage – on J registration cars it is quite common to find filiform corrosion, a spidery growth of rust beneath the top colour coat.

The lack of cohesive strength of the various coats of paint to one another and to the sheet steel requires more substantial paint repair work than a mere scratch or single stone chip would warrant. In the two above-mentioned age groups it may pay to have a professional job carried out if good appearance is required. It means cutting back to bright metal and applying etch primer to get a good key to the metal surface, filler surfacer to blend in paint levels, and finally a matching colour coat. The problem of undercoat adhesion of the complex paint system plagued the MGB again on some of the L registration cars. Here, however, stone damage usually extends to the chipping off of the top coat only, allowing for a brush touch-up if caught in time, say within 2 weeks.

Serious structurally significant inside corrosion of hollow and double-skinned sections such as doors and sills is not a feature of cars within the VISAR survey age groups, but it did affect some of the earlier cars produced prior to the introduction of the electrocoat painting system in 1966.

Some F/G registration cars suffer from hardening and age-cracking of underbody protection compounds, and there is thus a rapid rise in the incidence of general corrosion of underbody frame members and floor pressings.

The twin SU carburettors need regular balancing and do not respond kindly to owners neglecting to top up the dashpot with thin oil. The result of such neglect can be an erratic response by the engine when the throttle is opened quickly. Fuel leaks can be cured by tightening unions and push-on flexible plastic pipes. The carburettor float level should be checked too.

The 1788cc engine is inclined to be fairly noisy, although it is a reliable hard slogger. Leaking head gaskets are associated with the introduction of the V-8 engine in late 1973 in the MGB GT. Initial batches of back axles for V-8 engined cars were noisy, but they do not fail prematurely. On older cars moisture ingress and the corrosion of electrical connections are a likely cause of failure of lights and horn.

Specification of AA tested car

See p. 124

Make & model	MGB
Production years	1964–present
Body alternatives	Sports Roadster 2-door, fixed head Coupé (GT)
Engine variants	1798cc OHV
	3528cc OHV
Data: AA test version	MGB Sports roadster. 1971 model
Engine	In-line 4-cyl, watercooled, front-mounted
	Bore 80.3mm, stroke 88.9mm, 1798cc. Comp ratio 8.8:1
Fuel system.	2 SU variable-jet carburettors. Electric pump.
	12-gallon tank
Transmission	4-speed & reverse, synchromesh on all forward gears. Rear-wheel drive.
	Diaphragm-spring clutch, 8″ diameter dry plate, hydraulically operated
Suspension front	Independent. Coil spring, wishbone, lever damper
Suspension rear	Leaf-sprung live axle, lever arm damper
Steering	Rack & pinion. 3 turns between full locks
	Turning circle 32 feet
Wheels	14″ diameter. Rostyle, 5J rims
Tyres	155SR14 radial-ply (Dunlop SP68 fitted)
Brakes	Hydraulic, disc front/drum rear. Optional servo fitted
Dimensions	Length 12′9¼″ Width 5′0″ Height 4′1¼″ Wheelbase 7′7″
(overall)	Ground clearance 3⅛″ Kerb weight (full tank) 20½ cwts
Max speed (in gears)	First 31mph, second 49mph, third 76mph, top 105mph
Overdrive	O/D third 95mph, O/D top 104mph
Acceleration	0–60mph 11.8 seconds; standing-¼ mile 18.4 seconds
Fuel consumption	overall 23.9mpg
	steady 50mph 36.3mpg (top gear)
	steady 70mph 28.5mpg (top gear)
Fuel	Super Premium 5-star

What VISAR reveals

Worse than average ◼ | Average ▢
Better than average ▨ | No data ▢

All chart figures are percentages

	Age in years:	6–8	5–6	4–5	3–4	2–3	1–2
	Registration Suffix:	FG	H	J	K	L	M
Corroded front doors		36	15	21	6	13	0
Corroded rear doors							
Corroded front wings		32	13	20	6	8	2
Corroded rear wings		31	8	19	6	8	0
Corroded front underwings		8	2	6	0	3	0
Corroded rear underwings		7	2	6	0	2	0
Corroded body sills		44	22	31	5	6	5
Corroded jacking points		13	4	10	4	5	0
Corroded floor		23	2	6	2	2	0
Corroded underbody frame members		12	4	5	1	3	0
Defective undersealing		30	11	12	7	8	10
Loose/misaligned driver's seat		3	1	0	0	5	0
Attend to engine mountings		2	1	0	0	0	0
Evidence of head gasket leaks		4	0	3	3	8	5
Noisy valve gear		31	34	39	41	34	26
Evidence of engine oil leaks		20	27	12	19	7	17
Attend to carburettor tuning		42	46	45	49	51	30
Evidence of fuel leaks		7	7	5	6	8	9
Final drive noise		5	3	5	3	7	0
Unsatisfactory gear change		4	2	1	1	0	0
Unsatisfactory auto gear change							
Clutch judder		0	1	1	0	2	0
Attend to front wheel bearings		8	9	4	5	14	5
Attend to steering box/rack		10	11	11	10	5	10
Attend to footbrake		9	8	5	8	3	5
Attend to handbrake		21	29	16	19	17	5
Corroded brake pipelines		18	6	13	4	2	0
Defective obligatory lights		27	9	10	16	6	10
Attend to charging system		2	0	2	0	0	9
Attend to horn		10	0	6	7	3	0

Traditional sporting qualities

Just lately the MGB has come in for a certain amount of criticism with adjectives such as 'dated' and 'uninspiring' being bandied about. Is the car really past its prime?

The MGB is certainly no traffic-light dragster. It's more of a fast but not furious roadster, comparing closely in performance with a 2-litre Capri. Top speed is 105, but what is impressive is the strong feel of the smooth, untemperamental engine. Optional extra overdrive greatly adds to the B's easy-going nature and improves cruising fuel economy; the test car averaged 24mpg with extremes of 21 and 31mpg. The medium-weight clutch has a progressive takeup and the stubby gear lever slices precisely, if rather stiffly, through the very narrow gate.

The firm suspension gives a generally restless ride, although single road faults like a sunken manhole cover are rounded off surprisingly well. Cross-ply tyres are standard, but the test car was on SP68 radials, which squealed early and did not have outstanding grip, particularly in the wet. Nevertheless, ease and safety of handling at breakaway point are very impressive. The car feels well balanced and final oversteer occurs with plenty of warning. Steering heaviness decreases as the car gets into its stride and sensible gearing plus plenty of road feel greatly add to one's sense of complete control. The optional extra servo gives the brakes just the right amount of assistance. Fade-free and undeterred by a watersplash soaking, the discs and drums provide reassuring stopping power, and the handbrake, too, is powerful.

Well shaped and comfortable though the seats are, all is not well for the driver because the pedals are awkwardly offset, and toe-and-heeling is almost impossible. Although he can sit well back from the wheel, through which there is a clear view of the speedometer and tachometer, the smaller dials tend to be masked. Apart from the overdrive and ignition switches, the remaining controls are easy to reach, though not all are labelled. Except for a blind spot by the hood's side framework, all-round vision is very good. The wipers, however, sweep only a small area of the shallow screen.

The hood is easy to pull up over one's head in a sudden downpour, but a dozen press studs must be secured to complete the job. At more than 50mph wind pressure keeps the hood taut; there is only a slight draught to the rear of the stiff wind-up windows, and there are no rattles from the well-engineered framework. The heater seems unable to do very much right, though. It is slow to warm up, difficult to regulate and sends too much heat to the screen when one wants it all to the floor. In addition, the rotary controls are completely impractical.

The interior is neatly trimmed and the practical inelegance of the rubber floor mats is offset by thick fitted carpeting on the tunnel and rear luggage deck. Below the padded fascia roll there are several sharp edges and protruding switches which could cause injury in an accident. Anyone not wearing a comfortable seat belt could well come into contact with the exposed windscreen surround and hood toggle fasteners.

Boot space is modest and restricted by the spare wheel. Sound paintwork and thick underseal are reassuring but there are bad mud traps under the front wheel arches. Servicing accessibility is reasonably good, but greasing is of the old-fashioned kind – eight points needing attention every 3,000 miles.

The MGB is not without its shortcomings, and indeed lacks several of the currently fashionable sports car ingredients. Its appeal, however, lies in the fact that it contains a strong element of traditional sporting qualities which gives it character and distinction.

Morris Marina 1800 Saloon Super De Luxe

MORRIS MARINA
ENGINEERS' COMMENTS
Stands up to a thrashing

This very orthodox design has by and large been troubled far less with initial production problems or serious faults than most makes. Its mechanical components are well proven and reliable, requiring little attention other than routine maintenance. The 'A' and 'B' engines, never noted as quiet, still soldier on with a valve gear as noisy as it was a decade or more ago. Both are consistently above average in terms of oil tightness, however.

Some of the early-production back axles were noisy, but failure rate in service is very low. Carburettor attention is in most cases a matter of straightforward adjustment of the idling speed. The TC versions, of course, require periodic balancing of the two carburettors. Some excessive second and third gear synchromesh wear occured on 1971–2 production cars, but it has since been overcome by improvements in manufacturing specification. The 1.3-litre power unit is more prone to clutch judder than the 1.8-litre one. It pays to check for leaks from the clutch slave cylinder.

The steering rack should be checked to ensure that it is securely fastened and that the gaiters are free from splits and tears which allow lubricant to escape and wear-inducing dirt to enter. Corrosion of brake pipelines is in the nature of surface rusting only.

Attention to the charging system need be only a matter of ensuring better connections to and from the generator or adjusting fan belt tension or idling speed. A few of the first generation alternators had problems with their solid state rectifiers, since overcome by Lucas design changes. Some water ingress into the rear light cluster, in particular, accounts for an above-average rate of bulb failure.

Early Marinas suffered from an annoying brake squeal and even hot-running front wheel bearings, which has been overcome by manufacturing changes. In common with many contemporary cars the Marina uses spacerless taper roller bearings, which have more of an in-built end float and rock than previous designs. If in doubt, consult a Morris dealer. He will have all the latest service bulletins, including those which tell how to check for front suspension knock, a fault which can be cured.

In its first year of production, water ingress

past bulkhead caulking sealers into the passenger compartment and past the rear wheel arch into the boot was not uncommon. Rusting under the floor covering has disappeared with improvements in manufacture, however.

The results of early electrocoat paints were disappointing, but changes in paint formulation and better control of phosphating metal pre-treatment have brought about an improvement. However, flying stones can chip through the top coat of painted panels to the sheet steel. Rust spots develop and spread like a fine mesh underneath the top coat and ultimately, unsightly blisters erupt. Lower sections of the rear door, front and rear wings, the sills and the front bumper valance are prone to this purely external and localised corrosion.

The visual impact of the Marina's painted panels may not always be great, but they give consistently good protection against the formation of rust on the outside, in hollow sections, and in spot-welded seams and junctions. The factory-applied under-wing and underbody protection is proving effective. In J registration cars, poor factory application largely accounts for the unusually high level of underbody protection coverage faults.

Attention to the footbrake and handbrake is generally a matter of routine servicing rather than repair or replacement of anything more costly than disc brake pads. As a rule, it is considered unwise to buy an entirely new type of car during its first 9 months of manufacture, yet we bought Marina number 256 off the production line, and gave it minimum attention and maximum thrashing for $2\frac{1}{2}$ years. It still performs well as a pool car in the hands of many indifferent drivers, does not look its age and has hardly ever been off the road to date.

Specification of AA tested car

Make & model	MORRIS MARINA	See p. 128
Production years	1971–present	
Body alternatives	2-door Coupé, 4-door Saloon, Estate	
Engine variants	1275cc OHV, 1798cc OHV	

Data: AA test version	Marina 1.8 Super, 4-door Saloon. 1973 model
Engine	In-line 4-cyl, watercooled, front-mounted
	Bore 80.3mm, stroke 88.9mm, 1798cc. Comp ratio 9:1
Fuel system	1 SU variable-jet carburettor. Mechanical pump.
	11.25-gallon tank
Transmission	4-speed & reverse, synchromesh on all forward
	gears. Rear-wheel drive.
	Diaphragm-spring clutch, 8″ diameter dry plate,
	hydraulically operated
Suspension front	Independent. Torsion bar, lever damper, wishbone
Suspension rear	Leaf-sprung live axle, telescopic damper
Steering	Rack & pinion. 4 turns between full locks
	Turning circle 32 feet
Wheels	13″ diameter, $4\frac{1}{2}$C rims
Tyres	145SR13 radial-ply (Dunlop SP68 fitted)
Brakes	Hydraulic, disc front/drum rear. Optional servo fitted
Dimensions	Length 13′10″ Width 5′4$\frac{3}{4}$″ Height 4′6″ Wheelbase 8′0″
(overall)	Ground clearance 6″ Kerb weight (full tank) 19$\frac{3}{4}$ cwts
Max speed (in gears)	First 35mph, second 56mph, third 78mph, top 96mph
Overdrive	Not applicable
Acceleration	0–60mph: 12.8 seconds; standing-$\frac{1}{4}$ mile: 19.6 seconds
Fuel consumption	overall: 31.5mpg
	steady 50mph: 37.7mpg (top gear)
	steady 70mph: 27.5mpg (top gear)
Fuel	Premium 4-star

What VISAR reveals

	Worse than average		Average
	Better than average		No data

	Age in years:	6–8	5–6	4–5	3–4	2–3	1–2
All chart figures are percentages	Registration Suffix:	FG	H	J	K	L	M
Corroded front doors				5	5	2	2
Corroded rear doors				10	5	1	2
Corroded front wings				13	5	1	1
Corroded rear wings				12	5	3	1
Corroded front underwings				1	1	0	0
Corroded rear underwings				0	0	0	0
Corroded body sills				21	14	4	1
Corroded jacking points		N	N	5	5	2	1
Corroded floor		O	O	11	0	1	0
Corroded underbody frame members		–	–	2	2	1	0
Defective undersealing		T	T	23	9	7	7
Loose/misaligned driver's seat		C	C	2	2	2	0
Attend to engine mountings		U	U	3	2	1	0
Evidence of head gasket leaks		D	D	0	2	2	6
Noisy valve gear		O	O	24	26	32	29
Evidence of engine oil leaks		R	R	20	17	21	19
Attend to carburettor tuning		P	P	24	31	26	33
Evidence of fuel leaks				2	1	1	0
Final drive noise		N	N	11	3	4	6
Unsatisfactory gear change		–	–	4	6	7	2
Unsatisfactory auto gear change							
Clutch judder		T	T	4	2	7	6
Attend to front wheel bearings		O	O	27	34	29	26
Attend to steering box/rack		N	N	5	6	10	14
Attend to footbrake				19	15	9	12
Attend to handbrake				24	15	9	8
Corroded brake pipelines				11	9	2	1
Defective obligatory lights				33	23	14	5
Attend to charging system				0	4	2	3
Attend to horn				2	2	2	1

MORRIS MARINA 1.8

From AA Road Test Report 295, 1973

Practical but without flair

With its sombre, no-nonsense appearance and equally staid road manners, the test car presented an uninspiring prospect at first. After a few days of its stolid running reliability and surprising turn of speed, however, enthusiasm for the Marina began to warm. There is plenty of top gear acceleration right from the word go and so long as the rear axle is prevented from leaping up and down, standing-start times are very brisk.

It will rev willingly to 6,000rpm, yet pulls cleanly from 20mph in top too. Although it wobbles at idle, the power unit is absolutely trustworthy. The crude starter motor proves temperamental on cold starts though.

When making fuel consumption comparisons, the Marina 1.8 looks even more remarkable. Here is the classic example of the larger engine version that is more economical to run when subjected to typical use. There is no doubt that this blend of performance and economy make the 1.8 engine the best proposition for the Marina.

The Marina owes its basic gearbox design to the Toledo and in some ways it is disappointing for one so recently conceived. The lever movements are long and slightly sticky, making an indifferent comparison with the Escort or Avenger.

With revised front suspension, the 1.8 feels very game for rapid bend swinging on good roads. It is when the bends and bumps come together that the Marina feels distressed. Even by cart-spring standards, it is disappointingly prone to patter and bump steering. This is one of the least successful live-axled cars in current production.

In spite of this, the 1.8's straight-line ride is merely indifferent, rather than thoroughly bad. Admittedly, some potholes cause the most fearful crashing noises. Yet on normal British roads, the Marina 1.8 jogs and rocks its way along after a fashion that feels quite tolerable, although there is the feeling that in this aspect particularly, one gets what one pays for.

There is no word of contempt for the brakes, though. Response is progressive and steady and capable of producing a genuine 1.0g stop, which confirms the conviction that British brakes really are best.

One's opinion of the driving position may depend on height. Six-footers feel at home straight away, but shorter people find the seat too low, making them feel they have to stretch up to peer over the wheel.

Although the 1.3 is more impressive, the 1.8 still merits praise for mechanical quietness. There are too many sizzles from fascia and fittings, however.

Smart, roomy interior

All four doors open wide, but rear foot entry is restricted and belt reels make things worse. Once inside, however, one appreciates the generous back seat – it makes Escorts and Vivas look cramped. In fact, it is comparable to the Avenger's.

The interior decor is quite smart and is executed with a care not always applied to recent Austin/Morris products. There are no glue marks, for instance, on the headlining, and the carpet both fits and wears well.

Likewise the air-blending heater is good and the general results are very satisfactory. The ventilation system is less convincing, but there appears to be nothing in its general construction and equipment that would cast doubt on reliability. Its sheer mechanical simplicity will be an incentive to DIY types and there is a certain design thoughtfulness that will gratify them too.

The Marina is, in fact, one of the most blatant current examples of the family car as a domestic utensil. It is devoid of any real flair or enthusiast appeal but eminently practical, safely and effectively designed for its job, and offered at a keen price.

Morris Traveller

MORRIS MINOR
ENGINEERS' COMMENTS
Corrosion threatens long life

In its day, the Morris Minor was one of the most robust and long-lasting of little cars. While not a sparkling performer, it was easy to service, required little attention and did not deteriorate greatly with age. Then the salt age descended upon the British Isles; local authorities liberally spread salt and grit in ever increasing volume on trunk roads and motorways and in urban centres to keep traffic flowing freely regardless of frost, snow and ice. When the Morris Minor was launched, some 45,000 tons of this corrosion-promoting rock salt were dumped annually on Britain's roads. By 1971, when production of this car stopped, the figure had risen to over 1.3 million tons per annum. Production of the Traveller continued for a further 2 years.

Underwing perforation
The underwings of cars of F/G or earlier registration suffer badly from erosion by salt-rich mud at the point where they join the bulkhead and the front door pillar. This area readily packs with mud and road salt, and traps moisture and dirt. These deposits can be washed off by vigorous application of a jet from a garden hose, a task which should be undertaken at least two or three

times annually. If it is neglected, the front 'mudwings' will eventually be perforated from the inside.

Good outward appearance
The old Roto-dip painting system – highly successful for many years – rarely produced good, continuous protective layers of phosphate and primer paint on the areas where the three body panels – bulkhead, wing and door frame or 'A' post – join. The shape of the car makes it an easier car to paint than more recently introduced models. The outward appearance of older Minor cars therefore may give a better impression than the structure of the car warrants. Under load, jacking points readily tend to break away from the rust-riddled sill and lower body structure. The rear underwing-sill junction has a plastic sealer strip which shrinks and hardens with age, thus allowing corrosion a foothold around and behind it.

DIY repairs
Body sills, though not the most structurally vital, eventually suffer rust perforation, starting from the inside. It is possible to effect some chickenwire and plastic filler repair without fear of the body's impending

collapse, for the Minor has more of a chassis frame than many other small cars. But there are areas in which no attempt at patch-up repairs should be contemplated. For example, the torsion bar anchorage point in the bulkhead reinforcement, where the loads from road shocks and the weight of the car are absorbed. This part of the structure does occasionally rot away with time, but it generally takes a good many years before there is any danger of this anchorage pulling away under a sudden shock loading.

Timber treatment

The Minor Traveller with its part-timber structure presents problems of its own. Timber must be treated to keep out moisture, particularly where open-grained sections are exposed to the weather and the industrial environment, if it is not to rot away at the points where it joins the metal panels.

Beware of painted woodwork; instead, the wood should have been re-varnished from time to time. Look for evidence of filler application concealing perforation from the inside of the lower parts of door panels or sills, let alone wing-body junctions. A simple magnet can be used to test panels in question. If it does not 'stick' to a panel, a filler may have been applied.

Durable engine

The 998cc BLMC 'A' series engines, while not quiet, are durable; the slight oil seepage does not greatly matter. Owing to their fiercer operation, some older type clutches develop a judder. Nonetheless, they transmit power effortlessly to the rear wheels. It is possible to adjust the clutch operating mechanism. If routine brake maintenance is neglected, a pull to one side is not uncommon. Poor earth return accounts for the failure of horns and the rear obligatory lights.

Specification of AA tested car

Make & model	MORRIS MINOR	See p. 132
Production years	1948–1971	
Body alternatives	2-door Saloon, 4-door Saloon, Convertible, Estate	
Engine variants	918cc side valve, 1948–52, 803cc OHV 1952–56 948cc OHV 1956–62, 1098cc OHV 1962–71	
Data: AA test version	Minor 1000 "Traveller" Estate. 1965 model	
Engine	In-line 4-cyl, watercooled, front-mounted Bore 64.6mm, stroke 83.7mm, 1098cc. Comp ratio 8.5:1	
Fuel system	1 SU variable-jet carburettor. Electric pump. 6.5-gallon tank	
Transmission	4-speed & reverse, synchromesh on three higher forward gears. Rear-wheel drive $7\frac{1}{4}$" diameter dry plate clutch, mechanically operated	
Suspension front	Independent. Torsion bar, lever damper, wishbone	
Suspension rear	Leaf-sprung live axle, piston-type damper	
Steering	Rack & pinion. $2\frac{1}{2}$ turns between full locks Turning circle 33 feet	
Wheels	14" diameter, $3\frac{1}{2}$" rims	
Tyres	5.20×14 cross-ply (Dunlop C41 fitted)	
Brakes	Hydraulic, drum front/drum rear	
Dimensions (overall)	Length 12'5" Width 5'1" Height 5'0$\frac{1}{4}$" Wheelbase 7'2" Ground clearance 7" Kerb weight (full tank) 15$\frac{5}{8}$ cwts	
Max speed (in gears)	First 25mph, second 46mph, third 68mph, top 83mph	
Overdrive	Not applicable	
Acceleration	0–60mph: 20.5 seconds; standing-$\frac{1}{4}$ mile: 22 seconds	
Fuel consumption	overall: 38.4mpg steady 50mph: 50.0mpg (top gear) steady 70mph: 32.0mpg (top gear)	
Fuel	Premium 4-star	

What VISAR reveals

Legend: ▓ Worse than average | ▒ Average | ▨ Better than average | ☐ No data

All chart figures are percentages

	Age in years: 6–8	5–6	4–5	3–4	2–3	1–2
Registration Suffix:	FG	H	J	K	L	M
Corroded front doors	13	16	9			
Corroded rear doors						
Corroded front wings	17	12	7			
Corroded rear wings	16	11	12			
Corroded front underwings	14	8	5			
Corroded rear underwings	11	8	4			
Corroded body sills	28	27	14			
Corroded jacking points	21	13	9	N	N	N
Corroded floor	13	7	0	O	O	O
Corroded underbody frame members	24	21	7	I	I	I
Defective undersealing	30	11	0	T	T	T
Loose/misaligned driver's seat	6	0	0	C	C	C
Attend to engine mountings	7	2	0	U	U	U
Evidence of head gasket leaks	4	0	0	D	D	D
Noisy valve gear	29	25	36	O	O	O
Evidence of engine oil leaks	41	30	35	R	R	R
Attend to carburettor tuning	26	31	43	P	P	P
Evidence of fuel leaks	3	7	5			
Final drive noise	13	5	4	F	F	F
Unsatisfactory gear change	4	3	0	O	O	O
Unsatisfactory auto gear change						
Clutch judder	16	15	23	T	T	T
Attend to front wheel bearings	9	2	17	U	U	U
Attend to steering box/rack	12	4	14	O	O	O
Attend to footbrake	18	8	17			
Attend to handbrake	24	8	17			
Corroded brake pipelines	12	15	9			
Defective obligatory lights	27	33	19			
Attend to charging system	1	3	0			
Attend to horn	7	13	0			

MORRIS MINOR 1000 TRAVELLER

From AA Road Test Report 116, 1965

A tough, lively performer

This four-seater estate car version of the world-famous Minor is now powered by BMC's 1100 engine, but otherwise it is much the same uncomplicated mechanical mixture as before.

The engine is a quick-warming unit giving lively performance, and is happy to burble along smoothly in top at 18mph or work hard at an impressive maximum speed of 83mph. Nevertheless, it becomes boomy when pressed, the noise no doubt amplified by the 'sounding box' body shape. With care outstanding economy can be achieved. The overall test figure of 38½mpg includes various kinds of driving, but if the throttle is spared 43 is possible. Aided by a smart, light clutch, gear changing is beautifully quick and precise. Synchromesh on the upper three ratios is unbeatable and the gear lever moves through the box without protest.

Light steering, safe handling

The Traveller's seven-leaf rear springs make the ride pretty bouncy and harsh, but cornering roll is minimal. On the other hand, if a pothole is caught in mid-bend the tail gives a noticeable hop sideways. Handling is safe and predictable, aided by the light, accurate steering which tends to knock on rough surfaces. It takes a firm push to achieve maximum braking, but the all-drum system is well balanced and resists fade well. The handbrake is powerful, too.

The front seats are too upright and offer little support, which can result in backache on a 50 mile run. The steering wheel is too big and too high for some too. Forward vision is marred by the thick windscreen pillars and poor windscreen wiper sweeps. The interior mirror covers the rear windows adequately but the door-frames create a centre blind spot. Twin wing mirrors are standard, but are poorly placed for easy rearward vision. A floor-mounted switch dips the powerful headlamps, while remaining switches (apart from the indicator stalk) are in the fascia centre around the big speedometer with its small inbuilt fuel gauge. They are all easy to see and reach.

Only the driver's seat can be adjusted, but both front seats tip up to provide reasonable entry and exit for passengers. The interior is neatly trimmed in leather-cloth but the carpets, which are unbound, detach from their fasteners and soon look unsightly. The heater provides a pleasant flow of warmth to the front footwells – though little to the back – and a good flow of cool, fresh air in hot weather, boosted if necessary by a fairly quiet single-speed fan. Occasionally exhaust fumes are sucked into the car through the radiator grille duct, which can be unpleasant in dense traffic.

Generous cargo area

It is easy to load the flat cargo area at the rear through wide-opening back doors. The space it offers is generous enough, but shooting two bolts and folding the back seat forward doubles the volume to 40 cubic feet. Removing the spare wheel from its underfloor compartment is no joke with a boot full of luggage.

Sound, durable-looking paintwork covers the sturdy body. All the timberwork joints are well finished and varnished and the stainless steel window surrounds and other brightwork parts are of good quality. Routine servicing is simple, with all mechanical components very easy to work on. Ten grease nipples should be given the gun at 3,000 mile intervals. This seems a bit much, but it's nice to know the joints are properly lubricated.

The Minor has been in production for 17 years and its looks and ride betray its age. Nevertheless, it is well developed and in its latest 1100 guise provides a lively performance on a modest thirst. The estate is noisier than the saloon and suffers from jerkier ride and handling, but it offers the family man or business representative a tough little car with generous load space at a reasonable price.

Moskvich 412

MOSKVICH 412

ENGINEERS' COMMENTS

Maintenance counts

In attempting to assess the Moskvich 412 one must make due allowance for the adverse press publicity the car received during the autumn of 1973. As a result, many owners were frightened into submitting their cars for close scrutiny by AA engineers.

The overall impression of this exceptionally low-priced car is unfavourably affected by certain unarguable factors. For one, it is dated in many of its concepts. Also, the anti-corrosion treatment amd paint system are disappointing. They no longer meet current UK operating conditions, although they may be better suited to Russian winter conditions. An essentially dry Continental environment, even with hard frosts, slows down corrosion attack very markedly compared with the high humidity of Britain. It is therefore not surprising that ugly rust stains – which appear earlier on the Moskvich than on most other cars – are all too common on many body seams.

Body sill corrosion, which starts as a superficial rust rash following bombardment by road grit and slush, can become more widespread on older cars. However, we have no record of rusting out from the inside or a significant loss of structural strength of this robust car.

Poor dealer work

The underside usually has a protective compound layer which seems to be adequate to keep underfloor and under-wing areas free from corrosion. Water ingress into the passenger compartment was a major problem, but it has been cured on the latest models by improved sealing of doors and body seams. The problem of water leakage into the boot, however, has yet to be eliminated. Some of the defects found upon inspection could have been rectified by franchised dealers; originally their work was very poor – as seen, for instance, in post-accident repair – but there has been a discernible trend towards improvement. The quality of work, however, is still well below average.

Comments regarding the need for attention to the driver's seat , engine mounting, carburettor tuning, accelerator and choke linkages, fuel leaks and the horn are more an indication of poor dealer preparation than a reflection on the basic quality of Soviet workmanship. Relatively poor transit protection and long periods of storage

▶

account for moisture ingress into light units, which in turn produces poor earth return and a high rate of bulb failure. During the past 12 months the importers have taken steps to minimise owner complaints by building a large importation centre where quality checks and rectification are carried out prior to delivery to dealers.

Back axle noise speaks for the quality of cutting of the hypoid gears, but it does not mean failure is imminent or likely. There are basically two real areas of concern on this car: brakes and steering. The peculiarities of the brake system layout and the materials used tend to result in brake fade when repeatedly braking from speed, with quite an alarming pull to one side. The abruptness of the servo action takes a bit of getting used to as well.

If one turns the steering hard over to full lock, under dynamic conditions occasional rubbing contact between tyre and body and also the flexible brake hose can result. Driver restraint, a call to the franchised dealer for a check, and possibly some rectification work are highly desirable on the part of owners or would-be purchasers of a pre-1974 model.

Most of the fundamental shortcomings of materials, assembly and adjustment have now been overcome by the concerted action of the manufacturer and sole importer. It is, however, a mistake to assume that because the Moskvich is a very low-priced, relatively uncomplicated car, it requires no maintenance or regular service attention. The steering column gear change is a case in point. Neglect of linkage adjustment soon leads to needless wear and rough gear changes. The handbrake system, too, should not be neglected. Dynamic balancing of all wheels will improve the ride comfort of the roomy 412.

Specification of AA tested car

See p. 136

Make & model	MOSKVICH 412
Production years	1970–1974; from 1974 renamed Moskvich 1500
Body alternatives	4-door Saloon, Estate
Engine variants	1478cc OHC
Data: AA test version	412 4-door Saloon. 1973 model
Engine	In-line 4-cyl, watercooled, front-mounted
	Bore 82mm, stroke 70mm, 1478cc. Comp ratio 8.8:1
Fuel system	1 twin-choke carburettor. Mechanical pump.
	10-gallon tank
Transmission	4-speed & reverse, synchromesh on all forward gears. Rear-wheel drive.
	Diaphragm-spring clutch, 7.9″ diameter dry plate, hydraulically operated
Suspension front	Independent. Coil spring, wishbones, anti-roll bar, damper
Suspension rear	Leaf-sprung live axle, telescopic damper
Steering	Worm & roller. 4 turns between full locks.
	Turning circle 33 feet
Wheels	13″ diameter, 4½J rims
Tyres	6.45×13 cross-ply (Michelin ZX fitted)
Brakes	Hydraulic, drum front/drum rear. Servo
Dimensions	Length 13′5″ Width 5′1″ Height 4′10½″ Wheelbase 7′10½″
(overall)	Ground clearance 7″ Kerb weight (full tank) 20¼ cwts
Max speed (in gears)	First 28mph, second 47mph, third 72mph, top 90mph
Overdrive	Not applicable
Acceleration	0–60mph: 16.0 seconds; standing-¼ mile: 20.6 seconds
Fuel consumption	overall: 28.5mpg
	steady 50mph: 36.7mpg (top gear)
	steady 70mph: 28.0mpg (top gear)
Fuel	Premium 4-star

What VISAR reveals

Worse than average ▓ | Average ▒
Better than average ▨ | No data ☐

All chart figures are percentages

Age in years:	6–8	5–6	4–5	3–4	2–3	1–2
Registration Suffix:	FG	H	J	K	L	M
Corroded front doors				15	9	2
Corroded rear doors				9	8	2
Corroded front wings				15	8	2
Corroded rear wings				8	8	4
Corroded front underwings				0	2	2
Corroded rear underwings				0	1	2
Corroded body sills				15	3	2
Corroded jacking points		N		8	3	0
Corroded floor		O		30	10	0
Corroded underbody frame members		I		8	2	3
Defective undersealing		T		0	8	13
Loose/misaligned driver's seat		C		0	7	8
Attend to engine mountings		U		0	1	2
Evidence of head gasket leaks		D		0	3	0
Noisy valve gear		O		16	17	12
Evidence of engine oil leaks		R		15	35	13
Attend to carburettor tuning		P		46	47	43
Evidence of fuel leaks				0	20	11
Final drive noise		N		20	22	15
Unsatisfactory gear change		I		17	9	5
Unsatisfactory auto gear change						
Clutch judder		T		0	0	0
Attend to front wheel bearings		O		17	15	10
Attend to steering box/rack		N		33	46	51
Attend to footbrake				64	55	58
Attend to handbrake				18	34	36
Corroded brake pipelines				0	1	0
Defective obligatory lights				8	35	22
Attend to charging system				0	3	3
Attend to horn				8	8	11

135

MOSKVICH 412

From AA Road Impression 101, 1973

Russian orthodox

 Any family saloon that can be put on the road for £200 less than its rivals merits a closer look. The Russian-built Moskvich is a conventional 1½-litre car with dimensions and accommodation similar to those of the Marina.

Straight-line performance is respectable for a 1500cc family saloon which is comparable, for example, with a Hunter GL or Cortina 1600, but there are some irritating flat-spots on half throttle. The engine makes a clatter which the testers didn't find objectionable until past 60mph, but by 70mph the car feels harsh and noisy, with a lot of wind noise too. The gear shift, though notchy into the lower gears, is generally light and precise, contrasting with most of the other controls. Fuel consumption runs between 26mpg and 32mpg and filling is easy, once one remembers to operate the boot release each time the filler flap needs to be opened. Four-star fuel is essential, and even then, some pinking is evident.

The Moskvich rides most British roads with a basic suppleness that insulates passengers well. However, sloppy damping and bouncy seats create too much after-reaction for proper relaxation, and pronounced tilt builds up on corners. When it comes to handling, the 412 is recalcitrant. Its ungainly steering, spongy accelerator and stolid cornering manners quickly persuade one that hurrying is a waste of time and effort. This conviction is reinforced by the brakes, which need an initial firm push and then suddenly work with a vengeance, slewing the car as the back wheels lock. The test car's handbrake would not have passed the DoE test. Cornering ability is quite respectable and safe on Michelin ZX radials, which were fitted on the test car. Russian-made cross-plies are standard.

The interior evokes memories of ration books and utility furniture, and the fascia is reminiscent of a pre-war Packard or Studebaker but the speedometer is deadly accurate, surprisingly enough. Uncompromisingly tough rubber covers the floor and the plain plastic-trimmed seats lack shape, yet the driving position proves most acceptable; the seats are generously proportioned and one has a good forward view.

Reasonable legroom extends to the back, and there are four armrests, a cigarette lighter and notable features like a radiator shutter and four supplementary instruments. The interior design does not promote safety consciousness, however. The fascia and fittings are very solid, the static seat-belts are inconvenient and the heater controls are way beyond reach when one is belted in. The heater looks cumbersome, but it has a reasonable output when the crude water valve is yanked fully open.

There are no ventilation outlets, just swivelling quarter-lights that waver in the breeze. Boot space is generous, but the spare wheel and black tool sack take up a lot of room. The tool-kit is crude but conscientious, and contains much more than one gets in a British car at twice the price.

The 6-month-old test car showed evidence of rust-pimpled door handles, while closer inspection revealed several chipped and coarse areas marring the paintwork. The bonnet and boot lids appear incredibly flimsy, but at least the underbody has a good dose of undersealing, although some of the brightwork will harbour moisture and promote corrosion.

Although the Moskvich is cheap and has a reputation for low-cost ruggedness, one should consider the limitations of the car's road manners above its showroom appeal. Since the original test, several improvements have been made, including better braking and a neatly padded fascia concealing a more effective heater. Even so, there are still many good used cars around for about £750!

Reliant Scimitar

RELIANT SCIMITAR GTE
ENGINEERS' COMMENTS
Best of many worlds?

Although the sample size on which our comments are based is small, some interesting features come to light. When the car was introduced, the E was variously referred to as Estate, Executive, or Extra; there was never any attempt to play down its 'grand tourism' appeal. The Scimitar GTE has established a following among an exclusive set of executives, and it attempts to combine the best of many worlds: well-tried mechanicals such as a Ford V–6 power unit and gear box and a Salisbury back axle with limited slip differential to give good traction under power on unpredictable road surfaces. The glass-reinforced fibre body, constructed for lightness, has clean, distinctive lines.

The ladder-type fabricated chassis frame is made up of deep sections of hollow rectangular boxes, tubes, and open channels. The plan view of the chassis frame is not unlike that of the Triumph TR6, but it is stiffer; it has to provide practically all the torsional and bending strength of the car. The Scimitar's makers decided that its potential market was insufficient to warrant the considerable cost of laying down presses and forming tools to hammer out sheet steel or aluminium panels. All the dynamic loads – regardless of whether they are due to power unit, drive line, final drive, brake or road reaction – are taken by the chassis, not the glass-reinforced fibre body. The roof is reinforced by a roll stiffener made up of two steel tubes which serve as the upper anchorage of the seat-belts.

One would naturally expect a total absence of body corrosion on an all-plastic car, but this is not the case. Surprisingly, a number of over-anxious owners have had under-body compound applied. This is quite unnecessary as far as the non-metallic underfloor is concerned, and does very little to prolong the chassis frame life. Surface corrosion of the chassis is quite pronounced, in fact. The original factory-applied metal anti-corrosion treatment and protective paint system are not as good as those of mass-produced cars, particularly on the inside of hollow sections. After a number of winters' exposure to corrosive salt and slush, rusting is most evident where plastic and steel join. J registration cars have a high incidence of water ingress into the boot.

Brake pipelines suffer from an early onset of corrosion, particularly of union connectors. Earth returns in electrical systems may have to be given some extra attention by dealers and owners to ensure that all legally required lights always function correctly. The powerful footbrakes pull the car up squarely, but the handbrake needs frequent routine adjustment. Telescopic damper units and their attachments should be checked periodically.

The rack-and-pinion steering should be examined for tightness of damping to the chassis and damaged gaiters which allow lubricants to escape. There is a significant incidence of fuel leaks, which are usually found on the feed pipe from petrol pump to carburettor. Because of the increased fire risk of glass-reinforced fibre bodies, no fuel leak should be left unattended.

The back axles of some K registration Scimitars are noisy due to poor assembly, but they do not have a high failure rate. Attention to front wheel bearings does not imply imminent bearing collapse, but rather indicates that swivel joints and track rod ends as well as taper roller bearing end play should be checked against the manufacturer's tolerance range.

The power unit is basically the same V–6 as that used in the Ford Granada/Consul and the comments made in that section on engine oil leaks, cylinder head gasket leaks and valve gear noise also apply to the Scimitar. There is no need for alarm, however. The Ford engine and gear box can take a good deal of fairly high revving and hard slogging.

Glass-reinforced fibre does tend to shatter rather than crumble in serious collisions. Contrary to popular belief, it is not as easy to repair a damaged body panel in this car as it is to knock out a dent in a steel or aluminium one.

Specification of AA tested car

See p. 140

Make & model	RELIANT SCIMITAR GTE
Production years	1968–present
Body alternatives	Fixed head Coupé 3-door
Engine variants	V-6 2994cc OHV

Data: AA test version — Scimitar GTE 2994cc. 1972 model

Engine	V6-cyl, watercooled, front-mounted
	Bore 93.7mm, stroke 72.4mm, 2994cc. Comp ratio 8.9:1
Fuel system	1 Weber twin-choke carburettor. Mechanical pump. 17-gallon tank. Low-level warning
Transmission	4-speed & reverse, synchromesh on all forward gears. Rear-wheel drive. Diaphragm-spring clutch, 9" diameter dry plate, hydraulically operated
Suspension front	Independent. Wishbones, coil spring, anti-roll bar
Suspension rear	Coil-sprung live axle, trailing arms, Watts linkage
Steering	Rack & pinion. 3½ turns between full locks. Turning circle 36 feet
Wheels	14" diameter, 5½J rims
Tyres	185HR14 radial-ply (Cinturato CN72 fitted)
Brakes	Hydraulic, disc front/drum rear. Servo
Dimensions (overall)	Length 14'3" Width 5'4½" Height 4'4" Wheelbase 8'3½" Ground clearance 5" Kerb weight (full tank) 23¼ cwts
Max speed (in gears)	First 42mph, second 60mph, third 93mph, top 118mph
Overdrive	Optional O/D third 115mph, O/D top 115mph
Acceleration	0–60mph: 9.1 seconds; standing-¼ mile: 17.3 seconds
Fuel consumption	overall: 21.2mpg steady 50mph: 35.9mpg (top gear) 37.7mpg (O/D top) steady 70mph: 27.3mpg (top gear) 30.0mpg (O/D top)
Fuel	Premium 4-star

What VISAR reveals

All chart figures are percentages

	Age in years:	6–8	5–6	4–5	3–4	2–3	1–2
	Registration Suffix:	FG	H	J	K	L	M
Corroded front doors				0	0	0	
Corroded rear doors							
Corroded front wings				0	0	0	
Corroded rear wings				0	0	0	
Corroded front underwings				0	0	0	
Corroded rear underwings				0	0	0	
Corroded body sills				0	0	0	
Corroded jacking points				0	5	6	
Corroded floor				0	0	0	
Corroded underbody frame members				13	14	18	
Defective undersealing							
Loose/misaligned driver's seat				0	0	0	
Attend to engine mountings				0	0	0	
Evidence of head gasket leaks				6	0	0	
Noisy valve gear				13	10	5	
Evidence of engine oil leaks				31	29	18	
Attend to carburettor tuning				33	9	9	
Evidence of fuel leaks				0	5	4	
Final drive noise				0	19	0	
Unsatisfactory gear change				0	0	0	
Unsatisfactory auto gear change							
Clutch judder				0	5	0	
Attend to front wheel bearings				33	23	13	
Attend to steering box/rack				14	23	9	
Attend to footbrake				13	0	10	
Attend to handbrake				44	34	9	
Corroded brake pipelines				13	14	0	
Defective obligatory lights				0	23	15	
Attend to charging system				0	5	0	
Attend to horn				0	0	0	

RELIANT SCIMITAR GTE

From AA Road Test Report 303, 1973

Fast, grippy, fun to drive

The GTE is Reliant's glass-fibre-bodied trendsetter that replaced the ageing notchback Scimitar Coupé in 1968. Of late it has been flattered by imitations from BMW with their 2002 Touring and Volvo's 1800 ES.

Ford V-6 engine power gives vivid acceleration, making it faster than either the BMW 2002 or Triumph Stag. It is possible to reach 0–60mph in a spanking 9 seconds and 100mph comes up comfortably within half a minute, but one rarely employs Reliant's 6,000 rev limit because the engine sounds very harsh by 5,500. The automatic choke gives a steady fast idle and no flat-spots during the warm-up period which is hastened by a thermostatically-controlled cooling fan. Overdrive-equipped Scimitars like the test car have a wide gap between second and third gears, but thanks to improved engine torque this shortcoming is masked if not cured. Close spacing and long lever travel mar the gear change, but the synchromesh is unbeatable. Overdrive, at £50 extra, is money well spent; it provides marvellously relaxed high-speed cruising. Fuel consumption dropped to 17mpg on performance-testing day, but mixed mileages regularly gave 20–23mpg and the 17-gallon tank provides an excellent range between fill-ups.

Firm suspension

Unlike its new, softly sprung Capri rival – the 3000 – the Scimitar possesses no-nonsense suspension of almost vintage firmness, yet it is rare for occupants to be subjected to shocks over anything except bad potholes. Cornering roll is minimal, but the back axle is not entirely free from tremor. It is usually only a fast take-off on the turn that makes the axle jitter noisily, however. Road holding and handling give a tremendous feeling of security, with moderate understeer merging to balanced neutrality as cornering speeds are increased. Eventually the tail drifts out, but the excellent steering (spoilt only by knocking kick-back) instantly corrects any oversteer. Superb disc/drum brakes, albeit rather heavy, are an easy match for the GTE's performance.

Tasteful interior

At extra cost, luxurious leather trims the comfortable seats, which lack only lumbar support. Legroom is just adequate for a six-footer, and the pedals are well spaced despite narrow footwells; but while the instruments are clearly legible, the fascia rocker switches are fiddly to find, especially after dark. All-round vision is fair, but the tapered rear side windows restrict the driver's over-the-shoulder view, and the headlamps are useless for fast night driving. The back window's wash-and-wipe system is invaluable in dirty weather. It's optimistic to call the GTE a full four-seater, but as a 2+2 its rear accommodation is acceptable. The interior is tastefully trimmed in colour-keyed fabrics and warmed by an efficient heater, which, although slow to respond to the temperature control, will provide blissful cool air to the face while it toasts one's toes.

Although not perfect, the finish of the glassfibre body and paintwork is very impressive and should give reassurance to any long-term owner. No special protection is given to the chassis though. With the engine set so far back, access to the plugs and dipstick is awkward, but all the fillers are ideally placed for topping-up.

The testers collected the GTE with enthusiasm and returned it with reluctance. It's fast, it's grippy, it handles and stops like a sports car should, and it offers luggage accommodation that few estate cars can manage. Faults? Well, there's room for improvement in the switch layout, steering kickback, and window sealing. Nevertheless, as a sporty 2+2 that's fun to drive and offers estate car load-space when necessary, the GTE is a highly desirable hatchback that merits success and deserves imitation.

Renault 4 De Luxe

RENAULT 4
ENGINEERS' COMMENTS
Car with nine lives

Renault at one time had a reputation for building cars that suffered more from corrosion than most. This family trait is displayed by older 4s; despite considerable and continuing efforts by the manufacturers, the 4's rust resistance has been disappointing right up to K registration.

Iron phosphating metal pre-treatment followed by slipper-dip priming was rarely as effective as the manufacturers hoped in keeping rusting at bay on underbody panels and associated stiffening frames and body sills. Double skin construction of longitudinal and transverse stiffening members initially gives a strong, stiff bodyshell and total collapse of this part of the structure due to corrosion is rare. The method of fabrication, however, gives little chance of obtaining complete and durable anti-rust cover on the inside of hollow sections.

Poor sealing on cars up to K registration allows moisture to collect in the punt-type underbody platform beneath the floor covering; rusting inevitably follows. It is a sound practical procedure for a repairer to weld in new floor panels, however. The introduction of improved electrocoat primer painting in 1972 enhanced rust resistance radically and factory application of underbody protection compounds has further helped to retard deterioration by rust.

Drive line parts wear
Being a front-wheel-drive car, some of the 4's more expensive drive line components tend to wear more than those in conventional rear-wheel-drive layouts. Significant wear of outer driveshaft joints starts after about 2 years, and one out of eight 7- to 8-year-old cars was found to be in need of component replacement.

Dampers deteriorate fairly quickly and anti-roll bars tend to work loose after about 2 years' service and may require new rubber bushes. These are not expensive items to replace, however. On older cars, damaged gaiters on the rack-and-pinion steering can allow lubricant to escape and dirt and grit to enter. When a franchised dealer carries out checks for front wheel bearing rock, have him confirm that there is no undue wear in upper and lower swivel and steering joints. Generally such wear only becomes a problem in cars over 5 years old.

Engine mountings are rarely a source of

trouble. Valve gear noise can readily be reduced by attention to tappet clearance – a simple enough operation on the well-proven, sturdy little engine. Attention to carburettor tuning likewise is not difficult; it only involves idling and mixture strength adjustment. Most fuel leaks can be cured by attending to fuel pipe unions and renewing push-on nylon pipes when they show signs of hardening with age. Wear in linkages with age and usage accounts for most customer complaints of poor gear changes. On older cars, synchromesh action could be poor due to wear. In either case seek the advice of a franchised dealer and obtain an estimate of the cost of rectification.

Brake pipe corrosion

The unusually high number of inoperative or damaged lights, mainly on the rear, is due in part to accidental damage when reversing and also to poor earth return.

When adjusting the brakes, attend to the footbrake first, and then the handbrake. If in doubt, consult a franchised dealer. The hydraulic brake pipelines are partly sheethed in plastic, an arrangement which, while minimising stone bombardment damage, promotes corrosion. Brake pipe corrosion is concentrated at the point where the plastic sheeth ends.

The Renault 4 can take very considerable overloading, hard bouncing around, driver inconsideration, lack of maintenance and delay of long-overdue repair or replacement of some of the items referred to above – and still be driveable long after more sophisticated motor cars have ceased to function.

Although the sample size of M registration cars is small, and percentages are thus not qualified as above average, below average or average, the findings uphold developing trends.

Specification of AA tested car

Make & model	RENAULT 4	*See p. 144*
Production years	1962–1965 (R4) 1965–present (4)	
Body alternatives	4-door Saloon, 5-door Estate	
Engine variants	845cc OHV	

Data: AA test version	
Engine	Renault 4 Estate. 1968 model
	In-line 4-cyl, watercooled, front-mounted
	Bore 58mm, stroke 80mm, 845cc. Comp ratio 8.5:1
Fuel system	1 Solex carburettor. Mechanical pump.
	5.75-gallon tank
Transmission	4-speed & reverse, synchromesh on all forward gears. Front-wheel drive.
	Multi-spring clutch, $6\frac{1}{4}$" diameter dry plate, cable operated
Suspension front	Independent. Torsion bar, anti-roll bar, telescopic damper
Suspension rear	Independent. Trailing arm, telescopic damper, torsion bar
Steering	Rack & pinion. $4\frac{1}{2}$ turns between full locks.
	Turning circle $30\frac{1}{2}$ feet
Wheels	13" diameter disc type
Tyres	135×330 radial-ply (Michelin X fitted)
Brakes	Hydraulic, drum front/drum rear
Dimensions (overall)	Length 12'0" Width 4'10½" Height 5'1" Wheelbase 8'0"
	Ground clearance $7\frac{3}{4}$" Kerb weight (full tank) $12\frac{3}{4}$ cwts
Max speed (in gears)	First 20mph, second 39mph, third 59mph, top 68mph
Overdrive	Not applicable
Acceleration	0–60mph: 35.6 seconds; standing-$\frac{1}{4}$ mile: 23.9 seconds
Fuel consumption	overall: 40.0mpg
	steady 50mph: 47.6mpg (top gear)
	steady 70mph: N/A mpg (top gear)
Fuel	Regular 2-star

What VISAR reveals

Worse than average | Average | Better than average | No data

All chart figures are percentages

	Age in years: 6–8	5–6	4–5	3–4	2–3	1–2
Registration Suffix:	FG	H	J	K	L	M*
Corroded front doors	5	5	3	1	0	0
Corroded rear doors	4	5	2	1	0	0
Corroded front wings	22	8	11	3	0	0
Corroded rear wings	19	8	6	2	0	0
Corroded front underwings	11	5	5	1	3	0
Corroded rear underwings	4	5	3	0	3	0
Corroded body sills	26	19	18	6	0	0
Corroded jacking points	22	15	16	3	0	0
Corroded floor	35	47	37	9	0	0
Corroded underbody frame members	23	26	13	2	0	0
Defective undersealing	39	53	28	4	6	8
Loose/misaligned driver's seat	0	0	3	4	0	0
Attend to engine mountings	2	0	0	0	0	0
Evidence of head gasket leaks	1	3	1	1	0	0
Noisy valve gear	21	18	18	21	24	17
Evidence of engine oil leaks	43	45	36	28	21	25
Attend to carburettor tuning	23	26	21	12	14	8
Evidence of fuel leaks	0	5	4	1	0	0
Final drive noise	8	0	3	0	5	0
Unsatisfactory gear change	14	7	11	4	3	0
Unsatisfactory auto gear change						
Clutch judder	0	0	2	0	0	0
Attend to front wheel bearings	8	10	10	3	0	0
Attend to steering box/rack	12	2	4	1	0	0
Attend to footbrake	16	10	10	8	4	0
Attend to handbrake	23	29	26	20	14	25
Corroded brake pipelines	16	26	27	3	2	8
Defective obligatory lights	74	55	27	11	6	25
Attend to charging system	0	2	0	4	2	0
Attend to horn	4	5	5	1	2	0

* See Engineers' Comments, p.142

RENAULT 4

From AA Road Test Report 160, 1968

Practicality plus comfort

Motorways and farm tracks are all the same to this lightweight French holdall – one minute it is a family four-seater, the next a two-seater estate car.

Although the engine develops only 28bhp, it provides adequate acceleration to keep pace with briskly moving traffic. It does not compare with a Mini Traveller or a Husky, but at least the top speed of 68mph keeps one on the safe side of the legal limit! Pressed hard, the engine sounds revvy and clattery; driven gently, it hums along very quietly and gives a consumption of up to 47mpg on 2-star petrol. The worst consumption the test car achieved was 35mpg on a hard day's track-testing. The clutch is relatively heavy to operate and the push-pull gear lever emerging from the fascia takes some getting used to, although with practice it works very well. First gear is sometimes reluctant to engage and its synchromesh is weak.

The Renault's smooth, supple ride is spoilt by excessive cornering roll and too much harshness from the radial-ply tyres. However, road holding is first-class.

There is a lot of understeer, but sudden release of the accelerator in mid-corner produces only mild tuck-in. Light, low-geared steering becomes heavier when parking or cornering hard. Beware of very strong spring-back action, which can whizz the wheel back through one's hands and make the car rock sideways. Straight-line stability is excellent and the turning circle is compact. The progressive, fade-free drum brakes are powerful enough to cope with the car's performance, but they are fairly heavy and rear-wheel locking occurs early on a really hard stop. The 'bent-rod' handbrake cannot manage a gradient steeper than 1-in-4.

One sits *in* rather than *on* the resilient front seats, which, while comfortable, prove too upright for some. Similarly, tall drivers could use more rearward adjustment. As it is, the high, commanding driving position is a satisfactory compromise with a pleasant steering wheel-to-pedal relationship. Big windows give good vision, but the interior mirror is poorly sited. The wipers are efficient but irritatingly noisy and park in the driver's sight-line of the wing mirror. The testers like the three handy column stalks, but the choke control is too remote, and the three fascia rocking switches are too closely grouped for easy location at night. The weird speedometer is very French, and very optimistic. Apart from avoiding dangerous seat-belt loops, rear entry is easy. Neither headroom nor kneeroom is generous for tall passengers, but the seat offers plenty of width.

Interior fittings are as basic as the decor. The simple heater provides front occupants with a good flow of warmth and it is fairly easy to achieve intermediate temperature settings. Simple fascia flaps admit plenty of fresh air but never seal completely when shut. There is plenty of interior storage space, but the boot is particularly impressive. Roomy enough for most purposes, it can be converted to a 47-cubic-foot load area simply by folding the back seat. Loading is easy, as the flat floor is at bumper height and accessible through the back doors.

The panelwork seems, and sounds, more flimsy than most, but it is protected by well-applied paintwork and a comprehensive underspray. The testers noticed rust on certain sharp edges and corners, however, and some of the chrome had deteriorated badly. Apart from distributor access, routine servicing is uncomplicated – a good thing, because engine and transmission oils should be changed every 3,000 and 6,000 miles respectively. There are no grease points.

Do not dismiss the Renault 4 because of its unorthodox appearance; it is a thoroughly practical and economical small car, offering exceptional comfort in its class, and it is very realistically priced.

Renault 6 TL

RENAULT 6
ENGINEERS' COMMENTS
Reputation for durability

Since the 6 has many design concepts and basic manufacturing processes in common with its slightly smaller brother, the 4, many of our comments apply to both. Until J registration, both had the same power unit: combined engine, gear box and final drive. Since then, two options have been available – the old 845cc engine and the 1108cc power unit common to the 8 and early models of the 10. Front and rear suspension on the 4 and 6 are basically alike, ingeniously using telescopic dampers in conjunction with long torsion bars. But whereas the 4's rack-and-pinion steering had a strong centralising spring up to H registration, the 6 never did. Thereafter both are the same.

Good body protection

Although the appearance and size of the two car ranges are distinctly different, both have a punt-platform floor to which the body is fixed by some 41 bolts on the 6, and only 19 on the 4. Being a later design the bodyshell of the 6 is better engineered to keep moisture, dust and slush out of important sections such as the passenger compartment and boot. The boot is remarkably free of traces of water ingress

and rust. Underwing and underbody protection has been improved by the factory application of a fairly thick bitumastic sound-deadening and anti-rust compound, which, however, was neither extensive enough nor fully effective until about J registration. Since K registration the treatment of some hollow closed sections has been added where complete anti-rust protection is otherwise difficult to achieve: a petroleum-based material is applied as a covering film, but the body sections thus sprayed need subsequent re-treatment every 2 years to remain fully effective.

Oil leaks

Oil leaks from the combined engine, gear box and final drive unit increase with age and mileage as the seals wear; fitting new valve rocker-cover and sump gaskets reduces oil seepage. Gear change quality depends on correct linkage adjustment. With age and usage this may need a franchised dealer's attention and possibly renewal of synchromesh.

Poor maintenance

Deterioration of driveshaft universal joints is usually associated with undue wear caused by the entry of grit and dust after a protective gaiter has been damaged. Its frequency of occurence is similar to that of the 4, amounting to about 6% of the J registration cars inspected. The 6's all-drum brakes are similar to the 4's. The braking system has been greatly improved with the introduction of disc brakes on the front on the larger-engined 6 – 1108cc – in October 1970, J registration. Because of lack of routine service maintenance, including renewal of brake linings and adjustment of free pedal play, about one quarter of the H registration cars inspected pulled to one side when brakes were tested.

Trouble-free suspension

A number of insecure attachments of anti-roll bars after only 2 or 3 years motoring was also found, together with front damper bush wear. But on the whole the front suspension is remarkably trouble-free – more so than the 4's. Tail and number plate lights suffer from accidental damage which often goes unnoticed.

Being a well-built motor car, the Renault 6 has rightly gained a reputation for durability – and not only in this country.

Specification of AA tested car

Make & model	RENAULT 6	See p. 148
Production years	1969–present	
Body alternatives	5-door Saloon	
Engine variants	845cc OHV, 1108cc OHV	

Data: AA test version	Renault 6-850 5-door Saloon. 1970 model
Engine	In-line 4-cyl, watercooled, front-mounted
	Bore 57.9mm, stroke 79.5mm, 845cc. Comp ratio 8:1
Fuel system	1 Solex carburettor. Mechanical pump.
	8.75-gallon tank
Transmission	4-speed & reverse, synchromesh on all forward gears. Front-wheel drive.
	Diaphragm-spring clutch, $6\frac{1}{4}$" diameter dry plate, cable operated.
Suspension front	Independent. Torsion bar, anti-roll bar, telescopic damper
Suspension rear	Independent. Trailing arm, torsion bar, telescopic damper
Steering	Rack & pinion. $3\frac{1}{4}$ turns between full locks. Turning circle 32 feet
Wheels	13" diameter, 4J rims
Tyres	135×13 radial-ply (Michelin ZX fitted)
Brakes	Hydraulic, drum front/drum rear
Dimensions (overall)	Length 12'7$\frac{1}{2}$" Width 5'0$\frac{1}{2}$" Height 4'11" Wheelbase 8'0"
	Ground clearance 5" Kerb weight (full tank) $14\frac{3}{4}$ cwts
Max speed (in gears)	First 23mph, second 41mph, third 61mph, top 72mph
Overdrive	Not applicable
Acceleration	0–60mph: 27.1 seconds; standing-$\frac{1}{4}$ mile: 23.3 seconds
Fuel consumption	overall: 38.1mpg
	steady 50mph: 45.4mpg (top gear)
	steady 70mph: 31.0mpg (top gear)
Fuel	Regular 2-star

What VISAR reveals

Legend: Worse than average · Average · Better than average · No data

All chart figures are percentages

	Age in years: 6–8	5–6	4–5	3–4	2–3	1–2
Registration Suffix:	FG	H	J	K	L	M
Corroded front doors		7	2	0	0	
Corroded rear doors		3	3	0	0	
Corroded front wings		7	3	0	0	
Corroded rear wings		4	2	0	0	
Corroded front underwings		4	0	0	0	
Corroded rear underwings		4	0	0	0	
Corroded body sills		7	8	6	0	
Corroded jacking points	N	8	6	1	0	
Corroded floor	O	10	9	2	7	
Corroded underbody frame members	–	6	2	0	0	
Defective undersealing	T	30	11	11	7	
Loose/misaligned driver's seat	C	0	0	0	0	
Attend to engine mountings	U	0	1	0	0	
Evidence of head gasket leaks	D	0	0	0	0	
Noisy valve gear	O	24	26	18	26	
Evidence of engine oil leaks	R	43	35	20	11	
Attend to carburettor tuning	P	21	26	20	11	
Evidence of fuel leaks		0	5	3	6	
Final drive noise	N	0	8	0	0	
Unsatisfactory gear change	–	25	4	0	5	
Unsatisfactory auto gear change						
Clutch judder	T	0	2	1	5	
Attend to front wheel bearings	O	0	7	4	0	
Attend to steering box/rack	N	3	7	3	0	
Attend to footbrake		22	7	4	5	
Attend to handbrake		19	13	9	5	
Corroded brake pipelines		7	22	4	5	
Defective obligatory lights		11	22	18	28	
Attend to charging system		3	4	1	0	
Attend to horn		0	2	1	0	

RENAULT 6-850

From AA Road Test Report 225, 1970

Improved, and worth the extra

The 6 has much in common with Renault's rustic 4 and is really, as the commercials would say, 'the new improved 4 – now with added styling'.

An extra 6bhp compensates for a weight increase of exactly 2cwt, and although top-gear acceleration shows little improvement, maximum speed is up by 4mph and the 0–60mph time is down by a whopping 8½ seconds. This means that it is now as fast as an 850 Mini. The engine is not quiet, but it is certainly game, very flexible, and economical. Fuel consumption ranges from 32mpg to 45mpg and 2-star petrol is adequate. One soon masters the unfamiliar action of the 'walking stick' gear lever emerging from the fascia, but some drivers found the spring loading a little heavy. First gear does not always engage first time and its synchromesh is weak. The other ratios are fine.

Smooth ride

Like the 4, the 6 has a smooth and supple ride, impaired only by excessive thumping from the radial tyres on cat's eyes and road joints. There is a lot of cornering roll, but road holding is first-class. Strong understeer increases with speed and the steering wheel must be gripped tightly in a fast corner or the rim recoils through the hands.

Although rather heavy when parking, the steering lightens when the car is on the move. Early rear-wheel locking spoils the smooth, fade-free drum brakes, but pedal pressures feel just right. The heavy handbrake will hold the car easily on a 1-in-3 hill.

Driver's seat

Individual front seats are an extra, proving splendidly resilient, with large handwheels setting the squabs to any desired angle. However, there is not much thigh support, and taller drivers would prefer to sit an inch or two further back. Legroom to the left is cramped too, and it is a pity that the accelerator is so remote from the brake.

Big windows give a panoramic outlook, but poor arcs swept by the noisy wipers leave a bad blind spot for the driver. The cleverly moulded fascia contains a curious-looking instrument display comprising an optimistic speedometer flanked by a voltmeter and fuel gauge. All dials are easy to see through the steering wheel. While the switches and column stalks are handily placed, the 'bent-rod' handbrake is remote under the fascia. The headlamps are excellent.

Easy rear entry

High sills and untidy seat belts are the only obstacles to easy rear entry. Tall passengers have very little headroom and their knees contact the front seats when right back, however. Fittings are minimal, but a heater is standard. It's far more effective than its controls would have one think, providing instant temperature changes and an even spread of warmth right across the front footwells. Fascia-top vents quietly provide fresh air at face level, but are not as versatile as the 'eyeball' type. In contrast to the large areas of untrimmed metal and exposed spot welds, the seats and door panels are nicely finished. Rubber covers the floor over thick underlays.

Spacious boot

The spacious boot can be made even bigger by hingeing down the back shelf to make room for tall objects, or by folding the back seat forward, thus more than doubling the load space. The area is fully lined and easy to load.

The panelwork appears flimsy in certain areas, but is generously painted, with a reasonable finish, and the underside is protected by an oil-based spray. Components requiring regular service are not particularly easy to get at; perseverance is required. There are no grease points.

Compared with the Renault 4, the 6 is a usefully improved car all round except where price is concerned, but £100 is not really too much extra to pay for the added refinement that this pert and practical vehicle has to offer.

Renault 12TL

RENAULT 12
ENGINEERS' COMMENTS
Well engineered and durable

If one were asked to single out a car of French manufacture which has demonstrated that a moderately sized package can appeal to a large number of motorists almost anywhere in Europe, be well engineered and yet sensibly priced and economical to run, the Renault 12 would be high on the final short list. Do the VISAR data support this? Does the car live up to its good reputation when one considers long-term ownership rather than a 2 to 3 year period between trade ins?

The 12 is of modern all-steel construction; the sheet metal flooring panels are deeply corrugated by giant presses to give strength and stiffness with minimum weight and similarly, vital castings are lightweight and stiffened by numerous ribs. In this respect, the 12 differs from a great number of its contemporaries. Such ribbed designs, incidentally, make the car much quieter. Further, improvements in welding, metal pre-treatment and paint technology have helped to produce a body structure which stands up well in worldwide comparison with the best.

Underbody protection

The underbody protection compound – bitumen and PVC – is factory-applied and effective, as is the injection into sills of anti-corrosion petroleum-based compounds. A small number of M registration cars were affected by dealer-buyer differences regarding satisfactory dealer preparation of cars still covered by the manufacturer's warranty. In such instances, a local re-application of underbody protection compound, probably damaged during work on the car, or attention to a flickering light or blown bulb due to a poor earth return would have mollified the owners and obviated complaints.

Bodyshell well protected

The bodyshell is well provided with elongated holes to allow effective metal cleansing and phosphating, a necessary anti-corrosion metal pre-treatment. The next step is the application of primer by the electrocoating process, which leaves the entire bodyshell – even the interior of the many hollow closed sections – generally well protected by a more or less uniform, thin paint film. Structural weakening with age and exposure to Britain's corrosively aggressive environment is therefore low. Even so, stones may occasionally pene-

149

trate the paint protection, opening the way for light surface rusting on body sills of early electrocoat-treated cars; Renaults, like other cars, suffered from initial proneness to stone-chip damage when this paint system was adopted. The early application of fine-brush paint touch-in, however, usually deals quite effectively with such damage. The rear brake pipelines on older cars tend to corrode superficially, but not to the point of danger.

Excellent power unit

Front-wheel driveshaft universal joints sometimes wear with age and high mileage, but this is not a common problem, and replacement, though not cheap, is easily effected. The engine and gear box are among the best front-wheel-drive power units; driver complaints of engine oil seepage and troublesome or jerky gear change are virtually non-existent. The alternators on some L registration cars exhibited solid-state rectifier failures, but this problem has since been satisfactorily resolved. The occasional collapse of the driver's seat frame due to age and heavy usage is a surprising feature. Seat replacement is not necessary, though. A small welding job will solve the problem. All in all, Renault have produced a soundly engineered and durable car. They have undoubtedly come a very long way since their Dauphine and Caravelle rear-engined, rear-wheel-drive concept days.

Specification of AA tested car

See p. 152

Make & model	RENAULT 12
Production years	1970–present
Body alternatives	4-door Saloon, 4-door Estate
Engine variants	1289cc OHV
Data: AA test version	Renault 12TL 4-door Saloon. 1971 model
Engine	In-line 4-cyl, watercooled, front-mounted
	Bore 73mm, stroke 77mm, 1289cc. Comp ratio 8.5:1
Fuel system	1 Solex single-choke carburettor. Mechanical pump.
	11-gallon tank
Transmission	4-speed & reverse, synchromesh on all forward
	gears. Front-wheel drive.
	Diaphragm-spring clutch, $6\frac{3}{4}$" diameter dry plate,
	cable operated
Suspension front	Independent. Wishbone, coil spring, anti-roll bar
Suspension rear	Rigid axle, radius arm, coil spring, telescopic damper
Steering	Rack & pinion. $3\frac{1}{2}$ turns between full locks.
	Turning circle 35 feet
Wheels	13" diameter, $4\frac{1}{2}$B rims
Tyres	145SR13 radial-ply (Michelin ZX fitted)
Brakes	Hydraulic, disc front/drum rear
Dimensions	Length 14'3" Width 5'4½" Height 4'8½" Wheelbase 8'0"
(overall)	Ground clearance 6" Kerb weight (full tank) 17 cwts
Max speed (in gears)	First 28mph, second 45mph, third 68mph, top 88mph
Overdrive	Not applicable
Acceleration	0–60mph: 15.6 seconds; standing-¼ mile: 20.3 seconds
Fuel consumption	overall: 34.5mpg
	steady 50mph: 40.7mpg (top gear)
	steady 70mph: 28.5mpg (top gear)
Fuel	Premium 4-star

What VISAR reveals

	Worse than average		Average
	Better than average		No data

	Age in years:	6–8	5–6	4–5	3–4	2–3	1–2
All chart figures are percentages	Registration Suffix:	FG	H	J	K	L	M
Corroded front doors				2	3	0	0
Corroded rear doors				3	2	0	0
Corroded front wings				6	5	0	0
Corroded rear wings				4	4	0	0
Corroded front underwings				0	2	0	0
Corroded rear underwings				0	1	0	0
Corroded body sills				9	10	3	4
Corroded jacking points		N		3	2	1	0
Corroded floor		O		0	0	0	0
Corroded underbody frame members		I		1	4	0	0
Defective undersealing		T		5	8	9	21
Loose/misaligned driver's seat		C		7	1	4	0
Attend to engine mountings		U		0	1	0	0
Evidence of head gasket leaks		D		0	1	0	0
Noisy valve gear		O		16	8	17	4
Evidence of engine oil leaks		R		12	17	7	0
Attend to carburettor tuning		P		23	13	17	35
Evidence of fuel leaks				3	0	0	0
Final drive noise		N		1	0	1	0
Unsatisfactory gear change		I		1	0	0	0
Unsatisfactory auto gear change							
Clutch judder		T		1	1	3	0
Attend to front wheel bearings		O		1	2	0	0
Attend to steering box/rack		N		4	6	3	0
Attend to footbrake				1	4	1	0
Attend to handbrake				8	4	11	4
Corroded brake pipelines				15	9	1	0
Defective obligatory lights				22	17	8	12
Attend to charging system				0	1	5	0
Attend to horn				1	1	0	0

RENAULT 12TL

From AA Road Test Reports 232, 1971
and 318, 1973

A civilised family saloon

Renault's trend-setting five-door 16 and clever 5 make this mid-range saloon look conventional. It is a surprisingly large 1300–longer overall than the 16 in fact. Nonetheless, performance is impressive against a stop-watch, leaving several domestic rivals in its shadow. However, it lacks the silkiness of the 16, and as speeds rise one is constantly made aware of the engine's 'baritone' proximity, with too many boom periods. Economy is good, giving over 40mpg when the car is driven quietly, although brutal driving will depress this figure to around 25mpg, so the 12 is more than usually sensitive to different techniques. The gear shift has an uncertain, obstructive action which made it less popular with the testers than the column or fascia shifts from Renault.

The clever suspension is designed to introduce just a hint of rear-wheel steering under power when the rear is lightly laden. The result is the same progressive understeer through every corner, with a delightfully languid tuck-in even if the accelerator is cut in panic. A full boot makes no difference either. The steering has lots of feel but is too heavy at the standard pressures. The testers discovered that equalising them cures this, and there are no unpleasant repercussions–thanks to the clever suspension.

If the fascia did not keep fretting, the 12's unflurried ride would allow passengers to think that the road was smooth all the time! It takes another French car of the same class to match this one's ride comfort. An earlier test car could only manage a 0.85g best stop in the wet, but the testers got a true 1.0g on a later car with a lead-sensitive rear valve that prevents premature skidding. The TL requires just the right amount of effort, and fade resistance is excellent. But bad rub and squeals still afflict Renaults, it seems. The newer centre handbrake works better, holding on a 1-in-3 gradient.

The driver unaccustomed to Renaults immediately appreciates two things: the deep glass areas to front and sides and the luxurious driving seat. A longer acquaintanceship reveals irritations, however, like an impeded rear view, noisy wipers, pedal pads that are too high, and a big step up between accelerator and brake. The fascia presentation is reasonable and minor controls are convenient. The heating and ventilation give a well-diffused spread rather than localised blasts.

The rear seat is designed to give something special by way of comfort, not so much in terms of legroom as in proper support. The high roof line contributes to this, making possible both an elegant entry and a higher cushion once inside. Front door locking arrangements are irritating–the doors can only be secured by key, and outside. The trim is a trifle austere, although there is carpeting on the rear shelf, which prevents things sliding about. The boot is very large but the floor steps up and rear-spring housings intrude on width.

Putty is daubed over some joins and the front grille flinches under the weight of a wash leather. However, the science of rust resistance involves more than making one's rust traps thick-skinned. The Tectyl underbody coating is a move in the right direction–if only Renault would apply it more conscientiously. Chrome plating is distinctly inferior to British standards. Routine servicing access is excellent, though; the 12 is better than any other Renault and one of the testers' front-wheel drive favourites in this respect. However, later cars no longer have a starting handle.

The 12 possesses a rare combination of virtues – roominess, liveliness, and thriftiness–and its blend of ride and handling cannot be matched by domestic offerings. Despite Renault's inability to quell unwanted noises, or their lack of interest in doing so, the 12 remains one of the most civilised family saloons at the price.

Renault 16

RENAULT 16
ENGINEERS' COMMENTS
A good car bettered

The 16 demonstrates that by changes in manufacturing technology and attention to detail it is possible to improve further a basically sound motor car. Originally, anti-corrosion treatment consisted of the conventional phosphating and slipper-dip immersion of the fabricated bodyshell in a bath containing a solvent-based primer paint. Then Renault, in common with most British and other European manufacturers, adopted the electrocoat priming process which Ford USA had patented and successfully applied several years previously. This method provides a thin, even coating of primer paint on those difficult-to-cover areas and closed sections which the conventional system all too often failed to protect adequately against eventual rusting.

On J registration cars, Renault experienced intercoat adhesion problems with early electrocoat paints: stones and grit bombarding the car panels chipped the paint away in places down to bare metal, causing localised rusting if not touched in quickly. Stone bombardment can be reduced by fitting mud flaps. On F/G registration cars painted by the older system, corrosion can be more extensive, particularly where owners have neglected to remove mud and dirt trapped behind front wing ledges and around the headlamp units. Rusting starts from the inside and slowly eats its way through paint and metal until it appears as paint blistering on the outside of panels. Salt spray and slush readily penetrate the body sills, eventually causing inside-out corrosion.

Corrosion on early 16s is usually confined to some rust 'bleeding' out of spot-welded joints and door outer-skin-panel lap joints. The long-term effectiveness of underwing protection compounds and boot sealants has been greatly improved starting with H registration. In addition, the injection of petroleum-based anti-rust compounds into body sills and other hollow sections started with K registration cars. So all in all the car has been consistently good in terms of corrosion resistance since that time.

While front brake lines are generally rust-free, brake pipelines to the rear, by virtue of their location, tend to suffer from some localised mud packing. Rear brake lines on cars over 5 years old should be checked for corrosion deterioration. A

◗

dealer inspection for wear in outer steering joints and front suspension swivel joints is also recommended on cars of this age. Dampers may need replacing too. Poor electrical connections are the most likely cause of horn malfunction and a defective charging system. Light units, particularly stop lights and front and rear side lights, tend to fill with water which has leaked past seals or cracked coloured plastic covers. Cylinder head leaks, a problem on some older cars, have been eliminated on subsequent builds by modification to gasket and engine block.

Carburettor spindle wear and an excessively high cold-engine idling speed due to the design of the automatic choke are minor problems on early engines. With high fuel costs it pays not only to replace age-deteriorated plastic fuel feed pipes in order to eliminate fuel leaks but also to have a re-conditioned carburettor fitted.

Automatic gear boxes, which are comparatively rare on UK-registered 16s, rarely give trouble, although dirty electrical connections can affect the smoothness of auto gear changes. Basically the gear box is of sturdy design. Occasional synchromesh wear, where encountered, is largely due to poor driving habits. Provided the gaiter covering the output shaft has not been damaged, thus allowing lubricant to escape and dirt to enter, the front wheel driveshaft – somewhat costly to replace – should not wear unduly over the years.

We found that an all-purpose car which readily doubles as an estate car will receive harsher treatment and more owner neglect than a city saloon. This is particularly noticeable on F/G registration cars. Generally speaking, this well-built car of strong unitary construction is a source of little trouble and provides its owners with a good deal of versatile motoring.

Specification of AA tested car

See p. 156

Make & model	RENAULT 16
Production years	1965–present
Body alternatives	4-door Saloon
Engine variants	1470cc OHV (1965–70)
	1565cc OHV (1968–present), 1647cc OHV (1974)
Data: AA test version	Renault 16TL, 4-door Saloon, 1565cc. 1972 model
Engine	In-line 4-cyl, watercooled, front-mounted
	Bore 77mm, stroke 84mm, 1565cc. Comp ratio 8.6:1
Fuel system	1 Weber twin-choke carburettor, manual choke.
	Mechanical pump. 11-gallon tank
Transmission	4-speed & reverse, synchromesh on all forward gears. Front-wheel drive.
	Diaphragm-spring clutch, 7.9″ diameter dry plate, cable operated
Suspension front	Independent. Coil spring, anti-roll bar, telescopic damper
Suspension rear	Independent. Torsion bar, anti-roll bar, telescopic damper
Steering	Rack & pinion. 4 turns between full locks.
	Turning circle 34 feet
Wheels	14″ diameter, 4½J rims
Tyres	145SR14 radial-ply (Michelin ZX fitted)
Brakes	Hydraulic, disc front/drum rear. Servo
Dimensions	Length 13′10½″ Width 5′5″ Height 4′9¼″ Wheelbase 8′8″
(overall)	Ground clearance 4½″ Kerb weight (full tank) 20 cwts
Max speed (in gears)	First 30mph, second 48mph, third 72mph, top 93mph
Overdrive	Not applicable
Acceleration	0–60mph: 15.1 seconds; standing-¼ mile: 20.7 seconds
Fuel consumption	overall: 29.5mpg
	steady 50mph: 38.8mpg (top gear)
	steady 70mph: 30.1mpg (top gear)
Fuel	Premium 4-star

What VISAR reveals

Legend: ▨ Worse than average | ▦ Average | ▧ Better than average | ☐ No data

All chart figures are percentages

	Age in years:	6–8	5–6	4–5	3–4	2–3	1–2
	Registration Suffix:	FG	H	J	K	L	M
Corroded front doors		5	1	12	4	2	4
Corroded rear doors		6	1	11	1	3	4
Corroded front wings		25	3	10	6	3	4
Corroded rear wings		1	1	12	6	1	4
Corroded front underwings		2	4	2	2	2	0
Corroded rear underwings		2	4	2	2	0	0
Corroded body sills		23	8	13	9	9	0
Corroded jacking points		5	4	7	5	2	0
Corroded floor		4	0	2	0	0	0
Corroded underbody frame members		15	5	6	3	4	0
Defective undersealing		30	7	7	7	9	0
Loose/misaligned driver's seat		0	2	5	1	0	0
Attend to engine mountings		3	2	0	0	0	0
Evidence of head gasket leaks		5	0	0	0	0	0
Noisy valve gear		24	18	15	15	15	0
Evidence of engine oil leaks		48	21	19	18	12	4
Attend to carburettor tuning		31	18	10	15	9	9
Evidence of fuel leaks		5	2	0	2	2	0
Final drive noise		5	4	2	0	0	0
Unsatisfactory gear change		0	0	0	0	0	0
Unsatisfactory auto gear change				0	0	8	0
Clutch judder		5	0	2	1	0	0
Attend to front wheel bearings		2	4	2	1	0	0
Attend to steering box/rack		5	0	2	0	0	4
Attend to footbrake		12	10	5	3	7	4
Attend to handbrake		7	12	17	8	9	4
Corroded brake pipelines		42	18	9	8	2	4
Defective obligatory lights		41	23	35	23	18	14
Attend to charging system		0	4	0	0	0	0
Attend to horn		5	10	0	0	2	0

RENAULT 16TL

From AA Road Test Report 291, 1972

Unobtrusive, comfortable holdall

The first of the five-door saloons, Renault's 16 has been around for the best part of a decade, yet its appeal seems unabated. The TL uses the TS engine size but lacks its special cylinder head and produces 16bhp less. Nonetheless, its silky tractability down to 22mph, with a brisk pull-away and a gay willingness to sail to 6,000rpm, certainly does not feel very second best. Starting is prompt and the tick-over smooth and remote, but hot starting requires some motor churning at times.

Precise gear change

The gear change is clean, precise, and on the column. Despite British prejudice against the idea, its linkage goes direct to the box and results are better than the Maxi's. The clutch is fine, but the wheels will patter on brisk starts in the wet. Fuel consumption is reasonable and quieter tactics – which fit the car's character –give up to 35mpg.

Up to 60mph, the 16 treats its occupants to a general sense of insulated well-being that is still unsurpassed. Part of the credit goes to its mechanical smoothness, and part to its sumptuous seating. Yet the car's suspension gives a restfulness few can match; long, soft springing and clever damping mop up the bumps with disdain. The absence of rattles helps here and contrasts strongly with the Maxi. There is some price to pay in its cornering behaviour, however, as it is prone to exaggerated roll. The weightiness that builds up in the steering makes it more difficult for the driver – strong fight shows itself when accelerating round tighter turns. Basic stability is very safe and dependable, nevertheless.

Normal check braking is fine, with a light pedal action. In an emergency, however, the front wheels skid prematurely. The handbrake location is very poor – down on the right, under the fascia – yet it can hold on a 1-in-3 gradient.

Entry is easy because of the 16's lofty build, although the check links are ineffective. The front seats' inviting sumptuousness is almost matched by that of the back, despite its fold-away versatility. There is a profusion of armrests and the vinyl upholstery feels cosy, with excellent legroom too, because the cushion is at a good height. Yet a range of permutations is available to convert the 16 into a van or an estate car where the dog or carrycot can ride behind the passengers, yet stay in touch. The tail-gate opens easily and shuts with a nudge, and there is an automatic light too, although the load sill is high. The heater gives unobtrusive warmth but there is uneven flow – the driver gets less than the passenger. The 'toast rack' screen rail vent suffers the same fault and its flow gets too warm and stuffy if the floor heat is increased a bit.

Messy fascia

Offset pedals and a messy fascia layout still spoil the TL. The speedometer is wildly optimistic too. There is some muffled tyre rumble, but the 16 feels exceptionally smooth and subdued to 60mph. After that, however, a drone blots its copy-book on the motorway and does not abate until illegal speeds are reached.

Well painted

Although some panels are thin and dent easily, the 16 is well painted and extra wax-based sealer is applied underneath, although it is skimpy in places. Chrome is of poor quality and it is a pity that stainless steel bumpers are no longer fitted. Home mechanics will find routine servicing within their means, although some items are tortuous to get at. The spare wheel and tools are conveniently located at the front end, away from the luggage.

With its fastidious comforts and remarkable adaptability, it is easy to appreciate the 16's unabated appeal. For those whose priority is 'softly, softly', it may still be considered without rival at the price.

Rover 2000

ROVER 2000/3500
ENGINEERS' COMMENTS
Yesterday's body, today's engine

When the Rover Company decided to depart from tradition and build a car with a strong base-unit structure forming a chassis skeleton, it appeared likely that this would become the future form of construction of quality, mass-produced cars, allowing for a very long model life with minimal cost penalty to the manufacturer. While this method of construction does make it easy to change body styling features, since all exterior panels are bolted to this skeleton – a fact which should benefit manufacturer, body repairer and owner alike – few of the advantages have been fully realised.

Little change in shape

Body shape has changed little over the past 11½ years. Apart from the natural evolution of specification updating and an increase in bore and output from the original 1978cc engine, only the introduction of the Borg Warner Automatic and the American-designed V-8 engine are significant developments. By having a fairly open fabricated skeleton base unit, metal pre-treatment – including phosphating solutions – can more readily reach many of the otherwise difficult-to-cover areas, and

it is thus possible to get good anti-corrosion protection.

There were initial problems with metallic paints, when factory-painted adjoining panels could appear to be of two different shades when in fact they were not. The visual appearance of solid colour and metallic paint has since been consistently good, however. The wing panels are painted as separate units before being attached to the body. This provides good paint coverage on all flanges, something which is difficult to achieve on many makes.

While corrosion deterioration over many years does not seriously reduce the strength of the base unit structure, long-term rust resistance of body panels is not a strong feature. Application of better paint technology since late K registration and of polyurethane covering on sills should improve the situation. Rusty door edges can be found where owners have failed to keep door drain holes clean and have skimped on the washing and drying of painted rear wheel arches and the door panels covering them. This applies mainly to older cars. The tops of front wings and their rear edge area close to the door pillar are potential rust danger areas. Rear wings in particular suffer from road grit abrasion and thus rust more readily at the bottom. Mud and dirt packing – hence rusting – can be minimised by the regular use of a pressure hose to clean the underwing areas.

Good underbody protection

Serious breakdown of the generally good factory-applied underbody anti-drumming, anti-rust compound is not found on cars within the VISAR age group, but the tendency towards cracking of the protective compound is already apparent on F/G registration cars where body sill and floor panels meet and rust creeps in. Check for any signs of cracking of the final drive mounting plate and for brake pipeline corrosion on older cars.

There are no inherent front wheel bearing, suspension or steering problems, but a franchised dealer's check on swivel-joint and steering-linkage wear and the steering damper is well worthwhile. Dynamic balancing of all five wheels is also recommended. The effect of age and lack of owner and garage attention is very marked on F/G registration cars.

Oil leaks from the final drive seals, though not sufficient to prejudice durability of the gearing and bearings, readily contaminate the rear discs. This results in uneven brake pull and poor handbrake performance. If in doubt, have seals and brake pads renewed. New cars could benefit from better dealer attention to such irritating minor points as setting of carburettor float levels and checking of fuel lines for leaks, as well as checking lights and horn for effective earth returns and power-assisted steering for proper belt drive tension and correct fluid level. A small cylinder head gasket problem on the V-8 engine has now been resolved.

Specification of AA tested car

See p. 160

Make & model	ROVER 2000/3500
Production years	1963–1973, (2200) 1973–present
Body alternatives	4-door Saloon
Engine variants	1978cc OHC (1963–73)
	2205cc OHC 1973–present, V-8 3528cc OHV 1968-present
Data: AA test version	Rover 2000 SC 4-door Saloon. 1970 model
Engine	In-line 4-cyl, watercooled, front-mounted
	Bore 85.5mm, stroke 85.5mm, 1978cc. Comp ratio 9:1
Fuel system	1 SU variable-jet carburettor. Mechanical pump. 12-gallon tank. 1.25-gallon reserve
Transmission	4-speed and reverse, synchromesh on all forward gears. Rear-wheel drive. Diaphragm-spring clutch, 8½" diameter dry plate, hydraulically operated
Suspension front	Independent. Coil spring, anti-roll bar, telescopic damper
Suspension rear	de Dion. Coil spring, Watts linkage, telescopic damper
Steering	Worm & roller. 3¾ turns between full locks. Turning circle 35 feet
Wheels	14" diameter, 5J rims
Tyres	165SR14 radial-ply (Dunlop SP41 fitted)
Brakes	Hydraulic, disc front/disc rear. Servo
Dimensions (overall)	Length 14'10½" Width 5'6" Height 4'7½" Wheelbase 8'7½" Ground clearance 5½" Kerb weight (full tank) 25¼ cwts
Max speed (in gears)	First 32mph, second 55mph, third 84mph, top 100mph
Overdrive	Not applicable
Acceleration	0–60mph: 14.1 seconds; standing-¼ mile: 19.7 seconds
Fuel consumption	overall: 25.0mpg
	steady 50mph: 35.6mpg (top gear)
	steady 70mph: 25.3mpg (top gear)
Fuel	Super Premium 5-star

What VISAR reveals

	Worse than average	Average
	Better than average	No data

| All chart figures are percentages | Age in years: | 6–8 | 5–6 | 4–5 | 3–4 | 2–3 | 1–2 |
	Registration Suffix:	FG	H	J	K	L	M
Corroded front doors		21	17	10	5	4	0
Corroded rear doors		22	18	12	5	3	2
Corroded front wings		23	16	9	8	2	0
Corroded rear wings		26	17	12	7	4	0
Corroded front underwings		11	5	1	2	0	0
Corroded rear underwings		7	4	0	2	0	0
Corroded body sills		36	23	13	9	9	2
Corroded jacking points		12	12	5	2	0	0
Corroded floor		13	2	0	0	0	0
Corroded underbody frame members		10	3	2	0	0	0
Defective undersealing		16	6	5	2	4	4
Loose/misaligned driver's seat		8	3	3	2	0	0
Attend to engine mountings		2	1	0	0	1	0
Evidence of head gasket leaks		4	2	1	1	1	7
Noisy valve gear		22	14	12	10	14	0
Evidence of engine oil leaks		38	32	29	23	20	12
Attend to carburettor tuning		39	35	30	26	30	16
Evidence of fuel leaks		5	4	4	3	1	8
Final drive noise		5	4	3	5	1	0
Unsatisfactory gear change		2	0	1	0	2	0
Unsatisfactory auto gear change		17	4	3	7	5	0
Clutch judder		2	3	3	6	4	0
Attend to front wheel bearings		12	10	14	12	13	8
Attend to steering box/rack		15	11	7	9	4	8
Attend to footbrake		15	11	7	8	2	0
Attend to handbrake		17	16	18	14	14	4
Corroded brake pipelines		21	6	6	2	1	0
Defective obligatory lights		19	27	11	9	3	12
Attend to charging system		2	3	5	2	2	0
Attend to horn		6	2	1	0	3	8

ROVER 2000 SC

From AA Road Test Report 222, 1970

Compact comfort with character

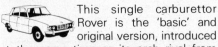 This single carburettor Rover is the 'basic' and original version, introduced at the same time as its arch rival from Triumph. The SC, TC and the 3500 V-8 have between them provided any buyer with all that he could wish for in performance, economy, and refinement. Unfortunately, one won't find all three attributes in one model! The SC achieves better flexibility and temperament than the faster TC but frequent gear changes are required to induce sufficient acceleration. On the open road it gets more into its stride, cruising past the legal limit without stress. Fuel consumption is most acceptable for so solid a car, although the TC was even better. The SC should manage 28mpg with restraint. The fuel reserve 'on tap' is a boon. The stubby gear shift feels notchy and obstructive but its action, like the clutch, is a great improvement on early cars.

The Rover's expensive suspension design made it a trendsetter in ride and handling in its heyday. Half a decade later it is still at the front of the field. Admittedly, there is pronounced roll and weighty steering, but no one could fail to be impressed by its sure-footed, balanced cornering behaviour, with gentle nose drift on a trailing throttle and equally orderly tail drift under power. Some rivals can now match the handling but few can attain its unflurried ride. Even at low speed, ridges are absorbed well, while minor bumps and hollows tend to pass unnoticed.

Although the brake servo comes in too suddenly and the pedal angle seems all wrong, the brakes do inspire confidence.

They performed a genuine 1.0g stop and were imperturbable in a fade test. The powerful handbrake lever is too close to the elbow to give a good working angle, however.

The ribbon speedometer and adjacent telltales all look and work well, and the shaped minor controls – with two column stalks – are sensibly spaced. The angle of the large steering wheel is adjustable and the driving seat responds well to initial adjustment, giving unobtrusive support and massive legroom if required. The friction clamp squab adjusters are excellent too. The screen rail is too high but the rear view is good. In fact, shallow windows are the only dating feature inside, and the blending of contemporary and traditional materials is both tasteful and practical. The seats are designed to take four in comfort and rear legroom is really better than it looks on casual inspection.

Boot space is definitely cramped with the spare wheel in situ, although interior oddments space is quite good. There are quieter 2-litre cars than the Rover for engine busyness, and, tyre roar intrudes at times and fittings fret over rough roads.

Heating and ventilation are both excellent – the strip vents give controllable flow where it is needed and the temperature of floor heat is instantly variable. Safety has been a major theme of the 2000 and it deserved the AA Gold Medal Award.

Panels are bolted on over a skeleton base, making panel corrosion less serious. Underbody protection looks good. In most respects, finish seems to confirm that 'a Rover is still a Rover'.

Second thoughts – 4 years later

Now 10 years old, the Rover's appearance has recently been smartened up in an attempt to disguise its ageing looks. There is no masking its limited boot and rear seat space, but the 2200 engine revision has given it a new lease of life, making it *smoother as well as quicker. The ride has been compromised by trying to make the cornering tauter, but the gear change is altered for the better. The 2200 remains a highly individualistic offering whose shortcomings are easier to forgive because of its strength of character.*

Rover 3½ litre Saloon

ROVER 3½ LITRE
ENGINEERS' COMMENTS
Air of solid dependability

The 3½ litre Rover is the last of a long line of old-image Rover cars exhibiting some of the features of a make long associated with an English tradition of solid dependability, sturdiness, class, fairly plush interior and, of course, weight. The sense of quiet motoring in style is underlined by the sound-deadening and anti-rust underbody protection compound which holds off corrosion on both front and rear underwings. Rust spotting of under-carpet floor panels – a feature of some of the older 3½ litre cars – is due to moisture ingress past door seals into the passenger compartment; this occurs when the rubber decays with age.

The car retains an ageless, glossy appearance of solid workmanship. During the last 18 months of its production run, the painting process was changed from the traditional solvent-based slipper dip primer to water-based electrocoat primer. This did not improve the resistance of the glossy top coat of paint to chipping by stones and road grit, however. Although the body does not have exaggerated curvatures – which means there is only an average risk of stone-chip damage to sills and lower

sections of door panels – the more brittle paint system of the electrocoat bodies tends to suffer some paint chipping and, as a consequence, odd surface rust spots. The chipping, where present, is generally slight, and spotting-in by fine-brush application of touch-in paint is usually all that is required to hide and rectify rust spots if caught in time.

Solid though the 3½ litre undoubtedly is in comparison with more recent cars, rusting emanating from the inside of such panels as door skins and body sills can nonetheless eventually perforate the metal on old and neglected cars. The freeing of all drain holes, which easily become clogged with leaves and dirt, should extend life considerably, however. The draining of trapped moisture will allow air to circulate and dry out the hollow sections.

The VISAR data suggest that above-average care in avoiding accidents is exercised by those who regularly drive older 3½ litre Rovers. This is not too surprising, since many of them are chauffeur-driven. Chauffeurs do not make the best engine tuners, however, as the twin SU carburettor installation is all too frequently poorly set in terms of balanced output per carburettor and idling speed adjustment. Periodic valve clearance rectification, not the simplest of tasks, should not be overlooked if quiet engine operation and fuel economy are one's aim.

Simple routine service maintenance, such as tightening of joints, can keep oil leaks down to a very low level. Adjustment of linkages and idling speed will ensure clean, crisp automatic gear selection; also, the runners of the heavy seats benefit from occasional re-tightening. Wear in suspension and steering joints is linked with age and mileage, and can easily be mistaken for wheel bearing wear. It is all too easy to strain the power-assistance pump by ignoring the pained noise it emits if steering is on full lock when parking in confined spaces. Attention to the steering system, where necessary, should concentrate first of all on curing leaks in the power-assistance pump and high-pressure hoses and on replacing worn or slipping belts to the hydraulic pump. Damaged gaiters of the rack-and-pinion steering should be replaced.

Even old solid Rovers suffer age deterioration, demonstrated by corrosion of brake lines, occasional poor earth contacts in the electric horn circuit and sloppiness in auto gear selection linkages. Those who value the air of diplomatic status and distinction and who do not mind the car's thirst for fuel may well find an old Rover 3½ litre a distinctly attractive car.

Specification of AA tested car

See p. 164

Make & model	ROVER 3½ LITRE
Production years	1967–1973
Body alternatives	4-door Saloon, 4-door fixed head Coupé
Engine variants	V-8 3528cc OHV
Data: AA test version	3½ litre 4-door Saloon Automatic. 1970 model
Engine	V8-cyl, watercooled, front-mounted
	Bore 88.9mm, stroke 71.1mm, 3528cc. Comp ratio 10.5:1
Fuel system	2 SU variable-jet carburettors. Mechanical
	pump. 14-gallon tank. 1.5-gallon reserve
Transmission	Automatic. Torque converter. 3-speed & reverse.
	Rear-wheel drive.
Suspension front	Independent. Torsion bar, telescopic damper, anti-roll bar
Suspension rear	Leaf-sprung live axle, telescopic damper
Steering	Worm & peg, power-assisted. 2.5 turns between full
	locks. Turning circle 40 feet
Wheels	15″ diameter. Rostyle, 5J rims
Tyres	670H×15 cross-ply (Dunlop RS5 fitted)
Brakes	Hydraulic, disc front/drum rear. Servo
Dimensions	Length 15′7″ Width 5′10½″ Height 5′1″ Wheelbase 9′2½″
(overall)	Ground clearance 6¾″ Kerb weight (full tank) 32 cwts
Max speed (in gears)	Low 50mph, intermediate 82mph, top 105mph
Overdrive	Not applicable
Acceleration	0–60mph: 11.9 seconds; standing-¼ mile: 18.5 seconds
Fuel consumption	overall: 17.8mpg
	steady 50mph: 25.6mpg (top gear)
	steady 70mph: 21.5mpg (top gear)
Fuel	Super Premium 5-star

What VISAR reveals

| | Worse than average | Average | Better than average | No data |

All chart figures are percentages

	Age in years: 6–8	5–6	4–5	3–4	2–3	1–2
Registration Suffix:	FG	H	J	K	L	M
Corroded front doors	9	7	16	11		
Corroded rear doors	11	10	13	11		
Corroded front wings	12	4	5	6		
Corroded rear wings	21	13	3	6		
Corroded front underwings	4	0	0	0		
Corroded rear underwings	3	0	0	0		
Corroded body sills	19	21	11	6		
Corroded jacking points	12	0	0	0	N	
Corroded floor	12	0	0	0	O	
Corroded underbody frame members	9	0	0	0	I	
Defective undersealing	23	4	0	12	T	
Loose/misaligned driver's seat	8	4	0	12	C	
Attend to engine mountings	0	0	0	0	U	
Evidence of head gasket leaks	0	0	0	0	D	
Noisy valve gear	18	4	0	11	O	
Evidence of engine oil leaks	31	27	33	13	R	
Attend to carburettor tuning	40	16	37	33	P	
Evidence of fuel leaks	6	0	5	6		
Final drive noise	0	4	6	0	F	
Unsatisfactory gear change					O	
Unsatisfactory auto gear change	20	4	13	0		
Clutch judder	3	0	0	0	T	
Attend to front wheel bearings	24	8	27	6	U	
Attend to steering box/rack	14	21	21	0	O	
Attend to footbrake	6	4	18	6		
Attend to handbrake	9	9	16	6		
Corroded brake pipelines	25	4	5	0		
Defective obligatory lights	11	4	23	12		
Attend to charging system	0	0	0	0		
Attend to horn	14	4	5	0		

ROVER 3½ LITRE SALOON

From AA Road Test Report 207, 1970

Dated looks, but good value

The news that a Rover was to be powered by a trans-atlantic V-8 must have been greeted with dismay by many British traditionalists. A pleasant surprise awaits those who sample the 3½ however, for in this case Anglo-American relations have never been better.

Smooth, silent power and an instant surge of acceleration typify the GM-based V-8 engine, and what a difference in performance compared with the old straight six! The 0–60mph time is cut by 5½ seconds and several seconds are lopped off the in-gear acceleration times; top speed was disappointing, however, at only 5mph better. Performance apart, it's the big lazy engine's silky refinement that is particularly impressive. Only when pressed does fan howl become insistent. Gentle driving gives 23mpg but in stop-start conditions 18mpg is normal. The 3½'s automatic transmission is 'de-tuned' to change earlier and thus more smoothly than, say, the 3500's more sporting shift-points, and it works well. It is only on full-throttle changes that a slightly undignified jerk can be felt.

Decorum needed on bends

Compared with its formidable (and cheaper) stablemate, the Jaguar XJ6, the Rover is far less tolerant of poor road surfaces, jerking and bumping uncouthly over deformities in a begrudging way. Fast corners create marked roll and a build-up of strong understeer, and the car feels wallowy through S-bends. Driven with appropriate decorum, all is well. But when it comes to bend-swinging, the Rover is a lady who doesn't like to be hurried. The dreadful power steering makes things worse. It's vague, over-light, and completely devoid of feel. The tyres object strongly to traversing raised white lines and the turning circle is a cumbersome 39½ feet. The 'all-or-nothing' over-servoed brakes provide a disappointing crash stop, and the 'umbrella' handbrake can barely

hold the car on a 1-in-3 hill.

Many seat adjustments

The large, luxurious and leather-covered front seats glide, rise, and recline, and thanks to ample support, long journeys create no twinges. One tends to slither on their slippery surface, though. With so many seat adjustments, most drivers are happy behind the wheel, but the dated body design is reflected by the lofty scuttle and the shallow windscreen and side windows. The wiper sweeps are poor too. Clear all-round vision is certainly not this model's strong point, nor is the muddled and fussy switchgear which takes a long time for the newcomer to learn.

Rear passengers sit in thick armchairs surrounded by walnut, good taste, and an air of gracious living, while pile carpet cushions their tread. Apart from the usual amenities, there are four individual courtesy lights, picnic tables, a tool-tray, door pockets, and a trinket box in the back seat, but safety equipment doesn't match the 2000's. Separate heating systems for both front and rear passengers ensure that warmth is properly circulated throughout the interior. There are no fresh-air fascia vents, but air-inlet flaps cool one's feet. Boot loading is easy, and there is room for a fair amount of luggage in the short, but deep illuminated depths.

Built-in thoroughness

Flawless paintwork and attention to detail, bumper mounts, jacking points, and so on reflect the thoroughness built in to the Rover from the start. Apart from the fuel pump, which is awkward to get at under the bonnet, servicing is quite straightforward.

Rover disprove the cliché that 'they don't build 'em like that anymore', but there is no doubt that the 3½ is now dated, both in looks and in specification. Nevertheless, it deserves all its success. The car is good value, a good investment, and there is still something irresistible about the feel and smell of real wood and leather.

Saab 96 V4

SAAB 95/96
ENGINEERS' COMMENTS
Improved resistance to rust

The Saab has only a limited UK following – mainly one of motoring enthusiasts – and thus comparatively small numbers have been inspected. Nonetheless, definite trends emerge.

The car is well protected against the corrosively aggressive environment by metal treatment, paint, factory-applied underbody compounds and latterly by injection of anti-corrosion material into hollow closed sections. This 'inner box' treatment must be repeated every other year to remain fully effective. The result of all this protection is an absence of corrosion on vital structures, underwings, underbody frame members and jacking points, underfloor pressings and boot.

Old Saabs rust

However, this has not always been the case. It must be remembered that the car started life way back in 1960, when it had a three-cylinder, two-stroke engine and a three-speed gear box plus driver-controlled free wheel. A good deal of the anti-corrosion measures currently taken by the factory were not applied at that time and old Saabs consequently rust badly. Door bottoms rust from the inside outwards and

underwing areas – on which it proved difficult to obtain a good durable covering by rubber-type protection compounds – also suffer. Front suspension spring and damper mount areas in the engine compartment innerwing structure and the rear suspension mount areas in the boot platform are also prone to rust.

Body protection

Premature rusting out from the inside of closed and semi-closed body sections was once such a prominent feature even of Swedish-built cars that something drastic had to be done to prolong their useful life. Sven Laurin of the Swedish Motoring Organisation (Motormännens Riksförbund) invented the process of injecting petroleum-based anti-corrosion compounds into difficult-to-protect hollow sections. This is referred to the world over as the M-L method. Hot dip galvanising of certain sheet steel sections has also been employed in an attempt to extend structural life.

Underbody compound test

The punt-type platform underbody of the integral steel body is common to both the Saab 96 and its estate version, the Saab 95.

Surprisingly, corrosion was found on floor sections of some 1968-built models, particularly where the mounts of the rear suspension radius links are attached. On pre-1968 cars the rate of deterioration due to corrosion is markedly higher than average, affecting such items as hollow sills and their junction to the floor. All this clearly demonstrates that the underbody compound can loose its effectiveness in time and needs thorough inspection on a hoist. By tapping it with the blunt end of a screwdriver, the potential buyer can determine whether the underbody protection is still securely attached to the steel panels. If any hollow-sounding areas are found, it will be necessary to strip back to metal and remove all traces of rust. The underbody should then be re-painted with a factory-approved primer paint before a fairly thick underbody protection compound is re-applied. A cracked and loosely attached compound, far from protecting the underbody against corrosion, accelerates the process.

Engine noise

The Ford V-4 is not a particularly quiet design, but attention to valve gear tappet clearance can lower the general noise level. A few final drive units tend to emit a typical hypoid whine but they are very robust and generally trouble-free. It is only after several years of motoring that the problem of excessive play in driveshaft inner universal joints arises.

The Saab, in common with other cars, experiences some water ingress past ageing seals which leads to premature rear and side light failures. Slight engine oil leaks and carburettor tuning faults are readily cured by routine service attention. Clutch action can be on the fierce side, but is a feature of this robust and mechanically reliable rally-tested car.

Specification of AA tested car

See p. 168

Make & model	SAAB 95/96
Production years	1963–present
Body alternatives	2-door Saloon (96), 2-door Estate (95)
Engine variants	3-cyl two-stroke 841cc (1961–67)
	V4 OHV 1498cc (1967–present)
Data: AA test version	Saab 96 841cc Saloon. 1963 model
Engine	3-cyl, 2 stroke, watercooled, front-mounted
	Bore 70mm, stroke 72.9mm, 841cc. Comp ratio 7.3:1
Fuel system	1 Solex single-choke carburettor. Electric pump. 8.8-gallon tank
Transmission	3-speed & reverse, synchromesh on 2nd and top gears. (4-speed option) Front-wheel drive
	Diaphragm-spring clutch, 7″ diameter dry plate, mechanically operated
Suspension front	Independent. Coil spring, anti-roll bar, damper
Suspension rear	Rigid axle, coil spring, telescopic damper
Steering	Rack & pinion. $2\frac{1}{4}$ turns between full locks. Turning circle 35 feet
Wheels	15″ diameter, 4J rims
Tyres	5.20×15 cross-ply
Brakes	Hydraulic, drum front/drum rear
Dimensions (overall)	Length 13′2″ Width 5′2″ Height 4′10″ Wheelbase 8′2″ Ground clearance $7\frac{1}{4}$″ Kerb weight (full tank) 16 cwts
Max speed (in gears)	First 22mph, second 56mph, top 75mph
Overdrive	Not applicable. Free-wheel fitted
Acceleration	0–60mph: 21.0 seconds; standing-$\frac{1}{4}$ mile: 23.6 seconds
Fuel consumption	overall: 32.8mpg Oil 1017mpg
	steady 50mph: 48.8mpg (top gear)
	steady 70mph: 35.0mpg (top gear)
Fuel	Regular petrol/oil mixture

What VISAR reveals

Legend: ■ Worse than average ▦ Average ▨ Better than average □ No data

All chart figures are percentages

	Age in years:	6–8	5–6	4–5	3–4	2–3	1–2
	Registration Suffix:	FG	H	J	K	L	M
Corroded front doors				7	4	0	
Corroded rear doors							
Corroded front wings				2	4	5	
Corroded rear wings				4	6	0	
Corroded front underwings				0	0	0	
Corroded rear underwings				0	0	0	
Corroded body sills				7	8	6	
Corroded jacking points				0	0	0	
Corroded floor				6	0	0	
Corroded underbody frame members				0	0	0	
Defective undersealing				3	0	12	
Loose/misaligned driver's seat				3	0	5	
Attend to engine mountings				0	0	0	
Evidence of head gasket leaks				0	0	0	
Noisy valve gear				13	24	21	
Evidence of engine oil leaks				20	19	32	
Attend to carburettor tuning				10	26	32	
Evidence of fuel leaks				0	0	0	
Final drive noise				3	0	16	
Unsatisfactory gear change				0	0	0	
Unsatisfactory auto gear change							
Clutch judder				0	8	11	
Attend to front wheel bearings				0	4	0	
Attend to steering box/rack				0	0	0	
Attend to footbrake				6	7	11	
Attend to handbrake				13	7	11	
Corroded brake pipelines				4	4	0	
Defective obligatory lights				31	0	5	
Attend to charging system				3	0	0	
Attend to horn				3	4	0	

SAAB 96 V-4

From AA Road Test Report 344, 1974

Staid but sturdy Swede

 The Saab 96 is an unusual car in many ways. In an age when many models are depressingly similar beneath the marketing tinsel, Saab continue to go their own way, concentrating on solid, unexciting values. The 96 tends to display its shortcomings early and reveal its virtue subsequently. Performance was undoubtedly given a shot in the arm when the old two-stroke gave place to the current V-4 engine. By current 1500 standards, however, acceleration is unremarkable. The quarrelsome column gear shift is not much encouragement either. Many will consider its remarkable economy handsome compensation, however. The test car nearly reached 40mpg in a traffic-free jaunt and the 35mpg recorded at a steady 70mph is incredibly good. Such economy is not difficult because the 96 feels cumbersome to drive briskly. Wearisome steering requires a strong pair of wrists and the car is heavy when parking too. Yet the 96's rally-bred ancestry was revealed in track-tests, when it didn't put a wheel wrong in a tight corner. Ride comfort is absorbent when driven in a leisurely fashion, but the car lurches and becomes restive if pressed too hard. The brakes have a professional feel. They are not so strongly servoed as most, yet give better control and progression. There is some fade, but they are immune to water and the unusual handbrake works well.

Comfortable driving position

Even the driving position feels old-fashioned. Nevertheless, its dining-chair posture is comfortable and it is easy to get in and out without stooping. The seat has insufficient lateral support and inset pedals are tiring. A Saab eccentricity is a lock on the gear lever instead of one on the steering column. Shallow windows do not interfere with the view as much as one would expect.

Deceptively roomy

The Saab is deceptively roomy. Apart from the limitations of two doors, it is comfortable enough for a full-sized family. A flat floor and high cushion allow reasonable legroom, even though it appears otherwise. Headroom is restricted, however, and door-locking arrangements are most confusing. Luggage space is both commodious and versatile; with the seat folded down, the boot can extend its load length forward, an eminently sensible provision which other saloon car makers should adopt. Despite its age, the 96 has stayed abreast of modern developments in heating and ventilation. In addition, it has advanced one or two ideas of its own, like the heated driving seat. Injury prevention features are very up-to-date too, with good structural protection.

Bowls along beautifully

There are one or two periods of resonance, especially at 65mph, but by 70mph all is subdued and the Saab bowls along beautifully most of the time, with just a trace of V-4 imbalance lurking in the background. Along country lanes, away from steep hills, the free wheel proves an asset, giving clutch-less gear changes on the move.

Body construction reassuring

For the longer term owner, standards of body construction and especially under body protection look most reassuring. Saab obviously know just what they are about and one couldn't wish for a better anti-rust treatment at the price. The paintwork on the test car appeared rather brittle, however, and this may prove one of those unusual models that will deteriorate less underneath than on top. Although there are easier cars to work on, routine maintenance can be tackled by home handymen; parts tend to be expensive, though.

The 96 has more to offer than casual consideration suggests. Although it is no bundle of fun, it will offer any owner-driver a practical investment that will do a good job and prove surprisingly economical.

Simca 1100 GLS

SIMCA 1100
ENGINEERS' COMMENTS
You can depend on it

It is not only cars built in Britain which have to deal with ever increasing severity of body corrosion caused by heavier salting of roads during winter and industrial pollution. French motorists, who for many years cared little about the appearance of their cars, have become conscious of rust-induced disfiguration and reduction in strength of car bodies. It is therefore not surprising that one sees a marked change in paint technology and internal section anti-corrosion treatment in the popular Simca 1100 range. Simca, in common with most French manufacturers and Daf of Holland, employ iron-phosphating rather than zinc-phosphating metal pre-treatment. Though providing less of an anti-corrosion barrier, it is cheaper, easier to control during application and tends to give better paint adhesion when panels are subjected to stone chipping or denting stemming from minor collisions.

Rust resistance
Simca first managed to produce reasonably rust-resistant cars when they changed over to electrocoat primer painting in 1972. Nonetheless, although the front and rear underwings are given a fairly thick bitumastic-type sound-deadening and anti-rust treatment during manufacture, the joints of front and rear wing to wheel arch tend all too often to corrode. Drain holes in doors easily become clogged and must be freed to allow trapped moisture to escape and air to circulate freely.

Body protection
Cars made since late 1972 are less likely to suffer comparatively early from rust 'bleeding' out of door seams or from inside-out corrosion of such hollow sections as the lower door, body sill, and underbody frame members and rusting from behind headlight units. The factory sprays a thin petroleum-based anti-corrosion compound into those areas most vulnerable to rusting. This treatment provides additional protection for about 2 years; the owner must then have it re-applied. On pre-L registration cars, stone chipping can lead initially to a sprinkling of rust which, if not attended to promptly, may be followed by more widespread paint lifting on front valances, front and rear wing stiffening flanges and the lower 3 to 4 inches of door panels. On early models, mud deposits and salt spray

can easily produce slow rusting away of the jacking points and of front-wing top panels, and eventual holing of the sill near its junction with the rear wing.

Lively engine

The lively five-main-bearing engine, capable of sustained high-speed operation, seeps oil significantly less than most and then only from the sump. Because it has a very traditional valve gear layout, with cam followers, long push rods and rockers, however, it is apt to be relatively noisy and will need regular tappet adjustment.

Poor location of the brake pipes accounts for the high incidence of corrosion.

The adjustment of the rear drum brakes (by two snail cams) is somewhat unusual and thus best left to a franchised dealer. The poor brake performance revealed by VISAR indicates that this adjustment was beyond the capability of some DIY enthusiasts.

Steering joint wear

The anti-roll bar bushes and lower swivel joints wear with age and mileage. In fact, some steering joint wear was found in cars only 2 to 3 years old. Water ingress in early production cars accounts for premature bulb failure and poor headlight performance. Number plate and rear lights and horns should be checked for a good earth return. Franchised dealers should be able to adjust the gear change linkages for more positive, clean action. The seat adjustment mechanism tends to work loose, yet tightening of the runners is not a difficult task, although it is sometimes forgotten in dealer preparation. Many amateur mechanics have found it is not easy to adjust the carburettor, and consequently have left it badly tuned.

Despite minor disappointments, the Simca 1100 has gained a reputation for sturdy dependability. It is a reputation well earned.

Specification of AA tested car

See p. 172

Make & model	SIMCA 1100
Production years	1967–present
Body alternatives	2- & 4-door Saloon, 2- & 4-door Estate
Engine variants	1118cc OHV
Data: AA test version	1100GLS 4-door Saloon. 1973 model
Engine	In-line 4-cyl, transverse, watercooled, front-mounted Bore 74mm, stroke 65mm, 1118cc. Comp ratio 9.6:1
Fuel system	1 Solex single-choke carburettor. Mechanical pump. 9.2-gallon tank. Low-level warning
Transmission	4-speed & reverse, synchromesh on all forward gears. Front-wheel drive. Diaphragm-spring clutch, 7.1" diameter dry plate, hydraulically operated
Suspension front	Independent. Torsion bar, wishbones, anti-roll bar
Suspension rear	Independent. Torsion bar, trailing arm
Steering	Rack & pinion. $3\frac{1}{4}$ turns between full locks. Turning circle $35\frac{1}{2}$ feet
Wheels	13" diameter. $4\frac{1}{2}$J rims
Tyres	145SR13 radial-ply (Dunlop radials fitted)
Brakes	Hydraulic, disc front/drum rear. Servo
Dimensions (overall)	Length 12'11$\frac{1}{4}$" Width 5'2$\frac{1}{4}$" Height 4'9$\frac{1}{2}$" Wheelbase 8'3$\frac{1}{4}$" Ground clearance 5" Kerb weight (full tank) 18$\frac{1}{4}$ cwts
Max speed (in gears)	First 27mph, second 46mph, third 69mph, top 85mph
Overdrive	Not applicable
Acceleration	0–60mph: 16.5 seconds; standing-$\frac{1}{4}$ mile: 19.7 seconds
Fuel consumption	overall: 33.2mpg steady 50mph: 40.4mpg (top gear) steady 70mph: 27.2mpg (top gear)
Fuel	Premium 4-star

What VISAR reveals

Worse than average | Average | Better than average | No data

All chart figures are percentages						
Age in years:	6–8	5–6	4–5	3–4	2–3	1–2
Registration Suffix:	FG	H	J	K	L	M
Corroded front doors			15	6	5	0
Corroded rear doors			12	11	4	0
Corroded front wings			15	11	3	0
Corroded rear wings			26	8	6	0
Corroded front underwings			12	0	3	0
Corroded rear underwings			12	0	0	0
Corroded body sills			16	13	8	0
Corroded jacking points			12	6	5	0
Corroded floor			0	0	5	0
Corroded underbody frame members			17	6	6	0
Defective undersealing			36	7	6	7
Loose/misaligned driver's seat			7	8	6	7
Attend to engine mountings			2	0	1	0
Evidence of head gasket leaks			0	0	0	0
Noisy valve gear			37	47	33	33
Evidence of engine oil leaks			16	17	11	7
Attend to carburettor tuning			42	22	28	33
Evidence of fuel leaks			4	0	0	0
Final drive noise			4	3	0	7
Unsatisfactory gear change			0	11	9	7
Unsatisfactory auto gear change						
Clutch judder			0	0	3	0
Attend to front wheel bearings			0	2	0	0
Attend to steering box/rack			4	0	3	0
Attend to footbrake			16	14	5	14
Attend to handbrake			8	14	21	28
Corroded brake pipelines			24	19	17	0
Defective obligatory lights			29	29	12	0
Attend to charging system			4	2	0	0
Attend to horn			0	9	3	0

SIMCA 1100 GLS

From AA Road Test Report 298, 1973

Best of Chrysler's Europe

There are two ways of evolving a competitive family car. One is to concentrate on well-tried, dated principles with good window dressing to disguise the staidness. The other is to go all out for technical merit and space utilisation, even if maintenance thereby proves more complicated. Chrylser played it both ways in their Avenger and Simca 1100.

In its standard tune, this 1118cc five-door car more than matches the acceleration of orthodox 1300 rivals, although it is an engine that tolerates rather than relishes trundling around. The car gets into its stride as its torque peak approaches and feels unburstable at high revs. Between 40mph and 70mph it scurries along sweetly in top, although the fussy chatter never completely disappears and road noise is prominent at times. The complicated gear linkage is spongy and imprecise and spoils an otherwise nice box. The clutch feels much smoother than on most transverse-engined cars, however. Fuel consumption is merely a good average; 40mpg was achieved on the test car only with the utmost restraint, whereas earlier versions seemed to be able to manage this in typical use. Tank range is modest but there is a low-level warning.

Extremely smooth ride

The Simca's level ride is excellent and the unknowing passenger may in fact attribute this to the smoothness of the road rather than the virtue of the car. With such a smoothy as the Simca around, one begins to wonder why any car less comfortable should be tolerated. Perhaps its proneness to cornering roll provides a partial answer. Enthusiastic driving also induces some steering fight, but in other respects, cornering remains impeccable. Besides lots of grip and steering 'feel', there is gentle 'tuck-in' when acceleration is cut. While previously the brakes required too much pedal effort, the additional brake servo on the latest cars is too fierce.

Comfortable driving position

A 5 foot 8 inch tester declared the driving position the most comfortable he had encountered on any smaller car. Actually, the GLS seat is better than the plusher Special's. Tall drivers find legroom restricted, but the pedals and wheel relate well to the seat and all-round vision is excellent, even in rain. Wiper arcs and minor controls could be better, but the headlamps are splendid, with instant beam trimmers to compensate for big loads. The instrument layout contains a surfeit of nooks and crannies and it neither looks nor works well.

The seat cushion automatically slides forward as the backrest is tipped, transforming a comfortable rear seat into a load platform 63 inches long. The rigid rear canopy removes to convert saloon into estate car when space is needed and although legroom is a bit tight, rear-seat support is excellent. There is good luggage space too. Unlike some heating systems that need a computer programmer to fathom their complexities, the Simca's slides speak for themselves and results are good too. The simple 'penny vent' fresh-air outlets on the fascia prove surprisingly effective and controllable.

Scanty undersealing

Panelwork is thin and the bitumastic sealer underneath is too scanty to be taken seriously. There are nasty crevices at the backs of front wings, and body trim strips seem none too secure. The under-bonnet layout looks daunting at first but removal of the air filter clears the way considerably to routine service items. The rearward tilt of the block helps too. Standard under-bonnet equipment is impressive.

The Simca 1100 GLS is an excellent family car thanks to its comfort and adaptability, yet it offers real enthusiast appeal at the same time. It is probably Chrysler's most competitive European model and remains on the testers' very short list of small cars they would be happy to live with.

Triumph Herald

TRIUMPH HERALD 13/60

ENGINEERS' COMMENTS

Corrosion threatens chassis

Features which set the Herald apart from cars of the 1960s are its tight turning circle and a chassis frame to which the body is bolted.

A light, oily film coating coming from the engine breather is quite common. This film attacks the rubber-bonded engine mountings, which need replacing from time to time. They are relatively cheap items, however.

Good paintwork

The paintwork is generally good, proving the durability of a good slipper-dip priming process and an alkyd top coat. Underwing areas stand up well, despite the absence of factory-applied underbody protective coatings, but body sills and jacking points do not. The latter tend to fill with mud and slush, rotting away from the chassis itself. The eventual holing of the body sill does not matter. It is not a structurally important member but is nonetheless exposed to external grit bombardment and the penetration of salt-laden spray into its hollow interior. The sill interior often lacks an effective paint barrier which would resist the early onset of general rusting from the inside out.

The chassis itself, after a number of years, eventually fails due to weakening by corrosion of vital frame members. This corrosion starts as surface rust on front and rear chassis outriggers and outer rail, the chassis extensions beneath the boot floor and the main chassis frame adjacent to the differential unit. The presence of this separate chassis frame makes the application of an underbody protection compound difficult.

Test for corrosion

The chassis frame and underfloor pressings can be tested for serious corrosion by putting a screwdriver against them. If the point or blade penetrates when pushed with moderate hand pressure, costly repairs may be necessary. Hardening and cracking with age of sealants is common in F to J registration cars, leading to water leakage into the boot and eventual rusting. While the brake pipes are not prone to serious corrosion within the time span of the survey, care should be taken with the front brake flexible hoses. They occasionally foul the tyres when the wheels are on extreme lock if the tension springs which locate them correctly have corroded away.

➡️

The drain holes in the door frame and the sill easily become blocked with dirt and leaves. For moisture to escape and air to circulate, they must be unblocked. Some water ingress past quarter-lights and seals is common in older cars.

Seat adjustment and runners need routine tightening if the tip-up seats are not to float about and rattle after a time.

Lowering the float level, fitting new plastic tubing and tightening fuel pipe unions will cure most fuel system leaks. Clutch judder may be due to slight leaks in the slave cylinder, which will affect the quality of clutch engagement. Adjustment can take care of handbrake cable stretch, although cables fray quite easily and thus need to be replaced from time to time. The horn earth return relies on a wire passing through the steering column; this wire may break after a few years' service. An alternative separate earth may be a better solution, particularly on older models. Rainwater gets into light units after a time and corrodes the earth return of the bulb holder.

A noisy back axle does not imply imminent failure of the gears. The unit should be inspected for excessive oil leaks and wear on the propeller and driveshaft universal joints. Replacement of these parts, if done in good time, is relatively inexpensive.

The convolutions of the gaiter on the rack and pinion steering occasionally get damaged, allowing lubricant to escape and dirt to enter. In addition, the clamps holding the steering rack to the frame tend to slacken with age and oil contamination. Among those components prone to wear are the track rod ends and the front suspension lower swivel joints. When checking the car for excessive front wheel bearing play, attention should be given to the above-mentioned items in particular.

Specification of AA tested car

See p. 176

Make & model	TRIUMPH HERALD
Production years	1960–1971
Body alternatives	2-door Saloon, Convertible, Estate
Engine variants	948cc OHV (1960–63) 1147cc OHV "1200" (1961–70) 1147cc OHV 12/50 (1965–67) 1296cc Ohv 13/60 (1967–71)
Data: AA test version	Herald 13/60, 2-door Saloon. 1968 model
Engine	In-line 4-cyl, watercooled, front-mounted Bore 73.7mm, stroke 76.0mm, 1296cc. Comp ratio 8.5:1
Fuel system	1 Stromberg variable-jet carburettor. Mechanical pump. 6.5-gallon tank. 0.75-gallon reserve
Transmission	4-speed & reverse, synchromesh on three higher gears. Rear-wheel drive. Diaphragm-spring clutch, 6½ diameter dry plate, hydraulically operated
Suspension front	Independent. Coil spring, wishbone, anti-roll bar, damper
Suspension rear	Independent. Swing axle, transverse leaf-spring, damper
Steering	Rack & pinion. 3½ turns between full locks. Turning circle 26 feet
Wheels	13" diameter, 3½J rims
Tyres	5.20×13 cross-ply (Dunlop C41 fitted)
Brakes	Hydraulic, disc front/drum rear
Dimensions (overall)	Length 12'9" Width 5'0" Height 4'4" Wheelbase 7'8" Ground clearance 6¾" Kerb weight (full tank) 16¾ cwts
Max speed (in gears)	First 24mph, second 44mph, third 68mph, top 82mph
Overdrive	Not applicable
Acceleration	0–60mph: 19.9 seconds; standing-¼ mile: 21.1 seconds
Fuel consumption	overall: 33.4mpg steady 50mph: 39.2mpg (top gear) steady 70mph: 27.0mpg (top gear)
Fuel	Premium 4-star

What VISAR reveals

Worse than average | Average | Better than average | No data

All chart figures are percentages

Age in years:	6–8	5–6	4–5	3–4	2–3	1–2
Registration Suffix:	FG	H	J	K	L	M
Corroded front doors	13	14	4			
Corroded rear doors						
Corroded front wings	19	8	5			
Corroded rear wings	17	9	6			
Corroded front underwings	9	4	1			
Corroded rear underwings	7	4	2			
Corroded body sills	36	42	20			
Corroded jacking points	7	11	0		N	N
Corroded floor	7	3	2		O	O
Corroded underbody frame members	37	36	19		I	I
Defective undersealing	56	31	20		T	T
Loose/misaligned driver's seat	14	8	2		C	C
Attend to engine mountings	23	17	19		U	U
Evidence of head gasket leaks	9	0	1		D	D
Noisy valve gear	9	15	2		O	O
Evidence of engine oil leaks	46	35	27		R	R
Attend to carburettor tuning	31	34	34		P	P
Evidence of fuel leaks	5	8	1			
Final drive noise	13	8	3		F	F
Unsatisfactory gear change	7	0	3		O	O
Unsatisfactory auto gear change						
Clutch judder	10	8	9		T	T
Attend to front wheel bearings	19	11	26		U	U
Attend to steering box/rack	13	7	1		O	O
Attend to footbrake	14	13	4			
Attend to handbrake	25	25	20			
Corroded brake pipelines	22	10	3			
Defective obligatory lights	15	24	9			
Attend to charging system	5	5	1			
Attend to horn	21	18	10			

(The vertical text running down the L and M columns reads "NO PRODUCT ... PRODUCT ...")

TRIUMPH HERALD 13/60

From AA Road Test Report 167, 1968

Trendsetter – 10 years later

When it was introduced in 1959 (the same time as the Mini) the Herald was acclaimed as a trendsetter. The 1300 engine is a derivative of the old Standard 8 original, still with three main bearings. Idling tends to be jittery and the accelerator feels heavy, yet once under way it is flexible and untroubled by harder work. The gear shift is precise but stiff in action, with a peculiar slant to the left into top. There is no synchromesh on first but the clutch action is smooth and light.

Fuel consumption is reasonable by 1300 standards; 35mpg should be possible touring and the tank's limited range is offset by a positive reserve controlled by a tap in the boot.

Initial cornering feels roll-free and alert, and the light, precise steering makes it easy to place the car accurately. Pressed harder, however, swing axle rear suspension makes the rear go completely awry. Lifting off the accelerator in panic only makes things worse and calls for really dexterous use of the steering. Less adventurous drivers may not contemplate pressing the Herald to that point, but an unexpectedly sharp bend on a wet night can be enough to start this train of events. Ride is firm but not choppy, and bigger individual bumps are dealt with well. The pleasant steering also offers that morale-boosting turning circle – the testers measured it at 24½ feet – enabling the Herald to occupy parking spots where others have given up and driven on. It's not kind to the tyre treads, though. The brakes are medium weight, but respond well right up to an excellent 0.97g best. The handbrake is heavy and unpleasant.

It's a squeeze to get in the front, let alone the back, and there is nothing to pull to shut the door properly. The 13/60 uses an improved driving seat with more shaping and lateral support; spanner work provides all sorts of adjustment permutations. The wheel has reach variation too. The only snag is that the inset wheel and offset pedals leave the driver hinged somewhere in the middle. Vision is superb all round. The engine makes itself heard between 50-60mph but is less intrusive thereafter. Wind noise and tyre thump and roar are more of an irritation and there are quieter 1300s than the Herald, although it compares favourably with other contemporary small saloons. Rear passengers know it's a small saloon – legroom is very cramped, knees splayed against the front seats. Wood veneers and good carpet with pleasant vinyl on the seats provide a congenial setting, but equipment items are sparse. There is a dearth of armrests, rear windows are fixed and there is no roof lamp. The water valve heater is difficult to regulate, with no foot warmth to the rear and no face-level ventilation to offset the stuffiness that develops at the front. Oddments stowage is sparse, too, although an unusually roomy boot offsets this complaint.

Despite the publicity emphasis on safety, the car's fascia seems unyielding, doors are not burst-proof and the front seats have no anti-tip restraints. The test car's chassis was showing rust already and the testers disliked the frameless door windows and general paint finish. Of course, a separate chassis with bolted-on panels takes some of the worry out of rusting and enables superb mechanical access on the Herald because the whole front tilts forward.

Despite its shortcomings, the 13/60 is compact and manoeuvrable without being too mini or unorthodox.

Second thoughts – 6 years later

Six years later the Herald looks very cramped and sparse when it comes to creature comforts and safety features. That swing-axle suspension deserved the criticism levelled at it, yet the concept of the up-market small car is still as popular as ever.

Triumph Spitfire IV

TRIUMPH SPITFIRE
ENGINEERS' COMMENTS
Middle-of-the-roadster

This popular, low-priced two-seater sports car shares many of its mechanical features with the Triumph Herald and the more powerful Vitesse, among them a cruciform backbone chassis of open channel section. Although this may become covered in flake rust and progressively diminish in strength with age, it is of sufficient thickness not to be weakened to the danger point by corrosion during the car's normal service life. On the other hand, the outrigger frame members to which the rubber-bushed rear suspension torque-reaction radius arms are attached can become structurally weakened if mud, road salt, and flake rust are not removed. The soundness of the metal of the box section and the weld should be verified periodically as a matter of routine maintenance, particularly on older cars.

With the changeover from slipper dip to electrocoat paint protection in 1970, some initial disappointment was experienced; later models have proved much more resistant to stone damage, however. Cars produced during the H and J registration period suffered an intercoat adhesion problem in the paint system; if stones chip through the top coat, corrosion may start to creep beneath it, lifting off the colour coat in blisters. The remedy is a procedure recommended in our comments on the MGB.

Mud packing under the wings is a common feature of this car. If left undisturbed, it will eventually cause more than just surface corrosion around the headlamps.

Small amounts of oil leak past the timing cover seal, rocker cover gasket, engine breather, oil-filler tube and sump gasket. It tends to get flung around the engine compartment, softening the rubber-bonded flexible engine mounts, which need periodic replacement.

Attention to the two SU carburettors should entail no more than balancing them, adjusting their idling speed and topping up the dashpot on each one. Where fuel leaks do occur, they are usually easy to cure by checking fuel unions and float level settings.

Clutch judder, a feature of earlier models, has virtually disappeared with clutch detail design changes. In any case, it pays to check for leaks on the slave cylinder of the hydraulically-operated clutch.

The steering rack is generally reliable, but occasionally works loose on the chassis or develops oil leakage past torn or deteriorated gaiters. Corrosion of the exposed working parts of the disc brakes is not uncommon on older models, nor is disc scoring if routine braking system maintenance, including periodic replacement of pads, is not carried out. The handbrake cables tend to stretch and fray with age. Hardening of body seals and water ingress past windscreen and tonneau are the result of deterioration with age; consequently, water accumulates beneath floor coverings, causing surface rusting once the paint cover has broken down. In contrast to the Herald 13/60, its derivative the Triumph Vitesse, and the Midget/Sprite, the boot of the Spitfire is remarkably watertight. The car does not receive an underbody protection compound at the factory, and where applied by dealers it is all too often poor, failing to penetrate behind the chassis frame or channel section or into critical zones around the attachment points of the final drive to the frame proper.

While wear in the differential unit may cause gradually increasing final drive noise, the unit itself rarely fails. However, the noise is more likely to be the result of worn needle bearings or partially loosened universal joints on the driveshafts or the propeller shaft. Proper investigation entails the use of a hoist and should be left to a qualified mechanic who is familiar with the model.

Specification of AA tested car

Make & model	TRIUMPH SPITFIRE	See p. 180
Production years	1962–present	
Body alternatives	Sports 2-door, soft-top or hard-top	
Engine variants	1147cc OHV (1962–67)	
	1296cc OHV (1967–present)	
Data: AA test version	Spitfire Mk 3, Sports 2-door, detachable hard-top. 1969 model	
Engine	In-line 4-cyl, watercooled, front-mounted	
	Bore 73.7mm, stroke 76.0mm, 1296cc. Comp ratio 9:1	
Fuel system	2 SU carburettors. Mechanical pump.	
	8.25-gallon tank	
Transmission	4-speed & reverse, synchromesh on three higher gears. Rear-wheel drive.	
	Diaphragm-spring clutch, $6\frac{1}{2}''$ diameter dry plate, hydraulically operated	
Suspension front	Independent. Wishbones, coil spring, anti-roll bar, damper	
Suspension rear	Independent. Swing axle, transverse leaf spring, damper	
Steering	Rack & pinion. $3\frac{1}{4}$ turns between full locks.	
	Turning circle 25 feet	
Wheels	13″ diameter, $4\frac{1}{2}$J rims, wire spoke wheels	
Tyres	145×13 radial-ply (Dunlop SP68 fitted)	
Brakes	Hydraulic, disc front/drum rear	
Dimensions	Length 12′3″ Width 4′9″ Height $3'11\frac{1}{2}''$ Wheelbase 6′11″	
(overall)	Ground clearance 5″ Kerb weight (full tank) $15\frac{1}{4}$ cwts	
Max speed (in gears)	First 27mph, second 47mph, third 73mph, top 93mph	
Overdrive	Optional. O/D 3rd 91mph, O/D top 90mph	
Acceleration	0–60mph: 14.2 seconds; standing-$\frac{1}{4}$ mile: 19.3 seconds	
Fuel consumption	overall: 32.1mpg	
	steady 50mph: 42.7mpg (top gear) 46.6mpg (O/D Top)	
	steady 70mph: 35.6mpg (top gear) 38.1mpg (O/D Top)	
Fuel	Premium 4-star	

What VISAR reveals

Legend:
- Worse than average
- Average
- Better than average
- No data

All chart figures are percentages

	Age in years: 6–8	5–6	4–5	3–4	2–3	1–2
Registration Suffix:	FG	H	J	K	L	M
Corroded front doors	14	13	8	2	5	
Corroded rear doors						
Corroded front wings	10	11	7	0	1	
Corroded rear wings	10	10	11	0	1	
Corroded front underwings	9	0	0	2	2	
Corroded rear underwings	12	0	0	0	2	
Corroded body sills	20	33	21	5	6	
Corroded jacking points	7	5	5	0	0	
Corroded floor	19	10	4	0	4	
Corroded underbody frame members	16	9	13	3	5	
Defective undersealing	44	7	23	14	10	
Loose/misaligned driver's seat	5	10	11	0	5	
Attend to engine mountings	21	21	10	12	3	
Evidence of head gasket leaks	0	3	5	4	2	
Noisy valve gear	4	16	4	25	39	
Evidence of engine oil leaks	45	40	36	29	35	
Attend to carburettor tuning	64	68	52	47	47	
Evidence of fuel leaks	2	10	4	2	2	
Final drive noise	38	21	2	21	15	
Unsatisfactory gear change	5	4	7	6	2	
Unsatisfactory auto gear change						
Clutch judder	10	7	2	2	0	
Attend to front wheel bearings	28	20	23	28	21	
Attend to steering box/rack	6	14	17	6	4	
Attend to footbrake	23	19	0	8	7	
Attend to handbrake	27	27	19	12	13	
Corroded brake pipelines	18	10	13	4	4	
Defective obligatory lights	25	19	16	16	10	
Attend to charging system	0	10	0	0	0	
Attend to horn	30	35	13	12	7	

TRIUMPH SPITFIRE Mk III (Overdrive)

Fun car with style

 The Spitfire has now reached the Mark III stage and in its basic form is a competitively priced car. A detachable hard-top and what the testers consider essential extras raise the price by nearly £150, however.

The 1300 TC engine cuts the previous smaller-engined Mark II's 0–60mph time by 3½ seconds and increases the maximum speed by 5mph. These are useful improvements, although the stretched power unit sounds and feels at the limit of its development. It is neither particularly smooth nor quiet, but will pull without objection from 20mph in top. Optional extra overdrive helps considerably in quelling the engine's busyness at speed and offers a choice of six ratios. It also engages very smoothly. Similarly, the gear change has an easy action but there is no synchromesh on first gear. Because of the 'quick' clutch and sudden throttle, brisk take-offs can be jerky. With restraint, up to 37mpg is possible, but those heavy on the throttle can expect about 28mpg. The quickly-filled tank is small and its contents can be heard sploshing about noisily.

While the ride is good on most major roads, it deteriorates noticeably on poorer surfaces, resulting in unpleasant thuds and thumps together with some scuttle shake. Radial-ply tyres (another extra) give plenty of grip, but be warned that the Spitfire's handling leaves much to be desired. Oversteer increases strongly with speed and if the throttle is closed suddenly in mid-bend the tail swings wide in dramatic fashion, especially in the wet; fun for the informed, but alarming for the inexperienced. Higher geared steering would make it possible to correct a tail swing more quickly, but no complaints about the remarkably small turning circle. Stability at

speed could be more reassuring, but the unservoed brakes prove excellent.

The seats, though too upright, hold one firmly in place and slide back far enough to accomodate comfortably a tall driver. The offset pedals cause aches after only a short spell of town driving , however. It's easy to see all four corners of the car despite hard-top blindspots but the interior mirror is too small. Single-speed wipers clear a wide area of the shallow screen. The fascia is attractive but impractical, as the speedometer is masked by the driver's left hand. The other dials can be seen at a glance and minor switchgear can be reached without much effort.

Plenty of leg length and a substantial grab handle keep passengers happy while their security is aided by anti-burst door locks, safety-locked seats and comfortable seat belts. Surprisingly, one pays £15 extra for the heater, which is a bit steep considering the crudity of its temperature regulation and distribution, the stuffiness at head level and the absence of fresh-air ventilation. Six bolts hold the hard-top in place, providing a snug interior spoilt only by draughts and wind noise via the frameless wind-up windows. The boot will take a suitcase and a couple of holdalls, and extra small luggage can travel on the carpeted deck behind the seats.

The paintwork is very impressive, but the underside is not protected by sealing compound. Engine accessibility is marvellous. Servicing is due every 6,000 miles and there are six grease points, but with such ease of maintenance, who cares? The Triumph's tool-kit is measly, however.

Those who liked earlier Spitfires will like the Mark III even more. Essentially a fun car, it has sufficient style, performance and road holding, but the testers wish its handling on the limit was more predictable.

Second thoughts–4 years later

A wider rear track and modified rear suspension were introduced in 1973, with the result that the former tendency towards violent oversteer on lift-off is eliminated.

Triumph Stag

TRIUMPH STAG
ENGINEERS' COMMENTS

Improvements undercut criticism

This sports car has only a limited following in the UK and consequently comparatively few have been inspected. The size of the sample is not large enough to allow one to draw firm conclusions, although certain trends are discernible.

Improved quality control

Since the car was launched, significant improvements in engineering specifications, paint technology and quality control have been introduced by Triumph and it is therefore not surprising that adverse criticism has decreased. In our experience it is a mistake to assume that a car with a comparatively high price tag and a limited market is superior in every respect to a volume-produced one. It takes nearly as much money, engineering resources and time to modify, improve and test a specialist car as it does, say, a BLMC 1800 or Ford Cortina.

Some engine defects

Early Stags can suffer from engine defects such as overheating and subsequent cylinder head gasket failure. The introduction of modified cylinder head gaskets in late M registration cars has eliminated this problem, however. The twin Strombergs,

of course, need more balancing than a single carburettor and early Strombergs had some diaphragm problems. While new diaphragms can be fitted, it is preferable to have re-conditioned exchange units fitted by a dealer. Fuel leaks are relatively easy to deal with; first check for and tighten any loose pipe unions. Also, the seal on the fuel tank unit may be poor. A Triumph dealer can fit an improved one, however, at modest cost.

Excessive valve gear noise can be minimised by valve-clearance adjustment, but this is not the easiest of operations and can be fairly expensive if carried out by a garage. The level of the noise transmitted from the final drive depends on the amount and type of rubber insulation between the back axle support bracket and the underfloor, since most of the noise is transmitted via the underfloor itself. One need not fear that the gears or final drive are about to collapse, as it is more likely that the needle bearings in the propeller shaft or short driveshafts need attention. This task is best left to a garage.

Steering, braking checks

The power-assisted steering tends to

develop oil leaks with age and mileage. The steering rack should be checked for tears in the rubber gaiters, where loss of oil and ingress of dirt can, if unchecked, result in premature wear. The footbrake and handbrake need regular maintenance to keep travel to an acceptable level, particularly if the car is habitually driven in a sporty manner. The gear change, much improved on later models, could at times be considered heavy and cumbersome for a sports car.

Engine oil leaks

Engine oil leaks can be minimised by attention to sump, rocker cover, and timing gear gaskets but it should be pointed out that the engine is not an oil user; these leaks take the form of weeps rather than constant drips.

Body protection

The application of an underbody protection compound at the factory is not standard and the underside of cars which have not had some such protective coating applied subsequently by a garage or specialist firm tend to suffer from stone and grit bombardment, which cuts right through the paint, giving rust a start. J registration cars are affected by the shortcomings of the early electrocoat primer paints which most manufacturers experienced when they switched from the conventional slipper-dip process. The intercoat adhesion of the multi-layer paint system proved inadequate on panels exposed to a high rate of stone and grit bombardment such as the reinforcing flange of the wing pressings, the underwings themselves, and the lower portion of doors and body sills.

Most of the corrosion which occurs on the Stag, including that of the brake lines, is of the surface type and in none of the cars inspected did it impair the structural or safety aspects of the car.

Specification of AA tested car

See p. 184

Make & model	TRIUMPH STAG
Production years	1970–present
Body alternatives	Convertible 2-door, 2+2 seater. Detachable hard-top option
Engine variants	2997cc OHC
Data: AA test version	Convertible 2+2 seater, 2-door soft/hard-top. 1971 model
Engine	V8-cyl, watercooled, front-mounted
	Bore 86mm, stroke 64.5mm, 2997cc. Comp ratio 9.25:1
Fuel system	2 Stromberg variable-jet carburettors. Electric pump. 14-gallon tank. Low-level warning
Transmission	4-speed & reverse, synchromesh on all forward gears. Rear-wheel drive. Overdrive. Diaphragm-spring clutch, 9″ diameter dry plate, hydraulically operated
Suspension front	Independent. MacPherson strut, anti-roll bar
Suspension rear	Independent. Semi-trailing arms, coil spring, damper
Steering	Rack & pinion. Power-assisted. 3 turns between full locks. Turning circle $33\frac{1}{4}$ feet
Wheels	14″ diameter, 5J rims
Tyres	185HR14 radial-ply (Michelin XAS fitted)
Brakes	Hydraulic, dual circuit, disc front/drum rear. Servo
Dimensions (overall)	Length 14′5$\frac{3}{4}$″ Width 5′3$\frac{1}{2}$″ Height 4′1$\frac{1}{2}$″ Wheelbase 8′4″ Ground clearance 4″ Kerb weight (full tank) 25$\frac{3}{4}$ cwts
Max speed (in gears)	First 39mph, second 56mph, third 85mph, top 115mph
Overdrive	O/D 3rd 104mph, O/D top 118mph
Acceleration	0–60mph: 10.2 seconds; standing-$\frac{1}{4}$ mile: 17.8 seconds
Fuel consumption	overall: 22.5mpg
	steady 50mph: 30.8mpg (top gear)
	steady 70mph: 24.7mpg (top gear)
Fuel	Premium 4-star

What VISAR reveals

Legend: Worse than average | Average | Better than average | No data

All chart figures are percentages

	Age in years: 6–8	5–6	4–5	3–4	2–3	1–2
Registration Suffix:	FG	H	J	K	L	M
Corroded front doors			14	2	4	
Corroded rear doors						
Corroded front wings			14	0	0	
Corroded rear wings			24	2	0	
Corroded front underwings			7	0	0	
Corroded rear underwings			7	0	0	
Corroded body sills			7	4	0	
Corroded jacking points			8	0	0	
Corroded floor			0	4	0	
Corroded underbody frame members			13	8	0	
Defective undersealing			11	33	6	
Loose/misaligned driver's seat			6	0	4	
Attend to engine mountings			0	0	0	
Evidence of head gasket leaks			14	4	0	
Noisy valve gear			33	6	4	
Evidence of engine oil leaks			27	38	37	
Attend to carburettor tuning			38	25	21	
Evidence of fuel leaks			6	3	4	
Final drive noise			0	7	8	
Unsatisfactory gear change			9	0	0	
Unsatisfactory auto gear change						
Clutch judder			0	0	4	
Attend to front wheel bearings			32	35	33	
Attend to steering box/rack			25	25	12	
Attend to footbrake			0	18	4	
Attend to handbrake			21	34	19	
Corroded brake pipelines			20	7	4	
Defective obligatory lights			21	4	23	
Attend to charging system			0	0	0	
Attend to horn			0	0	4	

(Left margin vertical text: NON-PRODUCTION ... NON-PRODUCTION)

TRIUMPH STAG

From AA Road Test Report 273, 1972

Luxurious yet disappointing GT

 The luxury grand tourer should combine sporting attributes of powerful performance and responsive handling with a high degree of refinement, a good control layout and plenty of comfort. Space and fuel economy are less important factors. How does the Stag measure up?

The V-8 power unit is, in effect, two Dolomite engines craftily stuck together. Power output is modest, however, and the Stag is no flyweight either, so performance is not shattering. The 2.5 PI or Capri 3000 can keep up with it but there is something special about the way a V-8 achieves it all with such refinement.

A grand tourer should not have to keep stopping for petrol; this one manages about 275 miles on a tankful. Consumption is reasonable and varies little with different usage. Overdrive was fitted to the test car, which helped. The gear shift works with easy precision and feels less obstructive now. There was some clutch judder on the test car, however, and drive-line vibration spoilt high-speed progress.

The steering and handling were a great disappointment. The steering is so light and uninformative that when the test car hit a patch of ice, the wheel retained its unalterable feel. Admittedly the car zooms round familiar bends with good grip and hardly any roll and makes light work of town driving. However, there is marked tuck-in if one cuts the power half way round a fast corner, followed by a distinct twitch – when one subsequently changes gear – as the drive shaft splines sort themselves out. It holds a good line on a windy motorway, though. Bump reaction is reasonably resilient but not quite in its price class. One doesn't expect a boulevard ride but even so its jittery agitation can be slightly disappointing. Normal use of the brakes reveals good progressive response but they look less impressive under duress. The control layout is generally good. Based on the 2000, the offset pedals are a nuisance. The seat is comfortable, though, with lots of adjustment, including a height setting. Similarly, the steering column tilts and telescopes to suit the driver. The minor controls, which are well placed, include those stalks and turret lighting control so successful on all Triumphs. The neat fascia includes supplementary instruments but some people may like more. The segmented warning light cluster completes the layout, with telltales for items like choke, handbrake and low fuel.

The hard-top is completely draught-free and the soft-top almost so, with electric door-glasses and face-level ventilation too. With the hood down but door-glasses up, front occupants can get their fresh air without frost-bite but it gets breezy in the back. The rear seat, with its scooped-out cushion and intruding tunnel, forces passengers into a contortionist position. The Capri looks positively spacious by comparison. Interior appointment is very civilised; there are seven interior lights and lots of oddments space. The carpeted boot is shallow, however. Perhaps it is best viewed as a civilised two-seater with two luggage areas. The hard top's removal is a two-man job, but one can manage the hood.

As an open car, the roll-over T-bar is the Stag's most conspicuous injury prevention feature, but the model is thoughtfully designed in this respect generally. The Stag has contoured wheel arches to prevent the accumulation of mud, but the undersealing is half-hearted. The engine bay gives reasonable accessibility, although one may not fancy valve adjustment by shims.

In spite of its smooth performance and thoughtful comforts for driver and front passenger, the Stag proved something of a disappointment. It is difficult to establish that affinity which should link driver with GT car. Somehow it seems to promise more than it has to give.

Triumph Toledo

TRIUMPH TOLEDO
ENGINEERS' COMMENTS
Conventional, robust-engined car

Outwardly the Toledo looks remarkably like a Triumph 1300/1500, housing all its mechanical components in what is virtually the same bodyshell. The Toledo, however, is a conventional front-engined, rear-wheel-drive car with a live axle. The four-door version became available after August 1971; J registration cars are exclusively two-door.

Surface corrosion

It is not surprising that the 1300/1500 and Toledo display a very similar pattern of gradual body corrosion deterioration with age. The corrosion is mainly of a surface nature, caused by stone chip damage to the paintwork which has not been touched in promptly. Triumph, in common with other makes, experienced a paint technology problem on the body sills of J registration cars. During that production period the paint manufacturers supplied primer and top coats which left a good deal to be desired. As the sills are subjected to periodic bombardment by small sharp stones or grit, the rather brittle colour coat occasionally splinters off and corrosion creeps unhindered under the colour coat. Stone chipping and subsequent mud and slush splashes account for surface corrosion of jacking points.

Water ingress

The sealing of the passenger compartment against water ingress is very good, but J and K registration cars have a high incidence of water leakage into the boot: one out of eight J registration cars and one out of thirteen K registration ones. Improvements in manufacture have virtually eliminated this problem. It is necessary to tighten the seat runners to the floor regularly.

Oil, fuel leaks

Oil leaks from the engine timing cover can readily soften the rubber-bonded engine mounts at the front. Such leaks are not generally substantial, and are easily reduced by tightening the gasket joint. It is more likely, however, that these leaks are the result of poor assembly of the oil filter rubber seal during routine servicing. Oil leakage past the tail shaft seal of the conventional four-speed all-synchromesh gear box eventually softens the rear mounting, which will then need replacing. Rubber insulation on front and rear subframes and radius rods tends to deteriorate with age. Fuel leaks on flexible plastic pipes are a feature of badly fitted twin SU carburettor units on the 1500TC. These twin units require balancing and idling adjustments as well as the topping up of dashpots with light engine oil. Basically, the engine is very robust and trouble-free.

Brake servicing

Lack of regular footbrake and handbrake servicing accounts for poor brake performance. On J registration cars nearly one in four pull to one side or the other when the brakes are suddenly applied.

Attention to front wheel bearings should alert purchasers to possible wear in swivel joints and wishbone bushes and deterioration of rubber elements in the front suspension. Because of the interaction of all these on steering precision and ride comfort, checks should be carried out by a franchised dealer. Routine service require-ments include attention to loose steering rack clamps which secure the rack assembly to the chassis and a check for worn or slack universal joints of the steering column. The gaiters should be free of tears, keeping lubricant in the rack-and-pinion assembly and wear-promoting dirt out.

Dealer preparation

Poor preparation by dealers of a number of cars still under the manufacturer's warranty accounts for the M registration percentages. Such simple operations as touching in small paint blemishes and adjusting tappet clearance and clutch and gear shift operating mechanisms would have improved the figures. The Toledo is a very conventional type of car and as such should be less demanding in terms of garage bills than its front-wheel-drive companion, the 1300/1500.

Specification of AA tested car

See p. 188

Make & model	TRIUMPH TOLEDO
Production years	1970–present
Body alternatives	2-door Saloon, 4-door Saloon
Engine variants	1296cc OHV
Data: AA test version	Toledo 2-door Saloon. 1971 model
Engine	In-line 4-cyl, watercooled, front-mounted
	Bore 73.7mm, stroke 76.0mm, 1296cc. Comp ratio 8.5:1
Fuel system	1 SU variable-jet carburettor. Mechanical pump.
	10.5-gallon tank
Transmission	4-speed & reverse, synchromesh on all forward
	gears. Rear-wheel drive.
	Diaphragm-spring clutch, 6½" diameter dry plate,
	hydraulically operated
Suspension front	Independent. Coil spring, wishbones, damper
Suspension rear	Coil-sprung live axle, four-link located, damper
Steering	Rack & pinion. 3¼ turns between full locks.
	Turning circle 34 feet
Wheels	13" diameter, 4J rims
Tyres	5.20×13 cross-ply (165×13 radials fitted)
Brakes	Hydraulic, drum front/drum rear
Dimensions	Length 13'0" Width 5'1¾" Height 4'6" Wheelbase 8'0"
(overall)	Ground clearance 6" Kerb weight (full tank) 17 cwts
Max speed (in gears)	First 26mph, second 43mph, third 67mph, top 85mph
Overdrive	Not applicable
Acceleration	0–60mph: 17.7 seconds; standing-¼ mile: 20.8 seconds
Fuel consumption	overall: 31.1mpg
	steady 50mph: 44.0mpg (top gear)
	steady 70mph: 30.4mpg (top gear)
Fuel	Premium 4-star

What VISAR reveals

Legend: ■ Worse than average ▦ Average ▨ Better than average ☐ No data

All chart figures are percentages

	Age in years: 6–8	5–6	4–5	3–4	2–3	1–2
Registration Suffix:	FG	H	J	K	L	M
Corroded front doors			10	8	4	6
Corroded rear doors				5	3	3
Corroded front wings			9	7	4	0
Corroded rear wings			5	8	1	3
Corroded front underwings			2	2	0	0
Corroded rear underwings			2	3	0	0
Corroded body sills			27	11	7	6
Corroded jacking points	N	N	8	7	3	0
Corroded floor	O	O	0	0	0	0
Corroded underbody frame members	–	–	7	5	2	0
Defective undersealing	T	T	11	11	6	6
Loose/misaligned driver's seat	C	C	5	2	0	3
Attend to engine mountings	U	U	5	3	1	0
Evidence of head gasket leaks	D	D	3	2	4	3
Noisy valve gear	O	O	16	18	26	27
Evidence of engine oil leaks	R	R	30	25	27	23
Attend to carburettor tuning	P	P	23	30	23	30
Evidence of fuel leaks			2	5	2	13
Final drive noise	N	N	0	3	1	0
Unsatisfactory gear change	–	–	2	4	4	11
Unsatisfactory auto gear change						
Clutch judder	T	T	2	1	2	7
Attend to front wheel bearings	O	O	54	54	35	22
Attend to steering box/rack	N	N	15	8	9	10
Attend to footbrake			19	10	1	0
Attend to handbrake			16	10	8	3
Corroded brake pipelines			11	6	3	0
Defective obligatory lights			21	15	13	11
Attend to charging system			2	3	1	0
Attend to horn			0	0	2	3

TRIUMPH TOLEDO

From AA Road Test Report 235, 1970

Tranquil family transport

By indulging in some clever spare-parts surgery, Triumph have created two new models from the 1300–the plush 1500 and the more basic Toledo, the latter destined to become the Herald replacement.

In fact, the Toledo performs very much like the Herald, gaining only slightly on through-the-gears acceleration. While not especially quick, it is extremely flexible, and remarkably quiet too. Indeed, it is hard to believe that the three-bearing engine dates way back to the Standard 8 of the early 1950s, for it feels as taut and finely balanced as ever. It is, however, rather less economical on fuel than its immediate Escort and Austin/Morris rivals which offer 4–5mpg extra overall; the Toledo's figures ranged from 26mpg to 35mpg. The clutch works with a smooth, light action and the gear box has an easy shift, but synchromesh on first gear can be beaten by a fast downchange.

Good road grip

The Toledo's live-axled ride is disappointing, for it seems unable to soak up bumps or ruts without making one aware of a constant underlying restlessness. Road grip proves very impressive, though, and thanks to its neutral handling at normal speeds the car is very mild-mannered. It understeers when pressed, but 'fail-safe' tuck-in occurs if one has to slow up suddenly in an ever tightening corner. Steering 'feel' is minimal, but it is a precise enough mechanism that demands little effort. The unwieldy turning circle of 34 feet is below par though. The drum brakes feel dead but prove most effective, if rather heavy, in an emergency stop. The handbrake is fine too, even on a 1-in-3 hill.

Toledo economies extend to the non-adjustable steering column, and only a simple (though generous) sliding adjustment for the seat. The testers would like more shoulder and lumbar support, but the driving position is quite acceptable because of a well-related layout. Vision is excellent, although the wipers could be better placed to reduce a blind spot that irritates tall drivers. The instruments, set in the attractively simple wooden fascia, are easily in view, while big square knobs on the minor controls make for easy action. There is also that familiar stalk on the column.

The front seats tilt forward to give good rear access. Headroom in the back is only marginal for tall passengers, who complain that the lowish seat and resultant 'knees-up' position provide no thigh support; foot space is also cramped. Most passengers, however, found the seat comfortably angled and kneeroom adequate–similar to the Avenger.

The heater is excellent, with a rapid warm up, instantly responsive temperature control and even distribution of footwell warmth. An ideal cool-face, warm-feet arrangement is possible, and fresh-air fascia vents and hinged front quarter-lights are provided. Comprehensive padding, very comfortable seat belts and quiet decor provide the Toledo with a safe and unfussy interior. There's a glove-box, two parcel shelves, and three ashtrays. The boot is not particularly spacious, but its boxy shape is useful. Loading is easy–if the head is ducked–as there is no rear sill.

The test car's paintwork had an impressive finish, and it is nice to see mud shields at the rear of the front wheel arches. It is a pity that there are such bad rust traps at the top of the arches, however, particularly as undersealing is not applied. The engine is a marvellous unit to work on and should encourage even the most wary DIY man 'to have a go'.

Except for its splendid heating and engine accessibility, the Toledo has nothing special to offer. However, it is a particularly easy, docile car to drive and certainly one of the quietest saloons in its class–and that counts for a lot.

Triumph TR6

TRIUMPH TR6
ENGINEERS' COMMENTS
Sound chassis is important

The TR6, though different from its less powerful Triumph stablemates, shares some basic engineering concepts with them – backbone chassis construction, for one. The TR6 has more suspension and rear-wheel-drive refinements, however, to take care of the extra power potential of the 125 horsepower engine. Double-jointing of the driveshafts improves road grip, safe handling at speed, and tyre life, but it introduces the need to accomodate lateral movement or 'plunge' of the short driveshafts even when full acceleration or braking torque tends to promote stickiness or binding on the sliding splines.

Final drive noise, often heard as a distinct 'clonk' when slack is taken up or power applied, is most likely due either to wear of the universal joint needle bearings on driveshafts or propeller shaft or to the working loose of the pre-loaded flange bolts. The protective gaiters on the driveshafts also tend to deteriorate with age, thus allowing penetration of harmful road grit. In the event of back axle noise, it is advisable to leave inspection and repair to a franchised dealer.

The need for attention to front wheel bearings does not imply undue wear of roller bearings or their imminent failure. It should, however, alert owners to probable wear of the swivel joints and bushes, since such wear produces a 'wobble' in the steering which might be mistaken for front wheel bearing trouble.

Steering checks

The rack-and-pinion steering should be examined for tears in the gaiters which will allow lubricant to escape and grit to enter, thus damaging the teeth. It also pays to check that the rack is tightly clamped to the chassis frame. A broken earth-return wire within the steering column accounts for many cases of inoperative horns.

Slight engine oil leaks such as weeps past the crankshaft seals, valve timing cover, rocker-cover joints and the sump gasket can produce a general oiliness. Handbrake maintenance is usually restricted to adjustment to allow for brake shoe lining wear and some lubrication of the long, covered operating cable.

The Lucas petrol injection system should not be tampered with by enthusiastic amateurs. It is a precise system and if 'chugging' of the engine is experienced during slow-speed town driving, try engaging a lower gear to increase engine speed. By maintaining the ignition in tip-top condition through regular attention, many of the problems complained of under the general heading of 'rough running engine' can be cured. If rough running persists, it may require attention by specially trained staff at a franchised dealer. The same applies to those fuel leaks which cannot be cured by tightening loose fuel line unions. Stone chipping of the paint, which is generally of good quality, was a problem on early TR6s, resulting in some surface rusting along the lower sections of door panels, door edges, and wing arch flanges. Body sills in particular suffer from gravel rash, which penetrates through the protective paint layers to the metal below. The structural stiffness and strength of the car are mainly provided by the box-type ladder frame, however. Engine, gear box, back axle and front and rear suspension are bolted to this frame via rubber-bonded bushes, as is the bodyshell itself.

Anti-rust coverage

It is difficult to get complete anti-rust coverage inside the box sections of the chassis frame and its outriggers. Deterioration by corrosion of these sections is generally fairly slow and within the period of inspection commented on here, no rust collapse has been reported. All the same, a sound chassis is most important in such a high performance sports car. The following check is an advisable one: put the blade or point of a screwdriver against the chassis or floor pressings and apply firm hand pressure. The point should not penetrate. If it does, the expense of restoring the car to its original strength will usually be too great to make the purchase worthwhile.

Specification of AA tested car

See p. 192

Make & model	TRIUMPH TR6 (PI)
Production years	1969–present
Body alternatives	2-door Roadster, 2-door Coupé hard-top
Engine variants	2498cc OHV
Data: AA test version	TR6 PI Overdrive, 2-door Roadster soft-top. 1970 model
Engine	In-line 6-cyl, watercooled, front-mounted
	Bore 74.7mm, stroke 95mm, 2498cc. Comp ratio 9.5:1
Fuel system	Fuel Injection system (Lucas).
	11.25-gallon tank
Transmission	4-speed & reverse, synchromesh on all forward gears. Rear-wheel drive. O/D standard from 1974. Diaphragm-spring clutch, 8½″ diameter dry plate, hydraulically operated
Suspension front	Independent. Wishbones, coil spring, anti-roll bar
Suspension rear	Independent. Coil spring, semi-trailing arm, damper
Steering	Rack & pinion. 3¼ turns between full locks.
	Turning circle 33 feet
Wheels	15″ diameter, 5½J rims
Tyres	165HR15 radial-ply
Brakes	Hydraulic, disc front/drum rear. Servo
Dimensions	Length 12′11″ Width 4′10″ Height 4′2″ Wheelbase 7′4″
(overall)	Ground clearance 6″ Kerb weight (full tank) 22½ cwts
Max speed (in gears)	First 37mph, second 58mph, third 88mph, top 117mph
Overdrive	Optional O/D 2nd 64mph, O/D 3rd 107mph, O/D top 111mph
Acceleration	0–60mph: 8.4 seconds; standing-¼ mile: 16.5 seconds
Fuel consumption	overall: 19.3mpg
	steady 50mph: 26.5mpg (top gear)
	steady 70mph: 25.0mpg (top gear)
Fuel	Super Premium 5-star

What VISAR reveals

Worse than average | Average | Better than average | No data

All chart figures are percentages

	Age in years: 6–8	5–6	4–5	3–4	2–3	1–2
Registration Suffix:	FG	H	J	K	L	M
Corroded front doors			14	14	17	
Corroded rear doors						
Corroded front wings			16	5	5	
Corroded rear wings			14	6	10	
Corroded front underwings			0	3	0	
Corroded rear underwings			0	3	0	
Corroded body sills			13	15	7	
Corroded jacking points			8	4	6	
Corroded floor			19	13	0	
Corroded underbody frame members			18	15	12	
Defective undersealing			30	24	17	
Loose/misaligned driver's seat			9	13	0	
Attend to engine mountings			5	2	0	
Evidence of head gasket leaks			0	0	0	
Noisy valve gear			10	3	9	
Evidence of engine oil leaks			41	43	32	
Attend to carburettor tuning			46	57	30	
Evidence of fuel leaks			9	17	0	
Final drive noise			15	11	5	
Unsatisfactory gear change			0	0	0	
Unsatisfactory auto gear change						
Clutch judder			5	7	0	
Attend to front wheel bearings			30	33	19	
Attend to steering box/rack			19	6	9	
Attend to footbrake			5	11	10	
Attend to handbrake			20	18	14	
Corroded brake pipelines			5	6	5	
Defective obligatory lights			0	20	0	
Attend to charging system			0	0	0	
Attend to horn			18	14	14	

No-nonsense sports car

Starting from humble origins, Triumph's TR range has grown bigger, heavier, and more sophisticated, reaching maturity in this latest TR6. The straight-six PI engine is a smooth and instantly responsive unit. Vivid performance is available provided the revs are kept up, but watch that flying tachometer needle. Cold starting is instantaneous, but the engine is reluctant to fire when warm, and does not idle steadily. The test car's overall petrol consumption on a shorter-than-usual test was just 19¼mpg, although 27mpg is easy to achieve with gentle driving.

Powerful synchromesh and a quick, light lever make the gear box a pleasure to use, but it takes a hefty push to free the firmly-biting clutch. With optional extra overdrive fitted, the driver has seven ratios at his command, providing a gear for all occasions as well as keeping the power coming in a long steady rush all the way to 117mph. Engagements are fast and smooth.

Great road grip

While proving fidgety and firm on poor surfaces, the suspension copes competently on most roads, with only an occasional pothole sending a shudder through the normally rigid body structure. Good damping and absence of body roll aid fast cornering, and ground clearance usually proves sufficient. The back of the car dips a good deal on a rapid take-off and also tends to twitch untidily if the throttle is closed when cornering quickly. However, provided the driver maintains a constant throttle opening, the TR sails around on an even line, displaying marked understeer and tremendous grip. Care is needed in the wet though, to prevent wheelspin. The light steering possesses reasonable feel but could be higher geared to advantage. Continual hard use from high speed will induce dramatic brake fade, but for normal purposes the disc/drum system is adequate. Pedal loads are not light, however; a panic stop from, say, 50mph demands a tread of 100 pounds.

The driving position is a very acceptable compromise for most people. The short-travel gear lever and stubby handbrake are just a hand's span away from the wheel. One soon forgets the pedal offset and appreciates, for example, the stretching space alongside the clutch. Bold instruments in the 'gunstock' wood fascia are seen at a glance, and clear all-round vision is helped by three flexible hood windows. None of the controls at the lower centre of the fascia is particularly easy to work, while the rocking switches for the wipers and washer can be reached only after trickily avoiding the column stalks.

Interior refinements

The quality of the interior trimming is a cut above cheaper Triumph sports cars. Refinements include a lockable glove-box, door pockets, and a courtesy light between the seats. The heater, being a water-valve controlled unit, either fries or freezes the occupants, but it is possible to roast one's toes while being cooled elsewhere by four fan-boosted fresh-air vents in and below the fascia.

It takes 1½ minutes to stow the hood properly, but it proves a snug, flap-free, and waterproof top. Like most convertibles, this one suffers from a lot of wind noise. Beyond 70mph it is terrifying–like being behind a jumbo jet on take-off.

The boot is a useful size and extra baggage can be stowed on the carpeted deck behind the seats. This area can also be used by a cramped third occupant sitting sideways. There is easy access to the handsome, though complex, engine and its auxiliary equipment.

With the demise of the big Healey 3000, the TR6 stands almost alone in its price range as an exhilarating, no-nonsense sports car–a potent, purposeful machine in the tinsel-trimmed world of pseudo GT cars.

Triumph 1300 TC Saloon

TRIUMPH 1300/1500
ENGINEERS' COMMENTS
A little bit of luxury

This range of front-wheel-drive cars bears a strong family resemblance to its bigger brother, the Triumph 2000, but shares comparatively few of the design and manufacturing features. The well-proven sturdy three-main-bearing, four-cylinder engine is generally trouble-free. It is combined with a reliable all-synchromesh four-speed gear box and final drive unit to form a compact power package which is not, however, mounted transversely. The 1300/1500 engine differs significantly from Austin/Morris front-wheel-drive cars in terms of accessibility for service, engine mount loading and durability, and final drive layout. The rubber-bonded engine mounts deteriorate slowly with age and are cheap to replace.

The final drive is a right-angle one, and being a hypoid pinion and crownwheel it occasionally emits a characteristic hypoid whine which can persist for many hundreds of miles of bedding in. Failure of the final drive is rare, but occasional checks should be made on bolt pre-load tension of the rubber-bonded Rotoflex universal joints on the driveshafts, since these can become contaminated by oil seepage from the driveshaft seals. Oil is also lost from crankshaft seals, engine sump, rocker cover and timing cover gaskets, but such leakage is not serious. Checks on the soundness and dust sealing of the gaiter on the constant-velocity joint of the driveshaft and the gaiter-securing clips are important. If these are not sound, wear can follow very quickly, resulting in needless expense on constant-velocity joint replacement. Despite some early statements to the contrary, extreme wear, even 'knocking' of this type of constant-velocity joint does not create a potential driving risk. This applies to the Mini, the 1100 and other front-wheel drives as well.

Front wheel bearings very rarely give trouble or need attention, but it pays to have a franchised dealer check for wear and play of swivel joints and suspension arm bushes if unusual tyre wear and road wheel vibrations manifest themselves. Steering rack mountings tend to work loose but are easily re-tightened. Steering rack gaiters should be checked for oil tightness. Gear change quality is affected by wear in the gear lever linkage, leading to excessive gear lever movement and 'chatter'. Seat runners tend to work loose on their attachment to the floor and need occasional re-tightening.

Since September 1968 those cars produced in Merseyside have been electrocoat primed. Prior to this, the comparatively shallow slipper-dip priming process did not give adequate anti-corrosion protection, particularly to hollow and complex sections such as sills, and to wings, underfloor pressings and door pillars. Substantial improvement in terms of corrosion resistance is evident from H registration onwards. The very marked improvement in the underwing area's resistance to corrosion is due to the fact that a protective compound has been sprayed on by garages.

The early Triumph 1300 has an unenviable reputation for rusting from the inside out on a number of body panels where moisture and dirt have collected in partly closed assemblies. Prominent areas of such rusting are the front wing outer panels (where the front scuttle joins them), inner panels near the suspension damper mounts, sill jacking points and the lower part of rear wing panels. Rust staining can also emanate from spot-welded seams and door frames.

Poor earth return due to a broken wire or corroded connections is the main cause of complaint for bad electrics, including horns and legally required lights. Handbrake maintenance is straightforward, but adjustment for cable stretch is frequently overlooked. Carburettor tuning involves the adjustment of idling speed and mixture strength after ensuring that tappet clearance and ignition settings meet with manufacturer's specifications. Apart from early production cars, few adverse comments regarding durability can be levelled at the 1300/1500.

Specification of AA tested car

See p. 196

Make & model	TRIUMPH 1300/1500
Production years	1965–1970 (1300cc), 1970–1973 (1500cc)
Body alternatives	4-door Saloon
Engine variants	1296cc OHV
	1493cc OHV
Data: AA test version	1300 4-door Saloon. 1966 model
Engine	In-line 4-cyl, watercooled, front-mounted
	Bore 73.7mm, stroke 76.0mm, 1296cc. Comp ratio 8.5:1
Fuel system	1 Stromberg variable-jet carburettor. Mechanical pump.
	11.75-gallon tank. Low-level warning
Transmission	4-speed & reverse, synchromesh on all forward
	gears. Front-wheel drive.
	Diaphragm-spring clutch, 6½" diameter dry plate,
	hydraulically operated
Suspension front	Independent. Wishbones, coil spring, telescopic damper
Suspension rear	Independent. Semi-trailing arm, coil spring, damper
Steering	Rack & pinion. 3¼ turns between full locks.
	Turning circle 31 feet
Wheels	13" diameter, 4J rims
Tyres	560×13 cross-ply (Dunlop C41 fitted)
Brakes	Hydraulic, disc front/drum rear
Dimensions	Length 12'11" Width 5'1¾" Height 4'6" Wheelbase 8'0½"
(overall)	Ground clearance 5½" Kerb weight (full tank) 18½ cwts
Max speed (in gears)	First 29mph, second 45mph, third 68mph, top 85mph
Overdrive	Not applicable
Acceleration	0–60mph: 20.7 seconds; standing-¼ mile: 21.3 seconds
Fuel consumption	overall: 27.9mpg
	steady 50mph: 36.1mpg (top gear)
	steady 70mph: 25.2mpg (top gear)
Fuel	Premium 4-star

What VISAR reveals

Legend: ■ Worse than average ▨ Average ▨ Better than average □ No data

All chart figures are percentages

	Age in years: 6–8	5–6	4–5	3–4	2–3	1–2
Registration Suffix:	FG	H	J	K	L	M
Corroded front doors	19	13	9	6	1	
Corroded rear doors	16	8	7	4	0	
Corroded front wings	41	21	12	6	0	
Corroded rear wings	28	13	10	6	0	
Corroded front underwings	31	3	4	2	0	
Corroded rear underwings	11	3	3	1	0	
Corroded body sills	38	39	18	13	2	
Corroded jacking points	17	12	6	5	0	N
Corroded floor	5	2	2	1	0	O
Corroded underbody frame members	22	11	6	4	2	I
Defective undersealing	32	11	9	8	0	T
Loose/misaligned driver's seat	7	6	8	6	3	C
Attend to engine mountings	5	1	2	2	1	U
Evidence of head gasket leaks	3	2	2	3	3	D
Noisy valve gear	22	16	22	27	24	O
Evidence of engine oil leaks	54	43	41	38	38	R
Attend to carburettor tuning	43	34	33	28	27	P
Evidence of fuel leaks	3	4	3	3	4	
Final drive noise	8	4	4	4	8	F
Unsatisfactory gear change	7	9	9	5	3	O
Unsatisfactory auto gear change						
Clutch judder	8	6	5	2	0	T
Attend to front wheel bearings	10	11	7	15	12	U
Attend to steering box/rack	24	22	22	9	17	O
Attend to footbrake	23	13	8	8	1	
Attend to handbrake	23	18	24	25	8	
Corroded brake pipelines	13	6	7	3	1	
Defective obligatory lights	16	24	17	7	9	
Attend to charging system	7	4	4	1	0	
Attend to horn	13	6	2	1	1	

(Column M reads vertically: OUT OF PRODUCTION)

TRIUMPH 1300 (with 1500)

From AA Road Test Reports 138, 1966 and 251, 1971

Tradition-backed modernist

Except for its engine, the 1300 is new all through – a compact family four-door, modern in concept, but following the traditional Triumph image.

Despite its years, the three-bearing engine runs very smoothly to maximum revs and will pull from as low as 12mph in top. It is brisk rather than quick in both acceleration and top speed, but refinement is important too. Anyway, there is always the livelier 1500 which is quicker to 60mph by 3 seconds, and a little less thirsty as well – 28mpg with the 1300, 29½mpg with the 1500. Newcomers tend to stall the engine because the clutch has a vague engagement and there is a lot of sudden jerking if the accelerator is used abruptly. The gear change is generally smooth and synchromesh excellent, but first balks occasionally.

Firm ride

The ride is firm without being harsh, although there is no doubt that the 1500's beam axle provides better all-round insulation. With the 1300 there are thuds and thumps, but these are heard more than felt. Even so, the car's structure feels reassuringly solid. Handling has typical front-wheel-drive predictability, the turning circle is a handy 29 feet, and parking effort is reasonably light. Road shocks are sometimes felt through the wheel, however. Road grip at both ends is excellent and side winds cause little deviation. The 1500's disc/drum brakes are an improvement on the 1300's thanks to servo assistance, although the 1300 has ample stopping power. The handbrake holds even on a 1-in-3 hill.

Many driving positions

Triumph provide an incredible permutation of driving positions – the seat slides, raises and lowers, and the steering column adjusts in and out, up and down. The passenger's seat is not quite so versatile, and more shoulder support would not come amiss. Some people are never satisfied! A small interior mirror and poor wiper settings mar what is otherwise clear all-round vision, but the visors cannot be pivoted sideways. All three pedals are comfortable to work and the instruments are easy to read, particularly the 'half orange' warning light cluster. Static seat-belts make reaching some of the switches awkward.

Interior trimming

There is plenty of width in the back for two burly passengers, but kneeroom is only fair when the front seats are right back. Headroom, too, is restricted for six-footers. The seat itself (with folding armrest) is comfortably angled and faced with ventilated PVC. Interior trimming is neatly executed, with polished walnut and thick carpeting providing a luxury appearance. There are also nice touches like courtesy switches on all doors and a map-reading lens in the swivelling roof light. Better safety features are needed, however.

The heater is splendid. It warms up rapidly, is easy to adjust quickly, and gives well-distributed heat – albeit only to the front occupants. It is a pity that the 1300 has no fresh-air vents, however.

Lined and lit, the shallow boot is easily loaded, if one ducks, and it will carry a useful load of luggage. The 1500's 'stretched' boot is even better, of course. Spare wheel and tools are stowed under the leathercloth mat.

Skimpy undersealing

The paint appears well applied and brightwork is kept to a minimum, but there are bad corrosion traps under the front wheel arches. Undersealing is skimped; in fact there is less evidence of superior finish outside this small prestige saloon than there is inside.

All routine tuning/servicing items are extremely easy to work on.

The 1300 is a welcome addition to the ranks of home-produced cars; it is original where it helps, conventional where it makes sense, and modern throughout. The 1500 is its logical extension.

Triumph 2000 Mk II

TRIUMPH 2000/2.5

ENGINEERS' COMMENTS
Solid, well-tried saloon

This series has had a very long model run. As a well-conceived package, it enjoys considerable popularity. Since the Triumph and the Rover 2000 compete, let us see how they compare in the VISAR findings. Whereas since 1970 Rover have totally immersed the car body in a large electrocoat bath, Triumph continued with the older, conventional method of slipper-dip immersion until 1974, using gravity flow of the solvent-based primer paint to give anti-corrosion protection. The Triumph then receives a surfacer epoxy ester, followed by an alkyd melamine top coat; the Rover's top coat is a thermosetting acrylic. Some corrosion does gain a toehold on the Triumphs with age, particularly where regular washing has been neglected. Even so, for a period up to approximately 6 years from the time they emerged bright and shiny from their respective factories in Coventry, the Triumph is clearly in the lead in terms of outward appearance of painted body panels and absence of gravel- and salt-induced rust spots on sills and front and rear valances. Triumph's factory-applied underbody protection is an all-over

wax application which has only a short service life. Less than half the cars inspected had additional garage-applied protection; where it had been applied, such protection was not always properly keyed onto the underbody. Signs of surface rusting of underbody pressings and frame members – none of them structurally significant – are thus more likely to be found on the Triumph. As far as corrosion of underwings, boot, jacking points and under-carpet floor panels is concerned, it is a toss up; both the Triumph and the Rover have good corrosion resistance.

On neglected 6- to 8-year-old cars, the Triumph shows the first signs of the limitations of its anti-rust protection and painting processes. The rate of rusting increases after the partial local breakdown of primer cover. Inspection of 10-year-old cars shows that, with the exception of brake pipelines, Rovers are slightly more corrosion-resistant.

There is little to choose between the two cars' power units with regard to reliability. Tappet adjustment is much easier on the very smooth six-cylinder Triumph. Both have good gear change characteristics and reliable gear boxes. Where fitted, the Borg Warner type-35 automatic transmission gives little trouble provided routine service attention to external linkage adjustments and idling speed is carried out. The Triumph's two carburettors or petrol injection of course require more attention to tuning and curing fuel leaks than the Rover SC's simple single carburettor fitment. Reference to this can be found in the comments on the TR6 PI.

The final drive, braking, all-independent suspension and steering systems on the two cars have little in common, and thus their service and periodic component replacement requirements differ. Those on the more complex Rover require more skill and equipment, particularly when effecting component replacements or repairs. Noise in the final drive may be due to universal joint wear, to which reference is also made in comments on the TR6 PI.

Routine servicing often skimps the relatively simple adjustment required to compensate for handbrake cable stretch. Checks on fluid level and belt tension should not be forgotten on cars with power-assisted steering. All cars should be examined for damage to protective gaiters, loosening of steering rack mountings, and wear of steering couplings. The apparent need for attention to front wheel bearings should alert owners to the necessity of a check by a franchised dealer for wear of swivel joints and MacPherson strut deterioration. Lack of dealer attention to the rectification of minor faults accounts for some of the percentages for M registration cars.

The final choice between a Triumph 2000 and a Rover 2000 of roughly comparable ages – since it is primarily influenced by the cost differential – will always be a personal one.

Specification of AA tested car

See p. 200

Make & model	TRIUMPH 2000/2.5 (PI)
Production years	1963–present (Mk I 1963–1969, Mk II 1969–present)
Body alternatives	4-door Saloon, 4-door Estate
Engine variants	1998cc OHV 6-cyl
	2498cc OHV 6-cyl (petrol injection)
Data: AA test version	2000 Mk II 4-door Saloon. 1970 model
Engine	In-line 6-cyl, watercooled, front-mounted
	Bore 74.7mm, stroke 76.0mm, 1998cc. Comp ratio 9.25:1
Fuel system	2 Stromberg variable-jet carburettors. Mechanical pump.
	14-gallon tank. Low-level warning
Transmission	4-speed & reverse, synchromesh on all forward
	gears. Overdrive. Rear-wheel drive.
	Diaphragm-spring clutch, $8\frac{1}{2}''$ diameter dry plate,
	hydraulically operated
Suspension front	Independent. MacPherson strut, coil spring, damper
Suspension rear	Independent. Coil spring, semi-trailing arm, damper
Steering	Rack & pinion. Power-assisted. 3.1 turns between full
	locks. Turning circle 33 feet
Wheels	13" diameter, 5J rims
Tyres	6.50×13 cross-ply (175SR13 radials fitted)
Brakes	Hydraulic, disc front/drum rear. Servo
Dimensions	Length 15'2¼" Width 5'5" Height 4'8" Wheelbase 8'10"
(overall)	Ground clearance $5\frac{1}{2}''$ Kerb weight (full tank) 25 cwts
Max speed (in gears)	First 31mph, second 48mph, third 72mph, top 95mph
Overdrive	O/D 3rd 88mph, O/D top 94mph
Acceleration	0–60mph: 15.0 seconds; standing-¼ mile: 20.1 seconds
Fuel consumption	overall: 26.0mpg
	steady 50mph: 31.8mpg (top gear) 37.7mpg (O/D top)
	steady 70mph: 25.3mpg (top gear) 28.8mpg (O/D top)
Fuel	Premium 4-star

What VISAR reveals

Worse than average | Average
Better than average | No data

All chart figures are percentages

	Age in years:	6–8	5–6	4–5	3–4	2–3	1–2
	Registration Suffix:	FG	H	J	K	L	M
Corroded front doors		18	7	6	4	1	0
Corroded rear doors		15	9	5	2	1	0
Corroded front wings		22	9	6	3	4	7
Corroded rear wings		21	9	9	4	3	8
Corroded front underwings		9	7	5	2	2	0
Corroded rear underwings		7	5	4	1	2	0
Corroded body sills		31	22	17	9	7	0
Corroded jacking points		9	7	6	2	3	0
Corroded floor		0	2	0	0	0	0
Corroded underbody frame members		12	10	8	7	5	0
Defective undersealing		16	23	23	14	10	0
Loose/misaligned driver's seat		0	1	3	4	2	0
Attend to engine mountings		2	0	1	1	0	4
Evidence of head gasket leaks		6	1	1	0	0	0
Noisy valve gear		16	22	20	14	10	0
Evidence of engine oil leaks		41	29	28	31	33	29
Attend to carburettor tuning		35	45	39	28	37	42
Evidence of fuel leaks		4	3	3	9	4	7
Final drive noise		8	5	7	3	2	12
Unsatisfactory gear change		3	3	0	1	0	0
Unsatisfactory auto gear change		11	13	8	2	9	15
Clutch judder		4	4	8	3	3	0
Attend to front wheel bearings		37	25	36	37	35	8
Attend to steering box/rack		30	10	12	17	6	15
Attend to footbrake		11	7	8	7	4	8
Attend to handbrake		17	19	30	25	22	28
Corroded brake pipelines		8	4	9	7	2	8
Defective obligatory lights		26	23	15	10	13	16
Attend to charging system		2	1	2	1	1	0
Attend to horn		5	8	5	0	0	0

TRIUMPH 2000 MARK II

From AA Road Test Report 219, 1970

Versatile, with dignity and appeal

 With its relation by merger to Rover, the Triumph 2000 has established a new pattern of executive car ownership, demonstrating that a car does not have to be big to be comfortable.

The choice of a six-cylinder engine gives the Triumph a docility in traffic, with good top-gear response that the Rover 2000 lacks. Its twin carburettors add a touch of complexity, however, and idling can be flighty in the warm-up period. Overall gearing is on the low side, making the car rather fussy at motorway speeds, with fan howl especially apparent. The optional overdrive is almost essential for longer journeys; it probably improves typical fuel consumption by 2mpg. The test car gave as much as 30mpg with careful driving and use of the overdrive. A 300-mile range between fill-ups should therefore be possible, with a telltale to remind one. The gear lever is lighter than earlier versions, with less notchiness. Clutch judder on hill starts is a fault the testers noted before and a 1-in-3 hill start is too much to ask.

New suspension settings have improved cornering prowess, but ride comfort has been compromised in the process. Grippy road holding on radials is accompanied by well-balanced handling; final oversteer asserts itself so gently that the driver learns to use it to his advantage. When cornering briskly, more steering effort is needed, however, and the car is unwieldy to manoeuvre too. The optional power-assisted steering overcomes this dramatically, although it has insufficient feel.

The ride feels fine on good main roads, but becomes knobbly and unresilient over poor surfaces, with some particularly unwelcome diagonal rocking on bumpy bends. The brakes are powerful in normal use, but the rears lock too soon in hard use and the handbrake feels unwieldy.

Of all the revisions on the Mark II, the fascia and control layout are the most successful and significant. Attractive yet orderly, all telltales are in a segmented cluster, and nearly every minor control is at one's fingertips on the variable rake steering column. Two dials on a matt teak fascia contain all gauges, and the new seats are extremely comfortable. The only complaint unattended to is the offset pedal layout, although the accelerator feels lighter and more precise.

Wind noises

At cruising speed, wind noises are the most prominent. The front quarter-lights and centre fascia vents all hiss, while another wind noise – from the cooling fan – is the main mechanically-originated intrusion. The new ventilators work well without chilling the driver's hands, and the small outboard vents are especially powerful, although separate rear outlets help ventilate the car evenly.

Although it is 8½ inches longer, the 2000's interior space remains unaltered compared with the Mark I. Its rear seat can take three passengers more comfortably than the Rover, but typical legroom is not as good, in fact. Interior trim and fittings are very tasteful, and oddments space is quite generous. The boot is 4 inches longer than before, though the load sill is higher.

The Britax seat-belts are a significant advance but the absence of childproof latches on the rear doors is a real liability for families with young children. The underbody has to rely solely on its paint and primer for protection and the low-mileage test car revealed one or two rust speckles. All routine service items are prominent under the bonnet but the wheel-changing equipment is unworthy of this type of car. The designer's dilemma in trying to improve an already successful formula is that particular attributes can be enhanced only at the cost of undermining others. The testers still think the Rover is the better longer-journey car. Even so, the Triumph retains versatility, while its dignity and appeal have been heightened.

Vauxhall Firenza Sport SL 2.3 litre

VAUXHALL FIRENZA
ENGINEERS' COMMENTS
A Viva in all but name

For reasons best known in Detroit, Vauxhall have pursued a curious policy of retaining the name 'Victor' through thick and thin, when others would have been only too glad to lose it. The first generation Victor, known affectionately as the camel – or a horse designed by a committee – can hardly have been rated as a spacious, refined, durable, rustproof car in its day. All its faults were eliminated by very much improved, roomier, quieter and better handling successive Victors. Vauxhall seem to have been motivated by a mixture of pious hope that, because the new models were so much better, the purchasing public would forgive and forget, and a tenacity to prove that they can redeem a model name by producing a very different type of car.

In the case of the Firenza, one can argue that Vauxhall have attempted the opposite: they introduced a sports coupé version of the moderately powered 1256cc Viva and in naming it, followed the trend for Italianate model names practised by the opposition. Even with a more powerful 1599cc engine, the car was not a serious contender for the title of sports car. It tended to be a sheep in wolf's clothing, so it never caught on and we thus have only a small sample to judge it by.

After a brief interval, Vauxhall re-introduced the car in very limited numbers as a really racy car complete with front spoiler, a very powerful 2279cc engine and a ZF five-speed gear box for special saloon car racing events, and a top speed of 120mph plus. Very much a wolf in sheep's clothing compared with the cars inspected during 1973–4. The VISAR survey covers cars with the 1599cc or 1759cc engine, although a few 2000 SLs are also included. Basically the car is a two-door Viva up to the waist, with a distinct roof line. It therefore shares the metal preparation, slipper priming to waist level, and all subsequent paint and careful anti-corrosion treatment with its less extrovert brother, the HC Viva. Its apparently poorer performance – compared with the Viva – with regard to rust on front doors of L registration cars and underwing corrosion on K registration cars is in part due to poorly repaired minor accident damage. While the percentage of cars involved in minor accidents necessitating some body repair was slightly below average, there were a number of unsatisfactory repairs of such damage – mostly paint jobs. This poor quality of repair work was 50% above the all-makes average. In addition, there was a remarkably high incidence of underside damage which had required subsequent repair.

The above remarks tend to confirm the view that the Firenza had a harder life than the Viva. The majority of owners were enthusiastic drivers; they were inclined to put an extra strain on seats and their runners, which necessitates the re-tightening of a bolt here and there. At the same time, they were apparently unusually conscious of the need to 'see and be seen'. Their cars were liberally equipped with extra lights and few had defective obligatory lights. The footbrake and handbrake, however, were more frequently in need of periodic replacement of brake pads and adjustment of the handbrake mechanism to take up cable stretch.

Alternators, while generally highly reliable, occasionally give trouble on early models. The evidence of stone bombardment due to rougher-than-normal motoring was seen on the underbody protection compound, which nonetheless generally proved its worth as both a sound-deadening and anti-rust layer. Attention to carburettors is generally only a case of straightforward idling adjustment, but the twin Stromberg carburettors fitted on the top-of-the-range model also need balancing occasionally.

Attention to front wheel bearings should extend to checking for wear in upper swivel joints and deterioration of the rubber bushes of the upper wishbone. The effectiveness of dampers should also be checked. These tasks are best entrusted to a franchised dealer.

Taken overall, the Firenzas inspected were HC Vivas in all but name.

Specification of AA tested car

See p. 204

Make & model	VAUXHALL FIRENZA
Production years	1971–1973
Body alternatives	2-door Fixed Head Coupé
Engine variants	1159cc OHV, 1256cc OHV, 1599cc OHC
	1759cc OHC, 1975cc OHC, 2279cc OHC
Data: AA test version	Firenza 2000 SL, 2-door Coupé. 1971 model
Engine	In-line 4-cyl OHC watercooled, front-mounted
	Bore 95.3mm, stroke 69.5mm, 1975cc. Comp ratio 8.5:1
Fuel system	2 Stromberg variable-jet carburettors. Mechanical pump.
	12-gallon tank
Transmission	4-speed & reverse, synchromesh on all forward
	gears. Rear-wheel drive.
	Diaphragm-spring clutch, 8″ diameter dry plate,
	cable operated.
Suspension front	Independent. Coil springs, wishbone, telescopic damper
Suspension rear	Coil-sprung live axle, radius arms, telescopic damper
Steering	Rack & pinion. $3\frac{1}{4}$ turns between full locks
	Turning circle 34 feet
Wheels	13″ diameter, 5J rims
Tyres	165–7OHR13 radial-ply
Brakes	Hydraulic, disc front/drum rear. Servo
Dimensions	Length 13′6″ Width 5′4$\frac{3}{4}$″ Height 4′5″ Wheelbase 8′1″
(overall)	Ground clearance 5″ Kerb weight (full tank) 19 cwts
Max speed (in gears)	First 35mph, second 53mph, third 81mph, top 100mph
Overdrive	Not applicable
Acceleration	0–60mph: 11.4 seconds; standing-$\frac{1}{4}$ mile: 18.0 seconds
Fuel consumption	overall: 26.0mpg
	steady 50mph: 35.6mpg (top gear)
	steady 70mph: 25.0mpg (top gear)
Fuel	Premium 4-star

What VISAR reveals

Legend: ■ Worse than average · ▨ Average · ▨ Better than average · □ No data

All chart figures are percentages

	Age in years: 6–8	5–6	4–5	3–4	2–3	1–2
Registration Suffix:	FG	H	J	K	L	M
Corroded front doors				0	14	
Corroded rear doors						
Corroded front wings				0	0	
Corroded rear wings				3	0	
Corroded front underwings				5	0	
Corroded rear underwings				5	0	
Corroded body sills				0	0	
Corroded jacking points	N	N	N	0	0	
Corroded floor	O	O	O	0	0	
Corroded underbody frame members	–	–	–	0	0	
Defective undersealing	T	T	T	8	0	
Loose/misaligned driver's seat	C	C	C	4	13	
Attend to engine mountings	U	U	U	0	0	
Evidence of head gasket leaks	D	D	D	0	0	
Noisy valve gear	O	O	O	0	7	
Evidence of engine oil leaks	R	R	R	33	21	
Attend to carburettor tuning	P	P	P	26	31	
Evidence of fuel leaks				0	0	
Final drive noise	N	N	N	4	0	
Unsatisfactory gear change	–	–	–	0	0	
Unsatisfactory auto gear change						
Clutch judder	T	T	T	4	0	
Attend to front wheel bearings	O	O	O	21	0	
Attend to steering box/rack	N	N	N	4	0	
Attend to footbrake				8	13	
Attend to handbrake				16	13	
Corroded brake pipelines				8	0	
Defective obligatory lights				4	7	
Attend to charging system				4	0	
Attend to horn				0	0	

(The letters in columns FG, H and J read vertically: NOT CURRENT PRODUCTION)

VAUXHALL FIRENZA

From AA Road Test Report 257, 1971, 289, 1962 and 341, 1974

Quick – but uncouth

 The Firenza was Vauxhall's answer to the Capri, using the Victor engine in a fast-back coupé treatment of the Viva bodyshell.

Bad vibration

In 2000 form the excellent acceleration, especially good in top gear, is marred by bad vibration, which abates in mid-range but returns again between 60–70mph. The testers like what it does, but not the way it does it. Fuel consumption is typical for a compact 2-litre, in fact very similar to the Capri 2000. It improves to around 34mpg if shown real consideration and oil consumption is modest.

A Victor-style gear change can balk into first, and synchromesh is also weak here, but otherwise it moves cleanly with a longish action. The clutch is light but tends to judder, and a 1-in-3 hill start is out of the question. Gear whine in the lower gears disappears in direct drive.

Responsive handling

The Viva's thorough rear-axle location makes this Coupé version well suited to its role. With wider wheel rims, radials, and firmer spring rates, it feels responsive without too much nose heaviness and though weightier, the steering has still-manageable parking effort and good feel. Unwise use of the accelerator causes the tail of the car to swing out, but in such a tidy manner that the driver still feels master of the situation. The ride, however, feels less resilient, especially at slow speeds. This may deter some family motorists although sporty types will probably be content. The brakes work extremely well once one is used to the step up to the pedal pad. They are fade and flood free and attain a true 1.0g crash stop at an ideal pedal load.

Incongruous instruments

The Firenza has always had a good driving seat but the Viva instruments, including a swinging arc speedometer, looked incongruous; the later Magnum has an attractive and purposeful seven-dial fascia, however.

The peculiar pedal-seat-wheel relationship that makes the driver's torso hinge somewhere in the middle continues to be an unattractive feature.

Effective ventilation

Forward vision is good but the coupé treatment creates rear vision problems. The four round headlamps give a superior beam to the Viva but the monotone horn seems more suited to a Bedford commercial. Ventilation is very effective, even though there is no booster fan link. The heater too gives well-controlled warmth and easy adjustment, although latest cars have reverted to water-valve temperature control – a retrograde feature compared with the former air-blending arrangement. The ordinary Viva's back seat is cramped, so the testers were not expecting much in the Firenza. In fact, it is adequate for youngsters or a short trip for adults, but rear entry will be a problem for the less agile. There is an enormous boot – much roomier than the Capri's and it is easier to load.

Good undersealing

Unlike some makers, whose undersealing does more for sales promotion than body protection, Vauxhall's stands up to close scrutiny. Yet paint looks coarse around door-frames and welds. The uncouth Victor engine spoils refinement, but it fits into the available space without shoe horning. The time-based service interval is a Vauxhall approach that makes technical sense.

Too close to Viva?

Perhaps the Firenza/Magnum remains too close to the Viva to be taken seriously as a sporting Coupé. It is fast, handles tidily, and is reasonably economical but Vauxhall must do something about its harsh mechanical manners and cramped rear accommodation. Yet over the longer term it possesses many reassuring features. Refined, it could win friends with those who want their car conventional and quick but compact.

This model was also offered in saloon and estate car form from September 1973 when its name was changed to Magnum.

Vauxhall Victor

VAUXHALL VICTOR
ENGINEERS' COMMENTS
Bigger and better now

The first Victors – produced between 1957 and 1961 – looked like scaled-down Pontiacs and rusted rapidly. For years Vauxhall have deserved to be rid of the unfortunate association: Victor=rust.

The FD Series, produced from August 1967, was replaced in March 1972 by the current FE Series. The VISAR survey is only concerned with these two series and their derivatives, VX 4/90 and Ventora. Having steadily improved over the years they now share many features with GM's successful Opel Rekord – although design and manufacturing integration is not as advanced as Ford (Europe).

The Ventora is given a thorough anti-rust treatment. After spray phosphating all over – which provides both primary anti-rust protection and a key for the subsequent paint treatment – the body is submerged up to window height in a tank containing 5,000 gallons of anti-rust alkyd primer paint. This allows protection to reach all the important external and internal surfaces, even of partly closed and box sections. One-half gallon of this brown-coloured dip primer adheres as a thin film to the sheet steel. Because of its colour it is easily confused with rust, for the two coats of grey epoxy primer surfacer do not always cover it. About 1 gallon of this surfacer is hand-sprayed onto the body to build up a layer of protective paint $1\frac{1}{2}$ to $2\frac{1}{4}$ thousandths of an inch thick on outside panels, underbody and the inside of body sills. After this is stoved onto the bodyshell, a base coat of clear acrylic is applied as the first operation of GM's re-flow painting process; it is followed by three coats of thermoplastic acrylic lacquers ($2\frac{1}{2}$ gallons) which, when stoved, give a high-gloss, fade-proof, stone-chip resistant and durable colour coat $2\frac{1}{2}$ to $3\frac{1}{2}$ thousandths of an inch thick. Nearly 1 gallon of plastisol sealer, weld cream sealer, metal-to-metal adhesives and rubber resin cement are applied to hard-to-reach areas at various stages of body fabrication and baked on. The entire underbody, including the wheel arches, is sealed with a bituminous sound-deadening compound 1/16th of an inch thick to protect it against stone bombardment and rust. It is fused to the underbody in a stoving oven. For extra protection a measured amount of silver-coloured bituminous aluminium is sprayed under pressure into the body sill section. Finally, the complete underbody receives 1 gallon of wax deposit, intended to give 6 to 9 months protection. How effective is all this in keeping rust at bay?

On FDs in particular it is only a middling success, since we discovered some rusting on lower portions of doors and wings, body sills and some rust 'bleeding' out of weld seams. On L and M registration cars, however, it stands up well. Process control is better and the FE's wings shroud the tyres more effectively, thus reducing exposure of these reverse contoured lower portions of wings and doors and the sills to stone bombardment. But surprisingly, the stippled PVC coating which so effectively minimises surface rusting induced by gravel rash on Vivas is not applied to all FEs. Vauxhall's claim that these styling changes obviated extra protection – since gravel chips now strike at a gentler angle – is unsupported by our data.

Despite improvements in gaskets and oil seals, the slanted engines are still far from oil tight. Gear boxes, drive line and back axles are durable, but could benefit from being quieter. Models with the three-speed column change need occasional linkage adjustment by a franchised dealer. The comments on the Viva regarding attention to front wheel bearings, steering, brake pipelines, clutch cable, footbrake and handbrake, electrics, carburettor tuning, and fuel leaks apply to the Victor and its derivatives as well.

Front suspension dampers soften with mileage and occasionally need replacing when the ride becomes too 'wallowy'. While cheap to replace, the Panhard rod bushes on the rear suspension are not durable enough. It is a pity that after several years of motoring, this car loses a feeling of tautness, for it is basically a sound vehicle.

Specification of AA tested car

See p. 208

Make & model	VAUXHALL VICTOR
Production years	FC (1964–67) FD (1967–71) FE (1972–present)
Body alternatives	4-door Saloon, Estate
Engine variants	1595cc OHV (1964–67), 1599cc OHC (1968–71), 1975cc & 3294cc OHV (1968–71), 1759cc & 2279cc OHC (1972–present)
Data: AA test version	Victor 1600 OHC 4-door Saloon. 1969 model
Engine	In-line 4-cyl, watercooled, front-mounted
	Bore 85.6mm, stroke 69.5mm 1599cc. Comp ratio 8.5:1
Fuel system	1 Zenith downdraught carburettor. Mechanical pump. 12-gallon tank
Transmission	4-speed & reverse, synchromesh on all forward gears. Rear-wheel drive.
	Diaphragm-spring clutch, $7\frac{1}{2}''$ diameter dry plate, cable operated.
Suspension front	Independent. Wishbone, coil spring
Suspension rear	Coil-sprung live axle, radius arms, telescopic damper
Steering	Rack & pinion. 4.3 turns between full locks
	Turning circle 33 feet
Wheels	13" diameter, $4\frac{1}{2}$J rims
Tyres	560×13 cross-ply (Goodyear G8 fitted)
Brakes	Hydraulic, disc front/drum rear. Servo
Dimensions (overall)	Length 14'8" Width 5'7" Height 4'4" Wheelbase 8'6"
	Ground clearance 5" Kerb weight (full tank) 20 cwts
Max speed (in gears)	First 32mph, second 49mph, third 74mph, top 89mph
Overdrive	Not applicable
Acceleration	0–60mph: 16.3 seconds; standing-$\frac{1}{4}$ mile: 20.7 seconds
Fuel consumption	overall: 27.6mpg
	steady 50mph: 36.3mpg (top gear)
	steady 70mph: 27.3mpg (top gear)
Fuel	Premium 4-star

What VISAR reveals

Legend: ■ Worse than average ▨ Average ▨ Better than average □ No data

All chart figures are percentages

	Age in years: 6–8	5–6	4–5	3–4	2–3	1–2
Registration Suffix:	FG	H	J	K	L	M
Corroded front doors	24	18	8	7	4	4
Corroded rear doors	21	13	7	5	3	2
Corroded front wings	23	23	5	7	0	0
Corroded rear wings	19	15	6	11	1	0
Corroded front underwings	19	15	6	8	2	4
Corroded rear underwings	8	5	5	6	2	0
Corroded body sills	31	18	6	4	3	8
Corroded jacking points	14	11	3	3	2	4
Corroded floor	8	0	0	0	0	0
Corroded underbody frame members	12	12	3	4	2	0
Defective undersealing	23	10	10	6	3	4
Loose/misaligned driver's seat	0	0	1	0	0	0
Attend to engine mountings	1	2	1	1	0	0
Evidence of head gasket leaks	2	0	2	3	0	0
Noisy valve gear	21	26	18	10	12	21
Evidence of engine oil leaks	65	58	44	49	29	30
Attend to carburettor tuning	44	39	38	42	35	45
Evidence of fuel leaks	10	6	5	4	4	0
Final drive noise	18	9	10	5	12	0
Unsatisfactory gear change	8	9	11	11	9	0
Unsatisfactory auto gear change						
Clutch judder	2	5	2	3	2	0
Attend to front wheel bearings	22	9	22	14	7	4
Attend to steering box/rack	17	19	11	7	4	4
Attend to footbrake	27	17	18	12	2	4
Attend to handbrake	17	25	20	21	12	15
Corroded brake pipelines	31	16	8	16	4	0
Defective obligatory lights	30	19	20	24	10	9
Attend to charging system	7	3	2	1	1	0
Attend to horn	11	0	2	4	1	0

VAUXHALL VICTOR 1600 FD

From AA Road Impression 20, 1969

Sensible family car buy

The 1600 is Vauxhall's basic Victor with a 1.6-litre engine, a three-speed column gear change, unassisted drum brakes all round, and a bench front seat. However, a bewildering array of optional extras (including the 2-litre engine) enables the buyer to equip the car as he wants. The test car came with a four-speed floor-change and servoed disc/drum brakes.

The overhead cam engine is an easy starter, but slow to warm up; the test car had an irritating flat-spot. It is a flexible unit though (down to 18 in top if one likes) and provides fair performance, but it's not quite a match for a 1600 Cortina. There is no harshness or exhaust resonances and 70mph cruising feels unstrained. Fuel consumption? Well, the test car averaged 27½mpg, with a low of 22mpg and a best figure of 33mpg. The 12-gallon tank gives an excellent range between fill-ups. Because of the engine's flexibility there is no need to make frequent demands on the whiney gear box, which has a crisp change and powerful synchromesh, although first won't be rushed.

Fitted with a set of radial-ply tyres (cross-plies are standard) the Victor has the sort of road grip and handling poise that challenges the best of the 1½-litre class, while its compromise between versatile ride and handling leaves most family mediums comfortably behind; clever – because it's achieved with a live axle. Efficient damping eliminates pitch and bounce, and the upholstery seems to work with the suspension to give unruffled progress. The steering is low-geared and very light. Straight-line stability could be improved, however, and the testers disliked the way cross-ply tyres twitched on raised white road lines. The brakes provide good stopping power at light pedal loads. Little fade occurs when they are treated harshly, and watersplash recovery is immediate. Handbrake location to the right of the steering column is a necessary evil, but it works very well.

Plain, simple trim distinguishes this Victor from its costlier stablemates. There are no armrests and the metal fascia looks cheap in its matt finish. Instrumentation is minimal but the floor covering is a sensible compromise of carpeting and rubber mats. It's worth paying extra for the separate front seats and individually styled rear ones, because on the ordinary benches one rolls around a lot. Tall rear passengers have just adequate legroom when the front seat is right back. There is plenty of seat width for two, and the headroom and foot space are uncramped.

The powerful heater is spoilt by its tendency to cause stuffiness, so one often needs to resort to the efficient fresh-air vents in the fascia, which are not boosted by the two-speed fan.

The paintwork's gloss is impressive, but patches of rust were visible in less obvious areas – on door edges, for example. Undersealing is applied with a rare thoroughness, however. There is plenty of space to spare under the bonnet, but the rear of the canted engine is masked by the bulkhead. This makes the rear sparking plugs inaccessible, but other service items are easy to reach. The jack is slow and cumbersome; there are no other tools.

Although its performance is not outstanding, the 1600 is a quiet car with a modest thirst, impressive ride and handling, and light controls. But to equip it with essential extras raises its price by £63.

Second thoughts – 5 years later

Sixty-three pounds! That was a lot then, but it's not today. Those extras – individual seats, servo disc/drum brakes, armrests – are fitted as standard on the latest models, and there's a lot more besides. Now bigger engined and even better built, today's Victor comes high on the testers' 'Best Family Car Buy' list.

Vauxhall Viva SL

VAUXHALL VIVA
ENGINEERS' COMMENTS
Worth a second look

When Vauxhall introduced their boxy looking Viva in 1963 some areas of the car failed to get adequate anti-rust protection. As a result, the HA had a reputation for early rusting. Although continued after 1967 in van form – with better protection – the HA has not been covered in the VISAR survey. The subsequent HB and HC ranges differ from the HA in body shape and particularly in suspension concept – leaf springs are gone altogether.

During the 1967-9 period, drastic steps were taken to remedy serious corrosion problems. These are described in the comments on the Victor. All models produced at both Luton and Ellesmere Port now undergo the same complex, relatively costly and reasonably effective anti-rust and paint treatment. The car bodyshell is no longer immersed a mere 18 inches in a bath of alkyd primer paint, but instead is dipped waist deep. This change has eliminated the problem of rusting of wings around headlamps and rear light clusters, tops of wings, and halfway up door panels.

As the VISAR statistics show, Vauxhall's claim to have produced one of the most durable small family saloons received a

further boost with the steps taken on the HC to eliminate gravel rash-induced surface rusting. The HC series is 1¾ inches wider overall than the HB, giving a useful bit of elbow room to passengers and allowing less of the wings, lower 3 to 4 inches of door panels and underwing ledges to be exposed to stones and grit thrown off the tyres. The removal of the curious horizontal ledge partway up the wings' and doors' outer panels allowed the introduction of a practical, unobtrusive styling feature – a stippled semi-resilient PVC covering – which takes the shock of abrasive stones and keeps the paint underneath intact.

The factory-applied undersealing is a layer 1/16th of an inch thick, effective in keeping corrosion at bay for a number of years. Although F/G registration Vivas are excellent in terms of rust resistance there are clear signs of some deterioration with age: rust 'bleeding' out of the seams of door panels, boot and bonnet lids and even the floor under its felt covering.

Careful inspection and possible renewal of the metal and flexible brake pipelines are advisable on F/G registration cars. Both front and rear suspension use a great deal of rubber where these units are attached to the underframes of the unitary body. They are maintenance-free but eventually deteriorate with use and exposure to road salt. It is wise to check the steering column flexible rubber coupling and steering ball joint for signs of wear.

Attention to front wheel bearings should alert buyers to the need for a franchised dealer to check not only for bearing play but also for wear or slackness on upper swivel joints. Oil tightness on Vauxhall engines can be a disappointment, for it is easy to re-position the rocker gasket improperly. Crankshaft seals and gaskets deteriorate with age and mileage, resulting in general oiliness. Slight petrol leaks are often cured by renewal of the short, flexible plastic tube, which hardens with age.

The all-drum brakes common on HB Vivas tend to pull to one side and need frequent adjustment to remain fully effective. Later models with a disc front/drum rear brake system are much improved. The handbrake needs a check for fraying of the cable and frequent adjustment to allow for stretch. Clutch cables, once prone to early failure, have been improved. Alternators – standard on HCs – are a 'fit and forget' item, but back axle noise needs dealer investigation, though the unit rarely fails. Many of the cars inspected are a reflection on owner care and dealer service. With regard to M registration cars, several dealers fell down on such easy tasks as adjusting clutch free travel to avoid judder and tappet clearance to reduce valve gear noise, setting carburettor idling speed and checking rear trafficator lights for good earth returns.

In common with its Opel counterpart – the Kadett – the Viva is much improved and worth a second look.

Specification of AA tested car

See p. 212

Make & model	VAUXHALL VIVA
Production years	1963–present, HA (1963–66), HB (1966–70), HC (1970–present)
Body alternatives	2-door Saloon, 4-door Saloon, Estate
Engine variants	1159cc OHV, 1256cc OHV, 1599cc OHC
	1759cc OHC, 1975cc OHC, 2279cc OHC
Data: AA test version	Viva de luxe, 1159cc, 2-door Saloon. 1970 model
Engine	In-line 4-cyl, watercooled, front-mounted
	Bore 77.7mm, stroke 61.0mm, 1159cc. Comp ratio 8.5:1
Fuel system	1 Solex downdraught carburettor. Mechanical pump. 8-gallon tank
Transmission	4-speed & reverse, synchromesh on all forward gears. Rear-wheel drive.
	Diaphragm-spring clutch, $6\frac{1}{4}''$ diameter dry plate, cable operated
Suspension front	Independent. Coil spring, wishbones, telescopic damper
Suspension rear	Coil-sprung live axle, radius arms, telescopic damper
Steering	Rack & pinion. $3\frac{1}{2}$ turns between full locks
	Turning circle 34 feet
Wheels	12″ diameter, $3\frac{1}{2}$B rims
Tyres	5.50×12 cross-ply (Uniroyal Rain fitted)
Brakes	Hydraulic, drum front/drum rear.
Dimensions	Length 13'5″ Width 5'3″ Height 4'5″ Wheelbase 7'11$\frac{3}{4}$″
(overall)	Ground clearance 5″ Kerb weight (full tank) 15$\frac{3}{4}$ cwts
Max speed (in gears)	First 26mph, second 44mph, third 70mph, top 81mph
Overdrive	Not applicable
Acceleration	0–60mph: 18.6 seconds; standing-$\frac{1}{4}$ mile: 20.6 seconds
Fuel consumption	overall: 30.2mpg
	steady 50mph: 44.4mpg (top gear)
	steady 70mph: 27.0mpg (top gear)
Fuel	Premium 4-star

What VISAR reveals

Legend: ■ Worse than average · ▨ Average · ▨ Better than average · ☐ No data

All chart figures are percentages	Age in years:	6–8	5–6	4–5	3–4	2–3	1–2
	Registration Suffix:	FG	H	J	K	L	M
Corroded front doors		18	7	4	4	2	2
Corroded rear doors		17	11	2	3	3	0
Corroded front wings		31	16	8	5	2	2
Corroded rear wings		16	8	6	4	3	2
Corroded front underwings		13	6	3	3	3	2
Corroded rear underwings		9	3	1	1	1	0
Corroded body sills		29	23	8	5	1	2
Corroded jacking points		9	6	2	2	0	2
Corroded floor		13	9	3	1	0	0
Corroded underbody frame members		13	6	3	2	0	1
Defective undersealing		17	11	10	9	7	9
Loose/misaligned driver's seat		6	2	2	2	1	0
Attend to engine mountings		5	2	0	0	0	0
Evidence of head gasket leaks		6	3	2	2	1	2
Noisy valve gear		28	33	22	25	16	27
Evidence of engine oil leaks		54	47	45	35	32	35
Attend to carburettor tuning		34	26	23	25	28	40
Evidence of fuel leaks		5	3	3	3	3	2
Final drive noise		12	9	8	5	3	8
Unsatisfactory gear change		6	4	4	3	2	3
Unsatisfactory auto gear change							
Clutch judder		3	5	3	3	3	6
Attend to front wheel bearings		14	13	17	19	14	13
Attend to steering box/rack		15	8	6	4	3	0
Attend to footbrake		21	24	15	11	7	3
Attend to handbrake		20	30	22	14	7	9
Corroded brake pipelines		30	12	12	9	3	3
Defective obligatory lights		31	23	16	14	11	16
Attend to charging system		7	5	2	2	3	0
Attend to horn		7	6	3	1	1	0

VAUXHALL VIVA DE LUXE

From AA Road Test Report 210, 1970

Improved and worthy de luxe

 The Viva has changed a lot since its introduction in 1963. There is now a choice of engines, and two-door or four-door saloon and estate car bodywork. This de luxe is the cheapest version.

Considering its modest capacity and 47bhp power output, this smallest engined Viva performs well by current small car standards. However, it must be criticised on the grounds of noise, a harshness on acceleration, and a lack of smooth refinement compared with several of its contemporaries. Sympathetic drivers won't let top gear speed drop below 26mph; fortunately though, exhaust resonances have been successfully tuned out. The test car's overall fuel consumption of 30¼mpg is unimpressive compared with other 1100s, but possible if one treats the accelerator gently.

Good clutch, gear shift

Mediocre flexibility seems unimportant when one has changed gear a few times, for the featherweight clutch and snappy gear shift are among the best available. Typical Vauxhall gear whine will be familiar to many drivers, though.

Revised damping and improved seat springing have quelled the former 'plunge and bounce' ride. It is firmer and steadier now, and the car is also stable in cross-winds. The cross-ply tyres still object to raised white road lines, however. Even though the test car was on optional extra radial tyres, the Viva corners superbly for a live-axled car, wet or dry – even on cross-plies. There is scarcely any roll, very little axle tremor, and the alert steering will immediately correct a rare tail twitch. The de luxe's drum brakes need servo assistance, for they prove adequate but heavily insensitive. They are fade-free though, and the handbrake will just hold on a 1-in-3 hill.

Most people will want the driving seat well back to get far enough away from the considerably offset accelerator, but the steering wheel is better positioned on this latest version. The seats are also improved, with a more relaxed backrest angle, but the cushion should provide more thigh support. There is an unobscured view of the speedometer, and although at full stretch, the toggle switches can be reached by a harnessed driver. Vision is aided by deep windows, slim pillars, and smooth, silent wipers. The tail is out of sight when reversing, however.

Trimming, in smart vinyl and plush carpet, looks far from austere, and door pull/armrests, three ashtrays, an interior light and coat hooks dispel the 'basic car' image. Safety features are also well covered.

Wide opening doors and safety-locked, tip-up front seats make rear entry quite easy. More thigh and shoulder support is needed for those in the back, but kneeroom remains reasonable even when the front seats are right back; headroom is adequate. Everyone is well served by the fast-warming, though none too-powerful heater – the two-speed booster fan helps though, and temperature adjustments are reasonably progressive. The Viva's swivelling-flap, fresh-air vents are less controllable than the Victor's 'eyeballs', but they do their job well enough.

Good paintwork

There is useful interior oddments space and for a small car the boot is vast. Spoilt only by a high rear sill, the load space – trimmed in leathercloth – is a useful shape, with the spare wheel standing on the right. The paintwork has an excellent gloss, the underbody is efficiently sealed, and underwing splash-shields (albeit of fibreboard) help to keep mud and water at bay. Items for servicing are very accessible, and home mechanics will find routine maintenance well within their resources.

Unless one needs the extra urge of the '90' engine or the executive SL trim, there is little point in aspiring to anything higher than the worthy de luxe in the Viva range.

Volkswagen 1300 Beetle

VW BEETLE 1200/1300
ENGINEERS' COMMENTS
Ancient but reliable

Nothing ever remains quite the same for very long. Even Beetles are not what they used to be, though many prospective purchasers still think so. Admittedly the shape is roughly the same as it has been for the past 38 years; the easy-to-paint Beetle body is bolted to its separate sheet steel platform base, as is the rear-installed power unit – a flat-four air-cooled engine, gear box and final drive. But that is about as far as it goes.

Swing axle
Engine, gear box and final drive have been altered significantly over the years, particularly the last 20. Only in the 1192cc basic Beetle is the rear axle still the true swing axle. This can present problems when it comes to handling the car on a gusty day along a stretch of road with an undulating surface. Triumph and others also experienced rear-end jacking up under these conditions, and therefore dropped the true swing axle many years ago. Volkswagen have tamed the swing axle by double jointing, however, thereby eliminating large camber changes at the driving wheels. The 1302 S introduced in September 1970 has a MacPherson strut front suspension secured to the reinforced inner wing à la Ford and others. The introduction of rack-and-pinion steering in October 1974 is too recent a development for us to comment on.

Clutch, gear box changes
Compared with the mid-1950, early-1960 cars, both the clutch and gear box are different. Since 1964 the dim 6-volt lighting system has been replaced by prominent headlights, large trafficators and massive rear-end light clusters, now supplied by a 12-volt alternator. Passenger comfort and safety have been improved too. The 1584cc 1303 S Beetle introduced in 1974 even has self-stabilising steering which gives directional controllability under braking in case of a front tyre failure. This has been borrowed from Audi-VW models, which are earmarked eventually to take over the mantle of indestructability and long life which the Beetle has acquired.

Rust resistance
The model has gained a reputation for outstanding rust resistance, but this is not true for all parts of the car. Rear wing corrosion does occur, particularly on F/G and earlier registration cars. On the outside

of the wing, it is due to grit and slush attack above the residual running-board-to-wing-joint. The underside suffers in the same zone. Progressive styling and design changes have reduced the width and hence protection against stone bombardment of the rear wing, so even Beetles begin to deteriorate with age. The factory does not apply a long-life special underbody protection compound, employing a wax spray instead. Only about 44% of the cars inspected had garage-applied additional protective treatment, and that eventually ages and cracks.

The body structure and underbody parts do not really show signs of rusting for about 6 years or more, with the exception of the jacking points. Emission control carburettors on M registration cars sometimes disappoint. Only a franchised dealer can set them to eradicate a flat spot tendency and stay within the emission legislation requirements. The adjustment of the handbrake to take up wear has become more important with the introduction of modified, improved braking systems in 1972. Brake pipelines, which are in close proximity to the floor, tend to corrode. The flexible fuel pipe to the carburettor should be checked for leaks.

Dealer checks

Front wheel bearing clearance is designed to be rather greater than in most cars. A franchised dealer should carry out checks for oil seepage from the steering damper, unwarranted play in its locating bushes, and lower swivel joint wear, all of which can be problems on 6-year-old cars.

When considering the purchase of a VW Beetle it is as well to remember that though the car can live with minimum routine service – and all too often receives next to none – the next owner pays dearly for this 'economy motoring'.

Specification of AA tested car

See p. 216

Make & model	VOLKSWAGEN BEETLE
Production years	1954–present
Body alternatives	Saloon, Cabriolet, Convertible
Engine variants	1192cc OHV, 1285cc OHV, 1493cc OHV, 1584cc OHV
Data: AA test version	Beetle 1300, 1285cc 2-door Saloon. 1972 model
Engine	Flat 4-cyl, aircooled, rear-mounted
	Bore 77mm, stroke 69mm, 1285cc. Comp ratio 7.5:1
Fuel system	1 Solex downdraught auto-choke carburettor. Mechanical pump. 8.8-gallon tank
Transmission	4-speed & reverse, synchromesh on all forward gears. Rear-wheel drive.
	Diaphragm-spring clutch, 8″ diameter dry plate, cable operated
Suspension front	Independent. Torsion bar, trailing arms
Suspension rear	Independent. Torsion bar, swing axle
Steering	Worm & roller. $2\frac{3}{4}$ turns between full locks
	Turning circle $34\frac{1}{2}$ feet
Wheels	15″ diameter, 4J rims
Tyres	560×15 cross-ply (Goodyear G8 fitted)
Brakes	Hydraulic. Dual circuit, drum front/drum rear.
Dimensions (overall)	Length 13′2½″ Width 5′1″ Height 4′11″ Wheelbase 7′10½″
	Ground clearance $6\frac{1}{4}$″ Kerb weight (full tank) 17 cwts
Max speed (in gears)	First 25mph, second 46mph, third 65mph, top 75mph
Overdrive	Not applicable
Acceleration	0–60mph: 20.1 seconds; standing-$\frac{1}{4}$ mile: 22.0 seconds
Fuel consumption	overall: 33.2mpg
	steady 50mph: 37.7mpg (top gear)
	steady 70mph: 26.7mpg (top gear)
Fuel	Mixture 3-star

What VISAR reveals

Worse than average | Average | Better than average | No data

All chart figures are percentages

	Age in years:	6–8	5–6	4–5	3–4	2–3	1–2
	Registration Suffix:	FG	H	J	K	L	M
Corroded front doors		9	5	10	7	3	2
Corroded rear doors							
Corroded front wings		18	8	9	4	3	2
Corroded rear wings		20	8	9	4	4	0
Corroded front underwings		13	8	4	0	1	0
Corroded rear underwings		12	7	3	0	1	0
Corroded body sills		27	9	8	6	5	4
Corroded jacking points		22	5	5	2	8	0
Corroded floor		3	6	3	3	2	4
Corroded underbody frame members		18	5	5	3	1	0
Defective undersealing		29	19	4	13	0	8
Loose/misaligned driver's seat		2	0	1	1	1	0
Attend to engine mountings		0	0	0	0	0	0
Evidence of head gasket leaks			0	0	0	0	0
Noisy valve gear		18	19	15	18	31	25
Evidence of engine oil leaks		26	12	15	9	6	15
Attend to carburettor tuning		27	19	18	23	21	39
Evidence of fuel leaks		0	4	2	2	0	0
Final drive noise		4	6	3	2	0	4
Unsatisfactory gear change		4	5	3	1	1	0
Unsatisfactory auto gear change							
Clutch judder		10	3	2	0	3	0
Attend to front wheel bearings		15	13	13	16	13	4
Attend to steering box/rack		6	4	12	12	12	4
Attend to footbrake		6	13	10	13	17	14
Attend to handbrake		0	6	5	5	16	17
Corroded brake pipelines		12	13	8	9	3	4
Defective obligatory lights		16	27	24	17	14	4
Attend to charging system		2	0	0	1	0	0
Attend to horn		12	12	8	1	4	0

VW 1300 BEETLE

Back to basics

The Beetle tends to generate extreme reaction ranging from scorn to devout fanaticism. Yet can its preference be justified in the present scene?

Built to last rather than go fast, performance is mediocre by 1300 standards. High gearing gives unstressed cruising though and once one is accustomed to its innocuous clatter and waffle, the car will cruise at 70mph without strain on itself or its passengers. One may struggle to get past unco-operative heavies on cross-country routes, however. The gear shift has short, easy movements although it pays to be brutal into third to prevent balking. Later cars give improved consumption and the test car managed nearly 40mpg when driven quietly; mixed use always seemed to result in 33–35mpg. The external filler requires a little care and fumes get into the car via an open quarter-light if it is brimmed. This problem can spoil its effective range.

Changes in 1968 introduced a 'bump bar' and other suspension revisions which tamed this Beetle's tail happiness. Its limitations are still apparent but it's easier now to keep within them. There is some nose drift before final oversteer sets in; this is not too vicious if one heeds its warning twitches. If one exceeds these limits of discretion, a lot of quick steering correction is called for. Road holding is better on radial tyres and this Beetle rides on them well too. Although there are short vertical deflections, the torsion bars prevent any jolting or jarring. One has to concentrate on a windy day, though the light, 'well-oiled' steering is a great help, with gentle but true self-centreing. For normal British use the testers would be quite happy with standard drum brakes – they resist fade and water surprisingly well. The owner of a 10-year-old car would probably notice lots of details but basically nothing has changed inside with its upright, dining-chair seating and chummy proximity of the front occupants. This proves remarkably comfortable, if only driver legroom was better. Pedal arcs remain odd but a forgotten blessing is the ease of getting in and out of the front. It is difficult to obtain a good all-round view. The fascia is basic but the multi-purpose stalk is an admirable feature, flashing headlights by day and dipping them at night with the same action.

Rear entry is cramped by fixed front cushions and belt loops lurk to trap the unwary too. Rear kneeroom is restricted and the hard, flat profile of the seat offers no lateral support. An exception to the rear passengers' second-class treatment is heating – they have their own supply and warmth is spread evenly over the whole floor. Simple fresh-air slots are mounted in the fascia and they prevent the separate de-misters causing stuffiness. Trim is plain but durable and although rubber mats ruck easily, there is a carpet in the luggage well that can be extended by folding the back squab. The shallow front boot is useful only for soft luggage; one longs for a single sizeable compartment to dump things without a struggle.

Construction seems as thorough and fussy as ever, with the smooth platform chassis wax-coated and robust bumpers properly mounted. Mechanical accessibility is good only for those with VW know-how and tackle – grovelling to reach oil drainers or valve adjusters is no fun. The handbook is not much help, either.

Second thoughts – 2 years later

Important seating changes 2 years ago that traded headroom for all-round legroom have been disproportionately successful. Currently legroom is much better at the back and front. Despite remaining accommodation limitations and mediocre performance, the Beetle still feels reassuringly robust and is now competitively priced.

Volkswagen 1600 Fastback

VW TYPE 3 (1500/1600)

ENGINEERS' COMMENTS

A name is not enough

The Type 3 never achieved quite the same popularity or awe enjoyed by the remarkable Beetle, whose success has mesmerised other manufacturers. This VW model has none of its smaller brother's charisma and little of its special features – though the Type 3 shares many of the Beetle's basic limitations. The 1500/1600 has a similar power unit and platform frame to which all the mechanical components are attached; the body is bolted onto this frame in Beetle fashion. Hence the metal pre-treatment and paint application are very similar for both models and in both cases platform and bodyshell are painted separately.

Different body shape

A bright-trim strip, where fitted, covers the sill of the Type 3, replacing the residual running-board of the Beetle. This strip needlessly traps salt and corrosion-inducing moisture while failing to deflect stones and slush from the lower portion of the doors. The effect of this different body shape is very marked on F/G registration cars; front and rear wings tend to pack with mud and corrode. As on the Beetle, the underwings and jacking points of the Type 3 suffer the risk of mud trapping and slow deterioration with age.

Clutch action quality

Both models suffer from the decline of clutch action quality with age and usage. The need for brake system attention on the disc-front and drum-rear 1500/1600s differs from that of a basic all-drum Beetle 1200, but neither model presents problems if regular maintenance is carried out. Bulb failure rate and damage to transparent rear light covers are significantly higher than average due to water ingress and body styling.

Floor corrosion

The decay with age of door rubbers on H registration cars accounts for the collection of water under coverings on the platform floor wells and consequently, the start of corrosion. The section of the car most prone to corrosion is the sill, which on pre-F/G registration cars can be seen to rust from the inside outwards.

On older cars it pays to have a franchised dealer check for excessive play in the worm and roller steering gear, wear in outer steering joints, oil seepage from the steering damper, wear, of bushes and ▸

deterioration of the steering column flexible coupling. In addition, it may be necessary to replace swivel joints and upper pivots if regular routine servicing has been skimped. Dynamic re-balancing of tyres and wheels helps to improve the ride considerably. Front wheel bearings have been designed to operate with working clearances slightly greater than those found on many other makes. There should be no large amount of wheel rock, however.

Unusual or rapid tyre wear with cross-plies calls for a franchised dealer's expert knowledge and equipment to determine the cause and to rectify it. The rear suspension geometry check is very important. In fact, whereas a Beetle can be run with many components badly worn or improperly adjusted or serviced, the Type 3 is far less tolerant of such gross neglect and abuse.

Routine servicing

It is difficult for owners to change plugs and attend to many other routine service tasks. With the car on a centre-post hoist, however, a franchised dealer can carry out these tasks quickly enough after dropping the power unit for easy accessibility. Carburation setting should present no problem if carried out by a VW dealer; he will have all the necessary aids. This operation soon pays for itself in fuel saving and smoother running.

The appearance of older Type 3s can be misleading, but an objective road test will generally show up those defects largely due to lack of owner maintenance. This discontinued VW range is not likely to be the answer for those who want a car which can tolerate rough handling and infrequent routine maintenance – and still come up uncomplainingly for more abuse.

Specification of AA tested car

See p. 220

Make & model	VOLKSWAGEN 1500/1600
Production years	1500 (1961–65), 1500A (1965–66), 1600 (1965–73)
Body alternatives	5-door Saloon, 2-door Estate
Engine variants	1493cc OHV
	1584cc OHV
Data: AA test version	1600 Variant L
Engine	Flat 4-cyl, aircooled, rear-mounted
	Bore 85.5mm, stroke 69mm, 1584cc. Comp ratio 7.7:1
Fuel system	2 Solex multi-jet carburettors. Mechanical pump.
	8.8-gallon tank
Transmission	4-speed & reverse, synchromesh on all forward gears.
	Rear-wheel drive.
	8″ diameter dry plate, cable operated
Suspension front	Independent. Trailing arms, torsion bar, telescopic damper
Suspension rear	Independent. Semi-trailing arm, torsion bar, telescopic damper
Steering	Worm & roller. Telescopic damper. 3 turns between full locks.
	Turning circle 36½ feet
Wheels	15″ diameter, 4½J rims
Tyres	165SR15 radial-ply (Michelin ZX fitted)
Brakes	Front disc/rear drum. Dual circuit
Dimensions	Length 14′3″ Width 5′4½″ Height 4′10″ Wheelbase 7′10″
(overall)	Ground clearance 6″ Kerb weight (full tank) 20 cwts
Max speed (in gears)	First 24mph, second 51mph, third 67mph, top 85mph
Overdrive	Not applicable
Acceleration	0–60mph: 19.5 seconds; standing-¼ mile: 21.1 seconds
Fuel consumption	overall: 29½mpg
	steady 50mph: 42.4mpg (top gear)
	steady 70mph: 31.0mpg (top gear)
Fuel	Regular 2-star

What VISAR reveals

Legend: ■ Worse than average ▨ Better than average ▨(light) Average □ No data

All chart figures are percentages

	Age in years:	6–8	5–6	4–5	3–4	2–3	1–2
	Registration Suffix:	FG	H	J	K	L	M
Corroded front doors		21	3	4	1	4	
Corroded rear doors							
Corroded front wings		23	13	11	4	5	
Corroded rear wings		20	9	7	1	3	
Corroded front underwings		13	6	2	0	3	
Corroded rear underwings		11	3	2	0	3	
Corroded body sills		26	20	8	4	3	
Corroded jacking points		14	16	7	0	3	
Corroded floor		0	12	3	0	3	
Corroded underbody frame members		16	11	1	3	6	
Defective undersealing		41	13	11	22	3	
Loose/misaligned driver's seat		2	3	0	2	0	
Attend to engine mountings		0	0	0	0	6	
Evidence of head gasket leaks		0	0	0	0	0	
Noisy valve gear		10	15	25	18	19	
Evidence of engine oil leaks		24	27	23	19	28	
Attend to carburettor tuning		30	30	24	18	32	
Evidence of fuel leaks		2	3	2	2	0	
Final drive noise		0	6	3	0	0	
Unsatisfactory gear change		0	3	7	0	3	
Unsatisfactory auto gear change							
Clutch judder		7	6	2	2	3	
Attend to front wheel bearings		10	12	12	14	15	
Attend to steering box/rack		10	9	11	8	11	
Attend to footbrake		13	12	7	0	18	
Attend to handbrake		11	6	10	4	8	
Corroded brake pipelines		18	12	11	8	7	
Defective obligatory lights		48	35	24	26	3	
Attend to charging system		2	3	0	0	0	
Attend to horn		12	6	2	4	0	

From AA Road Test Report 215, 1970

VW 1600L VARIANT

Dull but dependable Type 3

When someone in the family becomes a legend, it is difficult for the others to make their own impact. The Type 3 VW emerged as a rebodied and mechanically refined Beetle in 1961, yet despite its advantages it has never achieved the acclaim of the original 'people's car'.

The car tested was an Estate, with its flat four-power unit cleverly laid out beneath the rear load platform. It takes 16½ seconds to run from 30mph to 50mph – so the Variant is no fireball. However, its high top gear maintains a leisurely, loping pace for main road cruising. It is not particularly flexible, but its modest revs and middling power output ensure that this is an engine that is going to last. Starting is customarily prompt and the slightly sloppy gear change nevertheless plops between one gear and another without a quarrel. Clutch pressure seems heavy and the clutch on the test car juddered too. Fuel economy is mediocre considering the level of performance, but the 1600 runs happily on Regular – 93 octane is best.

The Variant seems an inherently safe car because its road holding is better than its handling; disconcerting front-end float deters the driver before the rear of the car breaks away. With its latest semi-trailing arm rear suspension (like the Super Beetle and 411), the Variant feels remarkably tame for a rear-engined design. Steering with good sensitivity and quick response helps here too; it has a pleasingly precise, 'well-oiled' feel, although a windy day causes the car to dither about.

The ride is supple and 'all-of-a-piece', although the unladen front end bobs and rocks too much at speed over bumps. The springs smother waves and hump bridges well, however. Although the high pedal is awkward, the brakes have a firm, progressive feel. Ultimately all four wheels lock up at 0.86g – not very good by modern standards – and watersplash recovery is slow. Fade is no problem, however.

The firmly supporting driver's seat with adjustable back rest rake is surprisingly comfortable after long spells, but limited legroom could cause discomfort to taller drivers. The instrumentation is tidily set out but minor controls are indifferently placed. Full marks, though, for the easy ignition lock and multi-purpose column stalk for lighting and flashers. The Variant is easier to park than the Fastback saloon, with better rearward vision. The characteristic VW clatter is less obtrusive inside – even at speed – than the noise of many rivals that may register fewer decibels. Both tyre and wind noises are restrained and there was no creaking from the test car's bodywork and fittings.

Rear entry is easier on a Variant than a Beetle, but front cushions are still fixed. Teutonic firmness with no shaping affects rear passengers' comfort, and legroom – especially knee space – is tight. The seat is generously proportioned, however. The Variant's load space lacks height because of the engine room beneath, but it is a good, regularly shaped platform and there is another separate boot at the front. Heating is powerful to all occupants but difficult to control – it tends to be all or nothing. Screen vents prevent stuffiness by delivering fresh air on the move but there is no booster fan in slow traffic. More thought seems to have been given to injury prevention than on the Beetle. Constructional standards are similar, which is quite good enough to make it superior to most rivals, of course.

In fact, this bigger VW shares many of the ubiquitous Beetle's virtues – and vices. Although one can certainly enjoy more performance and sophistication for the money, the Variant feels relaxed, tireless and uncompromisingly well made. Far from being a vivacious plaything in which to indulge a flight of fancy, the Variant's quieter charms will appeal to those concerned with dependability and beauty that is more than skin deep.

Volvo 144 Grand Luxe

VOLVO 144/145
ENGINEERS' COMMENTS
Sturdy as a tank

The general public associates Volvo with solid construction, sturdy dependability, sound Swedish engineering, absence of rust, and longevity. The 144 has all these qualities, and the 145 estate version can accommodate more passengers and their luggage than most competitors.

Outwardly the car has changed little since its introduction in 1967. The sills and doors are designed to be ventilated – hence kept dry – by the passage of air through the hollow sections, a refinement which has helped to keep the internal corrosion rate relatively low. Where sweating and moisture trapping cannot be eliminated, hot-dip galvanised steel pressings are incorporated into the body structure. They do not show – except in the car's substantially longer structural life. There are many production control problems, however. For example, where the galvanised section is welded to ordinary mild steel, the spot weld zone and the joint line suffer a greater risk of corrosion than a conventional steel body which relies on electrocoat primer paint to keep moisture and oxygen away from the sheet steel. Over the years the Swedes have had a

great deal of bitter experience with the deterioration by road salt and slush of the car body structure, which has forced them to adopt costly anti-corrosion measures.

Factory-applied undersealing is good and keeps the whole underbody, including underframe members and underwing areas, remarkably free of rust. But the quality of the sealant compound and rubber strips sealing the boot deteriorates with age, even on Volvos. Consequently F/G registration 144s have an unusually high incidence of leaking boots: one in every eight cars.

Volvo have had some problems with minor stone chips on the edges and lower part of doors and wing panels. When they changed their paint protection process, some K and a few L registration cars displayed the weakness of inadequate paint intercoat adhesion in the form of surface rust patches. The shortcomings of these paints have since been overcome on M registration cars, however.

No amount of internal protection can deal effectively with outside rusting of body sills induced by gravel rash. Mudflaps help, but only a chip-resistant plastic coating on top of the paint would be really effective. Mechanically, Volvos are sturdy cars. But even they are not exceptionally resistant to deterioration with age and mileage, as can be seen from the VISAR data on engine oil leaks – mainly from crankshaft seals, attention to handbrake, increase in final drive noise and corrosion of brake pipelines. Handbrake cables tend to fray and may need replacing from time to time. But brakes and the back axle rarely give trouble. The worm-and-roller steering with its many linkages and swivel joints needs checking for leaks and wear by a franchised dealer. Also get them to check for excess play in front wheel bearings, suspension upper swivel joints, and bushes.

Volvos are not among the quietest of cars; the push-rod-operated overhead valve engine is inherently noisier than the single overhead camshaft engine which made its debut in 1974 on the Volvo 240 series, replacing the 140 series. However, tappet adjustment can reduce valve train clatter. The car benefits from dynamic balancing of all five wheels and a check that the rear damper mountings are not loose or worn. While clutch action tends to be firm and fierce, this doesn't appear to affect adversely either its service life or gear box durability, both of which are good.

The electrical system can give unsuspected trouble. Both batteries and their connections have at times been found to be in need of re-tightening. Rear, stop and number plate lights suffer from water ingress and accidental damage; hence their high premature failure incidence. Some early cars have headlamp failures due to poor sealing against water and slush. While perhaps not the most stylish of cars, like an armoured car it will take much punishment and outlast many more sophisticated vehicles.

Specification of AA tested car

See p. 224

Make & model	VOLVO 144/145
Production years	1966–1974
Body alternatives	4-door Saloon, 2-door Saloon, Estate
Engine variants	1780cc OHV (1966–8),
	1986cc OHV (1968–1974)
Data: AA test version	144 de luxe 4-door Saloon. 1971 model
Engine	In-line 4-cyl, watercooled, front-mounted
	Bore 88.9mm, stroke 80.0mm, 1986cc. Comp ratio 8.8:1
Fuel system	1 Zenith Stromberg emission control carburettor.
	Mechanical pump. 12.8-gallon tank
Transmission	4-speed & reverse, synchromesh on all forward gears. Rear-wheel drive.
	Diaphragm-spring clutch, $8\frac{1}{2}$" diameter dry plate, cable operated.
Suspension front	Independent. Wishbones, coil spring, anti-roll bar
Suspension rear	Coil-sprung live-axle, radius arm, telescopic damper
Steering	Cam & roller. 4 turns between full locks
	Turning circle 32 feet
Wheels	15" diameter, 5J rims
Tyres	165SR15 radial-ply (Cinturatos fitted)
Brakes	Hydraulic dual circuit, disc front/disc rear. Servo
Dimensions	Length 15'2$\frac{3}{4}$" Width 5'8$\frac{1}{4}$" Height 4'9$\frac{1}{2}$" Wheelbase 8'7"
(overall)	Ground clearance 7" Kerb weight (full tank) 23$\frac{1}{2}$ cwts
Max speed (in gears)	First 34mph, second 54mph, third 78mph, top 93mph
Overdrive	Not applicable
Acceleration	0–60mph: 13.8 seconds; standing-$\frac{1}{4}$ mile: 19.6 seconds
Fuel consumption	overall: 27.1mpg
	steady 50mph: 34.5mpg (top gear)
	steady 70mph: 25.6mpg (top gear)
Fuel	Premium 4-star

What VISAR reveals

Worse than average | Average | Better than average | No data

All chart figures are percentages

	Age in years:	6–8	5–6	4–5	3–4	2–3	1–2
	Registration Suffix:	FG	H	J	K	L	M
Corroded front doors		12	10	1	5	6	0
Corroded rear doors		8	8	1	7	2	0
Corroded front wings		22	9	3	11	2	0
Corroded rear wings		16	6	3	8	0	0
Corroded front underwings		0	0	0	0	0	0
Corroded rear underwings		0	0	0	0	0	0
Corroded body sills		27	24	15	18	10	2
Corroded jacking points		7	7	6	8	2	0
Corroded floor		0	0	0	0	0	0
Corroded underbody frame members		4	3	1	1	0	0
Defective undersealing		10	2	7	4	9	5
Loose/misaligned driver's seat		3	4	1	0	0	0
Attend to engine mountings		0	0	0	2	0	0
Evidence of head gasket leaks		0	0	0	1	0	0
Noisy valve gear		46	19	33	26	36	35
Evidence of engine oil leaks		36	29	25	20	7	11
Attend to carburettor tuning		36	26	27	23	23	23
Evidence of fuel leaks		0	4	5	0	2	0
Final drive noise		10	7	2	7	0	0
Unsatisfactory gear change		4	0	0	0	0	0
Unsatisfactory auto gear change		0	0	0	0	0	0
Clutch judder		0	5	6	8	5	5
Attend to front wheel bearings		10	7	7	12	8	0
Attend to steering box/rack		8	12	11	7	5	10
Attend to footbrake		0	0	1	0	4	5
Attend to handbrake		36	17	9	5	4	5
Corroded brake pipelines		13	7	7	7	0	0
Defective obligatory lights		27	54	16	16	31	5
Attend to charging system		0	0	4	3	2	0
Attend to horn		3	3	1	1	2	0

VOLVO 144/145 DE LUXE

From AA Road Test Report 187, 1969, 241, 1971 and 107, 1974

Solid, staid and conservative

There are more worthy contenders in the 2-litre saloon market than anywhere else. Volvo were early in the field and the evolution of the 144/145 has included bigger engines and continual safety and interior revisions.

The 2-litre de luxe has a single carburettor but produces enough power to stay level on acceleration with the Rover/Triumph duet. It is particularly sprightly in top gear pullaway, though it's not as silky as the Triumph. The car will cruise contentedly past the legal limit despite an incessant, 'close-to-the-works' feel and sound; both seem out of place in a car of this calibre. Fuel consumption is commendable, with test figures ranging from 20mpg to 30mpg. The gear change is thumb thick but slick in action, although one must overcome a strong bias to find first and second. The clutch demands a long and heavy movement and the accelerator is ridiculously weighty too.

The 144's handling feels even more dated as progress marches on, yet those who harbour absolutely no sporting pretentions find the model steady and reassuring. Wet road grip is limited but there's no mistaking the feeling through the steering as the car goes on tip-toe, about to skid. The ride has a certain steam-roller quality, rounding off the worst of the bumps. Bigger potholes make it feel more flurried, however, and it sways and bounces over undulations. The brakes' ultra-lightness seems strangely at odds with the other major controls, which all appear purpose-built for crane drivers. There's no doubt that the front seats give superb support, but driver comfort is spoilt by the long clutch and general pedal offset – he finishes up sitting too close to the wheel with a splayed right leg. Close grouping of certain minor switches causes some fumbling; inertia belts are a must if everything is to be reached. There's an excellent all-round view but parked wipers get in the way.

Interior design changed little until a new fascia with ventilation was introduced. The hard plastic moulding may not feel very absorbent but it will behave in the right sort of way in an accident. A laminated screen is standard and later cars have a warning system that causes much clicking and flashing until safety belts are fastened. The testers preferred the warning telltale that comes on if an external bulb fails.

The ventilation system was slow to be adopted but Volvo did it well eventually. All four outlets are boosted by a very quiet fan that serves the heater too, but around town the fan is needed constantly. Without ventilation, heating tends to be stuffy, although rear occupants do get plenty at foot level. Rear passenger comfort is spoilt by excessive firmness, although there's plenty of space to stretch. Boot space is excellent even if the second spare wheel well is occupied – the saloon's sill is high, though, requiring a mighty lift. The Estate car has a comfortable seat which folds to give a 75-inch load length with no sill to worry about. The tail gate is only 5 feet 7 inches high when open, though.

Durable construction

The quality and durability of Volvo construction shows little sign of half measure. The paint shines in unnecessary places and there are galvanised lower sections, with ventilated sills. The underbody seal is complete and mud flaps help too. The model's dull conservatism of design pays dividends in terms of easy maintenance – simplicity really is the keynote. The electrical equipment has a heavy-duty specification too.

'Solid' – that's the word to describe the Volvo 144. Its road manners may be staid, but for some it represents the ultimate in dependable personal transport. People who buy a Volvo and change after a year or so tend to suffer only the disadvantages without even discovering the longer term benefits.

Prices . . . a warning
The dangers of pre-determination

We have included in this book a guide to used car prices produced by the simple means of touring dealers throughout the country and noting the prices being asked. Apart from regional variations, which are quite common, there are often significant differences in prices within a given region. For example, in the North the price of a particular model in Newcastle could be very different from that of the same model in Liverpool. Similarly, prices will depend on the actual condition of the cars concerned and the fact that there can be 11 months difference in age between two cars registered in the same year. The prices were accurate as at 1 February 1975, but what about today's value?

At the present time it is extremely difficult to forecast the trend or depreciation due to the unprecedented rise in new car prices. For instance, many 1-year-old cars are listed at prices equal to or slightly above the recommended new price at the time they were purchased but, compared with the list price 1 year later, the depreciation is in the order of 25%, with earlier models showing roughly 15% depreciation per annum. It will be seen therefore, that the more expensive the car the greater the depreciation expressed in real money terms.

Our survey was carried out in February, so if you are thinking of buying a car in June it would be reasonable to look for a slight reduction in price. This is, of course, a very rough rule-of-thumb guide to give you some indication of the price you may expect to pay, but there are many factors which could cause significant differences. The trade, generally, bases the price of secondhand cars on Glass's Guide, a confidential trade publication which is produced monthly. The guide is compiled primarily on the basis of the age of the cars, the average annual mileage, and condition at the time of sale.

Although it is produced monthly, there are many factors which could rapidly outdate the guide and the dealer has to apply these to his selling price. Seasonal variations in demand, the effects of the economic situation, competition and the ever increasing price of new cars all have a significant effect. Add to this the current increases in staff wages and garage overheads, and the extent of repair work the dealer has to carry out on the cars before he can put them up for sale and you have a considerable arithmetical problem.

The price asked may also be affected by the extent of the dealer's warranty: it may be for 1, 3 or 6 months; it may cover parts only or parts and labour; it may exclude certain components or give complete cover. Due allowance will also be made for the expensive extras such as automatic gears, overdrive, and power steering but 'bolt-on goodies' such as radios, fog lamps or headrests rarely have a significant effect on the price asked.

Any guide on prices, whether generally available to the public or in restricted circulation, can only be a guide and must never be taken as gospel by either the seller or the buyer. If the car which has caught your eye seems to be overpriced, check first before accusing the vendor of being a rogue or, alternatively, rushing to buy the car and regretting it afterwards. They say 'there is one born every minute' and this applies particularly to the man longing for a 'new' car with the money burning a hole in his pocket.

If you intend to part exchange your present car and are trying to estimate its value as part payment on a replacement model, do not expect to be offered anywhere near the price asked by dealers for comparable cars. You will probably get something between 15% and 30% less than the selling price depending on the age and type of car you wish to trade in. Why should there be such a substantial difference between the selling and buying price? The simple answer is that the dealer is in business to make a profit, but much of this is eaten up by the cost of preparing cars for sale and storing them until they are sold. It used to be accepted that the cost of servicing and cleaning a car for sale was £20, but garages are now spending around £50 preparing a popular car for sale and as much as £100 on the more exclusive models. Add the overheads to this and the profit margin starts to look a little sick.

Nevertheless, the differential is an important factor which has led to a considerable increase in the level of private sales at something nearer the asking price of dealers. Private selling may save you money but beware of private buying. If you know a lot about cars you may well find a bargain but if you 'buy a pup' you have no legal redress against the seller. Furthermore, if you are unfortunate enough to have bought a stolen car and it is impounded by the police you will have the problem of taking legal action against the seller assuming, of course, that you can find him. If you are a layman the best advice is to buy from a reputable dealer having good workshop facilities. You may pay a little more but the chances are that the car will have been prepared for sale, it will have warranty cover, the garage will have facilities for repair if things go wrong, you will have the protection of the Trades Description and Supply of Goods (Implied Terms) Acts and if the car turns out to be stolen you can hold the garage responsible.

There are, therefore, many good reasons why prices may vary from one showroom to another and from dealer to private seller, but a guide is still useful in helping you to get an idea of what your expenditure may be.

The question now is, how much can you afford to spend? All too often buyers get into difficulties because they spend the maximum they can afford on a replacement car, leaving nothing in reserve. Do not forget the insurance, which could well be much higher than your present rate if you are changing to a model which, in the eyes of the insurer, is a greater risk. Leave something to cover servicing and repair, as even the best of cars may well need some work carried out before the end of the year

and keep a little in hand for unforeseen extras. Until you have owned a car for a few months it is almost impossible to decide if you will need any extras. You may need fog lights, reversing lights, a rear window demister or more comfortable seat-belts. They all cost money and shortage of ready cash to buy them frequently causes owners to become discontented with the car itself.

It is a fact that most people end up paying more for a car than they intended, so what can you do to keep within your budget?

1 Decide the maximum amount you can afford to spend.

2 Deduct one-quarter of this to cover insurance and extra commitments. Remember, if you are under 25 years of age or are buying a high-risk car you may need to save even more to meet insurance premiums.

3 Decide what size and type of car you need. There is no point in buying a two-seater sports car if twins are on the way, or a high performance saloon for short journeys.

4 Check the price guide to make a choice of two or three models which would suit your purpose and your purse.

5 Resist the urge to rush off and buy the first car you see, no matter how persuasive the salesman may be; take your time, compare prices, mileage and condition.

6 Once you have made a decision, wait before committing yourself. If possible, hire a similar car for a day, or better still, for a weekend, to find if it really suits you. Time and time again we get complaints because people have, literally, bought cars which do not suit them; this applies particularly when husband and wife share a car.

7 When you have finally made up your mind, check the details of the warranty offered.

8 Read the small print before you sign the agreement or the order form.

9 Enjoy your motoring with a car which suits you and leaves a few pounds in your pocket for emergencies.

Guide to used car prices showing variations by age

Prices shown in the following tables were established by a team of AA Inspectors surveying their respective regions on 1 February 1975. Please refer to notes on prices in the preceding article, and see page 255 for a Voucher to cover information concerning cars not included in the tables and up-to-date prices of those which are.

South-east England

Model chosen from the range — Age in years / Registration suffix:	6-8 FG	5-6 H	4-5 J	3-4 K	2-3 L	1-2 M
Austin Allegro 1300 Super					960 / 1015	925 / 1220
Austin Maxi 1750			700 / 879	750 / 1012	945 / 1295	1260 / 1625
Austin/Morris Mini 1000	245 / 467	340 / 595	410 / 660	555 / 795	640 / 925	835 / 1050
Austin/Morris 1300 Super	265 / 478	360 / 560	595 / 685	650 / 800	845 / 1068	930 / 1045
Austin/Morris 1800	430 / 525	440 / 685	625 / 775	635 / 1095	990 / 1295	1220 / 1575
Chrysler 180			770 / 845	700 / 985	990 / 1332	1300 / 1680
Citroën GS Club				740 / 930	880 / 1210	1080 / 1400
Daf 44 Estate	295 / 450	335 / 550	415 / 670	480 / 800	780 / 960	970 / 1200
Fiat 850	180 / 300	240 / 410	390 / 495	440 / 685	685 / 750	
Fiat 127				660 / 740	715 / 835	870 / 1010
Fiat 128 Saloon		560 / 590	585 / 679	595 / 855	785 / 955	965 / 1130
Fiat 124 Special	405 / 495	520 / 610	600 / 735	695 / 845	930 / 1065	1180 / 1300
Ford Capri 1600 GT	580 / 680	690 / 840	820 / 925	950 / 1129	1025 / 1315	1270 / 1605
Ford Corsair	350 / 495	450 / 520				
Ford Cortina 1600E	350 / 590	575 / 775				
Ford Cortina 1600XL			765 / 895	845 / 1025	970 / 1249	1210 / 1655
Ford Escort 1100L	350 / 455	525 / 605	600 / 755	690 / 825	840 / 990	1025 / 1230
Ford Granada 3000GXL				1295 / 1450	1345 / 1820	1995 / 2495
Ford Zodiac MkIV	195 / 495	350 / 695	525 / 699	600 / 795		

Model chosen from the range	Age in years: Registration suffix:	6–8 FG	5–6 H	4–5 J	3–4 K	2–3 L	1–2 M
Hillman Avenger 1500 GL			550 / 670	660 / 795	725 / 895	855 / 1045	1060 / 1298
Hillman Hunter GL		500 / 595	590 / 685	750 / 820	795 / 1000	975 / 1250	1145 / 1490
Hillman Imp		220 / 380	333 / 500	435 / 680	550 / 700	675 / 850	785 / 980
Jaguar XJ6 4.2		950 / 1200	985 / 1610	1515 / 2100	2000 / 2650	2223 / 3250	2925 / 4350
MG Midget MkIII		260 / 550	395 / 525	480 / 675	530 / 790	640 / 1000	955 / 1100
MGB		340 / 750	560 / 985	650 / 1100	965 / 1300	1060 / 1595	1525 / 1825
Morris Marina 1.8 4-dr Saloon				655 / 825	780 / 975	895 / 1099	1050 / 1350
Morris Minor Traveller 1000		300 / 500	425 / 605	560 / 695			
Moskvich 412			160 / 210	215 / 370	345 / 390	410 / 545	560 / 630
Reliant Scimitar GTE		810 / 1050	920 / 1300	1380 / 1580	1500 / 1970	1750 / 2350	2250 / 2900
Renault 4		310 / 430	390 / 530	480 / 600	560 / 730	699 / 825	795 / 1050
Renault 6			425 / 530	545 / 650	600 / 785	700 / 890	800 / 995
Renault 12 TL			600 / 695	675 / 800	780 / 910	875 / 1025	1050 / 1295
Renault 16 TL				780 / 820	810 / 1075	900 / 1290	1200 / 1400
Rover 2000 SC		502 / 790	725 / 890	825 / 1100	1090 / 1210	1290 / 1495	1650 / 2200
Rover 3½ litre Saloon		540 / 775	795 / 947	950 / 1225	1075 / 1409	1400 / 1800	
Saab 96		275 / 400	420 / 595	550 / 725	630 / 855	780 / 1030	1000 / 1360
Simca 1100 GLS		295 / 450	440 / 595	525 / 685	625 / 770	645 / 905	895 / 1160
Triumph Herald 13/60		345 / 462	345 / 525	500 / 695	680 / 730		
Triumph Spitfire		285 / 399	400 / 575	540 / 600	650 / 850	900 / 1080	1100 / 1275
Triumph Stag			1250 / 1400	1295 / 1675	1590 / 2150	1940 / 2565	2250 / 3040
Triumph Toledo				645 / 795	762 / 840	835 / 1005	1090 / 1258
Triumph TR6 PI			745 / 890	825 / 990	900 / 1255	1185 / 1495	1395 / 1695
Triumph 1300		405 / 517	510 / 631	580 / 697			
Triumph 2000 MkII		553 / 660	635 / 958	820 / 1198	1050 / 1425	1300 / 1632	1510 / 2048
Vauxhall Firenza 2000 SL					725 / 900	875 / 995	990 / 1050
Vauxhall Victor		225 / 408	375 / 500	458 / 785	665 / 860	900 / 1230	1113 / 1490
Vauxhall Viva HB		332 / 460	400 / 555	505 / 678			
Volkswagen 1300 Beetle		300 / 410	415 / 550	520 / 679	650 / 705	720 / 982	900 / 1045
Volkswagen 1600 Super Beetle			570 / 625	650 / 700	700 / 825	810 / 950	900 / 1040
Volvo 144 De luxe		495 / 670	745 / 895	895 / 1130	1095 / 1390	1200 / 1610	1550 / 2008

Guide to used car prices showing variations by age

REGISTRATION LETTERS

The following suffix letters have been issued by Licensing Authorities.

1963 A	1967 (Jan/July) E	1970/71 (Aug/July) J
1964 B	1967/68 (Aug/July) F	1971/72 (Aug/July) K
1965 C	1968/69 (Aug/July) G	1972/73 (Aug/July) L
1966 D	1969/70 (Aug/July) H	1973/74 (Aug/July) M

Prices shown in the following tables were established by a team of AA Inspectors surveying their respective regions on 1 February 1975. Please refer to notes on prices in the preceding article, and see page 255 for a Voucher to cover information concerning cars not included in the tables and up-to-date prices of those which are.

Metropolitan London

Model chosen from the range	6–8 FG	5–6 H	4–5 J	3–4 K	2–3 L	1–2 M
Austin Allegro 1300 Super					900 / 955	975 / 1195
Austin Maxi 1750			749 / 850	945 / 1045	1075 / 1225	1225 / 1425
Austin/Morris Mini 1000	295 / 475	479 / 525	525 / 695	625 / 785	800 / 895	895 / 1050
Austin/Morris 1300 Super	350 / 495	475 / 645	695 / 745	735 / 895	825 / 965	975 / 1015
Austin/Morris 1800	425 / 525	575 / 735	825 / 895	895 / 1025	995 / 1345	1350 / 1555
Chrysler 180			690 / 775	775 / 999	1080 / 1455	1650 / 1795
Citroën GS Club				795 / 899	995 / 1265	1195 / 1350
Daf 44 Estate	340 / 495	425 / 525	425 / 669	630 / 750	805 / 925	975 / 1209
Fiat 850	225 / 325	325 / 425	435 / 495	435 / 655	675 / 723	
Fiat 127				620 / 740	725 / 875	925 / 980
Fiat 128 Saloon		570 / 590	620 / 675	660 / 880	795 / 940	1025 / 1120
Fiat 124 Special	390 / 490	520 / 610	600 / 725	730 / 855	925 / 1065	1165 / 1260
Ford Capri 1600 GT	600 / 700	705 / 845	865 / 989	955 / 1030	1125 / 1230	1275 / 1395
Ford Corsair	370 / 420	420 / 515				
Ford Cortina 1600E	545 / 590	660 / 775				
Ford Cortina 1600XL			769 / 855	860 / 975	1150 / 1249	1380 / 1655
Ford Escort 1100L	400 / 530	525 / 595	635 / 745	665 / 780	820 / 995	1035 / 1210
Ford Granada 3000GXL				1445 / 1559	1525 / 1820	1999 / 2355
Ford Zodiac MkIV	295 / 485	405 / 658	525 / 610	599 / 795		

Model chosen from the range	6–8 FG	5–6 H	4–5 J	3–4 K	2–3 L	1–2 M
Hillman Avenger 1500 GL		595 / 620	690 / 735	750 / 825	860 / 995	1000 / 1290
Hillman Hunter GL	490 / 590	595 / 620	700 / 755	800 / 975	980 / 1195	1085 / 1325
Hillman Imp	255 / 325	395 / 425	495 / 540	550 / 685	705 / 900	845 / 895
Jaguar XJ6 4.2	1000 / 1215	1095 / 1610	1570 / 2060	2090 / 2475	2370 / 2995	3295 / 4280
MG Midget MkIII	285 / 400	360 / 500	495 / 695	540 / 730	630 / 940	955 / 1125
MGB	385 / 720	575 / 835	650 / 1000	950 / 1295	1005 / 1580	1530 / 1840
Morris Marina 1.8 4-dr Saloon			735 / 880	850 / 980	930 / 1015	1125 / 1395
Morris Minor Traveller 1000	300 / 500	450 / 620	650 / 745			
Moskvich 412		160 / 210	220 / 375	350 / 430	420 / 560	590 / 640
Reliant Scimitar GTE	990 / 1090	1095 / 1305	1345 / 1575	1550 / 1935	1855 / 2305	2275 / 2799
Renault 4	260 / 400	400 / 445	460 / 530	575 / 760	735 / 850	800 / 1100
Renault 6		420 / 495	545 / 650	665 / 795	730 / 920	875 / 1020
Renault 12 TL		610 / 700	645 / 780	725 / 875	895 / 1025	1060 / 1280
Renault 16 TL			810 / 830	850 / 1095	1100 / 1295	1245 / 1485
Rover 2000 SC	495 / 795	725 / 895	875 / 1175	1175 / 1295	1395 / 1540	1755 / 2295
Rover 3½ litre Saloon	540 / 765	825 / 995	995 / 1245	1050 / 1435	1495 / 1850	
Saab 96	275 / 410	430 / 590	550 / 730	630 / 860	795 / 1040	1000 / 1370
Simca 1100 GLS	380 / 495	400 / 565	585 / 690	650 / 775	760 / 920	990 / 1195
Triumph Herald 13/60	380 / 495	450 / 575	565 / 695	690 / 730		
Triumph Spitfire	295 / 350	395 / 580	545 / 650	700 / 900	1020 / 1095	1100 / 1280
Triumph Stag		1260 / 1450	1350 / 1690	1600 / 2200	2000 / 2580	2350 / 3080
Triumph Toledo			655 / 780	750 / 860	870 / 1010	1070 / 1290
Triumph TR6 PI		750 / 850	815 / 1050	900 / 1300	1150 / 1500	1400 / 1800
Triumph 1300	420 / 520	570 / 680	590 / 700			
Triumph 2000 MkII	550 / 750	770 / 1000	915 / 1200	1150 / 1430	1320 / 1650	1550 / 2050
Vauxhall Firenza 2000 SL				810 / 930	900 / 1000	1000 / 1100
Vauxhall Victor	250 / 420	400 / 535	500 / 790	685 / 875	940 / 1250	1200 / 1480
Vauxhall Viva HB	370 / 450	420 / 560	510 / 680			
Volkswagen 1300 Beetle	330 / 450	420 / 580	550 / 680	690 / 735	645 / 890	890 / 1050
Volkswagen 1600 Super Beetle		580 / 645	660 / 690	710 / 845	850 / 950	910 / 1100
Volvo 144 De luxe	500 / 750	780 / 970	850 / 1200	1115 / 1450	1200 / 1700	1550 / 2045

Guide to used car prices showing variations by age

REGISTRATION LETTERS

The following suffix letters have been issued by Licensing Authorities.

1963 A	1967 (Jan/July) E	1970/71 (Aug/July) J
1964 B	1967/68 (Aug/July) F	1971/72 (Aug/July) K
1965 C	1968/69 (Aug/July) G	1972/73 (Aug/July) L
1966 D	1969/70 (Aug/July) H	1973/74 (Aug/July) M

Prices shown in the following tables were established by a team of AA Inspectors surveying their respective regions on 1 February 1975. Please refer to notes on prices in the preceding article, and see page 255 for a Voucher to cover information concerning cars not included in the tables and up-to-date prices of those which are.

Midlands

Model chosen from the range	Age in years: Registration suffix:	6–8 FG	5–6 H	4–5 J	3–4 K	2–3 L	1–2 M
Austin Allegro 1300 Super						869 / 1080	950 / 1495
Austin Maxi 1750				600 / 875	675 / 1065	1045 / 1375	1125 / 1595
Austin/Morris Mini 1000		290 / 425	420 / 565	525 / 695	550 / 925	770 / 995	865 / 1065
Austin/Morris 1300 Super		200 / 475	380 / 679	469 / 725	635 / 895	699 / 995	800 / 1025
Austin/Morris 1800		250 / 595	500 / 665	595 / 845	650 / 1050	795 / 1150	1095 / 1325
Chrysler 180				620 / 800	950 / 1100	895 / 1250	1325 / 1695
Citroën GS Club					725 / 950	1165 / 1275	1165 / 1495
Daf 44 Estate		400 / 510	500 / 610	610 / 725	595 / 800	860 / 950	945 / 1120
Fiat 850		195 / 290	300 / 450	400 / 580	740 / 795	800 / 865	
Fiat 127					699 / 780	773 / 845	800 / 1100
Fiat 128 Saloon			450 / 580	545 / 620	550 / 849	800 / 945	945 / 1125
Fiat 124 Special		370 / 450	430 / 550	600 / 800	785 / 950	850 / 1100	1000 / 1300
Ford Capri 1600 GT		475 / 525	560 / 765	660 / 999	775 / 1075	950 / 1395	1300 / 1495
Ford Corsair		135 / 445	379 / 580				
Ford Cortina 1600E		395 / 485	500 / 725				
Ford Cortina 1600XL				525 / 880	675 / 1055	699 / 1295	1025 / 1595
Ford Escort 1100L		210 / 510	425 / 589	595 / 779	599 / 925	629 / 985	895 / 1225
Ford Granada 3000GXL					895 / 1370	995 / 1995	1500 / 2500
Ford Zodiac MkIV		260 / 350	400 / 495	425 / 599	595 / 700		

Model chosen from the range	Age in years: 6–8 — Registration suffix: FG	5–6 H	4–5 J	3–4 K	2–3 L	1–2 M
Hillman Avenger 1500 GL		475 / 625	600 / 745	700 / 949	775 / 1095	1055 / 1335
Hillman Hunter GL	450 / 650	600 / 795	675 / 895	825 / 1005	900 / 1195	1045 / 1499
Hillman Imp	135 / 370	350 / 470	485 / 595	555 / 745	730 / 895	825 / 1020
Jaguar XJ6 4.2	829 / 1000	875 / 1650	1199 / 2125	1495 / 2695	1895 / 3300	2750 / 3595
MG Midget MkIII	310 / 405	395 / 500	540 / 600	600 / 685	625 / 895	855 / 1099
MGB	500 / 615	525 / 795	650 / 995	885 / 1150	995 / 1495	1275 / 1875
Morris Marina 1.8 4-dr Saloon			600 / 795	599 / 999	795 / 1195	985 / 1325
Morris Minor Traveller 1000	350 / 485	500 / 595	600 / 700			
Moskvich 412		210 / 300	300 / 390	330 / 420	400 / 545	555 / 685
Reliant Scimitar GTE	1000 / 1150	1100 / 1320	1290 / 1600	1395 / 1990	1775 / 2225	2250 / 2695
Renault 4	295 / 380	375 / 505	580 / 650	695 / 785	760 / 880	890 / 980
Renault 6		450 / 580	595 / 745	640 / 850	745 / 1025	1175 / 1225
Renault 12 TL		650 / 700	700 / 799	880 / 950	850 / 1200	1250 / 1525
Renault 16 TL			600 / 865	850 / 1050	899 / 1550	1245 / 1625
Rover 2000 SC	225 / 750	645 / 895	700 / 1095	850 / 1345	1000 / 1700	2095 / 2295
Rover 3½ litre Saloon	390 / 900	750 / 950	800 / 1225	1000 / 1850	1975 / 2200	
Saab 96	395 / 495	500 / 625	645 / 840	800 / 965	1025 / 1105	1225 / 1395
Simca 1100 GLS	250 / 400	425 / 575	595 / 760	659 / 895	810 / 980	945 / 1145
Triumph Herald 13/60	290 / 409	400 / 570	569 / 765	740 / 800		
Triumph Spitfire	350 / 499	450 / 585	500 / 655	620 / 790	880 / 1080	995 / 1295
Triumph Stag		1475 / 1575	1625 / 1650	1795 / 2095	2095 / 2490	2100 / 3150
Triumph Toledo			675 / 699	695 / 895	825 / 1050	995 / 1199
Triumph TR6 PI		600 / 790	890 / 1000	1000 / 1295	1220 / 1470	1295 / 1895
Triumph 1300	245 / 495	385 / 595	635 / 690			
Triumph 2000 MkII	340 / 650	650 / 945	950 / 1145	869 / 1450	1195 / 1795	1850 / 2455
Vauxhall Firenza 2000 SL				699 / 850	820 / 1000	1035 / 1060
Vauxhall Victor	299 / 495	440 / 645	450 / 750	650 / 995	825 / 1200	1275 / 1499
Vauxhall Viva HB	299 / 445	360 / 525	490 / 779			
Volkswagen 1300 Beetle	350 / 455	430 / 600	550 / 795	645 / 865	750 / 965	865 / 1085
Volkswagen 1600 Super Beetle		660 / 720	690 / 770	760 / 895	895 / 995	1000 / 1100
Volvo 144 De luxe	750 / 840	850 / 950	1000 / 1320	1195 / 1695	1660 / 2095	1985 / 2295

Guide to used car prices showing variations by age

Prices shown in the following tables were established by a team of AA Inspectors surveying their respective regions on 1 February 1975. Please refer to notes on prices in the preceding article, and see page 255 for a Voucher to cover information concerning cars not included in the tables and up-to-date prices of those which are.

Wales and West England

Model chosen from the range / Registration suffix:	6–8 FG	5–6 H	4–5 J	3–4 K	2–3 L	1–2 M
Austin Allegro 1300 Super					790 / 1255	1025 / 1495
Austin Maxi 1750			730 / 895	750 / 1095	1045 / 1350	1195 / 1695
Austin/Morris Mini 1000	300 / 525	545 / 675	595 / 695	650 / 795	725 / 945	850 / 1035
Austin/Morris 1300 Super	300 / 525	425 / 645	525 / 780	625 / 875	825 / 1095	935 / 1150
Austin/Morris 1800	225 / 545	450 / 700	495 / 795	700 / 1095	875 / 1245	1050 / 1345
Chrysler 180			600 / 860	695 / 1075	1110 / 1295	1350 / 1675
Citroën GS Club				695 / 810	1095 / 1295	1150 / 1545
Daf 44 Estate	475 / 525	580 / 620	640 / 690	625 / 820	890 / 985	985 / 1125
Fiat 850	200 / 305	375 / 490	450 / 580	690 / 790	750 / 825	
Fiat 127				645 / 795	825 / 875	795 / 1075
Fiat 128 Saloon		440 / 575	550 / 655	650 / 845	780 / 995	900 / 1175
Fiat 124 Special	385 / 430	425 / 500	600 / 800	795 / 990	850 / 1095	1095 / 1300
Ford Capri 1600 GT	475 / 525	545 / 795	695 / 995	795 / 1095	995 / 1375	1295 / 1550
Ford Corsair	195 / 525	425 / 585				
Ford Cortina 1600E	400 / 495	550 / 765				
Ford Cortina 1600XL			590 / 805	675 / 995	725 / 1295	950 / 1587
Ford Escort 1100L	225 / 555	470 / 600	645 / 890	675 / 910	705 / 1005	850 / 1200
Ford Granada 3000GXL				995 / 1495	1095 / 2050	1550 / 2550
Ford Zodiac MkIV	260 / 395	395 / 495	425 / 645	660 / 760		

Model chosen from the range	6-8 FG	5-6 H	4-5 J	3-4 K	2-3 L	1-2 M
Hillman Avenger 1500 GL		535 / 655	655 / 775	725 / 945	765 / 1105	1075 / 1345
Hillman Hunter GL	475 / 650	675 / 750	675 / 825	845 / 1025	925 / 1195	990 / 1425
Hillman Imp	155 / 445	375 / 465	495 / 645	625 / 765	750 / 875	839 / 1095
Jaguar XJ6 4.2	845 / 1000	895 / 1650	1195 / 2295	1525 / 2745	2500 / 3650	3350 / 4025
MG Midget MkIII	325 / 405	405 / 505	545 / 605	620 / 700	699 / 935	985 / 1125
MGB	550 / 695	695 / 795	640 / 1095	875 / 1195	1095 / 1495	1200 / 1845
Morris Marina 1.8 4-dr Saloon			615 / 795	625 / 995	795 / 1195	1025 / 1305
Morris Minor Traveller 1000	350 / 495	495 / 605	595 / 695			
Moskvich 412		220 / 305	300 / 420	325 / 425	395 / 550	550 / 680
Reliant Scimitar GTE	995 / 1200	1220 / 1300	1295 / 1595	1395 / 1995	1995 / 2350	2200 / 2800
Renault 4	350 / 425	395 / 575	640 / 700	745 / 815	795 / 925	920 / 980
Renault 6		475 / 525	580 / 755	695 / 850	740 / 1045	900 / 1195
Renault 12 TL		675 / 725	695 / 850	800 / 995	895 / 1225	1225 / 1425
Renault 16 TL			795 / 940	650 / 1095	1145 / 1225	1100 / 1595
Rover 2000 SC	350 / 700	795 / 1065	995 / 1200	975 / 1495	1295 / 1600	1400 / 2090
Rover 3½ litre Saloon	355 / 900	799 / 1095	895 / 1350	995 / 1995	1955 / 2180	
Saab 96	325 / 450	550 / 650	625 / 885	880 / 985	935 / 1115	1199 / 1400
Simca 1100 GLS	275 / 430	435 / 570	565 / 675	695 / 850	790 / 975	990 / 1195
Triumph Herald 13/60	295 / 475	435 / 640	539 / 715	715 / 805		
Triumph Spitfire	373 / 475	475 / 690	510 / 640	650 / 800	890 / 1030	1000 / 1195
Triumph Stag		1450 / 1550	1575 / 1695	1800 / 2095	2050 / 2495	2300 / 3195
Triumph Toledo			715 / 750	695 / 850	895 / 1180	1000 / 1295
Triumph TR6 PI		825 / 870	900 / 1015	995 / 1215	1250 / 1500	1395 / 1895
Triumph 1300	375 / 595	495 / 625	650 / 690			
Triumph 2000 MkII	395 / 785	775 / 1095	900 / 1195	1095 / 1445	1200 / 1695	1850 / 2465
Vauxhall Firenza 2000 SL				775 / 870	855 / 1000	1020 / 1040
Vauxhall Victor	295 / 595	450 / 675	505 / 795	720 / 1045	895 / 1345	1200 / 1575
Vauxhall Viva HB	250 / 425	400 / 595	545 / 765			
Volkswagen 1300 Beetle	325 / 475	495 / 625	525 / 795	745 / 900	795 / 995	925 / 1095
Volkswagen 1600 Super Beetle		650 / 710	700 / 785	790 / 950	945 / 1045	1100 / 1200
Volvo 144 De luxe	785 / 850	905 / 1115	1095 / 1395	1225 / 1790	1795 / 2195	1945 / 2300

Guide to used car prices showing variations by age

REGISTRATION LETTERS

The following suffix letters have been issued by Licensing Authorities.

1963 A	1967 (Jan/July) E	1970/71 (Aug/July) J
1964 B	1967/68 (Aug/July) F	1971/72 (Aug/July) K
1965 C	1968/69 (Aug/July) G	1972/73 (Aug/July) L
1966 D	1969/70 (Aug/July) H	1973/74 (Aug/July) M

Prices shown in the following tables were established by a team of AA Inspectors surveying their respective regions on 1 February 1975. Please refer to notes on prices in the preceding article, and see page 255 for a Voucher to cover information concerning cars not included in the tables and up-to-date prices of those which are.

North of England

Model chosen from the range / Age in years: Registration suffix:	6–8 FG	5–6 H	4–5 J	3–4 K	2–3 L	1–2 M
Austin Allegro 1300 Super					880 / 1225	1093 / 1425
Austin Maxi 1750			560 / 845	640 / 1020	825 / 1310	1000 / 1495
Austin/Morris Mini 1000	185 / 495	400 / 630	525 / 680	495 / 860	595 / 950	700 / 1050
Austin/Morris 1300 Super	170 / 495	380 / 645	495 / 725	550 / 795	650 / 1025	760 / 1070
Austin/Morris 1800	240 / 500	450 / 650	495 / 795	550 / 1050	810 / 1245	1020 / 1350
Chrysler 180			525 / 800	599 / 1005	880 / 1195	1250 / 1675
Citroën GS Club				675 / 850	885 / 1200	1050 / 1345
Daf 44 Estate	350 / 500	480 / 595	580 / 700	590 / 820	850 / 950	900 / 1100
Fiat 850	200 / 300	300 / 450	400 / 595	750 / 800	790 / 865	
Fiat 127				595 / 725	725 / 895	780 / 995
Fiat 128 Saloon		400 / 595	575 / 650	535 / 848	780 / 985	900 / 1150
Fiat 124 Special	380 / 440	420 / 550	600 / 775	770 / 895	800 / 1010	950 / 1295
Ford Capri 1600 GT	465 / 545	530 / 770	667 / 950	780 / 1050	980 / 1375	1250 / 1475
Ford Corsair	140 / 495	350 / 560				
Ford Cortina 1600E	390 / 450	495 / 655				
Ford Cortina 1600XL			595 / 825	620 / 1005	725 / 1295	1050 / 1595
Ford Escort 1100L	200 / 550	392 / 550	595 / 750	560 / 895	645 / 995	845 / 1200
Ford Granada 3000GXL				990 / 1450	995 / 2000	1469 / 2450
Ford Zodiac MkIV	280 / 400	400 / 500	425 / 630	600 / 720		

Model chosen from the range (Age in years / Registration suffix)	6-8 FG	5-6 H	4-5 J	3-4 K	2-3 L	1-2 M
Hillman Avenger 1500 GL		500 / 645	660 / 775	695 / 925	735 / 1075	1065 / 1355
Hillman Hunter GL	380 / 585	595 / 720	650 / 850	785 / 1050	895 / 1150	995 / 1450
Hillman Imp	135 / 400	330 / 455	495 / 625	595 / 725	745 / 895	820 / 1065
Jaguar XJ6 4.2	800 / 1000	900 / 1625	1200 / 2150	1500 / 2650	1895 / 3300	2800 / 4000
MG Midget MkIII	280 / 380	400 / 500	540 / 635	610 / 765	705 / 995	935 / 1099
MGB	485 / 630	550 / 800	650 / 1050	830 / 1195	1095 / 1495	1250 / 1895
Morris Marina 1.8 4-dr Saloon			610 / 795	600 / 1000	780 / 1170	1050 / 1350
Morris Minor Traveller 1000	375 / 480	500 / 600	595 / 685			
Moskvich 412		200 / 260	280 / 395	365 / 450	410 / 565	500 / 680
Reliant Scimitar GTE	975 / 1100	1090 / 1350	1290 / 1600	1395 / 1950	1880 / 2315	2195 / 2750
Renault 4	350 / 400	385 / 480	475 / 685	680 / 795	750 / 900	845 / 940
Renault 6		400 / 580	585 / 695	600 / 825	690 / 965	935 / 1195
Renault 12 TL		630 / 695	625 / 810	800 / 995	880 / 1200	1050 / 1425
Renault 16 TL			575 / 865	695 / 1045	900 / 1275	1095 / 1400
Rover 2000 SC	285 / 795	600 / 995	650 / 1100	850 / 1350	1295 / 1650	1295 / 2395
Rover 3½ litre Saloon	385 / 850	675 / 1000	785 / 1200	990 / 1700	1195 / 2200	
Saab 96	300 / 425	480 / 625	520 / 895	840 / 995	850 / 1150	1240 / 1325
Simca 1100 GLS	240 / 425	415 / 525	500 / 620	675 / 820	740 / 995	995 / 1150
Triumph Herald 13/60	245 / 450	400 / 595	500 / 745	730 / 780		
Triumph Spitfire	360 / 460	400 / 600	500 / 615	670 / 785	895 / 1025	1125 / 1160
Triumph Stag		1350 / 1550	1550 / 1695	1775 / 2095	2050 / 2500	2050 / 3150
Triumph Toledo			695 / 730	665 / 850	765 / 1025	995 / 1265
Triumph TR6 PI		795 / 800	800 / 1000	900 / 1250	1125 / 1500	1340 / 1850
Triumph 1300	275 / 550	499 / 600	645 / 695			
Triumph 2000 MkII	325 / 690	675 / 950	850 / 1095	895 / 1350	1125 / 1680	1670 / 2295
Vauxhall Firenza 2000 SL				680 / 885	850 / 1005	1020 / 1045
Vauxhall Victor	225 / 460	395 / 650	485 / 695	650 / 985	800 / 1225	1095 / 1550
Vauxhall Viva HB	260 / 459	365 / 575	500 / 725			
Volkswagen 1300 Beetle	295 / 480	450 / 625	550 / 725	699 / 925	745 / 945	905 / 1145
Volkswagen 1600 Super Beetle		655 / 700	690 / 775	700 / 900	925 / 1010	1000 / 1150
Volvo 144 De luxe	750 / 850	860 / 1025	985 / 1325	1200 / 1725	1695 / 2000	1900 / 2395

Guide to used car prices showing variations by age

REGISTRATION LETTERS		
The following suffix letters have been issued by Licensing Authorities.		
1963 A	1967 (Jan/July) E	1970/71 (Aug/July) J
1964 B	1967/68 (Aug/July) F	1971/72 (Aug/July) K
1965 C	1968/69 (Aug/July) G	1972/73 (Aug/July) L
1966 D	1969/70 (Aug/July) H	1973/74 (Aug/July) M

Prices shown in the following tables were established by a team of AA Inspectors surveying their respective regions on 1 February 1975. Please refer to notes on prices in the preceding article, and see page 255 for a Voucher to cover information concerning cars not included in the tables and up-to-date prices of those which are.

Scotland

Model chosen from the range / Age in years / Registration suffix:	6–8 FG	5–6 H	4–5 J	3–4 K	2–3 L	1–2 M
Austin Allegro 1300 Super					950 / 1250	1200 / 1450
Austin Maxi 1750			670 / 900	800 / 1045	950 / 1295	1200 / 1595
Austin/Morris Mini 1000	300 / 495	390 / 585	475 / 725	580 / 850	795 / 950	860 / 1035
Austin/Morris 1300 Super	350 / 485	400 / 600	600 / 735	675 / 825	725 / 945	825 / 1050
Austin/Morris 1800	395 / 525	485 / 675	635 / 795	695 / 1025	900 / 1295	1200 / 1485
Chrysler 180			690 / 800	705 / 950	975 / 1250	1300 / 1600
Citroën GS Club				750 / 925	805 / 1140	945 / 1290
Daf 44 Estate	275 / 450	380 / 575	450 / 700	400 / 750	760 / 1000	905 / 1125
Fiat 850	195 / 350	275 / 410	400 / 495	400 / 640	600 / 760	
Fiat 127				660 / 745	700 / 905	860 / 995
Fiat 128 Saloon		495 / 585	575 / 660	575 / 845	775 / 930	915 / 1140
Fiat 124 Special	390 / 495	495 / 590	585 / 730	690 / 880	870 / 1060	1075 / 1280
Ford Capri 1600 GT	580 / 650	650 / 825	825 / 995	900 / 1195	1050 / 1290	1280 / 1600
Ford Corsair	250 / 485	450 / 565				
Ford Cortina 1600E	325 / 595	575 / 795				
Ford Cortina 1600XL			695 / 800	800 / 965	825 / 1250	1200 / 1595
Ford Escort 1100L	395 / 525	520 / 650	695 / 825	695 / 810	775 / 910	950 / 1200
Ford Granada 3000GXL				1330 / 1430	1200 / 1770	1850 / 2400
Ford Zodiac MkIV	250 / 480	350 / 795	495 / 645	550 / 750		

Model chosen from the range	Age in years: Registration suffix:	6–8 FG	5–6 H	4–5 J	3–4 K	2–3 L	1–2 M
Hillman Avenger 1500 GL			520 / 660	650 / 725	725 / 835	830 / 1025	995 / 1280
Hillman Hunter GL		375 / 440	435 / 575	650 / 835	800 / 1015	900 / 1250	1090 / 1450
Hillman Imp		250 / 305	340 / 495	425 / 505	500 / 615	625 / 895	795 / 1025
Jaguar XJ6 4.2		900 / 1205	995 / 1635	1595 / 2095	2025 / 2650	2320 / 3150	3250 / 4200
MG Midget MkIII		260 / 425	395 / 505	455 / 600	505 / 710	625 / 925	925 / 1150
MGB		300 / 700	595 / 875	635 / 1035	950 / 1325	1060 / 1510	1540 / 1910
Morris Marina 1.8 4-dr Saloon				675 / 825	735 / 975	890 / 1075	1100 / 1385
Morris Minor Traveller 1000		250 / 495	375 / 590	560 / 695			
Moskvich 412			150 / 200	200 / 360	320 / 390	410 / 525	540 / 600
Reliant Scimitar GTE		990 / 1090	1000 / 1275	1300 / 1575	1575 / 1880	1880 / 2255	2255 / 2850
Renault 4		150 / 325	300 / 405	375 / 500	525 / 725	620 / 720	775 / 1000
Renault 6			390 / 460	480 / 620	560 / 780	680 / 840	800 / 985
Renault 12 TL			590 / 650	580 / 775	650 / 820	800 / 950	1005 / 1275
Renault 16 TL				775 / 805	805 / 975	900 / 1290	1245 / 1360
Rover 2000 SC		400 / 700	680 / 875	810 / 1100	950 / 1205	1200 / 1325	1575 / 2200
Rover 3½ litre Saloon		350 / 685	675 / 830	895 / 1055	1000 / 1500	1400 / 1735	
Saab 96		250 / 395	395 / 550	495 / 710	610 / 800	750 / 1000	940 / 1340
Simca 1100 GLS		260 / 395	385 / 435	475 / 550	595 / 675	625 / 850	850 / 1150
Triumph Herald 13/60		285 / 425	395 / 460	495 / 695	680 / 725		
Triumph Spitfire		200 / 300	395 / 500	480 / 560	600 / 800	850 / 1000	1000 / 1200
Triumph Stag			1200 / 1400	1270 / 1550	1500 / 2050	1795 / 2325	2200 / 2925
Triumph Toledo				600 / 700	690 / 800	760 / 995	985 / 1195
Triumph TR6 PI			695 / 825	800 / 975	850 / 1095	1000 / 1375	1350 / 1645
Triumph 1300		250 / 520	400 / 600	565 / 650			
Triumph 2000 MkII		400 / 550	500 / 750	750 / 1010	1000 / 1300	1200 / 1545	1450 / 2000
Vauxhall Firenza 2000 SL					705 / 900	820 / 980	975 / 1050
Vauxhall Victor		200 / 390	350 / 460	440 / 750	650 / 850	880 / 1150	1100 / 1450
Vauxhall Viva HB		250 / 445	350 / 525	490 / 665			
Volkswagen 1300 Beetle		200 / 405	415 / 575	505 / 570	590 / 895	695 / 995	900 / 1055
Volkswagen 1600 Super Beetle			565 / 615	640 / 695	695 / 810	800 / 900	870 / 1000
Volvo 144 De luxe		400 / 650	695 / 820	840 / 1095	1025 / 1295	1200 / 1550	1505 / 2005

Guide to used car prices showing variations by region

Prices shown in the following tables were established by a team of AA Inspectors surveying their respective regions on 1 February 1975. Please refer to notes on prices in the preceding article, and see page 255 for a Voucher to cover information concerning cars not included in the tables and up-to-date prices of those which are.

F and G Registration 6–8 years old

Model chosen from the range	South-east England	Metropolitan London	Midlands	Wales and West England	North of England	Scotland
Austin Allegro 1300 Super						
Austin Maxi 1750						
Austin/Morris Mini 1000	245 / 467	295 / 475	290 / 425	300 / 525	185 / 495	300 / 495
Austin/Morris 1300 Super	265 / 478	350 / 495	200 / 475	300 / 525	170 / 495	350 / 485
Austin/Morris 1800	430 / 525	425 / 525	250 / 595	225 / 545	240 / 500	395 / 542
Chrysler 180						
Citroën GS Club						
Daf 44 Estate	295 / 450	340 / 495	400 / 510	475 / 525	350 / 500	275 / 450
Fiat 850	180 / 300	225 / 325	195 / 290	200 / 305	200 / 300	195 / 350
Fiat 127						
Fiat 128 Saloon						
Fiat 124 Special	405 / 495	390 / 490	370 / 450	385 / 430	380 / 440	390 / 495
Ford Capri 1600 GT	580 / 680	600 / 700	475 / 525	475 / 525	465 / 545	580 / 650
Ford Corsair	350 / 495	370 / 420	135 / 445	195 / 525	140 / 495	250 / 485
Ford Cortina 1600E	350 / 590	545 / 590	395 / 485	400 / 495	390 / 450	325 / 595
Ford Cortina 1600XL						
Ford Escort 1100L	350 / 455	400 / 530	210 / 510	225 / 555	200 / 550	395 / 525
Ford Granada 3000GXL						
Ford Zodiac MkIV	195 / 495	295 / 485	260 / 350	260 / 395	280 / 400	250 / 480

Model chosen from the range	South-east England	Metropolitan London	Midlands	Wales and West England	North of England	Scotland
Hillman Avenger 1500 GL						
Hillman Hunter GL	500 / 595	490 / 590	450 / 650	475 / 650	380 / 585	375 / 440
Hillman Imp	220 / 380	255 / 325	135 / 370	155 / 445	135 / 400	250 / 305
Jaguar XJ6 4.2	950 / 1200	1000 / 1215	829 / 1000	845 / 1000	800 / 1000	900 / 1205
MG Midget MkIII	260 / 550	285 / 400	310 / 405	325 / 405	280 / 380	260 / 425
MGB	340 / 750	385 / 720	500 / 615	550 / 695	485 / 630	300 / 700
Morris Marina 1.8 4-dr Saloon						
Morris Minor Traveller 1000	300 / 500	300 / 500	350 / 485	350 / 495	375 / 480	250 / 495
Moskvich 412						
Reliant Scimitar GTE	810 / 1050	990 / 1090	1000 / 1150	995 / 1200	975 / 1100	990 / 1090
Renault 4	310 / 430	260 / 400	295 / 380	350 / 425	350 / 400	150 / 325
Renault 6						
Renault 12 TL						
Renault 16 TL						
Rover 2000 SC	502 / 790	495 / 795	225 / 750	350 / 700	285 / 795	400 / 700
Rover 3½ litre Saloon	540 / 775	540 / 765	390 / 900	355 / 900	385 / 850	350 / 685
Saab 96	275 / 400	275 / 410	395 / 495	325 / 450	300 / 425	250 / 395
Simca 1100 GLS	295 / 450	380 / 495	250 / 400	275 / 430	240 / 425	260 / 395
Triumph Herald 13/60	345 / 462	380 / 495	290 / 409	295 / 475	245 / 450	285 / 425
Triumph Spitfire	285 / 399	295 / 350	350 / 499	373 / 475	360 / 460	200 / 300
Triumph Stag						
Triumph Toledo						
Triumph TR6 PI						
Triumph 1300	405 / 517	420 / 520	245 / 495	375 / 595	275 / 550	250 / 520
Triumph 2000 MkII	553 / 660	550 / 750	340 / 650	395 / 785	325 / 690	400 / 550
Vauxhall Firenza 2000 SL						
Vauxhall Victor	225 / 408	250 / 420	299 / 495	295 / 595	225 / 460	200 / 390
Vauxhall Viva HB	332 / 460	370 / 450	299 / 445	250 / 425	260 / 459	250 / 445
Volkswagen 1300 Beetle	300 / 410	330 / 450	350 / 455	325 / 475	295 / 480	200 / 405
Volkswagen 1600 Super Beetle						
Volvo 144 De luxe	495 / 670	500 / 750	750 / 840	785 / 850	750 / 850	400 / 650

Guide to used car prices showing variations by region

REGISTRATION LETTERS		
The following suffix letters have been issued by Licensing Authorities.		
1963 A	1967 (Jan/July) E	1970/71 (Aug/July) J
1964 B	1967/68 (Aug/July) F	1971/72 (Aug/July) K
1965 C	1968/69 (Aug/July) G	1972/73 (Aug/July) L
1966 D	1969/70 (Aug/July) H	1973/74 (Aug/July) M

Prices shown in the following tables were established by a team of AA Inspectors surveying their respective regions on 1 February 1975. Please refer to notes on prices in the preceding article, and see page 255 for a Voucher to cover information concerning cars not included in the tables and up-to-date prices of those which are.

H Registration   5–6 years old

Model chosen from the range	South-east England	Metropolitan London	Midlands	Wales and West England	North of England	Scotland
Austin Allegro 1300 Super						
Austin Maxi 1750						
Austin/Morris Mini 1000	340 / 595	479 / 525	420 / 565	545 / 675	400 / 630	390 / 585
Austin/Morris 1300 Super	360 / 560	475 / 645	380 / 679	425 / 645	380 / 645	400 / 600
Austin/Morris 1800	440 / 685	575 / 735	500 / 665	450 / 700	450 / 650	485 / 675
Chrysler 180						
Citroën GS Club						
Daf 44 Estate	335 / 550	425 / 525	500 / 610	580 / 620	480 / 595	380 / 575
Fiat 850	240 / 410	325 / 425	300 / 450	375 / 490	300 / 450	275 / 410
Fiat 127						
Fiat 128 Saloon	560 / 590	570 / 590	450 / 580	440 / 575	400 / 595	495 / 585
Fiat 124 Special	520 / 610	520 / 610	430 / 550	425 / 500	420 / 550	495 / 590
Ford Capri 1600 GT	690 / 840	705 / 845	560 / 765	545 / 795	530 / 770	650 / 825
Ford Corsair	450 / 520	420 / 515	379 / 580	425 / 585	350 / 560	450 / 565
Ford Cortina 1600E	575 / 775	660 / 775	500 / 725	550 / 765	495 / 655	575 / 795
Ford Cortina 1600XL						
Ford Escort 1100L	525 / 605	525 / 595	425 / 589	470 / 600	392 / 550	520 / 650
Ford Granada 3000GXL						
Ford Zodiac MkIV	350 / 695	405 / 658	400 / 495	395 / 495	400 / 500	350 / 795

Model chosen from the range	South-east England	Metropolitan London	Midlands	Wales and West England	North of England	Scotland
Hillman Avenger 1500 GL	550 / 670	595 / 620	475 / 625	535 / 655	500 / 645	520 / 660
Hillman Hunter GL	590 / 685	595 / 620	600 / 795	675 / 750	595 / 720	435 / 575
Hillman Imp	333 / 500	395 / 425	350 / 470	375 / 465	330 / 455	340 / 495
Jaguar XJ6 4.2	985 / 1610	1095 / 1610	875 / 1650	895 / 1650	900 / 1625	995 / 1635
MG Midget MkIII	395 / 525	360 / 500	395 / 500	405 / 505	400 / 500	395 / 505
MGB	560 / 985	575 / 835	525 / 795	695 / 795	550 / 800	595 / 875
Morris Marina 1.8 4-dr Saloon						
Morris Minor Traveller 1000	425 / 605	450 / 620	500 / 595	495 / 605	500 / 600	375 / 590
Moskvich 412	160 / 210	160 / 210	210 / 300	220 / 305	200 / 260	150 / 200
Reliant Scimitar GTE	920 / 1300	1095 / 1305	1100 / 1320	1220 / 1300	1090 / 1350	1000 / 1275
Renault 4	390 / 530	400 / 445	375 / 505	395 / 575	385 / 480	300 / 405
Renault 6	425 / 530	420 / 495	450 / 580	475 / 525	400 / 580	390 / 460
Renault 12 TL	600 / 695	610 / 700	650 / 700	675 / 725	630 / 695	590 / 650
Renault 16 TL						
Rover 2000 SC	725 / 890	725 / 895	645 / 895	795 / 1065	600 / 995	680 / 875
Rover 3½ litre Saloon	795 / 947	825 / 995	750 / 950	799 / 1095	675 / 1000	675 / 830
Saab 96	420 / 595	430 / 590	500 / 625	550 / 650	480 / 625	395 / 550
Simca 1100 GLS	440 / 595	400 / 565	425 / 575	435 / 570	415 / 525	385 / 435
Triumph Herald 13/60	345 / 525	450 / 575	400 / 570	435 / 640	400 / 595	395 / 460
Triumph Spitfire	400 / 575	395 / 580	450 / 585	475 / 690	400 / 600	395 / 500
Triumph Stag	1250 / 1400	1260 / 1450	1475 / 1575	1450 / 1550	1350 / 1550	1200 / 1400
Triumph Toledo						
Triumph TR6 PI	745 / 890	750 / 850	600 / 790	825 / 870	795 / 800	695 / 825
Triumph 1300	510 / 631	570 / 680	385 / 595	495 / 625	499 / 600	400 / 600
Triumph 2000 MkII	635 / 958	770 / 1000	650 / 945	775 / 1095	675 / 950	500 / 750
Vauxhall Firenza 2000 SL						
Vauxhall Victor	375 / 500	400 / 535	440 / 645	450 / 675	395 / 650	350 / 460
Vauxhall Viva HB	400 / 555	420 / 560	360 / 525	400 / 595	365 / 575	350 / 525
Volkswagen 1300 Beetle	415 / 550	420 / 580	430 / 600	495 / 625	450 / 625	415 / 575
Volkswagen 1600 Super Beetle	570 / 625	580 / 645	660 / 720	650 / 710	655 / 770	565 / 615
Volvo 144 De luxe	745 / 895	780 / 970	850 / 950	905 / 1115	860 / 1025	695 / 820

Guide to used car prices showing variations by region

REGISTRATION LETTERS

The following suffix letters have been issued by Licensing Authorities.

1963 A	1967 (Jan/July) E	1970/71 (Aug/July) J
1964 B	1967/68 (Aug/July) F	1971/72 (Aug/July) K
1965 C	1968/69 (Aug/July) G	1972/73 (Aug/July) L
1966 D	1969/70 (Aug/July) H	1973/74 (Aug/July) M

Prices shown in the following tables were established by a team of AA Inspectors surveying their respective regions on 1 February 1975. Please refer to notes on prices in the preceding article, and see page 255 for a Voucher to cover information concerning cars not included in the tables and up-to-date prices of those which are.

J Registration — 4–5 years old

Model chosen from the range	South-east England	Metropolitan London	Midlands	Wales and West England	North of England	Scotland
Austin Allegro 1300 Super						
Austin Maxi 1750	700 / 879	749 / 850	600 / 875	730 / 895	560 / 845	670 / 900
Austin/Morris Mini 1000	410 / 660	525 / 695	525 / 695	595 / 695	525 / 680	475 / 725
Austin/Morris 1300 Super	595 / 685	695 / 745	469 / 725	525 / 780	495 / 725	600 / 735
Austin/Morris 1800	625 / 775	825 / 895	595 / 845	495 / 795	495 / 795	635 / 795
Chrysler 180	770 / 845	690 / 775	620 / 800	600 / 860	525 / 800	690 / 800
Citroën GS Club						
Daf 44 Estate	415 / 670	425 / 669	610 / 725	640 / 690	580 / 700	450 / 700
Fiat 850	390 / 495	435 / 495	400 / 580	450 / 580	400 / 595	400 / 495
Fiat 127						
Fiat 128 Saloon	585 / 679	620 / 675	545 / 620	550 / 655	575 / 650	575 / 660
Fiat 124 Special	600 / 735	600 / 725	600 / 800	600 / 800	600 / 775	585 / 730
Ford Capri 1600 GT	820 / 925	865 / 989	660 / 999	695 / 995	667 / 950	825 / 995
Ford Corsair						
Ford Cortina 1600E						
Ford Cortina 1600XL	765 / 895	769 / 855	525 / 880	590 / 805	595 / 825	695 / 800
Ford Escort 1100L	600 / 755	635 / 745	595 / 779	645 / 890	595 / 750	695 / 825
Ford Granada 3000GXL						
Ford Zodiac MkIV	525 / 699	525 / 610	425 / 599	425 / 645	425 / 630	495 / 645

Model chosen from the range	South-east England		Metropolitan London		Midlands		Wales and West England		North of England		Scotland	
Hillman Avenger 1500 GL	660	795	690	735	600	745	655	775	660	775	650	725
Hillman Hunter GL	750	820	700	755	675	895	675	825	650	850	650	835
Hillman Imp	435	680	495	540	485	595	495	645	495	625	425	505
Jaguar XJ6 4.2	1515	2100	1570	2060	1199	2125	1195	2295	1200	2150	1595	2095
MG Midget MkIII	480	675	495	695	540	600	545	605	540	635	455	600
MGB	650	1100	650	1000	650	995	640	1095	650	1050	635	1035
Morris Marina 1.8 4-dr Saloon	655	825	735	880	600	795	615	795	610	795	675	825
Morris Minor Traveller 1000	560	695	650	745	600	700	595	695	595	685	560	695
Moskvich 412	215	370	220	375	300	390	300	420	280	395	200	360
Reliant Scimitar GTE	1380	1580	1345	1575	1290	1600	1295	1595	1290	1600	1300	1575
Renault 4	480	600	460	530	580	650	640	700	475	685	375	500
Renault 6	545	650	545	650	595	745	580	755	585	695	480	620
Renault 12 TL	675	800	645	780	700	799	695	850	625	810	580	775
Renault 16 TL	780	820	810	830	600	865	795	940	575	865	775	805
Rover 2000 SC	825	1100	875	1175	700	1095	995	1200	650	1100	810	1100
Rover 3½ litre Saloon	950	1225	995	1245	800	1225	895	1350	785	1200	895	1055
Saab 96	550	725	550	730	645	840	625	885	520	895	495	710
Simca 1100 GLS	525	685	585	690	595	760	565	675	500	620	475	550
Triumph Herald 13/60	500	695	565	695	569	765	539	715	500	745	495	695
Triumph Spitfire	540	600	545	650	500	655	510	640	500	615	480	560
Triumph Stag	1295	1675	1350	1690	1625	1650	1575	1695	1550	1695	1270	1550
Triumph Toledo	645	795	655	780	675	699	715	750	695	730	600	700
Triumph TR6 PI	825	990	815	1050	890	1000	900	1015	800	1000	800	975
Triumph 1300	580	697	590	700	635	690	650	690	645	695	565	650
Triumph 2000 MkII	820	1198	915	1200	950	1145	900	1195	850	1095	750	1010
Vauxhall Firenza 2000 SL												
Vauxhall Victor	458	785	500	790	450	750	505	795	485	695	440	750
Vauxhall Viva HB	505	678	510	680	490	779	545	765	500	725	490	665
Volkswagen 1300 Beetle	520	679	550	680	550	795	525	795	550	725	505	570
Volkswagen 1600 Super Beetle	650	700	660	690	690	770	700	785	690	775	640	695
Volvo 144 De luxe	895	1130	850	1200	1000	1320	1095	1395	985	1325	840	1095

Guide to used car prices showing variations by region

REGISTRATION LETTERS

The following suffix letters have been issued by Licensing Authorities.

1963 A	1967 (Jan/July) E	1970/71 (Aug/July) J
1964 B	1967/68 (Aug/July) F	1971/72 (Aug/July) K
1965 C	1968/69 (Aug/July) G	1972/73 (Aug/July) L
1966 D	1969/70 (Aug/July) H	1973/74 (Aug/July) M

Prices shown in the following tables were established by a team of AA Inspectors surveying their respective regions on 1 February 1975. Please refer to notes on prices in the preceding article, and see page 255 for a Voucher to cover information concerning cars not included in the tables and up-to-date prices of those which are.

K Registration   3–4 years old

Model chosen from the range	South-east England	Metropolitan London	Midlands	Wales and West England	North of England	Scotland
Austin Allegro 1300 Super						
Austin Maxi 1750	750 / 1012	945 / 1045	675 / 1065	750 / 1095	640 / 1020	800 / 1045
Austin/Morris Mini 1000	555 / 795	625 / 785	550 / 925	650 / 795	495 / 860	580 / 850
Austin/Morris 1300 Super	650 / 800	735 / 895	635 / 895	625 / 875	550 / 795	675 / 825
Austin/Morris 1800	635 / 1095	895 / 1025	650 / 1050	700 / 1095	550 / 1050	695 / 1025
Chrysler 180	700 / 985	775 / 999	950 / 1100	695 / 1075	599 / 1005	705 / 950
Citroën GS Club	740 / 930	795 / 899	725 / 950	695 / 810	675 / 850	750 / 925
Daf 44 Estate	480 / 800	630 / 750	595 / 800	625 / 820	590 / 820	400 / 750
Fiat 850	440 / 685	435 / 655	740 / 795	690 / 790	750 / 800	400 / 640
Fiat 127	660 / 740	620 / 740	699 / 780	645 / 795	595 / 725	660 / 745
Fiat 128 Saloon	595 / 855	660 / 880	550 / 849	650 / 845	535 / 848	575 / 845
Fiat 124 Special	695 / 845	730 / 855	785 / 950	795 / 990	770 / 895	690 / 880
Ford Capri 1600 GT	950 / 1129	955 / 1030	775 / 1075	795 / 1095	780 / 1050	900 / 1195
Ford Corsair						
Ford Cortina 1600E						
Ford Cortina 1600XL	845 / 1025	860 / 975	675 / 1055	675 / 995	620 / 1005	800 / 965
Ford Escort 1100L	690 / 825	665 / 780	599 / 925	675 / 910	560 / 895	695 / 810
Ford Granada 3000GXL	1295 / 1450	1445 / 1559	895 / 1370	995 / 1495	990 / 1450	1330 / 1430
Ford Zodiac MkIV	600 / 795	599 / 795	595 / 700	660 / 760	600 / 720	550 / 750

Model chosen from the range	South-east England	Metropolitan London	Midlands	Wales and West England	North of England	Scotland
Hillman Avenger 1500 GL	725 / 895	750 / 825	700 / 949	725 / 945	695 / 925	725 / 835
Hillman Hunter GL	795 / 1000	800 / 975	825 / 1005	845 / 1025	785 / 1050	800 / 1015
Hillman Imp	550 / 700	550 / 685	555 / 745	625 / 765	595 / 725	500 / 615
Jaguar XJ6 4.2	2000 / 2650	2090 / 2475	1495 / 2695	1525 / 2745	1500 / 2650	2025 / 2650
MG Midget MkIII	530 / 790	540 / 730	600 / 685	620 / 700	610 / 765	505 / 710
MGB	965 / 1300	950 / 1295	885 / 1150	875 / 1195	830 / 1195	950 / 1325
Morris Marina 1.8 4-dr Saloon	780 / 975	850 / 980	599 / 999	625 / 995	600 / 1000	735 / 975
Morris Minor Traveller 1000						
Moskvich 412	345 / 390	350 / 430	330 / 420	325 / 425	365 / 450	320 / 390
Reliant Scimitar GTE	1500 / 1970	1550 / 1935	1395 / 1990	1395 / 1995	1395 / 1950	1575 / 1880
Renault 4	560 / 730	575 / 760	695 / 785	745 / 815	680 / 795	525 / 725
Renault 6	600 / 785	665 / 795	640 / 850	695 / 850	600 / 825	560 / 780
Renault 12 TL	780 / 910	725 / 875	880 / 950	800 / 995	800 / 995	650 / 820
Renault 16 TL	810 / 1075	850 / 1095	850 / 1050	650 / 1095	695 / 1045	805 / 975
Rover 2000 SC	1090 / 1210	1175 / 1295	850 / 1345	975 / 1495	850 / 1350	950 / 1205
Rover 3½ litre Saloon	1075 / 1409	1050 / 1435	1000 / 1850	995 / 1995	990 / 1700	1000 / 1500
Saab 96	630 / 855	630 / 860	800 / 965	880 / 985	840 / 995	610 / 800
Simca 1100 GLS	625 / 770	650 / 775	659 / 895	695 / 850	675 / 820	595 / 675
Triumph Herald 13/60	680 / 730	690 / 730	740 / 800	715 / 805	730 / 780	680 / 725
Triumph Spitfire	650 / 850	700 / 900	620 / 790	650 / 800	670 / 785	600 / 800
Triumph Stag	1590 / 2150	1600 / 2200	1795 / 2095	1800 / 2095	1775 / 2095	1500 / 2050
Triumph Toledo	762 / 840	750 / 860	695 / 895	695 / 850	665 / 850	690 / 800
Triumph TR6 PI	900 / 1255	900 / 1300	1000 / 1295	995 / 1215	900 / 1250	850 / 1095
Triumph 1300						
Triumph 2000 MkII	1050 / 1425	1150 / 1430	869 / 1450	1095 / 1455	895 / 1350	1000 / 1300
Vauxhall Firenza 2000 SL	725 / 900	810 / 930	699 / 850	775 / 870	680 / 885	705 / 900
Vauxhall Victor	665 / 860	685 / 875	650 / 995	720 / 1045	650 / 985	650 / 850
Vauxhall Viva HB						
Volkswagen 1300 Beetle	650 / 705	690 / 735	645 / 865	745 / 900	699 / 925	590 / 895
Volkswagen 1600 Super Beetle	700 / 825	710 / 845	760 / 895	790 / 950	700 / 900	695 / 810
Volvo 144 De luxe	1095 / 1390	1115 / 1450	1195 / 1695	1225 / 1790	1200 / 1725	1025 / 1295

Guide to used car prices showing variations by region

Prices shown in the following tables were established by a team of AA Inspectors surveying their respective regions on 1 February 1975. Please refer to notes on prices in the preceding article, and see page 255 for a Voucher to cover information concerning cars not included in the tables and up-to-date prices of those which are.

L Registration — 2-3 years old

Model chosen from the range	South-east England	Metropolitan London	Midlands	Wales and West England	North of England	Scotland
Austin Allegro 1300 Super	960 / 1015	900 / 955	869 / 1080	790 / 1255	880 / 1225	950 / 1250
Austin Maxi 1750	945 / 1295	1075 / 1225	1045 / 1375	1045 / 1350	825 / 1310	950 / 1295
Austin/Morris Mini 1000	640 / 925	800 / 895	770 / 995	725 / 945	595 / 950	795 / 950
Austin/Morris 1300 Super	845 / 1068	825 / 965	699 / 995	825 / 1095	650 / 1025	725 / 945
Austin/Morris 1800	990 / 1295	995 / 1345	795 / 1150	875 / 1245	810 / 1245	900 / 1295
Chrysler 180	990 / 1332	1080 / 1455	895 / 1250	1110 / 1295	880 / 1195	975 / 1250
Citroën GS Club	880 / 1210	995 / 1265	1165 / 1275	1095 / 1295	885 / 1200	805 / 1140
Daf 44 Estate	780 / 960	805 / 925	860 / 950	890 / 985	850 / 950	760 / 1000
Fiat 850	685 / 750	675 / 723	800 / 865	750 / 825	790 / 865	600 / 700
Fiat 127	715 / 835	725 / 875	773 / 845	825 / 875	725 / 895	700 / 905
Fiat 128 Saloon	785 / 955	795 / 940	800 / 945	780 / 995	780 / 985	775 / 930
Fiat 124 Special	930 / 1065	925 / 1065	850 / 1100	850 / 1095	800 / 1010	870 / 1060
Ford Capri 1600 GT	1025 / 1315	1125 / 1230	950 / 1395	995 / 1375	980 / 1375	1050 / 1290
Ford Corsair						
Ford Cortina 1600E						
Ford Cortina 1600XL	970 / 1249	1150 / 1249	699 / 1295	725 / 1295	725 / 1295	825 / 1250
Ford Escort 1100L	840 / 990	820 / 995	629 / 985	705 / 1005	645 / 995	775 / 910
Ford Granada 3000GXL	1345 / 1820	1525 / 1820	995 / 1995	1095 / 2050	995 / 2000	1200 / 1770
Ford Zodiac MkIV						

Model chosen from the range	South-east England	Metropolitan London	Midlands	Wales and West England	North of England	Scotland
Hillman Avenger 1500 GL	855 / 1045	860 / 995	775 / 1095	765 / 1105	735 / 1075	830 / 1025
Hillman Hunter GL	975 / 1250	980 / 1195	900 / 1195	925 / 1195	895 / 1150	900 / 1250
Hillman Imp	675 / 850	705 / 900	730 / 895	750 / 875	745 / 895	625 / 895
Jaguar XJ6 4.2	2223 / 3250	2370 / 2995	1895 / 3300	2500 / 3650	1895 / 3300	2320 / 3150
MG Midget MkIII	640 / 1000	630 / 940	625 / 895	699 / 935	705 / 995	625 / 925
MGB	1060 / 1595	1005 / 1580	995 / 1495	1095 / 1495	1095 / 1495	1060 / 1510
Morris Marina 1.8 4-dr Saloon	895 / 1099	930 / 1015	795 / 1195	795 / 1195	780 / 1170	890 / 1075
Morris Minor Traveller 1000						
Moskvich 412	410 / 545	420 / 560	400 / 545	395 / 550	410 / 565	410 / 525
Reliant Scimitar GTE	1750 / 2350	1855 / 2305	1775 / 2225	1995 / 2350	1880 / 2315	1880 / 2255
Renault 4	699 / 825	735 / 850	760 / 880	795 / 925	750 / 900	620 / 720
Renault 6	700 / 890	730 / 920	745 / 1025	740 / 1045	690 / 965	680 / 840
Renault 12 TL	875 / 1025	895 / 1025	850 / 1200	895 / 1225	880 / 1200	800 / 950
Renault 16 TL	900 / 1290	1100 / 1295	899 / 1550	1145 / 1225	900 / 1275	900 / 1290
Rover 2000 SC	1290 / 1495	1395 / 1540	1000 / 1700	1295 / 1600	1295 / 1650	1200 / 1325
Rover 3½ litre Saloon	1400 / 1800	1495 / 1850	1975 / 2200	1955 / 2180	1195 / 2200	1400 / 1735
Saab 96	780 / 1030	795 / 1040	1025 / 1105	935 / 1115	850 / 1150	750 / 1000
Simca 1100 GLS	645 / 905	760 / 920	810 / 980	790 / 975	740 / 995	625 / 850
Triumph Herald 13/60						
Triumph Spitfire	900 / 1080	1020 / 1095	880 / 1080	890 / 1030	895 / 1025	850 / 1000
Triumph Stag	1940 / 2565	2000 / 2580	2095 / 2490	2050 / 2495	2050 / 2500	1795 / 2325
Triumph Toledo	835 / 1005	870 / 1010	825 / 1050	895 / 1180	765 / 1025	760 / 995
Triumph TR6 PI	1185 / 1495	1150 / 1500	1220 / 1470	1250 / 1500	1125 / 1500	1000 / 1375
Triumph 1300						
Triumph 2000 MkII	1300 / 1632	1320 / 1650	1195 / 1795	1200 / 1695	1125 / 1680	1200 / 1545
Vauxhall Firenza 2000 SL	875 / 995	900 / 1000	820 / 1000	855 / 1000	850 / 1005	820 / 980
Vauxhall Victor	900 / 1230	940 / 1250	825 / 1200	895 / 1345	800 / 1225	880 / 1150
Vauxhall Viva HB						
Volkswagen 1300 Beetle	720 / 982	645 / 890	750 / 965	795 / 995	745 / 945	695 / 995
Volkswagen 1600 Super Beetle	810 / 950	850 / 950	895 / 995	945 / 1045	925 / 1010	800 / 900
Volvo 144 De luxe	1200 / 1610	1200 / 1700	1660 / 2095	1795 / 2195	1695 / 2000	1200 / 1550

Guide to used car prices showing variations by region

Prices shown in the following tables were established by a team of AA Inspectors surveying their respective regions on 1 February 1975. Please refer to notes on prices in the preceding article, and see page 255 for a Voucher to cover information concerning cars not included in the tables and up-to-date prices of those which are.

M Registration   1–2 years old

Model chosen from the range	South-east England	Metropolitan London	Midlands	Wales and West England	North of England	Scotland
Austin Allegro 1300 Super	925 / 1220	975 / 1195	950 / 1495	1025 / 1495	1093 / 1425	1200 / 1450
Austin Maxi 1750	1260 / 1625	1225 / 1425	1125 / 1595	1195 / 1695	1000 / 1495	1200 / 1595
Austin/Morris Mini 1000	835 / 1050	895 / 1050	865 / 1065	850 / 1035	700 / 1050	860 / 1035
Austin/Morris 1300 Super	930 / 1045	975 / 1015	800 / 1025	935 / 1150	760 / 1070	825 / 1050
Austin/Morris 1800	1220 / 1575	1350 / 1555	1095 / 1325	1050 / 1345	1020 / 1350	1200 / 1485
Chrysler 180	1300 / 1680	1650 / 1795	1325 / 1695	1350 / 1675	1250 / 1675	1300 / 1600
Citroën GS Club	1080 / 1400	1195 / 1350	1165 / 1495	1150 / 1545	1050 / 1345	945 / 1290
Daf 44 Estate	970 / 1200	975 / 1209	945 / 1120	985 / 1125	900 / 1100	905 / 1125
Fiat 850						
Fiat 127	870 / 1010	925 / 980	800 / 1100	795 / 1075	780 / 995	860 / 995
Fiat 128 Saloon	965 / 1130	1025 / 1120	945 / 1125	900 / 1175	900 / 1150	915 / 1140
Fiat 124 Special	1180 / 1300	1165 / 1260	1000 / 1300	1095 / 1300	950 / 1295	1075 / 1280
Ford Capri 1600 GT	1270 / 1605	1275 / 1395	1300 / 1495	1295 / 1550	1250 / 1475	1280 / 1600
Ford Corsair						
Ford Cortina 1600E						
Ford Cortina 1600XL	1210 / 1655	1380 / 1655	1025 / 1595	950 / 1587	1050 / 1595	1200 / 1595
Ford Escort 1100L	1025 / 1230	1035 / 1210	895 / 1225	850 / 1200	845 / 1200	950 / 1200
Ford Granada 3000GXL	1995 / 2495	1999 / 2355	1500 / 2500	1550 / 2550	1469 / 2450	1850 / 2400
Ford Zodiac MkIV						

Model chosen from the range	South-east England	Metropolitan London	Midlands	Wales and West England	North of England	Scotland
Hillman Avenger 1500 GL	1060 / 1298	1000 / 1290	1055 / 1335	1075 / 1345	1065 / 1355	995 / 1280
Hillman Hunter GL	1145 / 1490	1085 / 1325	1045 / 1499	990 / 1425	995 / 1450	1090 / 1450
Hillman Imp	785 / 980	845 / 895	825 / 1020	839 / 1095	820 / 1065	795 / 1025
Jaguar XJ6 4.2	2925 / 4350	3295 / 4280	2750 / 3595	3350 / 4025	2800 / 4000	3250 / 4200
MG Midget MkIII	955 / 1100	955 / 1125	855 / 1099	985 / 1125	935 / 1099	925 / 1150
MGB	1525 / 1825	1530 / 1840	1275 / 1875	1200 / 1845	1250 / 1895	1540 / 1910
Morris Marina 1.8 4-dr Saloon	1050 / 1350	1125 / 1395	985 / 1325	1025 / 1305	1050 / 1350	1100 / 1385
Morris Minor Traveller 1000						
Moskvich 412	560 / 630	590 / 640	555 / 685	550 / 680	500 / 680	540 / 600
Reliant Scimitar GTE	2250 / 2900	2275 / 2799	2250 / 2695	2200 / 2800	2195 / 2750	2255 / 2850
Renault 4	795 / 1050	800 / 1100	890 / 980	920 / 980	845 / 940	775 / 1000
Renault 6	800 / 995	875 / 1020	1175 / 1225	900 / 1195	935 / 1195	800 / 985
Renault 12 TL	1050 / 1295	1060 / 1280	1250 / 1525	1225 / 1425	1050 / 1425	1005 / 1275
Renault 16 TL	1200 / 1400	1245 / 1485	1245 / 1625	1100 / 1595	1095 / 1400	1245 / 1360
Rover 2000 SC	1650 / 2200	1755 / 2295	2095 / 2295	1400 / 2090	1295 / 2395	1575 / 2200
Rover 3½ litre Saloon						
Saab 96	1000 / 1360	1000 / 1370	1225 / 1395	1199 / 1400	1240 / 1325	940 / 1340
Simca 1100 GLS	895 / 1160	990 / 1195	945 / 1145	990 / 1195	995 / 1150	850 / 1150
Triumph Herald 13/60						
Triumph Spitfire	1100 / 1275	1100 / 1280	995 / 1295	1000 / 1195	1125 / 1160	1000 / 1200
Triumph Stag	2250 / 3040	2350 / 3080	2100 / 3150	2300 / 3195	2050 / 3150	2200 / 2925
Triumph Toledo	1090 / 1258	1070 / 1290	995 / 1199	1000 / 1295	995 / 1265	985 / 1195
Triumph TR6 PI	1395 / 1695	1400 / 1800	1295 / 1895	1395 / 1895	1340 / 1850	1350 / 1645
Triumph 1300						
Triumph 2000 MkII	1510 / 2048	1550 / 2050	1850 / 2455	1850 / 2465	1670 / 2295	1450 / 2000
Vauxhall Firenza 2000 SL	990 / 1050	1000 / 1100	1035 / 1060	1020 / 1040	1020 / 1045	975 / 1050
Vauxhall Victor	1113 / 1490	1200 / 1480	1275 / 1499	1200 / 1575	1095 / 1550	1100 / 1450
Vauxhall Viva HB						
Volkswagen 1300 Beetle	900 / 1045	890 / 1050	865 / 1085	925 / 1095	905 / 1145	900 / 1055
Volkswagen 1600 Super Beetle	900 / 1040	910 / 1100	1000 / 1100	1100 / 1200	1000 / 1150	870 / 1000
Volvo 144 De luxe	1550 / 2008	1550 / 2045	1985 / 2295	1945 / 2300	1900 / 2395	1505 / 2005

New versus secondhand
Compare the values

You have a specific sum of money to spend? Should you buy a new car or will you be better off by buying a more expensively produced car, secondhand and at a similar price? Tables on this and the following pages give the current new prices (where applicable) of the 50 cars presented in this book, with three other secondhand models falling in a similar price bracket. Current AA insurance group ratings of the new models are also shown. The grouping of individual vehicles is determined by a number of factors: performance, repair costs, value and the make of the vehicle concerned. The performance of a vehicle is based not only on the engine's size and the top speed, but takes into account vehicle weight and dimensions, which in turn affect acceleration. The value and repair costs of a vehicle must also take into account the availability of spare parts and the time taken to replace or repair those parts. The results of these enquiries are combined and a group rate is decided by comparison with existing vehicles.

You will find these tables helpful and, in many cases, you will be surprised at what your nest-egg will buy. Prices were established at 1 February 1975 (but see page 255). The choice is yours . . . browse a little.

Make and Model		Price new incl. tax	Used alternatives available	Price used★
AUSTIN ALLEGRO		**£1499**	1974 Austin 1800 MkIII	**£1530**
1300 SDL 4-dr			1974 Morris Marina 1.8 TC	**£1525**
INS 2	(See p. 25)		1972 Volvo 145 Estate	**£1550**
AUSTIN MAXI 1750		**£1816**	1974 Humber Sceptre	**£1785**
			1974 Renault 17 FH Coupé TL Auto	**£1850**
INS 4	(See p. 29)		1974 Ford Capri 2000 GT	**£1805**
AUSTIN/MORRIS MINI		**£1184**	1973 Austin Allegro 1500 Super DL	**£1150**
1000			1974 Citroën GS Confort 4-dr	**£1215**
INS 1	(See p. 33)		1973 Ford Cortina 1600L 4-dr	**£1230**
AUSTIN/MORRIS 1100			1972 4-dr Austin/Morris 1100 MkIII	**£790**
Super MkIII		Discontinued	1972 Daf 746cc Variomatic	**£750**
INS 1	(See p. 37)		1971 Ford Escort 1300L 4-dr	**£775**
AUSTIN/MORRIS 1800 DL		**£1868**	1973 Fiat 124 1800 Sport FH Coupé	**£1720**
			1974 Datsun Saloon C 260	**£1890**
INS 3	(See p. 41)		1974 Renault 17 TL FH Coupé Auto	**£1850**
CHRYSLER 180		**£2217**	1974 MGB Fixed Head Coupé GT	**£2275**
1812cc			1974 Rover 2200 SC Automatic	**£2205**
INS 5	(See p. 45)		1974 Triumph 2.5 PI	**£2165**
CITROËN GS Club		**£1550**	1974 Ford Cortina 1600XL	**£1545**
1220cc			1970 Jaguar XJ6 4.2 Overdrive	**£1575**
INS 4	(See p. 49)		1974 Renault 16 TL Saloon Auto	**£1495**
DAF 44 DL		**£1255**	1974 Austin Allegro 1300 Super DL	**£1245**
Variomatic 844cc			1974 Hillman Hunter 1496cc	**£1285**
INS 3	(See p. 53)		1974 Mini Clubman Estate Auto	**£1230**

★ Maximum secondhand prices of models listed, ie in first-class condition with average mileage.

Make and Model	Price new incl. tax	Used alternatives available	Price used★
FIAT 850 (now imported as SEAT) *INS 1*　　*(See p. 57)*	**£899**	*1972 Morris Marina 1.3 litre* *1973 Mini 1000 MkII Saloon* *1972 Ford Escort 1100L*	**£920** **£905** **£880**
FIAT 127 2-dr DL *903cc* *INS 3*　　*(See p. 61)*	**£1140**	*1974 Datsun 120Y New Sunny* *1973 Austin Allegro 1500 Super DL* *1973 Triumph Toledo 1493cc Saloon*	**£1095** **£1105** **£1155**
FIAT 128 Saloon *1116cc 4-dr* *INS 3*　　*(See p. 65)*	**£1324**	*1974 Triumph Toledo 1296cc* *1974 Vauxhall Viva Estate 2-dr* *1973 Austin Maxi 1750 HL*	**£1295** **£1350** **£1315**
FIAT 124 Special *1197cc 4-dr* *INS 3*　　*(See p. 69)*	**£1475**	*1974 Vauxhall Magnum 1800 Auto* *1973 Humber Sceptre Automatic* *1974 Ford Capri 1600 GTXL*	**£1535** **£1395** **£1490**
FORD CAPRI 1600 GT *1593cc* *INS 4*　　*(See p. 73)*	**£2087**	*1974 Fiat 124 Sport 1800 FH Coupé* *1972 Jaguar XJ6 2.8 Automatic* *1974 Triumph 2000 MkII*	**£2065** **£2175** **£2035**
FORD CORSAIR V4 *1663cc* *INS 4*　　*(See p. 77)*	Discontinued	*1970 Ford Corsair De Luxe* *1969 Renault 16 De Luxe* *1969 Morris 1800 MkII*	**£570** **£545** **£530**
FORD CORTINA 1600E *1599cc* *INS 4*　　*(See p. 81)*	Discontinued	*1970 Cortina 1600E 4-dr Saloon* *1971 Cortina 1300L 2-dr* *1969 Rover 2000 SC*	**£745** **£745** **£740**
FORD CORTINA 1600XL *2-dr Saloon* *INS 2*　　*(See p. 85)*	**£1830**	*1973 BMW 2002 Fixed Head Coupé* *1974 Ford Consul 2500L Automatic* *1974 Opel Rekord II FH Coupé*	**£1875** **£1750** **£1800**
FORD ESCORT 1300XL *4-dr* *INS 2*　　*(See p. 89)*	**£1535**	*1974 Renault 16 TL Automatic* *1972 Volvo 144S De Luxe* *1974 Vauxhall Magnum 2300cc*	**£1495** **£1430** **£1540**
FORD GRANADA 3000GXL *Saloon* *INS 6*　　*(See p. 93)*	**£3344**	*1973 Jaguar XJ6 4.2 litre Automatic* *1971 Mercedes-Benz 300SEL 3.5* *1974 BMW 525 Saloon*	**£3250** **£3325** **£3400**
FORD ZODIAC MkIV *V6 2994cc* *INS 5*　　*(See p. 97)*	Discontinued	*1972 Ford Zodiac MkIV* *1969 Jaguar 420G with Overdrive* *1969 Rover 2000 TC*	**£730** **£695** **£755**
HILLMAN AVENGER GL *1599cc 4-dr* *INS 3*　　*(See p. 101)*	**£1626**	*1973 Audi 100LS Saloon* *1974 Austin 2200 Saloon* *1974 Vauxhall Victor 2300 FE*	**£1580** **£1650** **£1680**
HILLMAN HUNTER GL *1725cc 4-dr* *INS 3*　　*(See p. 105)*	**£1854**	*1974 Triumph Dolomite Automatic* *1974 Renault 16TX Saloon De Luxe* *1970 Mercedes-Benz 280SE*	**£1855** **£1850** **£1875**
HILLMAN IMP Super *875cc 2-dr* *INS 1*　　*(See p. 109)*	**£1261**	*1974 Hillman Avenger GL* *1974 Ford Cortina 1300L 2-dr* *1974 Austin Allegro 1500 2-dr*	**£1280** **£1290** **£1300**

★*Maximum secondhand prices of models listed, ie in first-class condition with average mileage.*

Make and Model	Price new incl. tax	Used alternatives available	Price used ★
JAGUAR XJ6L 4.2 4235cc (Automatic) INS 7 (See p. 113)	£4679	1966 Rolls Royce Silver Shadow 1972 Mercedes-Benz 300SEL 6.3 1972 Aston Martin DBS Vantage	£4725 £4850 £4750
MG MIDGET SPORTS 1493cc INS 5 (See p. 117)	£1418	1971 Audi 100GL 4-dr Saloon 1972 Morgan 4/4 Sports Tourer 1974 Ford Capri 1600 GT	£1460 £1390 £1490
MGB SPORTS ROADSTER 1798cc INS 6 (See p. 121)	£1939	1970 Porsche 911T FH Coupé 1974 Renault 17 FH Coupé TL Auto 1972 Reliant Scimitar GTE	£1900 £1850 £1870
MORRIS MARINA 1798cc 4-dr DL INS 3 (See p. 125)	£1578	1974 Ford Consul Saloon 2000L 1974 Chrysler 180 1974 Renault 16 TS	£1600 £1600 £1565
MORRIS MINOR 1000 1098cc INS 1 (See p. 129)	Discontinued	1970 Morris Minor Traveller 1969 Mini Clubman Estate 1970 Vauxhall Viva 4-dr De Luxe	£595 £600 £570
MOSKVICH 412 1478cc INS 4 (See p. 133)	£745	1971 Austin 1300 GT 1971 Ford Escort 1300L 1972 Hillman Hunter 1496cc	£670 £775 £775
RELIANT SCIMITAR GTE 2994cc INS 7 (See p. 137)	£3354	1973 Jaguar XJ6 4.2 Automatic 1971 Porsche FH Coupé 911S 1973 Mercedes-Benz 230/4 Auto	£3250 £3100 £3400
RENAULT 4 845cc INS 1 (See p. 141)	£1088	1973 Hillman Avenger 1295cc 1973 Ford Escort 1100 De Luxe 1973 Austin Mini Clubman Estate	£1090 £1000 £965
RENAULT 6 845cc INS 1 (See p. 145)	£1285	1973 Morris Marina Estate 1.8 1974 Vauxhall Viva HC 2-dr De Luxe 1974 Triumph Toledo 2-dr	£1255 £1235 £1255
RENAULT 12 TL 1289cc INS 3 (See p. 149)	£1544	1973 Triumph Dolomite Automatic 1974 Vauxhall Magnum Estate 1800 1974 Austin Maxi Automatic	£1520 £1585 £1595
RENAULT 16 TL 1565cc INS 3 (See p. 153)	£1741	1971 Jaguar XJ6 2.8 with Overdrive 1973 Rover 2000 TC 1974 Austin 2200 Automatic	£1700 £1710 £1730
ROVER 3500 S 3528cc INS 5 (See p. 157)	£3230	1973 Jaguar XJ6 4.2 Automatic 1971 Mercedes-Benz 300SEL 3.5 Auto 1972 Porsche 911E FH Coupé	£3250 £3325 £3250
ROVER 3½ litre 3528cc (Automatic) INS 5 (See p. 161)	Discontinued	1972 3½ litre Rover Saloon Auto 1969 Mercedes-Benz 280SE Auto 1972 Citroën Pallas DS 23	£1625 £1525 £1670
SAAB 96 V4 1498cc INS 3 (See p. 165)	£1722	1974 Ford Capri 2000 GT II 1974 Opel Rekord II 1897cc 1971 Jaguar XJ6 2.8 with Overdrive	£1805 £1720 £1700

★ Maximum secondhand prices of models listed, ie in first-class condition with average mileage.

Make and Model	Price new incl tax	Used alternatives available	Price used ★
SIMCA 1100 GLS 1118cc 5-dr INS 3 (See p. 169)	**£1437**	1974 Renault 16 TL Automatic 1974 Ford Cortina 1600XL 2-dr 1974 Austin Maxi 1500	**£1495** **£1495** **£1440**
TRIUMPH HERALD 13/60 1296cc INS 2 (See p. 173)	Discontinued	1970 Triumph Herald 13/60 Saloon 1970 Ford Escort 1100 2-dr 1969 Hillman Hunter MkII	**£555** **£570** **£530**
TRIUMPH SPITFIRE MkIII 1296cc INS 4 (See p. 177)	Discontinued	1970 Triumph Spitfire MkIII 1968 Rover 2000 SC 1969 Jaguar 240 Saloon	**£565** **£600** **£565**
TRIUMPH STAG Convertible 2997cc INS 7 (See p. 181)	**£3467**	1973 Jaguar XJ6 4.2 Automatic 1970 Aston Martin DB6 Convertible 1974 Volvo 164 TE Automatic	**£3250** **£3475** **£3420**
TRIUMPH TOLEDO 1296cc 4-dr INS 2 (See p. 185)	**£1532**	1974 Renault 16 TL Automatic 1973 (Nov) Humber Sceptre 1725cc 1974 Austin 1800 MkIII Automatic	**£1495** **£1485** **£1600**
TRIUMPH TR6 PI Roadster 2498cc INS 7 (See p. 189)	**£2366**	1972 Jaguar E Type V12 FHC 1974 Jensen-Healey Sports 1974 Audi 100 S FH Coupé	**£2400** **£2250** **£2540**
TRIUMPH 1300 Saloon 1296cc 4-dr INS 2 (See p. 193)	Discontinued	1970 Triumph 1300 4-dr Saloon 1971 Morris Marina 1.8 Coupé 1970 Cortina 1600L	**£685** **£725** **£715**
TRIUMPH 2000 MkII 1998cc INS 4 (See p. 197)	**£2486**	1974 Audi 100 GL Automatic 1972 Mercedes-Benz 220/8 Auto 1974 Rover 2200 Automatic	**£2480** **£2450** **£2200**
VAUXHALL FIRENZA 2000 SL 1975cc INS 5 (See p. 201)	Discontinued	1972 Vauxhall Firenza 2000 SL 1970 Ford Capri GT XLR 2000 1970 Renault 16 TS	**£820** **£815** **£780**
VAUXHALL VICTOR 1800 1759cc INS 3 (See p. 205)	**£1959**	1974 Rover 2200 SC 1974 Ford Consul Estate L 2500cc 1971 Daimler Sovereign 2.8 Auto	**£2075** **£1990** **£1850**
VAUXHALL VIVA Standard 1256cc INS 2 (See p. 209)	**£1354**	1974 Austin Allegro 1500 SDL 1974 Simca 1301 GL Saloon Special 1974 Peugeot 204 Saloon	**£1300** **£1345** **£1315**
VOLKSWAGEN 1300 1285cc INS 2 (See p. 213)	**£1284**	1974 Renault 12 L 1973 (Nov) Hillman Hunter GL 1974 Morris Marina 1.3 De Luxe	**£1215** **£1285** **£1270**
VOLKSWAGEN 1600L Variant Estate 1584cc INS 3 (See p. 217)	Discontinued	1970 VW Variant Estate 1600L 1971 Vauxhall Viva 1600 Estate 1970 Ford Cortina 1600 GT	**£740** **£750** **£780**
VOLVO 144 Automatic 1986cc INS 4 (See p. 221)	Discontinued	1973 Volvo 144 Automatic 1973 Rover 2000 TC 1971 Jaguar XJ6 2.8 Automatic	**£1795** **£1710** **£1750**

★ Maximum secondhand prices of models listed, ie in first-class condition with average mileage.

Free Service of Used Car Prices for AA Members

In the tables of used car prices, and elsewhere in this book, emphasis has been given to the fact that prices were established by a team of Regional Inspectors on 1 February 1975. The feature 'Prices . . . a warning' points out the danger of accepting the prices as final and the variations and fluctuation which will occur during one year. For the benefit of readers who wish to buy or sell either a car not listed in the fifty examples given, or at a time when those prices given are obviously out of date, the Voucher below may be completed and sent to The Manager, Technical Service Dept, Automobile Association, Fanum House, Basingstoke, Hants RG21 2EA. The AA will then forward, without charge, a current valuation.

PLEASE DETACH HERE

VOU[AA]HER

Please send me a current valuation based on the information I give below:

MAKE & MODEL *(full description, please)* _____

YEAR OF MANUFACTURE   **CUBIC CAPACITY**

MILEAGE   **MANUAL or AUTOMATIC**

ARE YOU PURCHASING PRIVATELY OR FROM A DEALER?

ARE YOU SELLING PRIVATELY OR TO A DEALER?

NAME _____

ADDRESS _____

AA MEMBERSHIP No. _____ **DATE** _____
(where applicable)